Terentia, Tullia and Publilia

How well do you know Cicero? It may be possible for us to feel as though we know him almost intimately, from his many orations, writings and hundreds of personal letters which survive. But what do you know about his family?

The women of Cicero's household are (being women) typically silent in extant texts, and survive only as secondary figures to Cicero. Yet there is an irony in this, at least with regard to his first wife Terentia: a strong, tempestuous woman of status and fortune, with an implacable desire to retain control of both.

Less is known of his daughter, Tullia; his second wife, teenaged Publilia, is shadowy and mysterious as the young submissive wedded to compensate for her predecessor's steely resolve and fiery temper.

This book reconstructs the lives of these three important women. It artfully assembles a rounded account of their personalities and experiences through the accumulation of references in Cicero's nine hundred personal letters, and with a study of ancient Rome during the years of upheaval on the cusp of the Republic and the Empire. In short, it creates a history for these figures who, through history, have not had voices of their own. Susan Treggiari creates a vivid impression of the everyday life of upper-class Roman women in Italy during the heyday of Roman power.

Susan Treggiari retired in 2001, after teaching chiefly at the University of Ottawa and Stanford University. Her previous publications include *Roman Freedmen during the Late Republic* (1969, 2000), *Cicero's Cicilian Letters* (2nd edition 1997), *Roman Marriage* (1991) and *Roman Social History* (2002).

Women of the Ancient World
Edited by Ronnie Ancona and Sarah B. Pomeroy

The books in this series offer compact and accessible introductions to the lives and historical times of women from the ancient world. Each book, written by a distinguished scholar in the field, introduces and explores the life of one woman or group of women from antiquity, from a biographical perspective.

The texts will be authoritative introductions by experts in the field. Each book will be of interest to students and scholars of antiquity as well as those with little or no prior knowledge of ancient history or literature, combining rigorous scholarship with reader-friendly prose. Each volume will contain a guide to further reading, a brief glossary, and timelines, maps, and images, as necessary.

Women of the Ancient World will provide an opportunity for specialists to present concise, authoritative accounts, uncovering and exploring important figures in need of historical study and advancing current scholarship on women of the past. Although there is a growing body of excellent scholarship on the lives and roles of women in the ancient world, much work remains. This series will be the first of its kind.

Olympias, Mother of Alexander the Great
Elizabeth Carney

Julia Domna, Syrian Empress
Barbara Levick

Julia Augusti, The Emperor's Daughter
Elaine Fantham

Cornelia: Mother of the Gracchi
Suzanne Dixon

Terentia, Tullia and Publilia: The Women of Cicero's Family
Susan Treggiari

Coming Soon:

Neaera
Madeline Henry

Julia Balbilla
Patricia Rosenmeyer

Terentia, Tullia and Publilia
The Women of Cicero's Family

Susan Treggiari

Routledge
Taylor & Francis Group
LONDON AND NEW YORK

First published 2007 by Routledge
2 Park Square, Milton Park, Abingdon, Oxon OX14 4RN

Simultaneously published in the USA and Canada
by Routledge
270 Madison Avenue, New York, NY 10016

Routledge is an imprint of the Taylor & Francis Group, an informa business

© 2007 Susan Treggiari

Typeset in Sabon by
Keystroke, 28 High Street, Tettenhall, Wolverhampton
Printed and bound in Great Britain by
Antony Rowe Ltd, Chippenham, Wiltshire

All rights reserved. No part of this book may be reprinted or reproduced or utilised in any form or by any electronic, mechanical, or other means, now known or hereafter invented, including photocopying and recording, or in any information storage or retrieval system, without permission in writing from the publishers.

British Library Cataloguing in Publication Data
A catalogue record for this book is available from the British Library

Library of Congress Cataloging in Publication Data
A catalog record for this book has been requested

ISBN 13: 978–0–415–35178–2 (hbk)
ISBN 13: 978–0–415–35179–9 (pbk)
ISBN 13: 978–0–203–69854–9 (ebk)

Coniugi nepotique suavissimis

Arnaldo Treggiari   Milo Emmett Parris

Contents

	List of illustrations	ix
	Preface	xi
	List of abbreviations	xiv
	Stemmata	xviii
	Maps: the Roman world; southern Italy; Rome in the late Republic	xx
1	The rank into which they were born	1
2	The world into which they were born	13
3	Cicero: from *eques* to consul	22
4	Terentia: the young wife	30
5	The life of mother and daughter	40
6	Living through disaster	56
7	Restoration	71
8	Finding the right man	83
9	Public and private quarrels	100
10	Three divorces, a wedding, a funeral and a baby	118
11	Death and survival	143
12	Conclusions	155

Chronology	165
Ages	168
Glossary	170
Notes	172
Bibliography	205
Index of persons and Gods	214
General index	223

Illustrations

Figures

Frontispiece: Portrait of a young woman		x
1.1	Luxury dinnerware	7
3.1	Farm oxen	23
4.1	Sheep of a transhumant shepherd	35
5.1	A Roman theatre	54
7.1	A Roman road in Italy	72
7.2	Italian hill country	82
11.1	Cicero in later life	146

Maps

1	The Roman world	xx
2	Southern Italy	xxi
3	Rome in the late Republic	xxii

Frontispiece: Portrait of a young woman: Romano-Egyptian mummy, 2nd century AD (Museum of Scotland, Edinburgh)

Preface

In writing this book I thought often of Emily Eden's classic novels, *The Semi-attached Couple* (1860, but written thirty years before) and *The Semi-detached House* (1859), which address marriage in the English aristocracy. The earlier book is especially illuminating on the difficulties which social conventions impose on a warm-hearted bride from a loving family. Roman women were caught up in a tension between the ideal of monogamous, affectionate and lifelong partnership and the social practice of separation of property, relatively easy divorce, the wife's strong ties to the family of her birth and restricted legal rights in her children. These affected both wives and daughters. A daughter was expected to be permanently attached to her family of birth. A wife was both semi-attached to her husband and semi-detached from him.

There are insuperable difficulties in writing a biography of any individual in the ancient world: the shortage of first-hand material from the individual and those who knew him or her; the nature of secondary sources; our ignorance of much of what was taken for granted. The difficulty is compounded for women, since few of their writings have survived. We have to study them through sources almost always written by men, or produced by and for men (sculptures, coins and so on). For the present study, we have literary sources. Terentia and Tullia are documented almost entirely by only one man, the husband and eventually ex-husband of one and the devoted father of the other. Many of the later references derive from him too. Only occasionally do we know what other contemporary men said or wrote of them. They are, however, the only Roman women of the classical period adequately documented by private letters. Publilia is known through the same writer, Cicero, and a handful of other references. The evidence is not consistently rich on all periods of their lives. The result is that some of the reconstruction of quite important events or circumstances is guesswork. It is impossible to produce a detailed account of all stages of their lives or a rounded portrayal of character.

In attempting to write their lives, I have fallen between two stools. I want to set out the evidence so that readers can make up their own minds and I want to see things from the women's point of view. I have veered towards the former, so that Cicero, who gives us the evidence, at times usurps centre-stage. My reconstruction of what is not documented in their lives, because it is guesswork, slips away from the footlights. In the end, I wanted readers to know what can be known and to fill in the gaps by using their own imagination.

The intention here is to set out the material we have. References to sources are therefore as full as I can make them. Those in parentheses in the text directly concern Terentia, Tullia or Publilia. The notes at the end cite other sources or moderns. I have cited scholarship selectively (mostly in English), when I thought it would help the reader, when it represented a divergent view and when it was entertaining. I am indebted to many of the scholars who have written on Greek and Roman society in the last half-century, even though they could not all be acknowledged here. The reader who wishes to do so will be able to trace many of them through the bibliography which I have cited. I have tried to approach the ancient sources with a fresh eye.

I have been helped by some scholarly and imaginative biographies or studies of other Roman women. In recent years there has been a flowering of books and articles on the position of Roman women as a category. I have naturally consulted recent biographies of Cicero, all of which pay at least passing attention to his wives and daughter. Much of what scholars say on them can be traced back to influential German compilations of the late nineteenth and early twentieth centuries (Drumann-Groebe, Schmidt, Weinstock). Much of their interpretation was suggested by Plutarch. We should focus on the contemporary source, Cicero, biased and egocentric as he was, and draw our own conclusions.

Work on Cicero is enormously facilitated by the work of D. R. Shackleton Bailey (1917–2005), especially the commentaries on the correspondence and the *Onomastica*. I use his dates for individual letters. For ease of reference, Shackleton Bailey's number is given alongside the traditional number: thus 'A 1.5/1.7' directs the reader to paragraph 7 of the letter traditionally known as Book 1 number 5, which is number 1 in Shackleton Bailey's edition of the letters to Atticus. Anyone in search of further information should usually begin with Shackleton Bailey's commentary on a passage. I refer normally to Shackleton Bailey 1965–70, 1977 (both cited by volume number) and 1980. Readers looking for a translation may wish to consult Shackleton Bailey's Penguin translations (now out of print), the American Philological Association reprint of *Ad Familiares* (1988) or his Loeb editions. The big Cambridge edition, *Cicero's Letters to Atticus*, has a translation of that text. Translations in this book are my own, unless I indicate otherwise. Without Shackleton Bailey's work, a book such as this would be impossible. Only those who studied Cicero before the appearance of *Cicero's Letters to Atticus* can understand the difference he made.

I was fortunate to have had a preview of Robert Kaster's full and informative translation and commentary, *Marcus Tullius Cicero: 'Speech on behalf of Publius Sestius'* (Oxford: Clarendon Press, 2006, Clarendon Ancient History Series).

I thank my editors, Ronnie Ancona and Sarah Pomeroy, for their invitation to write this book and for their encouragement. I am indebted, as always, to friends who also work on women's history, especially to Keith Bradley, Suzanne Dixon and Elaine Fantham. Professors Dixon and Fantham, who are also contributing to this series, shared their insights on writing biographies of women. Professor Bradley generously read the whole typescript at a crucial stage and gave me the benefit of his sharp eye for what needed to be added, expanded, emphasised or cut. He is not to be blamed for the imperfections of my account. I have learned much too from undergraduate and graduate students over many years. I should like to thank Richard Stoneman, that inspiring editor, for being always ready with good counsel. Now that he is leaving Routledge, it is time to acknowledge with gratitude and admiration the work he has done for ancient history. It has been a pleasure to work with the teams at Routledge and Keystroke, especially my sharp-eyed copy-editor, Philip Parr. Officers of the Museum of Scotland, English Heritage and the Ashmolean Museum responded with courteous efficiency to my requests for illustrations. I am especially indebted to Michael Vickers, Senior Assistant Keeper of the Department of Antiquities, for finding and supplying a photograph in the midst of the Ashmolean's major building programme. As ever, I am grateful for the resources of the Sackler Library and of the Bodleian. The Sub-Faculty of Ancient History at Oxford and Oxford University Computer Services have provided the practical help I needed. For support of all kinds, without which writing would be impossible, I thank, as ever, my husband, Arnaldo Treggiari.

Abbreviations

A	Cicero *Letters to Atticus*
A.	Aulus
Acad.	Cicero *Academica*
Ad Brutum	Cicero *Ad Brutum/Letters to Brutus*
AE	*Année Epigraphique*
Am.	Cicero *De amicitia/On friendship*
Ap.	Appius
App. BC	Appian *Civil war*
Arch.	Cicero *Defence of Archias*
Asc.	Asconius, cited by pages in the edition of A. C. Clark (e.g. 10C = 10Clark)
B. Afr.	*Bellum Africum*
Balb.	Cicero *Defence of Balbus*
Brur	Cicero, *Brutus* or On famous orators
C.	Gaius
Caec.	Cicero *On behalf of the plaintiff Caecina*
Cael.	Cicero *Defence of Caelius*
CAH	*Cambridge Ancient History*
Cat.	Cicero *Speeches against Catiline*
CIL	*Corpus Inscriptionum Latinarum*
Clu.	Cicero *Defence of Cluentius*
Comm. Pet.	?Q. Cicero *Commentariolum petitionis/Handbook to electioneering*
cos.	Consul
cos. suffect	Suffect consul
D.	Decimus
De or.	Cicero *De oratore/On the orator*
Dig.	*Digest of Justinian*
Div.	Cicero *De divinatione/On divination*
Div. Caec.	Cicero *Divinatio in Caecilium*
Dom.	Cicero *De domo/On his house*
Euseb. *Chron.*	Eusebius *Chronicles*
F	Cicero *Ad familiares/Letters to friends*

Abbreviations xv

Fin.	Cicero *De finibus*/*On the ends of good and evil*
Flacc.	Cicero *Defence of Flaccus*
Font.	Cicero *Defence of Fonteius*
Frag.	*Fragment*
Gell.	Aulus Gellius *Noctes Atticae*
Har. resp.	Cicero *De haruspicum responso*/*On the reply of the haruspices*
Hor. *Epodes*	Horace *Epodes*
Hor. *Epp.*	Horace *Epistulae*/*Epistles*
Hor. *Odes*	Horace *Odes*
Hor. *Sat.*	Horace *Satires*
Hort.	Cicero *Hortensius*
ILLRP	*Inscriptiones latinae liberae rei publicae*, ed. Attilio Degrassi (Florence: La nuova Italia, i² [1965], ii [1963])
Juv.	Juvenal
L.	Lucius
Laud. Tur.	*Laudatio 'Turiae'*
Leg.	Cicero *De legibus*/*On the laws*
Leg. ag.	Cicero *De lege agraria*/*On the agrarian law*
Lig.	Cicero *Defence of Ligarius*
Livy *Epit.*	Livy *Epitomae* (summaries of books)
LTUR	*Lexicon Topographicum urbis Romae*
LTUR Suburbium	*Lexicon Topographicum urbis Romae Suburbium*
M.	Marcus
M'.	Manius
Macrob.	Macrobius *Saturnalia*
Mil.	Cicero *Defence of Milo*
MRR	*Magistrates of the Roman Republic*, ed. T. R. S. Broughton, i (1951), ii 1952), iii (1986) (now published by Oxford University Press, New York)
Mur.	Cicero *Defence of Murena*
Nep. *Att.*	Nepos *Life of Atticus*
Nonius	Nonius Marcellus *De compendiosa doctrina*, ed. Wallace M. Lindsay (Leipzig: Teubner, 1903)
ns	New series
OCD³	*The Oxford Classical Dictionary*³ (Oxford: Clarendon Press, 1996)
Off.	Cicero *De officiis*/*On duties*
OLD	*Oxford Latin dictionary*
Or.	Cicero *Orator*
Ovid *Am.*	Ovid *Amores*
Ovid *Ars*	Ovid *Ars amatoria*
Ovid *Met.*	Ovid *Metamorphoses*
Ovid *Tr.*	Ovid *Tristia*
P.	Publius

xvi *Abbreviations*

Parad.	Cicero *Paradoxa Stoicorum/Paradoxes of the Stoics*
Phil.	Cicero *Philippics* (*Speeches against M. Antonius*)
PIR²	*Prosopographia imperii Romani*²
Pis.	Cicero *Invective against Piso*
Planc.	Cicero *Defence of Plancius*
Pliny *Epp.*	Pliny *Epistulae/Letters*
Pliny *NH*	Elder Pliny *Natural history*
Plut.	Plutarch
Plut. *Ant.*	Plutarch *Life of Antony*
Plut. *Cato mai.*	Plutarch *Life of Cato the Elder*
Plut. *Cato min.*	Plutarch *Life of Cato the Younger*
Plut. *Cic.*	Plutarch *Life of Cicero*
Plut. *Mar.*	Plutarch *Life of Marius*
Plut. *Quaest. conv.*	Plutarch *Quaestiones convivales*
Plut. *Pomp.*	Plutarch *Life of Pompey*
Plut. *Sulla*	Plutarch *Life of Sulla*
Polyb.	Polybius
Prov. Cons.	Cicero *De provinciis consularibus/On the consular provinces*
QF	Cicero *Letters to his brother Quintus*
Quinct.	Cicero *On behalf of the plaintiff Quinctius*
Quint. *Inst.*	Quintilian *Institutio oratoria*
Rab. Post.	Cicero *Defence of Rabirius Postumus*
RE	*Real-Encyclopädie der classischen Altertumswissenschaft*
Red. Pop.	Cicero *Post reditum ad populum/After his return to the People*
Red. Sen.	Cicero *Post reditum ad senatum/After his return to the Senate*
Rep.	Cicero *De Republica/On the Republic*
RP	Syme (1979–91)
s.	*sub*/under
sal.	salutation (heading of a letter)
Sall. *Cat.*	Sallust *Catiline*
Sall. *Jug.*	Sallust *War with Jugurtha*
Sall. *Hist.*	Sallust *Histories* (cited by book and fragment from McGushin 1992)
[Sall]. *Inv.*	[Sallust, attributed to] *Invective against Cicero*
SB *A*	Shackleton Bailey (1965–70)
SB *Cicero's letters to his friends*	Shackleton Bailey (1978b)
SB *F*	Shackleton Bailey (1977a)
Sen.	Cicero *De Senectute/On old age*

Sen. *Con.*	Elder Seneca *Controversiae*
Sen. *Ben.*	Seneca, *De beneficiis*
Sen. *Suas.*	Elder Seneca *Suasoriae*
Ser.	Servius
Sest.	Cicero *Defence of Sestius*
SHA	*Scriptores Historiae Augustae*
Sid. Ap. *Epist.*	Sidonius Apollinaris *Epistulae*
Soranus *Gyn.*	Soranus *Gynaecology*, tr. Owsei Temkin (Baltimore: Johns Hopkins University Press, 1956)
SRosc.	Cicero *Defence of Sextus Roscius of Ameria*
Stat. *Silv.*	Statius *Silvae*
Suet. *Aug.*	Suetonius *Life of Augustus*
Suet. *Jul.*	Suetonius *Life of Julius Caesar*
Suet. *Gr.*	Suetonius *On Grammarians*
Suet. *Tib.*	Suetonius *Life of Tiberius*
Sulla	Cicero *Defence of Sulla*
Syme, *RP*	Syme, *Roman Papers*
T.	Titus
Tac.	Tacitus
Tac. *Ann.*	Tacitus *Annals*
Tert. *virg. vel.*	Tertullian *De virginibus velandis*
Ti.	Tiberius
Top.	Cicero *Topica/Matters concerning commonplaces*
TP	Tyrrell and Purser 1885–1933
Tusc.	Cicero *Tusculan disputations*
Val. Max.	Valerius Maximus
Vat.	Cicero *Invective against Vatinius*
Vell.	Velleius Paterculus
Verg. *Aen.*	Vergil *Aeneid*
Verr.	Cicero *Prosecution of Verres*
Vitr.	Vitruvius

Stemmata

Tullii Cicerones and paternal kin

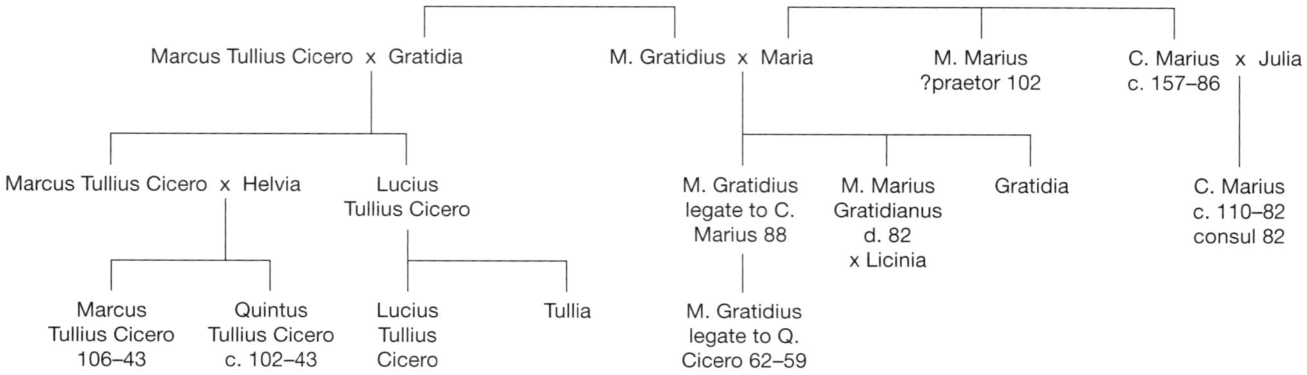

```
Marcus Tullius Cicero × Gratidia ─────────────────────── M. Gratidius × Maria ─────── M. Marius         C. Marius × Julia
        │                                                        │                    ?praetor 102       c. 157–86
        │                                                        │                           │
        │           Lucius Tullius Cicero                         │                           │
        │                   │                                    │                      M. Marius Gratidianus    Gratidia
        │                   │                                    │                      d. 82
        │                   │                                    │                      × Licinia
        │           Lucius Tullius Cicero   Tullia               │                                       C. Marius
        │                                                        │                                      c. 110–82
        │                                           M. Gratidius legate to C. Marius 88                 consul 82
        │                                           M. Gratidius legate to Q. Cicero 62–59
Marcus Tullius Cicero × Helvia
        │
   ┌────┴──────────────┐
Marcus Tullius    Quintus Tullius
Cicero            Cicero
106–43            c. 102–43
```

Tullii Cicerones and maternal kin

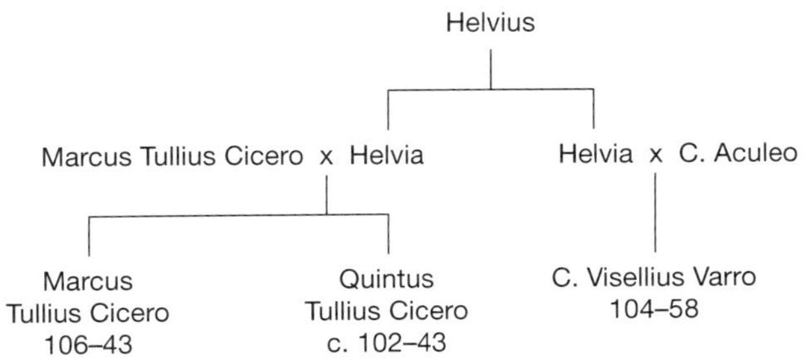

Helvius
├── Helvia × C. Aculeo
│   └── C. Visellius Varro
│   104–58
└── Marcus Tullius Cicero × Helvia
      ├── Marcus Tullius Cicero
      │   106–43
      └── Quintus Tullius Cicero
            c. 102–43

Cicero's immediate family

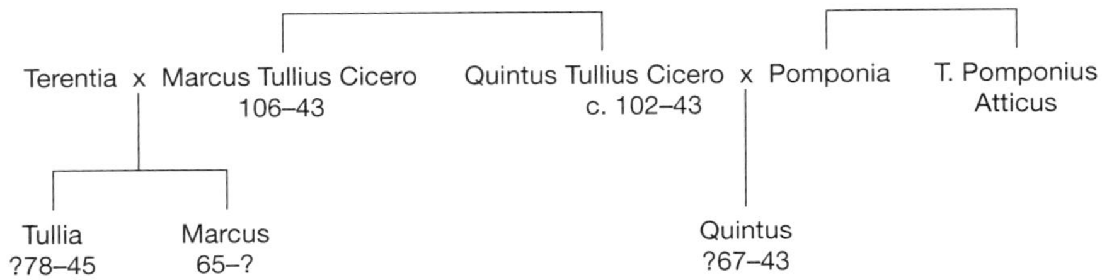

                                    ┌── T. Pomponius Atticus
                                    └── Pomponia × Quintus Tullius Cicero
                                                        c. 102–43
                                          └── Quintus
                                                ?67–43

Terentia × Marcus Tullius Cicero
              106–43
    ├── Tullia
    │   ?78–45
    └── Marcus
          65–?

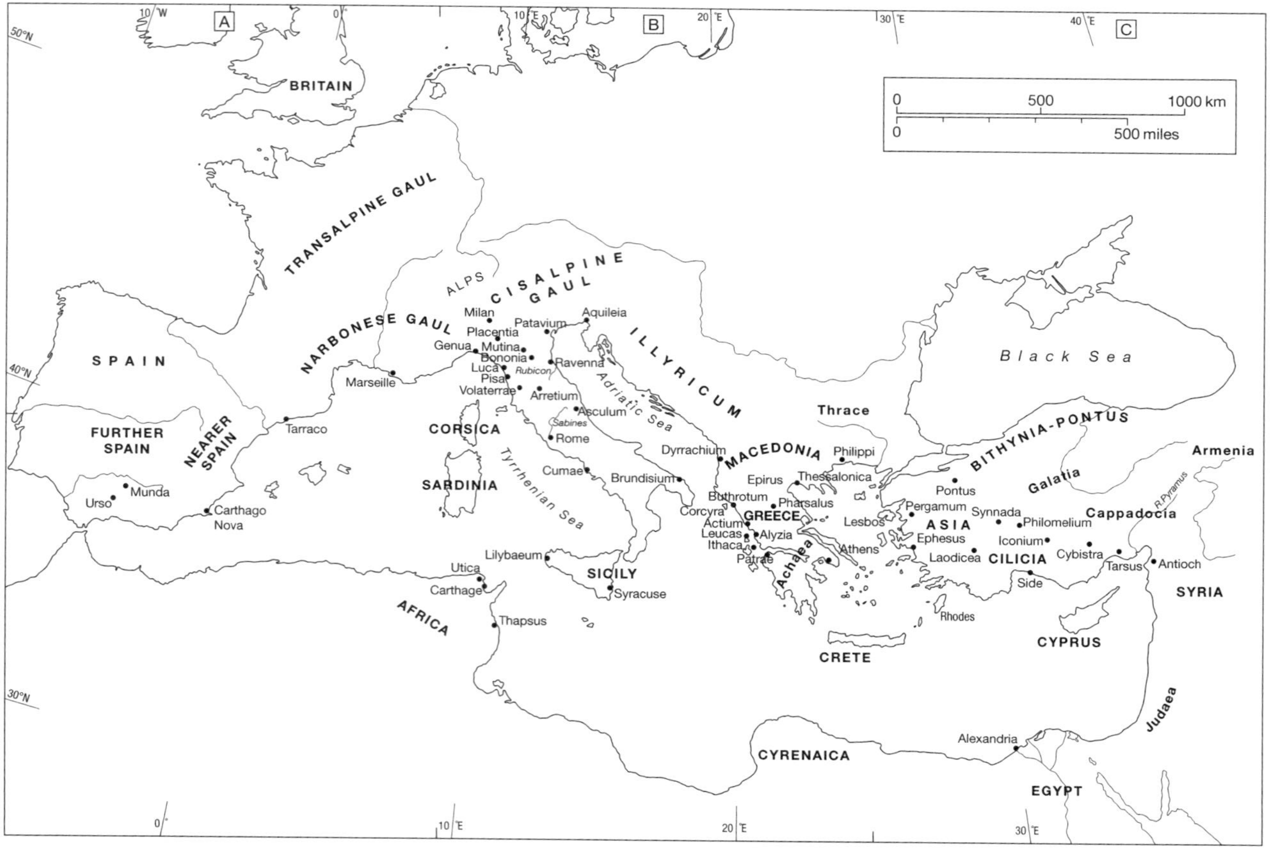

Map 1 The Roman World
Based on *CAH ix*² 566

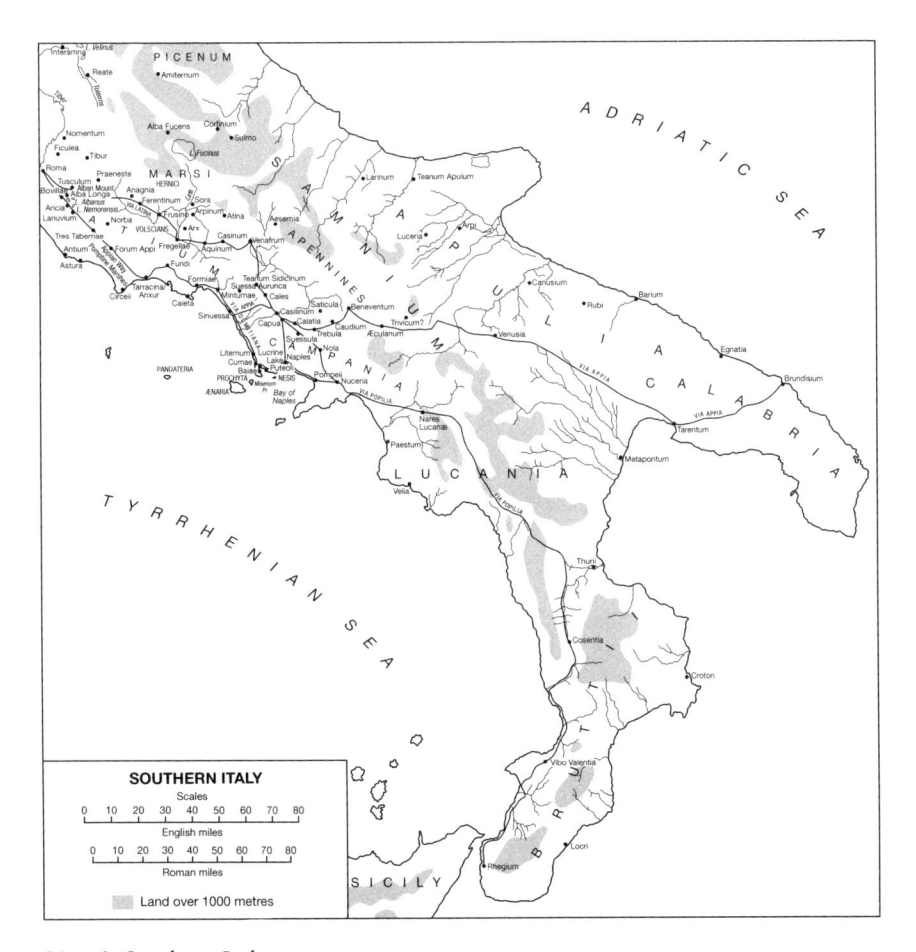

Map 2 Southern Italy
Based on SB *A* iii (end paper)

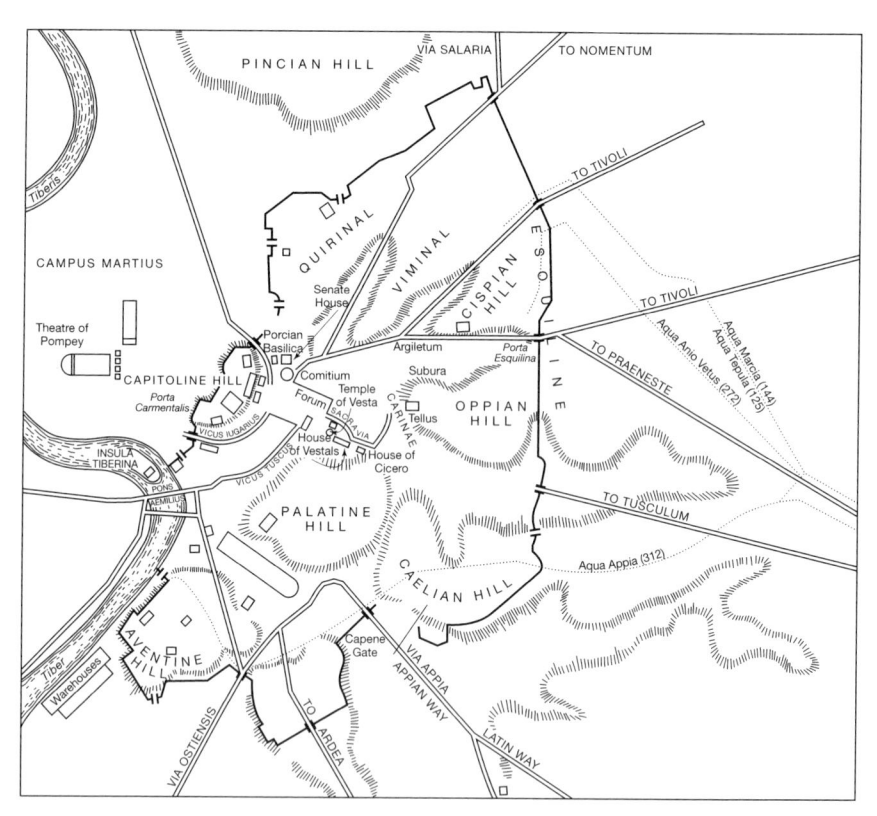

Map 3 Rome in the late Republic
Based on *CAH ix²* 70

1 The rank into which they were born

> ... certare ingenio, contendere nobilitate,
> noctes atque dies niti praestante labore
> ad summas emergere opes rerumque potiri.
>
> ... competing with inborn ability, striving with nobility, night and day struggling with outstanding effort to win through to the greatest resources and gain control of the world.
>
> Lucretius, *On the Nature of Things* 2.11–13

Terentia, her daughter Tullia and her husband's second wife, Publilia, who was young enough to be her granddaughter, were born into wealth, position and power, when the Roman Republic was relatively secure in its dominance of the Mediterranean, although domestic problems were intensifying. They were free, when others were slaves; they were Roman citizens; they shared in Graeco-Roman high culture. Since their socio-political status depended initially on that of their parents and later on that of their husbands, and since Terentia and Tullia at least were deeply involved in their husbands' politics, the context in which their men functioned is essential background. Apart from biology, they had less in common with women of lesser status than with men of their own class. Some six hundred senators and their families were at the vertiginous peak of a social pyramid, formed of tens of millions of inhabitants of the Roman Empire and a million in Rome itself.

People born into the upper classes, when Rome ruled all of the world which mattered, were extraordinarily privileged.[1] Given a sufficient fortune and a suitable education, a young male Roman might hope, by talent and hard work, to climb the political ladder, increase his property and, if he achieved a year of office as consul, control his world for a time. Those who began the race as members of senatorial families with high officials among their ancestors had the advantage of 'nobility' and had the best chance of reaching the top. Those who rose to the highest elected offices usually proceeded to govern a province, where they ruled supreme without colleagues and had opportunity to win glory and legitimate profit (not to mention rich illicit pickings which might give rise to prosecution and disgrace). The

Epicurean philosopher, like Lucretius (quoted above), might idealise contemplative detachment, but in practice any Roman man born into the upper classes was likely, out of duty or ambition, to get involved in public service. The possibilities were exciting.

Rome's position in the world also affected the lives of Roman women. This is the age of widowed mothers who pushed their sons into politics, of sisters who helped their brothers, of wives whose dowry and diplomatic abilities smoothed the career of their husbands and of daughters whose marital prospects were enhanced by their father's political promotion and who might influence his decisions and act as intermediaries between him and husbands' families.

Rome, Italy, the Empire

The Romans traced their origins to villages on the hills at the lowest crossing of the Tiber, which coalesced into a city-state around the eighth century.[2] Women were citizens with private rights (not the vote, the rights to stand for office or serve in the army) and transmitted the citizenship to their children in valid Roman marriage or outside marriage. By a process of conquest and absorption, the Romans gradually extended their power, first in the surrounding plain of Latium and then over neighbouring territories. From the beginning, as Cicero saw it, they had extended Roman citizenship to others:

> What in particular undoubtedly founded our empire and increased the race of the Roman People was that our leader, the creator of this city, Romulus, by his treaty with the Sabines taught us that we ought to increase this state by welcoming even those who had been our enemies. By his authority and example, our ancestors never left off their generosity in granting and sharing citizenship. So many from Latium, for example the citizens of Tusculum and Lanuvium, and whole races from other groups were welcomed into citizenship, for instance the Sabines, Volscians, Hernici.
>
> (*Balb.* 31)

In peninsular Italy, not only Latins (whose customs and language were the same as those of the Romans), but also Italic peoples of other languages and culture, whole city-states of the Etruscans or Greek colonies might become Roman. The Volscians, who swept into southern Latium from the Apennines in the fifth century and fought the Romans hard, were subdued by the late fourth century. Volscian Arpinum/Arpino, which was to be Cicero's hometown, received limited citizenship at that time, and full citizenship in 188. By the mid-second century, the map of peninsular Italy was a mosaic of Roman territory; cities (*coloniae*) founded by Rome and populated by people with full Roman or the more limited Latin rights; allied cities and tribes. But all were dominated by Rome and contributed to Rome's fighting forces.

Once Romans dominated the peninsula, they came up against foreigners beyond the sea, initially across the narrow straits which divide the toe of Italy from Sicily. As a result, in the mid-third century, Sicily became the first 'province': the Roman Empire had begun.

> For you ought to take care of all the allies and provinces, but especially, judges, you ought to take care of Sicily, for many just reasons, first of all because Sicily was the first of all foreign nations to attach herself to the friendship and good faith of the Roman People. She first of all was given the name of province, which is an ornament of empire; she first of all taught our ancestors how glorious it was to rule foreign races.
> (*Verr.* 2.2.2)

Like Italy itself, the Empire was a mosaic. It was not a geographical bloc with defined frontiers, but rather everything the Roman People could control, whatever fell under their power, *imperium populi Romani*, to which they could give orders (*imperare*) or (as I have translated above) which they could rule.[3] The startling expansion of the 60s and 50s must have impressed Terentia and Tullia, especially when Q. Cicero, with Caesar, crossed the terrifying Channel and could study the landscape and peoples of Britain.[4] The Empire included provinces administered by Roman governors, in which there would be cities with degrees of self-government, even 'freedom', and attached to which there might be whole kingdoms, allied to Rome but still ruled by kings. Members of the provincial elite might be granted Roman citizenship. There was a rich cultural mix. In the eastern Mediterranean, the common language for the upper classes and anyone involved in trade was Greek. In the West, Latin was making headway. Roman soldiers and merchants spread Roman ways. But the vast majority of the inhabitants of the Empire spoke their own native languages and followed their local customs and laws. Rome itself was a cosmopolitan city, of free foreign immigrants as well as slaves and ex-slaves of foreign origin.

The fundamental division in the world known to Romans was between slave and free.[5] Slaves were chattels, without legal rights. All the societies with which Rome came into contact practised slavery. The unusual characteristic of Romans was that, if they freed their slaves, they made them citizens.

In areas controlled by Rome, to be born not only free but Roman seemed to Romans to be a distinct privilege, as in the nineteenth century, for many reasons among which the existence of the Empire was prominent, being born British was a privilege.[6] The elite of a Greek city, say Naples, might despise Romans as culturally inferior and not cherish any wish to be offered Roman citizenship or to speak Latin, but the practical benefits of Roman private rights (marriage, contracts, owning Roman land, benefiting under Roman wills) and the right of appeal against Roman officials became obvious, by the second century, to Italians from allied communities who were trading in the provinces. The breakthrough the Romans made was to allow the acquisition of Roman citizenship without the renunciation of prior ties and loyalties. After the war with the allies, which brought about the extension of the Roman franchise to peninsular Italy, Cicero (*Leg.* 2.2.5.) could say of the natives of Italian towns, *municipia* (of which Arpinum was one): 'I hold that all citizens of *municipia* have two fatherlands, one according to nature and one according to the state.'

How did a person acquire citizenship? First, by birth, as the child of a valid Roman marriage. A marriage was valid when made by two Roman citizens as long as there was no incapacity, such as close relationship (marriage was forbidden between ascendant and descendant [e.g., parent and child] or collaterals closer than first cousins [e.g., brother and sister, uncle and niece]) or being under age. The right of intermarriage with Romans might also be acquired by citizens of other communities: if the father were Roman, then the marriage was valid in Roman law and the children acquired his citizenship. Second, a child born to a Roman woman not validly married in Roman law acquired her citizenship according to *ius gentium*, the law observed (in Roman thinking) by all human beings.[7] Next, citizenship might be acquired, by free aliens, a group or an individual person or family, through a law or by executive action on the part of a Roman official. It was also possible, and common, for an individual Roman citizen, man or woman, to transmit citizenship by the act of freeing a slave, for liberty and citizenship went together.

Citizens had the right of marriage with other citizens (*conubium*), the right to make contracts according to Roman law (*commercium*), the right of appeal against action by elected officials (*provocatio*), and, if male and adult, the vote, the right (in theory) to stand for public office and to serve in the army. The Roman People was sovereign: it met as a group in several differently organised assemblies to pass laws, decide on war or peace and elect men to annual office.

Within the citizen body, there was a marked hierarchy or, as Cicero would see it, a series of steps of varying worthiness and status (*dignitas*).[8] Social status depended in part on political rank and was supposedly associated with moral desert. At the top were the *ordines*, ranks (you could picture them in the front rows at the games or as soldiers drawn up for battle) of senators and *equites*. Beneath them was the *populus Romanus* or the Roman *plebs*, the common people, as a whole.

Senate and *equites*

If you wanted to find out if a man was a senator, you could check for his name on the list of senators or look and see if he was wearing the gold ring, *latus clavus* (a broad upright purple stripe on his tunic) or special red shoes (*calcei mullei* or *patricii*, if he had held curule office), which were senatorial privileges.

The Senate (*senatus*) was made up of men who had held elected office. In practice only men of considerable wealth and position could afford to stand. Candidates might be sons of senators or belong to wealthy families which had not yet achieved senatorial rank. These, the pool from which the Senate was drawn, were from 70 onwards known as *equites*, cavalrymen (though their connection with cavalry was historical rather than current, except that when they served in the army they, as officers, mostly rode with the infantry rather than marching on foot). Cicero tells us in 54 that standing for office had 'always been open to men risen from this equestrian order of ours' (*Planc.* 17).

The senators were elected by the People. Some senatorial families cease to be attested, perhaps because their fortunes were diminished, or because they failed to produce sons who reached the age at which they could stand for office. As a result, a constant intake of new blood was needed so this was not a closed hereditary aristocracy. A man who could not point to an ancestor in the direct male line who had been a senator was a new man, *novus homo*.[9] Many such men would reach only the lowest rung of senatorial office, the quaestorship, and remain among those in the Senate who were not called upon to speak but merely voted. Some might aspire to the praetorship, a more hotly contested office, and the rare few, the famous *novi*, of whom Cicero is the most famous, reached the consulship.

But the consulship, the summit of a senatorial career, open to only two men a year, was carefully guarded. As Sallust (*Jug.* 63), a former *eques*, wrote of the late second century: 'At that time, the *plebs* bestowed the other offices, but the nobility passed the consulship from hand to hand. Any new man, however distinguished he might be . . . , was held unworthy of this honour and spurned as if he were polluted.' These 'nobles' (*nobiles*) were those who could point to an ascendant who had held the consulship. (The adjective *nobilis* means 'known' or 'notable'). Such men had names which were recognised.[10] The Romans expressed dates by naming the consuls of the year. So schoolchildren had to learn the list of consuls. Having a consular ancestor was a marked advantage in one's own candidacy for a consulship. Similarly, having a praetor as an ancestor might help a man get the praetorship. The Romans had an aristocracy of office, recruited from those who had passed the test of being elected by an assembly of the People. There was competition between *nobiles*: not all could win.[11]

Sharp competition for recognition by peers and by the electorate meant that Roman politicians had to work hard. The year or two before the elections were a time of canvassing, in the city and sometimes in scattered country districts. Men kept themselves in the public eye by acting as advocates in trials held in the Forum (which provided a public spectacle), by making speeches on political questions at the invitation of senatorial colleagues, by seizing the opportunity of a family funeral to praise their distinguished kin (including, in the late Republic, women), by seeking glory in foreign wars, as commanders or subordinates.

Socially, despite some political and economic conflicts of interest, senators and *equites* were closely intertwined. Their families intermarried. Some *equites* were as rich as or richer than senators. A man whose uncle or elder brother had advanced from the equestrian order to the Senate would still count as a new man if he too attempted to enter the Senate. So would one whose mother was descended from a long line of consuls but whose father was an *eques* and descended from *equites*. Senators and *equites* went to dinner at each other's houses, invested in land, had similar cultural interests and education, served side-by-side on the councils of Italian towns. A man like Cicero's friend Atticus could claim a *social* superiority to a senator who traced his origin to an Italian town and whose family had held the citizenship for only a century, such as Cicero: 'Titus Pomponius Atticus, descended as he was from the remotest origins of the Roman race, retained uninterrupted the equestrian rank inherited from his forebears. His father was industrious, by the standards of those days rich, and a lover of literature' (Nep. *Att.* 1.1–2, tr. Horsfall [1989] 15). Lucretius might have had Atticus in mind when he recommended watching the struggles of others and standing aloof.[12]

Women fitted into this socio-political hierarchy. During the late Republic, they did not formally belong to the order of their father or husband. But people would know whether a woman was the daughter of a senator or an *eques*, whether she was patrician, what was the status of her husband, and these things would count. Upper-class married women might meet in a formal group for religious and social purposes. They would exclude disreputable women. They might even be regarded as an *ordo* (order).[13] There would also be informal but socially exclusive gatherings of married women or girls.

Nothing at this date marked out the wives and daughters of senators from women of equestrian families. But there was competition to show status through dress, jewellery (see frontispiece) and attendants. A long tunic called the *stola* distinguished the married woman on formal occasions: its shape did not vary but taste and wealth could be displayed in the choice of colour and fabric.

Senators and *equites* enjoyed riches and position which marked them off sharply from the rest of the population. They had most of their wealth in land, the securest form of investment. Senators could engage in trade and commerce through middlemen, particularly their freedmen. Conspicuous consumption was important as an assertion of their taste and liberality. Standards of living had been rising for some time, thanks to imperial expansion. Luxury meant fine cuisine, wine, scent and spices, rich fabrics and dyes, furniture, specialised slaves, grand houses and gardens (Figure 1.1).[14] It was normal in the late Republic for a senator to have not only a house in Rome (essential for political life), but several residences in different parts of Italy, usually equipped with profitable farms as well as pleasure-grounds.[15] They might also give a base for useful political contacts. The Bay of Naples was especially fashionable for recreation, which included beach

Figure 1.1 Luxury dinnerware: red Arretine bowl in moulded terracotta, which reflects styles in gold and silver, customs in dining and drinking and the association of wine with sexual pleasure. Even if the couple represented are an upper-class man and a courtesan, upper-class women probably used such vessels, most often in gold or silver (Ashmolean Museum, Oxford)

picnics, boating and swimming.[16] Senators' wives and daughters participated in their lifestyle, moving around as the season dictated. Terentia and Tullia were to have opportunities for holidays and tours. Pilia, Atticus' wife, on one occasion in early summer, borrowed Cicero's country-house (villa) on the Lucrine Lake (the *Cumanum*), with its servants and stores, for a holiday without her husband and small daughter.[17] We hear little of women's direct ownership of houses and villas, but that may be partly due to the bias of our sources, for they must sometimes have inherited them from fathers or husbands.[18] Partly, too, it may be because women did not need to boost their status in this way: they might prefer investment properties and portable wealth, such as jewels, which they could enjoy while their husbands provided the setting.[19]

The town-house (*domus*) was a headquarters, where the most important of the domestic staff were normally based.[20] It was the domicile to which important messages would be sent, the place to which clients would come for the formal morning-call (*salutatio*). It would need spacious reception-rooms and outdoor spaces for *salutatores*, meetings and arbitrations.[21] These were activities of the master of the house (*dominus*). Its mistress used the same spaces and had her own callers and meetings, but (presumably) at a later time of day, when her husband had gone to the Senate, law-courts or assembly. While big, semi-public events were in progress, she, the children and the domestic staff could get on with their own activities in other parts of the house: a light breakfast, dressing, giving orders for the day.[22] Because our literary evidence focuses on men and the archaeological evidence has to be interpreted, we tend to see the women and children fitting into the interstices of the life of the house, but they probably saw it differently. To them, the routine of the day and the uses to which the house was put were natural, and their lives flowed smoothly around the politician's schedule. The *atrium*, the main reception room, was the centre of domestic cult and the place where the ancestral portraits were kept. It was the hub of domestic life once the *salutatores* had gone. A ceremonial marriage-bed would indicate that the owner was married; a loom might demonstrate the industry of the mistress of the house.[23] The mistress would use it to oversee the running of the house. When a family member was absent, a system of couriers would be organised from there. When a courier was about to depart, the person in charge, often the wife if the husband was away, would send messages to friends, asking if they had letters they wanted to send.[24]

The common people

A woman of the senatorial or equestrian class would be aware of lower-class citizens when she went outside her home.[25] They were part of the seething crowds in the streets, at the races, plays or gladiatorial games. Only when the men and children (of either sex) were formally dressed in the toga or the married women in their native costume (the *stola*) could they be immediately identified as citizens and distinguished from foreigners and slaves. Working men, who usually wore tunics, might be day-labourers in the docks or on building-sites. They might be employees in the transport business, like, for instance, the drivers who might cause a nasty accident when they tried to help their mules drag a heavy wagon up the steep slope of the Capitoline.[26] The more fortunate might be craftsmen and shopkeepers, assisted by their wives, children or slaves and freed slaves.[27] Upper-class women might visit their shops (particularly those of goldsmiths, jewellers, makers of cloth, clothes and shoes, perfumers and so on) or summon them to give commissions. Pedlars visited rich houses. Farmers came into the city to sell produce. They might be known to the upper classes as their tenants or neighbours in the country. A wealthy woman might also have dealings with merchants and businessmen. Alongside the more successful farmers, these were at the upper end of the lower classes.

> Now what we have been taught [by philosophers] to think about crafts and ways of earning a living, which should be considered suitable for a free person and which are sordid, goes like this: First of all, occupations which incur people's hatred are considered bad – for instance the trade of a usurer. In the class of the sordid ways of earning a living, those unsuitable for a free person, come the jobs of all wage-earners who sell labour, not skill, for their very wages are recompense of a contract of slavery. We must also think sordid those people who buy from merchants and sell instantly, for they would get no profit unless they told outright lies, and there is nothing more shameful than deception. All labourers take part in a sordid skill, for the workshop has nothing freeborn about it. Least of all can we approve those crafts which serve sensual pleasures, 'Fishmongers, butchers, cooks, poultry-fatteners, fishermen', as Terence says; add to this group, if you like, perfumers, dancers and the whole *corps de ballet*. But skills in which either a greater degree of knowledge inheres or a greater than ordinary benefit is the object – such as medicine, architecture, teaching of honourable subjects – these are honourable for those to whose rank they are appropriate.
>
> (*Off.* 1.150–1)

Cicero goes on to make an exception for wholesale merchants. The upper classes might lump together all who were compelled to earn their living by physical labour or skill. The city wage-earner was uncomfortably close to a slave (since he had to take orders); even the independent workman or dealer ministered to others and (at least according to high-minded doctrine) their superfluous appetites. Cicero could refer to such humble people (at least when they were opposed to him politically) as 'dregs', both in private and for educated readers – 'the depraved and lowest dregs of the People', 'workmen and shop-keepers and all those dregs of communities', 'all the dregs of the city'.[28] To their betters, workmen seemed to be on the same side as slaves.[29] Crowds which came to protest in the Forum or in front of the houses of politicians (and sometimes took to violence) were no doubt mixed, including slaves, freed slaves, day-labourers, craftsmen and shopkeepers, foreigners and citizens. It was hard for the observer to tell which was which, but if the shops were shut for the day it would seem obvious that shopkeepers were involved.[30]

Even those who would in modern times be called 'professionals' – doctors, architects, teachers, philosophers, most of the poets – relied on others for their living. Some of these might be, or become, *equites*. Those who served the upper classes would often interact with the women of the household. They might live in the household, instruct children and dine with the family.

Upper-class women would know some of their own slaves and freed slaves more intimately than lower-class Romans. The wealthy Roman of either sex owned a considerable number of slaves, the majority of them farmworkers. More educated and valuable servants worked in the household, both in Rome and in the country, where it was also necessary to employ large numbers of 'labourers', humble cleaners or spinning women and so on, whom their owners never name in our literary texts and who leave no record at this period.[31] But the mistress of the household and her daughters would certainly have known by name and had a good deal to do with the steward, servants who waited at table, child-minders, nurses, hairdressers, spinning-women, footmen, valets, secretaries and ladies' maids. Some of these would be manumitted and become free Roman citizens, though they might continue to work in the household.

Sketch of political history, c. 150–80

The Greek historian Polybius belonged to the cultivated group which surrounded P. Cornelius Scipio Aemilianus. This group of friends is constantly evoked by Cicero when he sets his ethical or political dialogues in a kind of golden age, the time of his own grandfather: he puts philosophical teachings into the mouths of its eminent Roman members.[32] Polybius tried to explain to his Greek readers what kind of state had established its empire over 'almost the whole of the known world' within the short space of fifty-three years from the lead-in to the Second War with Carthage down to the collapse of the Hellenistic monarchy in Macedon (220–167). By the end of that period, Rome had little to fear from the remaining great powers in the Mediterranean, though wars continued to be endemic. Soon Carthage and Corinth were destroyed (146). By 133, the Romans had six provinces: Sicily, Sardinia and Corsica, Nearer Spain, Further Spain, 'Africa' (part of modern Tunisia) and Macedonia. By the end of the century she acquired 'Asia' (the old kingdom of Pergamum), Narbonese Gaul and Cilicia. Although Rome allowed a great deal of self-government, she took on the burden of defence and security. Tribute was exacted. Wealth flowed to Rome: loot, tax-collectors' profits, gifts, slaves and economic migrants. Trade preceded and accompanied the armies. New luxuries became fashionable, then commonplace as they came within the reach of more people.[33] The wars brought about a socio-economic revolution in traditional Italian society: the availability of confiscated land, improved farming techniques and slave labour allowed wealthier citizens to cash in. Peasants, the backbone of the army, were often displaced from their land. There was a demand for reforms, partially met by Tiberius Gracchus' law (133) distributing public land to the poor.

Increased legislative activity heightened political conflict. Two currents of thought can be distinguished, whose practitioners were labelled *boni* or *optimates* (the good, the best people) and *populares* (those supporting the People). 'Those who want what they say and do to be pleasing to the multitude were held to be *populares*; those who behave in such a way that their ideas win approval from the best people were thought *optimates*.'[34]

A sporadic succession of *popularis* tribunes over the years of the late second and early first centuries championed causes attractive to the common people such as the secret ballot, allotments of land, colonies, subsidised grain allowances, private rights (especially the appeal) and special commands for generals expected to win wars. They even proposed the enfranchisement of the Italian allies. Civil violence escalated in 133, when a senatorial mob lynched Tiberius Gracchus. Other reformers met a similar fate. Disappointed in their hopes of receiving Roman citizenship (first raised in 125) by the murder of M. Livius Drusus in 91, the Italians revolted. A bloody war left lasting bitterness, though the Romans quickly enfranchised loyal communities and individuals, and subdued and gradually brought the rest into full citizenship.[35] It was not until the time of Augustus that wounds were healed.

Competition for prized military commands became more unscrupulous. The general C. Marius, a new man from Arpinum, exploited a perception of senatorial incompetence and won the consulship and a special command in North Africa. He was subsequently the main architect of the defeat of the Cimbri and Teutones, wandering northern tribes who brought back memories of the barbarians who had sacked Rome in the fourth century. He was elected, unprecedentedly, to six consulships (107, 104–100). Plum commands became a bargaining tool. The shocking upshot was that in 88 L. Cornelius Sulla, indignant that a tribune had given the command assigned to him by the Senate to the aged Marius, marched on Rome and seized power. A dozen opponents were outlawed and fled or were killed. Once Sulla had departed to his province, the Marians in turn took over Rome in civil war. Marius held his seventh consulship, but died that year (86). Enemies were killed and their heads displayed on the speakers' platform. They included the great orator M. Antonius.[36] Sulla, theoretically representing senatorial legitimacy,[37] came back in 83 with his victorious eastern army, beat the Marians in a series of battles on Italian soil, proscribed his upper-class enemies (on one account 40 senators and 1600 *equites*) and massacred 8000 Samnite prisoners. He made himself dictator and attempted to restore stability by optimate reforms. Most of his constitutional settlement was undone by 70. His violence was branded on people's memory.[38]

Politics had also played on rivalry between senators and *equites*. By manning the extortion court (to try provincial governors) with a panel of judges who were specifically drawn from men who were neither senators nor close relatives of senators and whose duty was to try senatorial ex-governors, Gaius Gracchus created conflict of interest between the ruling class and a larger and disparate group, whose financial interests largely coincided with those of senators but which included wealthy tax-contractors who might quarrel with governors. The discontents of the masses produced a deeper rift in the citizen body. The war with the allies and the civil wars and proscriptions left a legacy of suffering which would not be forgotten for generations. Although women were not a target, they inevitably suffered in the transit of armies and in the aftermath of battles and because of what happened to their fathers, husbands and sons. All these events were part of the consciousness of Terentia as she grew up.[39]

2 The world into which they were born

Demographic and biological circumstances

Expectation of life in the Greek and Roman world was closer to that of other pre-industrial societies than to that of modern 'Western' countries. Life expectancy at birth was probably twenty-five to thirty years.[1] There must have been considerable local and social differences. Great cities, such as Rome itself, like early modern London, attracted new inhabitants and reduced their life expectancy. Infant mortality was very high. But the upper classes, with a better diet, access to doctors (not always salutary), freedom from hard physical work, the ability to visit the country and seaside and to stay out of the city through the worst of the summer heat, were more likely to enjoy a long life than the working class.[2] Even their domestic slaves had healthier lives than the poor citizens.

We are under-informed (even for the upper classes) about inability to conceive, miscarriages, premature births and children who died very young. Risks were highest around the time of birth and weaning; ordinary childhood illnesses were a threat. (Probably about 50 per cent did not survive to the age of ten.)[3] We naturally hear most about men who survived to adulthood and political careers. Women are under-represented, even in the epitaphs, except for wives who died pathetically young. Men who survived war or women who survived pregnancy and childbirth might live healthy lives to an advanced age, but their age cohort would be diminishing steadily.[4] The disparate experiences of Tullia and Terentia help illustrate the range of possibilities. Terentia allegedly lived to the age of 103 (Pliny *NH* 7.158). Tullia died as a result of childbirth in her thirties.

Women often escape attention in our literary sources. Cicero found occasion to mention the mother-in-law of the consul Piso as involved in the depredations of which he accuses him. He observes the usual rule that women should not be named in political speeches. Asconius, the diligent commentator who researched this speech in Nero's time, was unable to discover what she was called: 'I have not been able to find out who Piso's mother-in-law was. This is plainly because authors have not, in describing houses and households, handed down the names of women as they have those of men, unless they were distinguished' (Asc. 10C, commenting on *Pis.* 24).[5]

The Roman system of nomenclature made it difficult to identify women. In our period, citizen men usually bore two names: a forename (*praenomen*), such as Marcus, Quintus, Gaius; and a 'clan' name (*nomen gentile*), such as Tullius, Marius, Pomponius. Only a few forenames were in common use and choice was further restricted by the custom of using only a selection of these in a family. Women bore no forename and took the 'clan' name in the feminine: Terentia, Tullia, Publilia, Maria, Pomponia and so on. Upper-class men in the late second and early first centuries often had a third name, the *cognomen*, which might be passed from father to son (Cicero, Caesar), thus distinguishing an individual family from the 'clan', or adopted by an individual because of some experience or achievement (Atticus). Women were normally not distinguished from others in the same 'clan'. (The Caeciliae Metellae were pioneering the use of a *cognomen*; freedwomen had one too, since they kept their slave name as well as acquiring a 'clan' name.) Plebeians with the same 'clan' name were not necessarily related (for one thing they included freed slaves). It was usual to identify a woman by mentioning her father or husband. So we might find *Tullia Ciceronis f(ilia)*, 'Tullia, daughter of Cicero' or *Terentia Ciceronis*, 'Terentia (wife) of Cicero'.

Roman law, custom and religion

> In many articles of our law the position of women is worse than that of males.
> (*Dig.* 1.5.9, Papinian)[6]

Roman women were citizens, and bound by Roman law, but lacked the public rights which men enjoyed. They could give evidence, but making speeches in court or elsewhere was thought to be indecorous.[7] They could not therefore do everything that a Roman patron (*patronus*) could do for his clients. Similarly, they could not act as legal guardians to their own children. A woman throughout her life needed a man to act for her in certain legal transactions. This might be her father, husband or guardian. Fathers had peculiar powers in Roman law:

> For among Roman citizens some are fathers of households, others are sons of households, some are mothers of households, some are daughters of households. *Patres familiarum* are those who are in their own power, whether they have reached puberty or not, and similarly for *matres familiarum*. *Filii* and *filiae familiarum* are those who are in someone else's power. For a child born of me and my wife is in my power; in the same way a child born of my son and his wife, that is my grandson and granddaughter, is equally in my power, and my great-grandson and great-granddaughter and so on.
>
> (*Dig.* 1.6.4, Ulpian; cf. Gaius 1.55)

As long as a man was validly married in Roman law, all his children came under his paternal power (*patria potestas*) at birth (or that of his own father, if he were still alive). The *pater familias* (father of the household) had power of life and death over his children (rarely exercised), the power to send them into exile or marry them off or cause a divorce. The children owned no property in their own right: anything they acquired by gift, will or work belonged to him. But if he died without making a will, they were automatically his heirs to equal shares in his property. The father's death released all his children from power: they became legally independent. (Daughters did not fall under the control of their brothers.) Any child under age would need a guardian, but so did all independent women of any age.

If a father gave his daughter in marriage, she might enter the control (*manus*) of her husband, which gave him rights similar to those of a *pater familias*. This custom seems to have been rare by the late Republic and not to have applied to any of the women in whom we are interested. It was more usual for the father to retain his *patria potestas* over a married daughter. This in theory enabled him to dictate a divorce from her husband. He retained control of property. A father could, however, free his daughter (by *emancipatio*), which made her independent.[8] An independent woman needed a guardian to authorise the manumission of slaves, the giving of a dowry or the sale of land. As far as we can tell from the very limited evidence, this was more a formality or convenience than a severe restriction for upper-class women.[9] The guardian was often a kinsman or might be the husband or a freedman (who could be controlled). A woman could go to a magistrate and ask for her guardian to be changed.[10]

There were, after 169, limits on the amount that a father in the top property class could bequeath to a daughter. But this rule was thought to be so unfair that fathers got round it by leaving property in trust.[11] On the other hand, women could make wills, benefit under wills, own land and free slaves. Wealthy women often had extensive and complicated business interests.[12] In retailing and crafts, women worked alongside their husbands (and widows perhaps with sons) and were probably often joint owners of stock, tools and any slave staff.[13] Roman law was well developed by the late Republic and provided a flexible tool for people ready to exploit the opportunities of empire.

Roman legal institutions originally derived from the customs common to Latins. Statute law partially codified custom, or added to it. Praetors through jurisdiction clarified or simplified procedures. Much of what affected women comes from evolving custom: for example, the institution of *manus* and its diminished importance.

Monogamous marriage existed from the beginning. Its overt purpose was the production of legitimate children to carry on the husband's line. In developed Roman law and probably as early as the period with which we are concerned, a marriage was created by bilateral agreement, the consent of the two partners and of their *patres familiarum* (if they existed). (No external ratification was required, as long as the partners were legally capable of contracting the match.[14]) Its continuance depended on continued consent. Consequently, the withdrawal of consent by one of the parties sufficed to produce a divorce.[15] Husbands probably from the beginning had had the right to divorce adulteresses. Then they acquired the right to divorce virtuous but childless wives without penalty. Finally, divorce was available to either husband or wife (unless she was 'under her husband's control'), without it being legally necessary to give the reason. A wife could unilaterally divorce her husband, without any intervention from the state.[16] All this was custom. Officialdom developed rules about what was to happen to the dowry after a divorce, just as it built up rules about inheritance, based on ancient customs.

Customary, statute and praetorian law were not the only things which dictated how a woman should act. There were also religion, accepted morality and social convention. Religious beliefs were bound up with marriage, which was under the protection of Juno, the queen of the gods. The divine abstraction *Fides*, Good Faith, was supposed to control conjugal conduct. The gods were held to disapprove of sinful human behaviour. Accepted morality was to some extent enforced by the censors (especially on senators, who were ideally to set a standard)[17] and by families. Social convention in the first century seems to have been against unilateral divorce initiated by a woman. It would be more proper for a woman's *pater familias* (if she had one) to inform her husband that the marriage was over.

The household (*familia*), in Roman ideology, was extremely important. Individual *familiae* each governed by a single *pater familias*, were the units which made up society. The *pater familias* could discipline his dependants (women condemned by a court might be handed over to their fathers for punishment) and represent the family's interests in the public sphere.[18] There were corresponding limits on women's activity outside the home. For centuries, Romans attributed to wives and daughters a devotion to the family, and a preference for staying indoors and spinning wool (occupations which symbolised chastity): a woman should be *domiseda* and *lanifica*. If she did have to go out, she should be modestly dressed, chaperoned and attended by servants and have a specific and respectable purpose. Certain places and times and contacts might need to be avoided.[19] None of this could apply to lower-class women. Retailers and craftswomen needed to be in places of common resort; market-women needed to shout their wares just as they do in a modern Italian market. But even a butcher's wife could be praised for 'keeping herself to herself' ('not knowing the common herd').[20]

Assertiveness was not a feminine virtue in Roman eyes. Rather, modesty (*modestia*), restraint (*verecundia*), graciousness (*comitas*). *Pudicitia*, conventionally translated as 'chastity', was regarded as the chief feminine virtue, just as *virtus*, 'manliness' (including courage), was masculine.[21] Both these virtues were linked with a sense of honour, a horror of shameful actions, and a concern for reputation (the honour other people would allocate). The paradigm was Lucretia, who was forced to surrender to a rapist because he threatened to kill her and a slave and say he had found them in bed together. But next day she summoned her husband and male kin, told them what had happened and killed herself, rather than providing an excuse to wives who let themselves be seduced.[22] She reconciled private conscience and public reputation in an act which exemplifed honour. Lack of *pudicitia* in a woman would disgrace her parents, siblings and children, since it cast doubt on her nature and upbringing, on the legitimacy, nature and upbringing of her children. It was the duty of a father to defend his daughter against sexual threats. The relevant legend here is that of the teenaged Verginia, whose moral upbringing matched that of her parents.[23] Her father killed her when he could not rescue her from a lustful tyrant who claimed she was a slave.

One of Cicero's narratives shows that such a sense of honour would still resonate with senatorial judges in 70.[24] He attacks Verres for plotting to get a woman of good birth from the Greek city of Lampsacus into his clutches when he was on the governor's staff in Asia. In Cicero's lurid version, Verres gave his aides the job of finding out if there was any virgin (*virgo*) or sexually experienced woman (*mulier*) in the town who would make it worth his while to stay longer. A certain Rubrius reported that there was Philodamus, a man of birth, honour, wealth and reputation, whose daughter lived with her father because she was unmarried, a woman of outstanding beauty but also of integrity and *pudicitia*.[25] Despite Philodamus' protests that he was used to having governors quartered on him, not the hangers-on of a mere legate, he was forced to receive Rubrius as a house-guest and obliged by his sense of hospitality to lay on a banquet and allow Rubrius to control the guest-list. He took the precaution of sending his young son to dine elsewhere. The dinner-party rapidly turned into a drinking session and Rubrius suggested that Philodamus should invite his daughter to join them. Philodamus, much shocked, replied that it was not a Greek custom for women to join men on the couches at a drinking-party. There was shout of 'This is too much to stand for: let the woman be summoned'; Rubrius ordered his slaves to close and guard the door; Philodamus, realising that they intended to offer violence to his daughter, told his own slaves to defend her. A violent scene followed: boiling water was poured over Philodamus. His son came home in haste to defend his father's life and sister's *pudicitia*. He was backed up by the people of the town: a lictor was killed; several slaves and Rubrius wounded. At a meeting of the citizens of Lampsacus next morning it was decided that the Senate and Roman People could have no objection to provincials defending the *pudicitia* of their children. Violent protests outside the house where Verres was staying were only defused by the intervention of the Roman businessmen resident in the town. In all this, Cicero, while underlining the difference between Greek and Roman dining customs, insists on the value both Greeks and Romans put on sexual honour and identifies himself and his Roman audience with Philodamus by repeated use of the Roman concept *liberi* to describe Philodamus' offspring.[26]

Honour, then, was vitally important for both sexes. It was shown in *pudicitia*, which includes self-respect, and in good faith, *fides*, towards others. A eulogy of the time of Augustus shows how a woman might demonstrate her honour and win honour from others. Her husband composed a funeral oration for a woman whose name we do not know. Before her marriage, both her parents were murdered: in the absence of her future husband, she, with her sister, brought the killers to justice. She then moved to her fiancé's house and lived with his mother, to guard her *pudicitia*. She fought another legal case, in the interests of her duty (if the text is rightly restored) to her father, her dutiful love for her sister and her *fides* to her future husband. He praises her domestic virtues: *pudicitia*, obligingness, graciousness, tolerance, enthusiasm for wool-working, religion without superstition and so on. She was loving to her relations and as attentive to her husband's mother as she had been to her own parents. She had other merits in common with all married women of good repute. But she also had remarkable achievements of her own: she shared with her husband the administration of their property; she was generous to poor relations; she provided for her husband when he fled abroad (perhaps after Caesar's defeat of the Pompeians in 48) by stripping herself of her gold and jewels, and sent him slaves, cash and produce; she defended their house against a gang; she begged Caesar to allow him to return; then, in the triumviral proscription of 43, she hid him, and after the younger Caesar reinstated him, she protested that he had been restored, in the face of abusive violence from Lepidus; when they failed to have children, she offered an amicable divorce.[27] It is a remarkable record of an exceptional woman, commemorated by her husband in a formal eulogy and known from no other source, but it also gives an idea of what was possible to other women and what men thought they might aspire to, within the role of wife and daughter. Some of the more daring deeds of the anonymous woman are paralleled in what Terentia did: she faced violence in 58; she supplied Cicero when he was away; she interceded for him.

The ideology of marriage pulled a couple together: loyalty, affection, sharing resources, responsibility for children, a union dissolved only by death.[28] Law and some customs pulled them apart: the separation of property, the division of spheres of responsibility (the house for the wife, the Forum for the husband), the availability of divorce, the mortality rate, the likelihood that the husband would be abroad for years at a time. A couple might at some times operate as a unit of two yoke-fellows pulling together, at others independently, at others as if semi-detached. But 'semi-detached' implies also 'semi-attached'. Marriage was complex, its outcome unpredictable. Blood ties were permanent, which did not mean that relationships with kin were simple, only that people were indissolubly attached to parents and siblings.[29] Those ties could weaken or strengthen the conjugal bond. Terentia, Tullia and Publilia show the shifting demands of the natal family and of husbands.

Women's occupations, appearance, visibility

Roman ladies were not expected to be present at wild drinking sessions like the orgy at Lampsacus, but they acted as hostesses and dined out. This was a custom which shocked the Greeks and is defended by Cicero's contemporary Cornelius Nepos: 'what Roman is ashamed to take his wife to a dinner party? Where does the lady of the house not occupy the place of honour, and receive guests?' (*Prologue to the Lives of the Foreign Generals* 6; tr. Horsfall 1989: 29).[30] They also attended social events restricted to women of their class. These included (for married women) the nocturnal rites which were held for the Good Goddess once a year in the house of a senior official, who, along with all other males of the household, had to spend the night elsewhere.[31] There were other sacrifices and festivals which it was proper to attend. On great national occasions, it was essential that all social classes and age groups and both sexes be represented.[32] Upper-class women would be visible as they went in procession on foot or sat at the games or if they walked with their attendants around the city to visit their friends or to shop. If they rode in a sedan-chair or litter, they might be less easily seen (depending on whether the curtains were open or closed), but their attendants would cause a stir.

The rearing and education of girls

Marriage marked the transition to adulthood for a girl, whose life was more restricted and chaperoned before marriage. Some of her education must have prepared her to give orders on domestic matters; tradition demanded that she learned to spin. Elegant appearance and manners were also valued.[33] No doubt mothers or women slaves or freedwomen were mainly responsible for this side of a girl's training. There is remarkably little evidence on academic education. But most girls of the elite will have had Greek-speaking nurses and child-minders who brought them up bilingually; teachers of reading, writing and arithmetic; some education in Greek and Latin literature (especially poetry), and probably music and dancing.[34] Cicero held that women might speak a correct, old-fashioned Latin, passed down by their mothers.[35] Some women were highly cultured, like the Sempronia, who, Sallust says, was learned in Greek and Latin literature and could play the cithara and dance more elegantly than a good woman needed to do (that is, as well as a professional entertainer). She could make verses, joke and adopt various tones in conversation.[36] Her accomplishments and charm might have made her a good role-model for a Roman girl if she had not misbehaved scandalously. Sallust's portrayal suggests a keen interest in the social graces of the upper-class ladies whom he met at dinners or other occasions.

A Roman girl on the point of marrying was supposed to dedicate her toys to the household gods.[37] She was about to become a woman, an abrupt transition even though she had been brought up to expect it. The legal minimum age was twelve.[38] That need not mean that marriage with pre-pubertal girls was common or consummated. Epigraphic evidence for the Principate suggests that women of the classes which could afford an epitaph married for the first time in their late teens or early twenties.[39] The Augustan marriage legislation of 18 BC set twenty as the age by which women were expected to be mothers. It is likely that in all periods daughters of senators married younger than the general population.[40] Medical opinion favoured marriage soon after *menarche*, which was thought to occur, for well-nourished upper-class girls, at thirteen or fourteen,[41] although there was no doubt a much wider range for the population as a whole.[42] So we may expect them to marry between fourteen and eighteen. Livia, born in 58, probably married for the first time in about 44.[43] Caecilia Attica, an heiress, whose marriage her father started planning when she was about six, was born probably in 51 and her marriage to Agrippa was arranged in 37 and presumably took place soon after.[44] Betrothals often took place very early, but these were not binding.[45] For dynastic reasons, daughters of the most powerful men married youngest of all: Julia, daughter of Augustus, was born in 39 and married in 25; Agrippina the Younger, born in AD 15 or 16, married in 28.[46] But, even in Augustus' family, Antonia the Younger did not marry until she was twenty.

Source material

The evidence for the lives of republican women is almost entirely literary. Technical literature, such as writings on law, cast light on women in general, but for individuals we rely on historians, especially Sallust (?86–35 BC) and Livy (59 BC–AD 17); biographers such as Suetonius (c. AD 69–after 121) and Plutarch (before AD 50–after 120); poets such as Catullus (?84–?54); and, above all, the speeches, treatises and personal letters of Cicero (106–43).[47] So we hear of the aristocrat Sempronia: she receives a character sketch a paragraph long in Sallust. Or there is Aurelia, who gets occasional mention as the mother of Caesar. Servilia, the mother of Brutus and for a time Caesar's mistress, also moves in and out of the limelight; as does Clodia, sister of the demagogue Clodius and perhaps the mistress of Catullus. Wives, mothers and sisters of politicians, these and others (several Caeciliae Metellae, Calpurnia wife of Caesar, Cornelia wife of Pompey, Fulvia wife of Antony) enable scholars to make a composite picture of the possibilities open to women of the elite. We must not accept at face value the promiscuous and desperate Sempronia, the incestuous Clodia and the avaricious virago Fulvia represented by their political enemies.

   Since the structure of women's lives did not change rapidly, evidence from a later time casts light on living conditions. The vivid and sophisticated love elegies composed by Sulpicia show a Roman aristocrat capable of sexual passion, and the dramatisation of love affairs by other poets of the triumviral and Augustan period (especially Ovid) show a Roman *dolce vita* in the context of easy interaction between the sexes.[48] Epitaphs, more numerous after the fall of the Republic, document the qualities expected of women by their families. Apart from Sulpicia, whose work survives, other women wrote letters and memoirs, lost to us, which could be read by Romans who might transmit some of the substance to us, but none are known from the period of Terentia and Tullia.

The three women who are the subject of this book are documented almost entirely by Cicero, the husband of Terentia and Publilia and the father of Tullia. The evidence, chiefly his personal letters, is entirely different from that of public speeches or political history. It is 'more realistic'.[49] The women did not come from the top senatorial aristocracy, the old *nobilitas*. So direct comparison with the noblewomen just mentioned is risky, because they were not exactly on the same level, and also because the evidence on them is less slanted and more immediate. Terentia, Tullia and Publilia may turn out to be more typical of actual women in the wide senatorial/equestrian elite than the distorted images of Sempronia or Clodia.

The difficulty remains that all our sources are male and that the most important first-hand source is Cicero himself. Scholars writing on women and the family have often discussed this problem.[50] It is impossible to reconstitute fully a woman's life or her own point of view.

3 Cicero
From *eques* to consul

Cicero's family: Tullii, Gratidii, Marii, Helvii, Aculeones

Because little is known of Terentia's family, it will be best to begin with the family into which she was to marry. Perhaps her own family was similarly rooted in an Italian town. After her marriage, if not before, she was acquainted with the kin, friends and houses with which her husband had grown up. It is necessary, therefore, to introduce Cicero. His career has been described by many scholars.[1] Here I stress connections, events and achievements which are directly relevant to the lives of his wives and daughter. His experience of his close and extended family must have had a strong influence on him as husband and father.

Marcus Tullius Cicero was born on 3 January 106 at his grandfather's farmhouse near the River Liris, an easy ride outside the town of Arpinum.[2] He later described the estate, with an oak associated with the great Marius, tall poplars, the island where the Fibrenus plunged into the Liris, the lush banks contrasting with the rocks and mountains above.[3] At the time of his birth the house was small and old fashioned, but Cicero's father, who lived there most of the time as a studious invalid, renovated it. Cicero, who inherited it, liked to go on thinking of it as a countrified house, and there was still a farm attached, as there was in most country residences (Figure 3.1).[4] The icy streams made the grounds cool and beautiful on the hottest day.[5] This was what Cicero called his 'cradle',[6] the home of his boyhood and a place which held the memorials of his family, presumably including tombs.

Arpinum and its territory were his fatherland, part of the greater fatherland of Rome.[7] Leaving Rome, the traveller would go by the *Via Latina* and turn towards the hills at Frusino/Frosinone or Fregellae. The town, with its citadel at 627 metres defended by walls in polygonal masonry up to 6 metres high, is on the edge of the Apennines, commanding rich farming country, and 85 Roman miles from Rome.[8] The family no doubt had a town-house here, from which they helped run local politics. Cicero regarded the town as a safe refuge in time of danger, because of its walls and the loyalty of his fellow-townsmen.[9] The Tullii Cicerones were one of the great families of the town, but there is no epigraphic trace of Tullii at Arpinum.[10] Plutarch

Figure 3.1 Farm oxen, a sight as familiar to children in the first century BC as to the author's daughter Jo in 1967 (Roccasinibalda, Rieti; Treggiari)

was puzzled to find conflicting traditions about Cicero's father: one that he had been reared in a fuller's workshop and the other that he was descended from a Volscian king, Tullus Attius, who had fought the Romans.[11] The descent from a king must be what the Tullii themselves claimed: it would be politically useful for their prestige in Arpinum, as it was for their Roman contemporaries to claim descent from a god or hero.[12] Cicero, however, disclaimed a relationship with a Roman consul of the early Republic, who was necessarily a patrician, though he jokes that he belonged to the same *gens* as the Roman king Servius Tullius.[13] The link with a stinking fullery will be what Cicero's enemies claimed.[14] It is entirely possible that somewhere on land which belonged to the family there was a fullery (washing new wool and dirty clothes). Ancestors engaged in disreputable trades form an old theme in invective.[15] The truth behind this is probably a diverse portfolio of investments, such as Terentia herself was to have.

The Cicerones intermarried with other leading families. Cicero's grandfather (another M. Tullius Cicero) was a man of strong opinions and pungent expressions.[16] He married a Gratidia. Her brother M. Gratidius was learned in Greek literature and a noted orator, but was killed in 101 while serving under his close friend M. Antonius.[17]

On at least one occasion, the brothers-in-law were at loggerheads in Arpinum, when Gratidius proposed a law introducing the secret ballot in Arpinum, and Grandfather Cicero opposed him. This made the consul M. Aemilius Scaurus say he wished Cicero had chosen to engage in politics in Rome.[18] Gratidius married a Maria, sister to C. Marius, the great new man, who achieved seven consulships[19] and to M. Marius.[20] M. Marius adopted a son of Maria and Gratidius, who thus became Marius Gratidianus and went on to hold the praetorship twice in the 80s. Gratidius and Maria also had a daughter, who married L. Sergius Catilina, of Roman and patrician family. It was alleged that Catilina murdered his brother-in-law Gratidianus during the civil wars in 82.[21] As praetor in the Cinnan period, Gratidianus brought off a political coup which made him very popular with the common people: Cicero in the work on morals dedicated to his son deprecated the sharp practice but still stresses the fact that Gratidianus was one of the family. As Asconius says, the kinship was close.[22] All these kin illustrate the translation to Rome of Arpinate notables and the possibility of radically different political aims within groups of people connected by blood or marriage.

C. Marius was important to Cicero as the pioneer Arpinate in Roman politics.[23] At some point, Cicero wrote an epic called *Marius*. The memory of Marius was potent with the common people: Cicero was often to appeal to his exile and restoration as a partial precedent for his own. In a speech to the People, he claimed that he had seen the courage of his fellow-townsman and heard his brave words, when he showed himself unbroken by calamity. The implication must surely be that (as a young man of nineteen) he had been in company with Marius at Arpinum. Despite the infighting between relations by marriage in local affairs and the fact that Cicero had been serving under Sulla the year before, they could trust each other with their lives.[24]

Mixed or shifting as Cicero's view of the great Marius was, he must have been conscious of how Marius had put Arpinum on the map and pioneered careers in Rome for other Arpinates, especially his kin. While Terentia and Cicero were children, Marius was saving Rome from the northern barbarians. In the 90s, back in Rome, he was one of the great men, while Cicero was being inducted into the culture and traditions of the ruling class. Cicero was fortunately too young to take a part in the politics of 88–82, but the link must have been among the factors which would be assessed by anyone investigating him as a possible husband.[25]

Let us return to Cicero's other relations in the male line. Cicero's father had a younger brother, Lucius, who went out to Cilicia as an aide to M. Antonius (cos. 99), along with his uncle Gratidius, and had a son, also called Lucius, of about Cicero's age.[26] There seems also to have been a daughter. The younger Lucius was a fellow-student of Cicero and Quintus in Athens in 79 and helped Cicero with the prosecution of Verres in 70, but died in 68. In the first extant letter, Cicero tells Atticus how this loss grieved him: 'all the pleasant things which can come to a person from the kindness and character of another came to me from him' and later he recalled how Lucius loved him like a brother.[27] The relationship shows how affectionate family ties could be. Terentia must have seen a good deal of Lucius during the first decade of her married life.

Little is known of Cicero's mother, Helvia. Quintus tells an anecdote (below, p. 33). Plutarch says that she was of good birth and morals and transmits a pious fiction that she bore Cicero without pain.[28] Cicero never mentions her by name in his extant writings, but his general remarks about his parents are dutiful.[29] In his dialogue *Hortensius* he puts into his own mouth the sentence: 'My grandmother used to say what you are saying, that everything happens because of fate,[30] but my mother, a wise woman, thought not' (Mueller 1904: F v.103, pp. 326–7). Perhaps she died young, though not too early for her second son (born in about 102) to remember her. The Helvii (who need not have been from Arpinum or its region) had already appeared in the lists of Roman officials, with praetorships in 198 and 197.[31]

Helvia's sister married the *eques* C. Aculeo, a close friend of the orator L. Licinius Crassus. Aculeo had sons, one of whom was named C. Visellius Varro, who rose to the curule aedileship (c. 59) and had consular descendants.[32] He was to help Cicero by drafting a bill for his recall in 58.[33] There seems to have been a daughter who married L. Aelius Tubero, a close friend of Cicero's, who was to serve under Q. Cicero and to reach the praetorship.[34]

All these connections with upwardly mobile men show how Cicero had a firm base in both his native cities, Arpinum and Rome. In the region of either, there may have been contacts with Terentia's branch of the Terentii or with the family of her unknown mother.

Cicero's upbringing

Scholars can only conjecture whether Cicero had a happy or unhappy childhood.[35] There is little evidence to indicate whether the boys enjoyed a healthy relationship with their parents, but it is clear that they had roots in a privileged environment, surrounded by kin, with some of whom they were on affectionate terms, and the usual servants. Even family or national quarrels may have strained, not broken, a solid structure.[36]

In his treatise on the making of an orator, Cicero reminds his brother that in their boyhood it was commonly believed that the two great orators of the day, Antonius and L. Licinius Crassus (cos. 95), had thought little of education. But the boys could rebut this from their own knowledge. Their father, their kinsman C. Aculeo, who was a close friend of Crassus, and their uncle L. Cicero, who had travelled back from Cilicia with Antonius, could attest that both were highly cultured.[37] Cicero's father, that excellent and far-sighted man, was right to secure an education for his sons. He arranged for them to have access to Crassus' house in Rome, where they studied with the learned men who frequented it, and listened to Crassus conversing in Greek with them on matters of scholarly interest. The young Cicero had opportunities to put questions to Antonius, too.[38] It was this privileged education which allowed Cicero late in life to recreate the intellectual excitement of a conversation between Crassus and Antonius in the company of younger friends (*De oratore*). After Crassus' death in 91, Cicero came of age and studied law with Q. Mucius Scaevola, Crassus' father-in-law (cos. 117).[39] It is probably at this time that Cicero and Atticus were fellow-students, along with Q. Cicero, C. Varro (Cicero's cousin), C. Julius Caesar (nephew by marriage to Marius).[40] Scaevola would sit on a semicircular seat and hold forth, or the young men would shadow him as he went about the work of an advocate. Besides learning his job, Cicero was making friends who would be useful in a political career. After this Scaevola died in 88, Cicero transferred to an even greater lawyer of the same name (cos. 95).

Frequenting the houses of leading men meant that Cicero got to know the women of the household, too. He claims to have listened to the conversation of Scaevola's wife Laelia, the elder daughter of C. Laelius (cos. 140); of her daughters Mucia (wife of Acilius Glabrio) and Mucia (Crassus' wife), and the latter's two daughters, the Liciniae. Networks including women would be important in giving a young man knowledge of potential brides. The youths who were his friends might have sisters or cousins. We know that shared intellectual interests of older and younger men might result in marriages. So the younger Tubero, Cicero's connection by marriage, who became a distinguished lawyer, was to marry the daughter of Cicero's friend, the jurist Ser. Sulpicius Rufus, and their daughter married another jurist. How far this pattern means that the bridegroom had been in and out of the house as a student we cannot tell.

Cicero's early career

Military service in 89 during the war against the seceding Italian tribes (among them the Marsi, who lived in the Apennines behind Arpinum) will have broadened and deepened Cicero's friendships with his contemporaries and brought him to the notice of senior politicians. L. Tubero was among the young fellow-officers. Cicero served under Sulla and Pompeius Strabo.[41] He soon returned to civilian life, but the times were still turbulent. Little is known of him for the next few years, during which Rome was taken over first by Sulla and then by Marius and his ally Cinna. He continued with his studies and at the age of twenty-three composed a book on rhetoric, but he avoided any premature work as an advocate. Not until some stability had been established by the cruel victory of Sulla did he begin his career in the law-courts. His friend Atticus had avoided involvement in politics by going to live in Greece (c. 86), enjoying the intellectual life of Athens (from which he acquired his nickname of 'the man from Attica') and the beauties of an estate on the Adriatic coast. In mid-79, Cicero also went east to Greek lands in pursuit of culture, to sit at the feet of philosophers in Athens and to practise Greek rhetoric in Asia. He claims that he had been over-straining his voice and physique and needed to work on his technique and strength. Gossip probably suggested that he went because of fear of Sulla, but the latter was no longer dictator.[42] It must have been a difficult decision to interrupt his two-year-old practice, which was beginning to make a name for him in

Rome as an industrious and courageous defence counsel. On his return to Rome in mid-77, he would work hard with clients and start gathering support for a political career. For a new man could not rely on 'recommendation by his ancestors' in presenting himself to the voters. His family, in effect, started with him: he was 'descended from himself'.[43] In 76, he was elected to the quaestorship by the Tribal Assembly and spent the year 75 working on tax matters in Sicily at Lilybaeum. He resumed his work in the courts in 74. He boasted twenty years later about the gruelling routine of work which he managed. After telling an amusing anecdote about the lack of publicity his honest administration in Sicily had earned him, he went on:

> When I realised that the ears of the Roman People are not very sharp, but their eyes are keen and clear-sighted, I stopped thinking about what people were going to hear about me and I saw to it that from then on they would see me in person every day: I lived before their eyes, I walked about the Forum; my doorman never stopped anyone seeing me, even if I was asleep. What can I say about how my time was taken up, when even my leisure was never leisured? For the speeches which you say you like to read when you are at leisure, Cassius (the prosecutor), I wrote on religious holidays and days when the games were held, so that I should never have any leisure at all. For I always thought what M. Cato wrote at the beginning of his *Origins* was a noble sentiment: 'great and famous men must give an account of their leisure as well as of their work'.
>
> (*Planc.* 66)

Marriage

It was advisable for a young man to double his family by forming a marriage alliance before he stood for the quaestorship.[44] So we see most men who aspired to the Senate married, if not fathers, before the time of their first public office. Some, like Caesar, married in their teens. 'Boys assumed the toga of manhood in the vicinity of the fifteenth birthday, and a young *nobilis* might be spurred to activity in the law courts after no long delay. Likewise to matrimony.'[45] But others waited, for various reasons, until their late twenties.

When did Cicero marry Terentia? It is agreed that it must have been between 80 and 76. The only direct evidence is from what we know of his elder child, Tullia. If she was already married in December 63 (and this, as we shall see [p. 43], is not absolutely certain), she was at least twelve then, so she must have been born in 75 at latest. Since her birthday was 5 August, this puts her parents' marriage in 76 at latest.[46] Some conjecture 77.[47] But Tullia may have been born earlier and many scholars, on general grounds, put the marriage in 80 or 79, shortly before Cicero went to the East.[48] Others, by putting Tullia's birth in 79, show that they date the marriage to 80.[49]

We can fill in a little of what Cicero was doing in the relevant years. In 81, at the age of twenty-six, he delivered his first speech, *On behalf of Quinctius*, for the plaintiff in a civil case.[50] Later that year, or early in 80, he made a more celebrated appearance in a criminal case, defending, probably successfully, a man accused of parricide.[51] In Cicero's version, the charge had been trumped up and a freedman of Sulla was involved. Although Cicero exculpated the dictator himself and claimed to support him, it was a bold choice of brief and Cicero was bold to circulate a version of his speech in writing. By the middle of 79, after other cases, including another of political importance,[52] he went to Greek lands. By then, Sulla had retired to private life, but the times were still out of joint and Cicero may have thought it advisable to be away. Dangerous as some of his work may have been, it made his name and will have made him a more desirable match for a wealthy and well-connected woman. But if we suppose that Cicero married Terentia before he went to Greece, and got her pregnant with Tullia, then a two-year absence in the East looks odd. It is perhaps partly to avoid the assumption that he left his new bride that other scholars prefer the tight dating of the marriage after his return in mid-77. It seems to be universally assumed that Cicero could not have taken his wife abroad.[53]

But was it impossible? We have good evidence that it was not normal until the Augustan period for governors to take their wives abroad. But distinctions could perhaps be made between provinces. There is no reason why Calpurnia, a young woman who needed to produce an heir, should not have visited Caesar in Cisalpine Gaul, that is, northern Italy, during the winters he passed there. We know Octavia later briefly joined Antony in Athens. In the 80s Sulla claimed that when he had been declared a public enemy, his house and villas had been burned, so his wife Caecilia Metella took her children and fled to him in Greece: the fact of her journey is not disputed.[54] In time of civil war in the 40s, Cornelia followed Pompey as far as Lesbos; L. Metellus took his mother-in-law Clodia and probably his wife Licinia to Greece; and Pompeia went with Faustus Sulla to the campaign in Africa and then, as a widow, to Spain.[55]

But what of husbands who were travelling for pleasure and edification, not as public servants? We are hardly informed at all about women travelling as private individuals related to men who were not governors, but Terentia, Tullia and Atticus' wife undertook the journey to Brundisium/Brindisi.[56] That was in Italy, but journeys to the provinces are attested. As soon as he married her, Sestius took L. Scipio's daughter to Marseille, a Greek city in southern France, to see her exiled father.[57] The wife and daughter (or sister) of T. Ampius Balbus visited him in exile (possibly in Asia) in 46.[58] The sea voyage to Greece could be dangerous, but might also be more comfortable than overland travel. Athens, as a civilised and at the moment peaceful city, could have been visited by upper-class Roman women when their husbands were not on public business and so could attend to their needs.

If Terentia had no mother or suitable chaperone, it might well have seemed improper for her to remain in Italy while her husband was abroad.[59]

My preferred scenario is that Cicero married Terentia in about 80, when he was twenty-six, and that when, probably unexpectedly,[60] he decided to go to the East, he took her with him (at least to Athens, where he spent six months, and perhaps Rhodes, though not 'over all of Asia').[61] He must, like his son later, have taken comfortable accommodation in Athens for his family party, which included his brother and cousin, whose philosophical life made a happy memory.[62] This hypothesis allows us to conjecture that Tullia was born in 78, in Athens or Rhodes.[63] If being married made a man look like a serious citizen, having a child was even more important. To marry and then separate for two years would jeopardise this: even if Cicero left a pregnant Terentia in Rome, he would have sacrificed the hope of a second pregnancy. In any case, the 80/79 date for the marriage seems preferable, as it makes the schedule less tight.

We can only guess at Terentia's age when she married: almost certainly between sixteen and twenty. For the sake of argument I shall assume, conservatively, eighteen, but it could easily have been a year or eighteen months either side of that age. If eighteen, she was perhaps fully grown and relatively mature mentally and emotionally.

Coming back superbly prepared for the demands of a public career, Cicero secured election to the quaestorship, did a good job in Sicily, consolidated his fame with the prosecution of Verres in 70, and was elected head of the poll to the praetorship of 66. His hard work, networking, oratorical pre-eminence and reputation as an honest man were rewarded by election to the consulship of 63, the first new man for many years to get to the top.

4 Terentia
The young wife

Terentia's family

The woman who married Cicero was a daughter of a branch of the Terentii, but we do not know her father's *cognomen* (if he had one). The Terentii had appeared in the records of officials as far back as the war with Hannibal and there are several in the second century, but the most important senatorial branch was that of the Terentii Varrones, who traced descent from a new man who had held the consulship in 216. They were thus plebeian nobles, with a long track record. The fact that Cicero's cousin Visellius had the *cognomen* Varro suggests that Cicero may have already had a link with the Terentii Varrones. The most famous member of the family at this date was M. Terentius Varro of Reate (116–27), a polymath who rose to the praetorship. He owned a villa at Casinum/Cassino, not far from Arpinum, and was a friend of Cicero. It is possible that these links of family, friendship and vicinity came into play, if Terentia was the daughter of a Varro. Moreover, her father may have been a Marcus. An epitaph to freed slaves found six Roman miles outside Rome on the Appian Way, if genuine, seems to have been set up for staff of Cicero's family (or freed slaves of such a staff group). The use of the *praenomen* Marcus by two Terentii is compatible with their having been freed by a woman who would, according to the normal usage, have passed on her father's *praenomen* to her freedmen (since she had no first name of her own).[1]

Terentia had a sister who was a Vestal Virgin. Her name was Fabia.[2] This must mean that Terentia's mother married twice, producing daughters both for a patrician Fabius (a distinguished family, but 'in temporary eclipse'[3]) and a plebeian (but possibly noble) Terentius. We have no clue about the identity of the mother. If we suppose that the marriage with Terentius came first, then we may wonder if he died, thus making her available to Fabius. The early death of her father would help explain the lack of information about him and the wealth of Terentia. She might even have been his sole heiress. If this is the right reconstruction, Terentia would have been brought up in the household of a stepfather and had a younger half-sister. Conversely, Fabius may have been the first husband and Fabia the elder of the two half-sisters. Whichever scenario is right, the half-sisters may have spent little time together. Girls dedicated to the life of a Vestal left home before puberty.

In 73, Fabia was charged with unchastity with Catiline.[4] She was acquitted (*Cat.* 3.9). Cicero in 64 managed to attack Catiline without incriminating his sister-in-law: 'Your manner of life was such that there was no place so holy that your coming there did not give grounds for a criminal charge, *even if nothing wrong happened*' (quoted by Asc. 91C). Asconius comments on the italicised words that Cicero cast blame on Catiline, while sparing his relative. Others believed her guilty.[5]

Fabia is never named in the letters (which do not begin until 68, in the surviving collection): Cicero never sends the most minimal message of courtesy or talks of her being invited to a family event; he does not even mention the possibility of exploiting her influential position, for instance when Terentia was in need of help in 58. But Terentia did find refuge in the house of the Vestals in the emergency (p. 61), so Fabia (or, if she was now dead, her fellow-Vestals) must have protected her. Perhaps both Terentia and Cicero had few living relations, but there is also an odd absence of mention in Cicero's correspondence of the 60s onwards of any kin outside the immediate family, Marcus and Quintus and their wives and children, apart from an incidental piece of information on Visellius Varro (p. 67).

The wedding

Perhaps Terentia was about eighteen at the time of their marriage. (There is no suggestion that she was older because of a previous marriage.) That makes her about fifty-two at the time of the eventual divorce. There will have been the usual ceremonies: the traditional bride's dress of flame-coloured veil, the sealing of the dotal contract, the clasping of right hands in token of the exchange of faith, the feast at the bride's home, the torchlit procession of the bride, with her attendants, to the bridegroom's house, where she was formally received by her new husband and presented with water and fire as symbols of belonging to her new household. Attendants lifted her over the threshold to ensure she did not trip, which would have been a bad omen.[6] It must all have been exciting. The consummation of the marriage, also surrounded with ceremonial, must have been a major event for her, even though she was brought up to see the production of children in marriage as her task in life.[7] Whether Cicero was a skilled and considerate lover we cannot know: though he claimed in his fifties to have never been very interested in courtesans, this does not mean that he had not had sexual experience with slaves or other accessible women.[8] He was also capable of crude expressions about sexual intercourse (p. 134), but that common male pose does not cast any light on his practice. Let us hope that the beginning of the marriage was propitious.

Terentia will have received the usual wedding presents from close relatives.[9] She is known from outside sources to have brought Cicero a handsome dowry. Plutarch says it was ten myriads of *denarii*, that is, ten times ten thousand, 100,000 (400,000 sesterces).[10] Such round figures must be treated with caution, but Plutarch certainly intends us to understand a splendid injection of capital. Because 400,000 sesterces made a man eligible for the Senate, it is tempting to link the marriage with Cicero's launch into politics.[11] He had not yet inherited from his father nor touched much remuneration from advocacy: a rich marriage was vital. In the summer of 44, a letter to Atticus shows that the idea of getting Cicero's son Marcus married was in the air and that one sound reason was that his wife's dowry might maintain him.[12] He was then nearly twenty-one. Quintus wanted the same for his son, who was nearly twenty-three.[13]

Why was the match made? We can see that Terentia's connections were creditable and her fortune attractive. We cannot tell if Cicero also chose her for herself, though we cannot tell for sure that emotions played no part.[14] The most obvious qualifications he offered her were his ability and career prospects. If the marriage took place in 80 or 79, Cicero had given enough proof of his abilities as an orator to allow his bride to hope that he was launched on a prosperous career as an advocate and probably a senator. But, because of the political situation, it was also a gamble.

Cicero was almost certainly still a son-in-power, *filius familias*, dependent on his father. The dowry would in theory go to swell his father's property. But upper-class young men in practice enjoyed considerable independence, if we can judge from the young *eques* M. Caelius Rufus or from what was planned for Cicero's own son a few decades later.[15] They might live in apartments or rented houses, rather than the family home. We do not know if Cicero and Terentia had their own establishment or moved into the residence which had presumably been the home of Cicero and his brother during their education in Rome. It seems likely that Cicero's grandfather and father (if not earlier generations) had needed a base in Rome, so the house may have been in the family for some time. Cicero's father was to leave a house to his elder son.[16] This was in the fashionable district called the Keels (*Carinae*), the brow of the Oppian Hill running from the future site of the Baths of Titus to around the site of the later church of S. Pietro in Vinculis. The hills were favoured by the richer classes because they were healthier than the crowded valleys. Pompey also had a paternal mansion in the *Carinae*.[17] The house was very near the Temple of Tellus, the Earth goddess, and within easy reach of the Forum and of the shopping district of the Subura.[18] If Terentia did not live there, she must at least have visited her father- and brother-in-law fairly frequently.

Mater familias

Cicero professed conventional Roman ideas about households being run with good sense and discipline, so that they exemplified proper behaviour and clean living.[19] If we knew that Cicero's mother was still alive at the time of his marriage and if we knew that Terentia was very young, it would be tempting to think of Cicero entrusting his bride to his mother for training in housewifery. We know from Quintus that Helvia was a frugal manager. Quintus writes to his brother's secretary Tiro to ask him to keep the letters coming even if he has no news: he should just send an empty letter so that Quintus will know he is not being cheated of correspondence. This will be just like his mother, who used to seal all the empty wine-bottles so that she could tell that no unauthorised person was drinking the wine.[20] Considering that Quintus is writing to an ex-slave and that the household slaves would be the people most likely to be suspected of pilfering, this humorous story is not perhaps very tactful. One can imagine that Helvia's strictness was resented. Since Cicero in his youth had translated Xenophon's *Oeconomicus*, he was well aware of the theory of division of labour between partners, the idea that the husband worked out of doors and the wife at home, looking after the fruits of his labour. This did not apply solely to farmers. *Diligentia*, careful attention, one of the virtues of the advocate, was required of his wife in administering the home.[21]

Mothers, mothers-in-law, sisters, aunts and trusted servants must have given young brides helpful tips about household management. Being a good housekeeper was a prime virtue and day-to-day running of the house was primarily the wife's responsibility.[22] She was the guardian of her husband's property.[23] In his report on his young third wife, which he made to her aunt soon after the wedding, Pliny praises the upbringing the aunt had given her and glances briefly at her efficient and careful management.[24] The ability to spin wool had a symbolic significance: the woman who used every spare moment to turn the product of the farm into yarn with which clothes could be made for her family (especially the toga, that multi-purpose and quintessentially Roman garment) and household was obviously dedicated to the welfare of her husband and not to frivolity and to risking her chastity.[25] The well-ordered, old-fashioned household would have a loom in the atrium, the main reception room, and this too symbolised the industry and chastity of the mistress of the household.[26] But, although it was good for a woman to have learned to spin and to sit among her maids doing just that and to have a hand in clothes worn by her menfolk,[27] it may be doubted if Terentia and her upper-class contemporaries usually did more than make sure that a servant assigned daily wool-working tasks to slaves. It was not expected that the mistress would have hands-on experience of cooking (a male role in grand households) or cleaning. Much of the normal routine would be supervised by senior servants, especially by a steward, often a freedman, to whom the mistress would give orders.

We would expect that brides would bring servants of their own to their new household. The steward of whom we hear in Cicero's family (from 59 to 47) is indeed a freedman of Terentia's, Philotimus. A bride would also bring such confidential women servants as her dressers and perhaps her nurse to support her. If they were part of the dowry, slaves would in theory be her husband's property, as long as there was no divorce, but the fact that they came from the wife's side of the partnership would not be forgotten. More likely, they would be her chattels. We do not find any clear information on staff Terentia may have brought when she married.

If she did not enter *manus*, then the bride would bring two sorts of property to the marriage: the dowry, which became the husband's for the duration of the marriage; and her private property, often more important, which she retained. What we know (from slightly later evidence) of Terentia's property strongly suggests that she did not enter *manus*. The institution was becoming rare in this period. Although Cicero's father had legal control of her dowry (and probably allowed Cicero to use it for his and Terentia's expenses), she had other property. If her father (as seems likely) died before her marriage, she will have administered this independently, with the supervision of a guardian.

We know that in April 59 Cicero and Terentia had the satisfaction of going to inspect a *saltus* she owned (A 2.4/24.5, Antium, early April 59). This would be an estate of mountainous land with woods and pasture (Figure 4.1). Since Cicero compares it with Epirus (where Atticus had a ranch), saying that only the oak of Dodona (so big that it was sacred) is needed to make them feel they owned Epirus itself, it seems that it was a productive estate, perhaps with big trees. Such land could be exploited as pasture for sheep, with pigs in the woods feeding on beech-mast or acorns, as a source of hay or leaves for cattle-fodder, as hunting grounds, and for the timber. Trees were coppiced to produce long, straight beams, much in demand for building. The prunings would make the small branches and twigs needed for the production of charcoal, used in industry and for central-heating and warming the baths. Suitable trees included sessile oak, poplar, hornbeam and ash.[28] This was clearly an important investment property. It is mentioned only in passing, so we are left to conjecture that this was only one possession among many which escape attention.[29] Terentia was also occupying some public land, rent-free, in 59 (A 2.15/35.4, Formiae, c. 28 Apr. 59). She owned built-up land too, since she intended to sell a village or a double row of houses (*vicus*) when Cicero was in exile (F 14.1/8.5, dispatched from Dyrrachium, 25 Nov. 58).

There was also urban property in her dowry. This is identified with apartment blocks both in the Argiletum and on the Aventine, which passed to Cicero on the divorce, and the rents of which he and, no doubt, Terentia intended to form young Marcus' income while he was a student in Athens in 44.[30] We know that Cicero meant Marcus' allowance to be as generous as that of his fellow-students of comparable rank.[31] The ordinary annual amount was to be 80,000 sesterces, which was the total of the rents and would have enabled him to rent a house in Rome.[32] All this (and it is unlikely to be all she had) adds up to a substantial and diversified package of investments. Like other upper-class women, she enjoyed the independence which property gave and which would enable her, if necessary, to detach herself

Figure 4.1 Sheep of a transhumant shepherd at summer pasture in the high meadows (Sabine Hills near Vallecupola, 1000m, July 1985; Treggiari)

from her husband. The law made husband and wife separate persons and there is naturally a great deal of material in the abundant legal sources about property and the sorting-out of problems between family members. Nevertheless, society approved the idea of sharing between husband and wife. Cicero felt he shared Terentia's *saltus*. We shall find her later being generous in emergency.

When Cicero married, his responsibilities increased, but his financial position was enhanced. The dotal buildings in the Argiletum and on the Aventine would subsidise the couple's living expenses: 80,000 (if the rents were the same as in the 40s) would go a long way. (The frugal Atticus seems to have spent 3000 a month on his household expenses.[33]) Major capital expenditure, especially on houses, would in due course become possible, but nothing indicates that Terentia was directly responsible for any of that.

Getting married for an upper-class man meant that a symbolic marriage-bed would suddenly appear in his main reception room, the atrium.[34] Terentia on marriage became *mater familias*, 'mother of the household'. She shared with her husband responsibility for the servants (her own and her husband's slaves and freed slaves) and for religious worship inside the house. Offerings were made to the hearth, the household gods, the *Lares* and *Penates*, and to the guardian spirit of the husband, his *Genius*, who personified his procreative powers. Belief in the wife's guardian spirit, her *Juno*, was probably evolving.[35] Sacrifice was routinely offered to various gods as a thank-offering or before a serious undertaking, such as a journey.[36] Offerings to the gods were interwoven in meals and barbecues.[37] They were so much a part of ordinary life that it is not surprising that Cicero scarcely mentions them. There is evidence to suggest that Terentia took this responsibility seriously. There is an anecdote about her sacrificing (p. 44) and Cicero once claimed that she worshipped with ceremonial purity, though the gods had failed to repay her (*F* 14.4/6.1, Brundisium, 29 Apr. 58). In 49, he asked her to perform a sacrifice of thanksgiving to the god who had made him feel better by arranging for him to vomit bile (*F* 14.7/155.1, aboard ship, Caieta, 7 June 49). It was her habit to perform such worship dutifully and in a pure manner (*pie et caste*). The half-humorous request suggests that Cicero delegated much of the family cult to his wife. But he played the part of the *pater familias* in such religious ceremonies as the coming of age of his son, and as a Roman official he was constantly involved in sacrificing, though he rarely alludes to it. He claims to pray: perhaps we may conclude that Terentia and Tullia were also in the habit of praying for their own and their family's welfare.[38]

The presence of a wife also made a difference to a man's social life. She would act as his hostess at some of his parties and would invite the wives of his friends. (A single man seems not to have done this.) She would also accompany him to similar parties at his married friends' houses. But they did not always operate as a couple: they could be semi-detached. Cicero went out and entertained alone, and presumably so did Terentia.[39] Cicero notoriously went to one party where the only woman known to be present was not the sort who could mix with senators' wives. The dinner was at the house of P. Volumnius Eutrapelus and she, Volumnia Cytheris, was his freedwoman and had been his mistress and an actress, therefore disqualified on three counts from socialising with upper-class women.[40] But this was probably while Cicero was divorced and he seems not to have made a habit of this kind of thing.

Terentia would visit women friends, attend sacrifices and the games, move around Rome (properly escorted by footmen and women slaves), keep in touch with family and perhaps go on visits to country-houses without her husband. However, of all this we have no direct evidence for this period. She must also have been developing her relationship with her husband and hoping to have children. If we are right to conjecture that she went to the East with Cicero, they were often together, so opportunity was not lacking. But if they were married in 80 and Tullia was born in 78, they were not abundantly fertile, unless there had been a miscarriage.

The arrival of their first child must have been greeted with joy, as was young Marcus' birth over a decade later. Cicero subscribed to the concept of children as a gift of the gods and of love of children as a natural instinct.[41] When Atticus' only child, a daughter, was born, Cicero sympathised fully with the delight a baby and toddler could bring. Although Cicero must have wanted a son to follow in his footsteps and benefit from the position he could win in public life, he seems to have been unreservedly delighted to have a daughter, who called forth his protective instincts. (He talks of kissing small daughters and expected Attica to kiss him.[42]) He took an interest in child development.[43] Apart from his year's absence in Sicily (the year of her third birthday), he was to be in close touch with Tullia during her childhood, in contrast to his relationship with his son later, which was interrupted by the trauma of his exile, which the child understood all too well.[44] To look at the matter from a practical point of view, a daughter's education came considerably cheaper than a son's; her dowry, though a substantial capital sum, amounted to much less than a son would need to launch his career; and, by marrying in her late teens where a son married in his late twenties, she was likely to produce grandchildren when the grandparents could enjoy them.[45]

It was important for Cicero to develop a stable family life, since report of his domestic behaviour would spread to the outside world through clients, friends, relations and, especially, staff.[46] As he says of his friend Caelius:

> A young man of this age could not be adequately recommended to you if he were disapproved of by such a distinguished and serious-minded town, let alone by his excellent parent. I came to my good reputation among men from these springs and my work in the courts and my manner of life flowed to the opinion of men more widely thanks to the recommendation and judgement of my people.
>
> (*Cael.* 5–6)

Terentia had to contribute to this effort by behaving as a Roman matron should. If Plutarch (*Cic.* 20.2) is right, she did this willingly, since she was deeply interested in Cicero's political career: 'Terentia was not meek or naturally timid, but an ambitious woman and, as Cicero himself tells us, more inclined to take a share in his political concerns than to give him a share in her domestic ones'.

When Cicero came back from his postgraduate studies in philosophy and rhetoric and settled down to the hard slog which would bring him to office,[47]

> His way of life was liberal, yet moderate: he enjoyed the company of Greek and Roman scholars. He rarely came to the dinner-couch before sunset, not just because of work, but because his digestion was delicate. He was precise and fussy in the rest of his physical regimen, setting up a schedule of massages and walks. By managing his health in this way he kept his body free of disease and strong enough for his many hard struggles and efforts.
>
> (Plut. *Cic.* 8.2–3)

Terentia's life must to some extent have been built around his routine. Cicero claimed to have little interest in the games, parties early in the day, board-games or playing ball, but to have relaxed with literature. He worked at night and until old age did not take siestas.[48] The house was full of cultured men, who came to dinner or even lived there. Diodotus the Stoic, who died in 59 and left Cicero about 100,000 sesterces, had taught the young Cicero and lived many years in his house.[49] In the early 80s, Cicero had spent days and nights in study and worked on dialectic with Diodotus, which helped his oratory. Others, for instance a slave-boy of P. Crassus, frequented Diodotus.[50] For an undefined time before his death in 44, a doctor called Alexio gave Cicero the benefit of his professional skill and cultivated company.[51] Such resident intellectuals were often 'brain-drain' Greeks, though some were freedmen of friends.[52] Cicero also gradually acquired educated slaves, secretaries, readers, librarians and research assistants, who were vitally important for the preparation of speeches and for his writings.[53] So Terentia had no lack of clever people to talk to, and it is natural that later intellectuals assumed that she drank deep of philosophy from her husband, though he felt a wife was a distraction (Jerome *Against Iovinianus* 1.48; below p. 149). I do not think she was unable to participate in literary and intellectual conversation.[54]

But Cicero was in no ivory tower: his house had to be open to callers of all kinds. Foreign guests included surprising people like Diviciacus the Aeduan Gaul.[55] Citizens came on business to the morning reception. Cicero gives vivid pictures of advocates advising clients at home or being intercepted as they walked around Rome.[56] Terentia must have been keenly aware of the 'open house' policy,[57] the parties,[58] the sheer hard work: 'the unending toil of activity in the Forum and the employment of standing for office' (*infinitus forensium rerum labor, et ambitionis occupatio*).[59] Amid all this, we must imagine her going about her own activities and little Tullia running around the house and gardens.

Much of the structure of family life must have been created by Terentia. The new nuclear family would celebrate birthdays with presents and festivities. It would now be necessary for Cicero to mark the married women's festival of 1 March, the Matronalia, by a gift and a feast.[60] Terentia would expect him to meet her friends, to escort her to dinners, to co-operate with her arrangements for recreational travel.

Having a daughter meant that Cicero had 'issue', *liberi*, and could rank himself with responsible citizens. Even in the courts, he could bring in his family to evoke fellow-feeling. In 70, he criticised Verres for having stopped an estate going to an only daughter:

> I am sure that this seems harsh and unworthy to each of you, as it does to me. I delight in my daughter; you are moved by a similar feeling and kindness towards your daughters. What is there that nature meant to be pleasanter or dearer to us? What more deserves all our care and kindness [*diligentia, indulgentia*]? Cruel man, why did you do such injury to the dead P. Annius? Why did you brand this pain on his bones and ashes?

Why did you snatch away from his child the father's property which was handed down by her father's wish, by right and by the laws?
(*Verr.* 2.1.112–13)

He identifies with fathers' hopes for their posterity: 'We have small children' (*Verr.* 2.1.153). It was a father's duty, conscious that he might not live to protect his child, to make careful provision for her support as a minor, which even her mother and guardians might not be able to assure. Having a child meant that Cicero could show a warm side. It was not assumed for the sake of the other respectable fathers in his audience.

5 The life of mother and daughter

Early days

After the prosecution of Verres in 70 assured Cicero's leadership of the bar, he held his aedileship (69) and continued his work as advocate for the defence. Now the sources abruptly improve. From November 68, when he was thirty-eight, we have our first surviving letter from the substantial body (426 letters) of Cicero's correspondence with his friend T. Pomponius Atticus, still based in Greece.[1] The correspondence with Atticus and others becomes richer in the 50s and 40s.[2] One book of letters (Book 14), in the collection known as *Ad familiares* (F 1–16; 435 letters), is addressed to Terentia,[3] a total of 24 letters. Three books, a total of 27 letters, are preserved from his correspondence with his brother Quintus. It is these, along with the sixteen books to Atticus, which form the main body of evidence on Cicero's family life.[4] The density of the letters differs according to circumstance, and much has been lost, but they remain a uniquely valuable source. The letters which concern us were all written for the moment and for a specific recipient (though some might be shown to others: those which Cicero sent to Terentia from his exile might be read in whole or part by Tullia). Cicero did not intend them for posterity. Atticus, Quintus and Terentia were in his confidence more than any other human beings: he may not have revealed all of himself, but he came as close to it as he or any man could. They tell us of mundane facts of family life, of Cicero's intimate and sometimes transient feelings, and of the doings and reactions of Terentia and Tullia.

The letter, for Cicero and his upper-class contemporaries, was a vital way for keeping in touch when face-to-face contact was impossible. It might be written in one's own hand, or dictated to a secretary. It would be inscribed on a wax tablet or written with ink on papyrus, then carried by one's own courier or the servant of a friend. It might travel a short distance in Rome, go to a villa a hundred miles away or be delivered in a province months later. It might be a short, hasty note like an email or telephone call, or an important communication which had to be pondered. Distance meant that the exchange of views could be slow by modern standards,[5] but the Romans were prolific correspondents and we must assume that Terentia and Tullia used this way to keep in touch with friends as well as with Cicero. They had that much in common with Jane Austen or Queen Victoria.

In the very first letter we see Terentia doing her duty as Cicero's wife by cultivating the friendship of her new sister-in-law, Atticus' sister Pomponia, who had recently married Cicero's brother: 'We are expecting Quintus any day. Terentia has painful rheumatism. She is very fond of you and your sister and your mother and sends you warm greetings, as does my darling little Tullia [*Tulliola*]' (*A* 1.5/1.8, Rome, Nov. 68). The match between Quintus (now about thirty-four) and Pomponia (near her brother in age and he was born about 110, so probably at her second marriage, and older than her new husband) had not got off to a good start and Cicero was anxiously doing his best to help. In ordinary day-to-day contacts, Terentia would be more important than her husband.

Affectionate mentions of Tullia often end a letter: 'My darling little Tullia is demanding the present you promised and summons me as surety. But I would rather repudiate the debt than pay' (*A* 1.8/4.3, Rome, after 13 Feb. 67). The joke was still going on in early summer, when the family were at their country-house near Rome (*A* 1.10/6.6, Tusculum, c. May 67). The tone of this seems consistent with Tullia being ten. One gets the impression of an attractive child and of a loving and easy relationship, full of fun and jokes. Cicero was later to talk of the pleasure children give when he wrote to Atticus about *his* baby daughter:

> I rejoice that you are delighted with your little daughter and that you approve of the doctrine that affection for children is natural. For if this is not so, there can be no natural link between one human being and another: if that is taken away, social life is taken away.
> (*A* 7.2/125.4, Brundisium, 25 Nov.[?] 50)

Tullia's engagement

Soon after, Cicero communicates the news that he has arranged Tullia's betrothal. The language, except for an affectionate diminutive, is that of a formal engagement announcement: 'We have engaged Tulliola to Gaius Piso Frugi son of Lucius' (*A* 1.3/8.3, Rome, end of 67). Tullia was of an age to understand that this was an important occasion and to express formal consent. (Later, seven was the minimum age.) When Atticus later looked into possible suitors for his small daughter, Cicero suggested that among the criteria might be the character of the man, his family, his financial resources, his birth on both sides and the congeniality of his father.[6] Tullia's engagement seems to have been a coup for a new man who had yet to reach the praetorship, and must be owed to his success as an orator and to shared values. Piso was the son and grandson of praetors and great-grandson of a consul and meticulous censor, so he belonged to the plebeian nobility.[7] The

42   *The life of mother and daughter*

family deserved the *cognomen* Frugi, originally a tribute from his contemporaries to the consul, a model of probity.[8] The word is untranslatable,[9] but was applied, not exclusively, to well-behaved, useful, sober, thrifty and profitable slaves. The family was not only distinguished but of high moral standing, useful to the state and congenial to Cicero. It was connected with other Pisones who were friends of Cicero: M. Pupius Piso[10] and C. Calpurnius Piso (cos. 67).[11]

Negotiations had presumably taken place with the father, who was a few years senior to Cicero and certainly alive in 69/8 and a friend, at least in public life. There probably was – or had been – an elder son, Lucius. Tullia's betrothed was to be quaestor in 58, so he was born around 89. If Tullia was born in 78, then there was to be the typical gap of about ten years between young husband and wife.

Over the next few years we hear nothing more of any contact between the family and Piso or any reactions of Tullia to the arrangement made on her behalf. But this may be put down to the scantiness of the record. We may hope that the young girl saw something of her fiancé, whose mind was probably on his studies, military service and oratorical training. For he was a suitably scholarly and talented man. Cicero said years later:

> I have never met anyone who excelled my son-in-law C. Piso for enthusiasm and hard work, nor could I easily name his superior for talent. He never took any time off from speaking in the Forum or mental preparation at home or writing and thinking. So he made so much progress that he seemed to fly, not run; he chose his words elegantly and put them together appropriately and in rounded phrases; he worked out many strong arguments to prove his case and his ideas were sharp and neatly arranged; his deportment was so attractive that it looked as if he used a technique and trained movement, although he did not. I am afraid that it may seem that, out of affection, I say more than was really in him, but that is not so; even more important things can be said about him, for I do not think anyone of the same age could be compared with him for self-restraint, devotion or any kind of virtue.
>
> (*Brut.* 272)

Was he perhaps one of Cicero's students? We can imagine that Tullia, on the verge of her teens, was impressed by the budding orator and cavalry officer she expected to marry.

If Tullia was born in 78, then she reached the age of fourteen in 64. It was around the fourteenth year that the doctor Soranus, who no doubt treated the upper classes, expected most girls to develop breasts and begin to menstruate (Soranus *Gyn.* 1. 33). It was best to postpone sexual intercourse until after menstruation began (1.25, 33). He thought that most women were ready to conceive after the age of fifteen, but men who were looking for a bride in order to secure children and not just for pleasure should observe and investigate a candidate's physique (1.34). A girl's own family would be in a better position to assess whether she had reached the right stage of development. So about the time Cicero was concentrating on his hopes of the consulship, Tullia must have been adjusting to her developing body, monthly inconvenience or even discomfort, and the prospect of marriage in the near future.[12] The sources are silent on the emotional impact of puberty, but the Stoic philosopher Epictetus (*Encheiridion* 40) in the late first/early second century AD claimed:

> As soon as they reach the age of fourteen, women are called 'Lady' [*kyria*; in Latin *domina*, 'lady' or 'mistress'] by men. So, seeing that the only thing they have got is to sleep with men, they begin to beautify themselves and put all their hopes in this. We ought to take pains, then, to make them understand that what they are really respected for is showing themselves well behaved and chaste.

Epictetus, as a slave of Nero's secretary and later as a teacher of eminent Romans, had plenty of opportunity to observe upper-class girls of his day. His second sentence suggests that he even felt an obligation on himself and male members of their families to wean girls away from worldly frivolity and concentration on their sexual attractiveness. But his observation fits what we should expect to be the natural development of girls who were reared to expect marriage to be their career.[13]

We may look ahead to the wedding. In the year of Cicero's consulship, 63 (from which, since Atticus was in Rome, no letters survive), we know that Piso could be counted as one of the family. In a speech to the Senate on 5 December 63, Cicero calls him his son-in-law (*Cat.* 4.3). But this does not prove that the marriage had taken place, for the relationship theoretically came into effect on betrothal.[14] Piso might, as has been suggested, be awaiting the outcome of the crisis before marrying. This is also consistent with Tullia being in Cicero's house, though it would be perfectly natural for her to go there on visits and during such an anxious day, as a married woman. If they were not already married, it seems likely that the wedding took place before the end of Cicero's consulship or early in 62. Piso was around twenty-five and Tullia perhaps fifteen. Some time before the spring of 58, Cicero had the opportunity to make one of his excruciating jokes. Piso's gait was womanish; Tullia's energetic. So Cicero told his daughter, 'walk like a man' (Macrob. 2.3.16).

Back to the time of the engagement. Another milestone in 68 was the death of Cicero's father on 23 November, probably after a long illness.[15] Even before his death, Cicero had been involved in large capital expenditures, the purchase and remodelling of a country-house at Tusculum (the *Tusculanum*)[16] in the hills about twenty-five kilometres from Rome, easily reached for short breaks and 'the only place where we can rest from all annoyances and hard work'.[17] Cicero needed statues and adornments, which

44 *The life of mother and daughter*

Atticus was to buy and send for the colonnade and hall at Tusculum, 'Academia' where philosophical discussions took place.[18] He also acquired a library. In 60 he was given another library of Greek and Latin books.[19] Cicero also mentions another villa, the *Formianum*, between modern Formia and Gaeta, on the coast of Latium, which was also to be decorated with statuary: this house might already have been in the family, since it was within reach of Arpinum.[20] By 60, he also had a villa and land at Pompeii, an attractive town of mixed Greek and Roman culture on the Campanian coast, and a house in the town at Antium/Anzio, on the coast near Rome.[21] Cicero and Terentia had become comfortably established by early 66, when Cicero, having been elected at the minimum age and top of the poll, was the senior praetor. Their luxurious and beautiful homes must have given pleasure to Terentia and Tullia, who spent more time in them than Cicero could. They will have sat in the gardens, received visitors, walked in the grounds and read books. We should also imagine them getting out and about, in Rome and the country, to the houses of friends to visit other women, to the temples to attend sacrifices, to the games to watch tragedies and comedies in a temporary theatre or the chariot-races in the Circus Maximus and occasionally perhaps to gladiatorial contests and wild-beast hunts in the Forum.[22]

The new baby and the consulship

The following year, the letters show Cicero beginning to canvass for the elections of 64, and looking forward to Atticus switching his base to Rome. In the midst of this, in July 65, he wrote a rapid mock-solemn note, putting the birth of his son and the good condition of Terentia on a par with the election of the new consuls (*A* 1.2/11.1, Rome, July 65). The joy he shows makes us wonder why we know of only two children born in perhaps fifteen years of marriage. There may have been miscarriages, of which we would scarcely be informed. It is implausible that they produced babies and chose not to rear them. The Cicerones do not seem to have been prolific: Tullia certainly was not going to be. Terentia may not have been very fertile. It can be taken for granted that Cicero wanted a son to follow in his footsteps and that he would have welcomed other daughters.

Terentia's political involvement can be seen in the run-up to the elections of 64. According to a story which Cicero told in the poem he later wrote on his consulship, she had performed a sacrifice and was about to pour wine on the dying ashes when the fire flared up. This was taken as an omen that her husband would win the election.[23] More dramatically still, Plutarch and Dio put the incident – or a similar incident – in December 63 when the public sacrifice to the Good Goddess was performed by the Vestal Virgins in Cicero's house on the night of the 4–5th.[24] It may be the announcement of this which inspired the author of the *Invective against Cicero* (probably a later rhetorical exercise, but falsely attributed to Sallust) to accuse Terentia of sacrilege and perjury (2), for she, on the instructions of the Vestals, brought news of the omen to Cicero and told him to go ahead with the decisions he had made on behalf of their country. She strengthened Cicero's resolution, which was already made before he consulted the Senate on 5 December.[25] This story suggests a rooted belief in Terentia's influence. It seems possible that the omen was elicited on two occasions. If one account is to be preferred, it must be Cicero's. Even if he has adorned the truth, he too expresses Terentia's solidarity with his political ambitions.

At the crucial time, there is a gap in the letters, since Atticus was in Rome, so there is no correspondence on Cicero's triumph at the elections of 64 and his year as consul. Other sources contribute a little. Terentia and Tullia must have taken a keen interest in the busy political timetable of 63, especially in the months when Cicero was the presiding consul and had the twelve lictors in attendance (January, March, May, July, September, November). For the last months of the year, Cicero took the lead over his colleague in his battle against Catiline. Since women could not attend the Senate or the Assemblies, they got most of their political news at second hand, but they had it promptly from a major player.

There were other functions which the consul's wife and daughter could watch. The Latin festival lasted four days at the beginning of January. On 1 January, the new consuls, wearing the purple-bordered toga of their office for the first time, went in procession up the Capitoline Hill and sat on their ivory chairs.[26] Cicero addressed a meeting of the Senate in a speech devoted to the agrarian law of one of the tribunes: the opening of the speech, which would have included formal expressions to mark the occasion, is unfortunately lost.[27] As part of the festival, there was a major sacrifice on the Alban Mount (Monte Cavo in the *Castelli romani* south-east of Rome), when Cicero offered libations of milk to Jupiter.[28] On 3 December, after the arrest and confession of several of the conspirators, the Senate decreed a thanksgiving to the gods (*supplicatio*) in honour of Cicero, because he had freed 'the city from fire, the citizens from slaughter and Italy from war'.[29] *Supplicationes* were normally honours for generals: this was the first time a civilian had received one. That same day, a statue of Jupiter, decreed in 65, was erected with a different orientation.[30] Cicero must have arranged the timing. In his speech to the People, he told them to venerate Jupiter before returning home.[31] He also urged them to attend, with their wives and children, the ritual banquet for the gods which was to be held at all the temples during the (probably five-day) festival of thanksgiving.[32] It was essential that both sexes and all ages were represented at these great public occasions when both Senate and People took part.[33] All these religious ceremonies would have given Terentia and Tullia a prominent role among the Roman women, so they must have been memorable events for both of them. Terentia, who was careful in her religious observance in the house, was probably equally devoted to public cult.

That same night at the annual sacrifice by women to the Good Goddess, Terentia was hostess to the Vestals and high-born married women, since the ceremony was always held in the house of a high official, consul or praetor. If Tullia was already married to Piso, no doubt she was attending the rite for the first time. All male members of the household had to absent themselves.[34] The hostess must have felt that she had reached the summit of a Roman wife's social ambitions. In a house adorned with flowers and greenery, Terentia received the wives of Cicero's fellow-magistrates and all the great ladies, people like Caesar's widowed mother Aurelia. Politics must have been at the forefront of their minds. But, at a time of relief and fear, the occasion must have stimulated religious fervour as they prayed for the welfare of the Roman People. The ritual, so secret that we know few details, lasted all night. There was music and wine. Terentia's private religious feelings may also have been stirred by the signs and portents which were reported earlier in the year: a lunar eclipse, a man struck by lightning, an earthquake and ghosts.[35]

As consul's wife, Terentia was a source of patronage, especially for women. One contemporary source, the Sicilian Diodorus, gave an account of a plot of the Catilinarian conspirators which seems to be a doublet of the attempt to assassinate Cicero on 7 November (below). They thought of killing leading men by infiltrating their houses at the Saturnalia in December. It was this, according to Diodorus, which a young man (not named here) betrayed to his mistress (again, unnamed). She went to the 'wife of Cicero' and warned her (40.5, a fragment). In the usual version, Cicero got information from Fulvia, the mistress of Q. Curius, and Terentia is not mentioned. But, on the use of Terentia as an intermediary by a woman informant, Diodorus is convincing.[36]

The consular speeches, no doubt revised from transcripts taken down at the time, were copied and circulated in 60.[37] Of these, the speeches about the conspiracy of Catiline are relevant to our topic. When he firmly quashed the Catilinarian conspirators, Cicero foresaw a backlash and positioned himself as the protector of the families of others, though he put his own at risk (*Cat.* 4.1–3). Cicero claimed that the Catilinarians had tried to assassinate him at his morning reception on 7 November.[38] Everybody seems to have accepted that this was true. He could say that his wife and children might have been witnesses to violence: 'he would have slaughtered me in my residence, in the sight of my wife and children' (*Sulla* 18). He says that two Roman *equites*, at a meeting of the conspirators, promised to kill him before dawn, before he got out of bed, since one of them was a close enough friend to be able to count on being admitted to his bedroom, which was in any case Cicero's custom.[39] But he, after naming the men to witnesses, denied them admittance when they turned up. Terentia presumably normally slept with her husband, as Quintus expected his wife to do (p. 81), but she must have been in the habit of leaving the bedroom before her husband's *levée*. It was a time of high anxiety and she must have felt that violence had come dangerously close.

In the published version of the speech of 5 December, which was part of the Senate's debate on the dangerous topic of what to do with the arrested conspirators, Cicero lists his closest connections to pathetic effect:

> Death can be no disgrace to a man of courage; it cannot come too early to a man who has achieved the consulship, nor can a wise man think it sad. But I am not so hard-hearted as not to be moved by the sorrow of my dear and loyal brother, present here, and by the tears of all the men I see around me. And my thoughts are often called back home by my wife, who is fainting [*exanimata*], my daughter, who is prostrated by fear [*abiecta metu*], and my little son (whom, it seems to me, the Republic holds in her arms as a hostage for my good behaviour as consul) and by my son-in-law, who stands here in our sight, awaiting the outcome of this day.
>
> (*Cat.* 4.3)

In case of his death, he commended his infant son to the senators as the son of the man who had saved the state (*Cat.* 4.23). The pitiable vignette of the women, overcome by anxiety, and the two-year-old child is thrown into relief by the emotion of the senators, including Quintus, and contrasts with the standing figure of Piso, present as an observer (since he was not yet a member of the Senate). Perhaps he intended to take the news of the Senate's decision back to Cicero's house. Cicero himself was busy: when the Senate had voted for the death of the conspirators, he escorted the praetor P. Cornelius Lentulus Sura, who had admitted his guilt, to the prison, where the sentence was carried out on him and four others. He announced the execution to the crowds assembled outside: 'They have lived'.[40] Then he was escorted home through brilliantly lit streets by crowds acclaiming him as 'Father of his Country'.[41] Terentia must have seen to it that their house was illuminated with torches at the door and on the roof. Perhaps she received him ceremonially at the door.

In his speeches, Cicero exploited his love for his family to illustrate the sacrifice he was prepared to make for his country.[42] In fact, his execution of the conspirators came back to haunt him and to threaten his family. If Terentia, as hostess at the sacrifice to the Good Goddess, was responsible for announcing a favourable omen which steeled his resolution, she was morally implicated. Plutarch (*Cic.* 202) says she spurred him on. That rite was the high point of the year of the consul's wife, but it came at a moment of crisis: Terentia rose to both occasions.

If we conjecture that Tullia's marriage took place this year, it is difficult to guess at what date it would have been convenient to hold the ceremony. Yet it is tempting to suppose that Tullia was married from the consul's house. It would give the wedding the maximum publicity and do no harm to the political prospects of the bridegroom. The bride's torchlit procession, the decorated houses, the songs and shouts, the scattered nuts all made a spectacle for the Roman People.

Politics as usual

In 62, the rebels were defeated, Catiline killed and many alleged conspirators brought to trial under the Plautian law on violence.[43] The hostile tradition accused Cicero of cruelty and corruption and rigging trials with the complicity of his wife:

> Doubtless you are made famous by the policies you developed about the commonwealth after your consulship with your wife Terentia, when you passed judgements *at your home* under the Plautian law, you condemned some of the conspirators to exile, others to fines, when one of them built your villa at Tusculum, another your villa at Pompeii, another bought your house in Rome . . . If I'm accusing you falsely, give an account of how much you got as paternal inheritance, what you gained through court cases, what money you used to buy your house, to build your villas at Tusculum and Pompeii at vast expense, or, if you keep silence, who can doubt that all that luxury was achieved from the blood and suffering of your fellow-citizens?
>
> ([Sall]. *Inv.* 3; my emphasis)

Cicero would have replied that his money was obtained honestly from grateful beneficiaries of his advocacy. The slander was a commonplace of invective when it was credible that a wife was over-involved in politics: Cicero in 44 attacked Antony by claiming that his wife Fulvia was busy with falsification of documents and sales of state property from a base *in their house*.[44] It might well be believed that Fulvia – married in turn to P. Clodius Pulcher, a radical tribune responsible for a major legislative programme (killed 52), C. Curio, who switched to Caesar's side before the civil war (tribune 50, killed 49), and Antony – was a protagonist and not just a devoted wife. Terentia, at this period, could be seen as equally involved. Confirmation comes from an allegation, apparently false, made by Antony in 44. He claimed that Cicero had refused to release the bodies of the executed Catilinarians to their familes for burial.[45]

But a great deal of intervention by wives was acceptable and so normal that it was taken for granted and is rarely mentioned in our sources. For instance, in 62, Cicero wrote to P. Sestius, who was serving as proquaestor in Macedonia, about whether he wished to be replaced. An earlier letter from Sestius had suggested that he did, but one of his trusted agents had been to see Cicero and told him that the proquaestor wanted to stay in the province. Cicero had not been sure if this was right and Sestius had indeed changed his mind until he followed up the matter with a certain Q. Cornelius and Sestius' wife, Cornelia,[46] arranged a meeting with Terentia. Here we see Cornelia as the repository of the most up-to-date instructions from her husband, contacting the consular's wife quite formally to ensure that Cicero would oppose the recall of Sestius and persuade Sestius' other friends in the Senate

The life of mother and daughter 49

to do the same.⁴⁷ Terentia was a trusted intermediary. It was etiquette for the junior senator's wife to approach her and not Cicero himself.

A negotiation which was going on in late 62 and January 61 is more mysterious. Cicero begins a letter to Atticus abruptly: 'That Teucris is a slow brute and Cornelius has never got back to Terentia'. The business in question was clearly a loan, for Cicero goes on to consider other people he might approach: 'But, to go back to what I was saying before, I've never seen anyone as unscrupulous, crafty and procrastinating as she is. "I am sending a freedman." "I've given instructions to Titus." Excuses and postponements' (*A* 1.12/12.1, Rome, 1 Jan. 61). 'Teucris' is a made-up name. It seems to mask a woman, as the feminine pronoun suggests. Cicero was trying to secure a loan from C. Antonius, who had been consul with him in 63 and was now governor of Macedonia.⁴⁸ So 'Teucris' may be Antonius' wife or Sestius' wife Cornelia (as is suggested by the probability that the Cornelius mentioned here is the same as Sestius' agent and perhaps Cornelia's client, Q. Cornelius, of the letter to Sestius). 'Teucris' was still dragging her feet three weeks later, but carried out her promise by mid-February.⁴⁹ Again, we see a woman acting as a go-between and again we see that Terentia is involved, here explicitly in negotiations with Cornelius. We are not told that she was dealing with 'Teucris', although, since it was more proper for a woman to have confidential meetings with another woman, perhaps it was 'Teucris' and Terentia who had the direct contact and Cicero's vivid description of how 'Teucris' put him off is derived from Terentia's accounts of their conversations.

Twelve months after the sacrifice at Terentia's house in December 62, Rome enjoyed a spectacular scandal when a man, said to be the up-and-coming politician P. Clodius Pulcher, gate-crashed the Good Goddess' rites at the house of Caesar, at which Terentia, as the wife of a consular, was surely present, and probably Tullia as well. The enmity between Cicero and Clodius which resulted, because Cicero disproved Clodius' alibi at his trial for sacrilege, was to lead directly to his exile on the charge of having executed Catilinarians without trial. A titillating anecdote in Plutarch (*Cic.* 29.2–3) belongs to this period, but should be discredited as an invention of Cicero's slanderers, perhaps Antony in his reply to Cicero's attacks on his private life. The story goes that Cicero gave evidence against Clodius in order to disarm Terentia's suspicions about his contacts with Clodius' sister Clodia. She thought Clodia (then the wife of Metellus Celer) wanted to marry Cicero. The suspicion was supported by the fact that one of Cicero's intimates was going back and forth between the two houses. This man has been convincingly identified with the Greek poet Thyillus, who is attested as a client of Cicero. But the mediation was no doubt political.⁵⁰ Plutarch's characterisation of Terentia as difficult and domineering fits with his own picture of her as sharing in Cicero's political life, but also probably derives from a hostile source which wanted to show Cicero as weak, just as Cicero later claimed that Fulvia bossed Antony around. That said, we can well imagine

50 *The life of mother and daughter*

that Terentia, as the sister of a Vestal, took a more serious view of the sacrilege than Cicero initially did, when he thought it a splendid bit of gossip to relay to Atticus,[51] and spurred Cicero on against Clodius. Although Cicero as a consular was now a more desirable marriage partner than when he had married Terentia, it is wildly improbable that Clodia, a member of the proud patrician Claudii, would have preferred him to Q. Caecilius Metellus Celer (cos. 60), of the top plebeian nobility and a family closely linked with her own. That part of the story can be discounted, as can any rift between Cicero and Terentia.[52]

Domestic bliss

Meanwhile, family life continued. In 62, after the trial of Sulla,[53] so perhaps in the autumn, Cicero handed over the paternal house on the *Carinae* to Quintus and bought a fine place on the Palatine to reflect his position and to make himself more accessible.[54] He paid 3,500,000 sesterces, a large sum, but not disproportionate.[55] The house, which probably had two storeys above a basement (for servants' quarters and offices) which gave it impressive height and outlook, was to have elegant decor and gardens.[56] Cicero was still working very hard.[57] Eminent men courted him, crowds attended him.[58] He started thinking about improvements to the country-house at Arpinum.[59] He had also been borrowing money to spend on the villas at Tusculum and Pompeii.[60] Atticus' affection for him gave him great joy and only that of Quintus and his nuclear family was as important (*A* 1.17/17.5, Rome, 5 Dec. 61). The happy domestic scene is evoked in January 60, when Cicero, lonely for the companionship of an adult male with whom he could discuss his political perplexities, nevertheless finds consolation with his immediate family:

> the only repose I find is the time I spend with my wife and little daughter and my honey-sweet son Cicero. For my self-seeking and sham friendships make a fine show in the Forum, but give no satisfaction at home. So when my house is well filled in the morning, when we go down to the Forum packed tight with herds of friends, in all that great crowd I can find no one with whom I can joke freely or heave a sigh as with an intimate.
>
> (*A* 1.18/18.1, Rome, 20 Jan. 60)

Expensive home improvements continued.[61] Cicero invited Atticus to spend the New Year festival of the Compitalia with them in 60–59, perhaps at Antium or Tusculum; Terentia invited Pomponia (and presumably her son, born c. 67) and Atticus' mother Caecilia. (Quintus was away governing Asia.) Cicero planned to have the bath heated and to go for walks with Atticus.[62] The Compitalia (a movable feast) was a holiday from work for slaves and labourers as well as senators. It was celebrated by local groups, in the countryside or in towns, which lived around crossroads. A household would hang up a woollen doll for each free member and a woollen ball for each slave: so slaves were distinguished from the free, but they were included in the group.[63] Perhaps the women would have looked in on the religious rites of their social inferiors. It was a relaxed occasion, like the Saturnalia of 17 December.

By now, Cicero owned the ancestral villa and estate near Arpinum; the large new house on the Palatine with its splendid view, itself prominent when viewed from below; a country-house at Tusculum, convenient for short breaks, acquired in 68; a villa near Formiae on the sea, ideal for spring holidays, first mentioned in 66; a town-house at Antium/Anzio, also on the coast, which he owned from 60 at latest to 45 at latest, also convenient for short breaks, as when Cicero went there to avoid the gladiatorial games in Rome;[64] and a villa at Pompeii, first mentioned by Cicero in letters in 60 but also referred to in a dialogue, the dramatic date of which falls between 63 and 60.[65] The houses at Arpinum, Tusculum and Pompeii had agricultural land attached. But the villas which Cicero bought, like the house at Antium, which had a good library, were also intended for recreation and learned leisure, and the social life which overlapped with politics. They were in beautiful places, all easily accessible, and Cicero called them 'the pearls of Italy'.[66] There was criticism of the new man for getting above himself: he had acquired the house of Crassus in Rome;[67] he had bought the Tusculan villa which had once belonged to Lutatius Catulus;[68] he owned a place at Pompeii. If he visited the fashionable resort of Baiae to take the waters, that was uppity for a man from Arpinum. The Pompeian villa was also on the Bay of Naples and close enough to Baiae to suggest luxury and debauchery.[69]

Senators were, on the one hand, expected to have a standard of living appropriate to the rulers of the world, who might play host to foreign princes, and, on the other, supposed to remember an allegedly native Roman plain and even ascetic style. Even Pompey, it was said, built a modest house in Rome in the 50s.[70] But the general trend was for ever-increasing conspicuous consumption, in houses in Rome, suburban villas in extensive parks and villas by the sea and elsewhere. The richest senators competed with one another; men of more limited means, like Cicero, aimed at good taste, comfort and keeping up with the fashion for marble columns, statuary and gardens. It is possible that he spent more on his villas than most of his peers would have considered necessary. But the purpose was not just to 'keep up with the Joneses'. The villas provided recreation, a setting for study and healthy holidays. They allowed the family to get away from the din of the Forum and the noise and smoke of Rome.[71] Depending on their location, they could provide coolness; sea or mountain air; fresh produce, fish, meat and game, and outdoor activities. Women of the family, who had no work to do in the Forum, could get away to these estates for longer periods of time than their husbands and fathers.

52 The life of mother and daughter

In April and May of 59 we see the little family group (apparently without Piso) on holiday together, visiting an estate belonging to Terentia, then at the seaside at Antium and finally travelling south to Formiae. Cicero wanted to be away from Rome in order to avoid taking a stand on Caesar's legislation, but he did not want to appear to be engaged in frivolous amusement. Plans depended partly on when Atticus would join them.

Cicero found Antium blissfully quiet:

> I am not able to confirm the promise I made you in any earlier letter, that a piece of writing would come out of this trip. I have embraced leisure so eagerly that I cannot be torn away from it. So I am either enjoying myself with books, of which I have a charming collection at Antium, or counting the waves [a proverbial expression for wasting time], as the weather is unsuitable for mackerel-fishing. I do not feel like writing... I am even wondering if I might settle down here at Antium and use up all this period. I would rather have been chief magistrate here than at Rome. You made a wiser choice when you acquired your house at Buthrotum [in Epirus]. But this community of the Antiates comes a close second to that town. That there should be a place so near to Rome where many people have never set eyes on Vatinius [a tribune who was working for Caesar]... where nobody interrupts me and everyone likes me!
>
> (*A* 2.6/26.1, Antium, early April)

The possibility that Cicero was a fisherman is startling.[72] He was in an unusual mood, disillusioned (because he had little influence and nothing to do) with the political career at which he had worked so hard for nearly twenty years, at least sometimes attracted by a quiet life at home and listening to the rain pattering on the roof.[73] It would be pleasant to think that this means he spent more time enjoying the company of his wife and children. Perhaps Terentia or Tullia accompanied him in walks and talks on the beach.[74] Tiny indications suggest that the family was close. Letters of this period often include love from Terentia to Atticus (she appears to have read his letters) and little messages from Marcus, sometimes in Greek, in which he was making progress.[75] Atticus helped Terentia with some business affairs (*A* 2.15/35.4). When Cicero urges Atticus to come and visit them, he uses the plural 'we'. Although the pronoun elsewhere can mean only Cicero himself, the natural interpretation here is that it includes Terentia (and possibly the children): 'About 1 May we shall be either at the villa at Formiae or at Pompeii. If we are not at Formiae, please come to Pompeii. That will be delightful for us and not too far out of the way for you' (*A* 2.4/24.6, Antium, early Apr. 59). As Atticus was planning a visit to Buthrotum and would travel down the Appian Way to get to Brundisium/Brindisi, both these villas would make convenient stopping-places. Atticus, however, advised Cicero that a visit to Pompeii might look frivolous, so that part of the scheme was dropped. Instead, they would reach Formiae on 21 April and return to Antium on 3 May, so that Tullia could attend the games there on the 4/5th. A teenage daughter's wishes are taken into account. Tullia was probably interested in plays and perhaps there were other festivities too, as at Rome.[76] Cicero then intended to go north to Tusculum and then down the Latin Way to Arpinum and back to Rome by 1 June. This plan would allow Atticus to visit them at Formiae, Antium or Tusculum.[77] Shortly after, Cicero was more specific: he wanted to leave Formiae for Antium on 29 April and Antium for Tusculum on 7 May.[78] But then it occurred to him that it would look as if he were out only for enjoyment if he attended games, so he despatched a brief note while travelling: 'I will wait for you at the Formian villa until 7 May. Now let me know on what day we shall see you'.[79] It is not clear if Tullia was able to go to the games alone. It would have been perfectly proper for her to attend games, which consisted of plays and races, with suitable companions and attendants. At the races, women sat with men, while in the theatre auditorium they were segregated. But since women in general liked going to plays, 'to see and be seen', says Ovid cynically, the colonnades of theatres were places for young people to meet and chat (Figure 5.1). The games were recognised as one of the main diversions of women of the leisured classes.[80]

On 19 April, they set off for Formiae and joined the Appian Way at Tres Tabernae, where they spent the night.[81] Early next day, they travelled on down the Appian Way, reaching Forum Appii by the fourth hour, having covered about ten Roman miles. They probably spent the night at Tarracina/Terracina, nineteen Roman miles further on.[82] They should have reached Formiae on the 21st, as planned. As usual, Cicero does not tell us how he travelled, still less how his wife and daughter did. He probably rode a horse or was driven in a four-wheeled carriage, *raeda*, as, sometimes at least, he did in Cilicia and as Milo did when accompanied by his wife.[83] For the women, the choice was between a carriage and a slower but smoother litter carried by male slaves.[84] When they reached the villa near Formiae, Cicero was short of news of Rome and distracted from writing, not only by the common people who came to his receptions and left on time before the fourth hour, but by local gentry who kept dropping in, one of them wanting to talk philosophy, so the house was more like a basilica than a villa.[85] Cicero seems to have been relaxed, for he says that he was feeling sleepy after dinner one evening when a letter from Atticus arrived.[86] But he was writing long and frequent letters to Atticus. The plan now was to stay at Formiae until 6 May (that is, perhaps still leaving on the 7th) and then go to Arpinum, which he describes in Homer's words about Ithaca, as a rugged country which bred good men. Atticus would not be keen to travel there, he thought.[87] But apparently Atticus *was* willing: 'We shall see you at the house at Arpinum and welcome you to some country hospitality, since you have turned down this chance to visit us at the seaside' (*A* 2.16/36.4, Formiae, 29 April or 1 May).

Figure 5.1 A Roman theatre: stage-building, stage and seats for the audience (Orange, Provence, June 1998; Treggiari)

In his dialogue the *Laws*, which is set after the death of Clodius in January 52 and where the interlocutors are Atticus, Quintus and Cicero himself, Atticus is portrayed as getting to know the villa and its grounds for the first time.[88] This seems a device which enables Cicero to describe the setting and what it meant to him. It is not strong evidence that Atticus had never visited the villa before 52. But we cannot be sure he came in 59. There is a break in the letters between early May and June, by which time Cicero was back in Rome and Atticus had set off for his estates in Epirus.

Probably in August, there was an unsavoury political incident. A man called Vettius accused several young men of being in a plot to kill Pompey. Next day he emended his evidence at a public meeting and added new names, including Tullia's husband. He also accused 'an eloquent ex-consul' (clearly Cicero) of inflammatory remarks.[89] This scare led to no prosecutions, but shook Pompey and made things difficult for Cicero in future.

This series of letters is typical in what it says about politics and personal matters and what it omits. There were things which Atticus would know and which did not need to be explained. Often these are exactly the things we would like to know. The detail of the 60s eludes us. The marriage of Terentia and Cicero seems to have been a success: Cicero may even have written a poem called *Uxorius* (possibly 'The man devoted to his wife', *SHA* 20.3.2).

We know nothing of Tullia's education, except that her father's later praise of her intellectual qualities suggests that she probably had as much literary training as was usually given to daughters in the upper classes. We know nothing of her relationship with her mother. Her marriage got off to a good start, as far as we know. We know that Q. Cicero acquired a house next door to his brother's on the Palatine and that Cicero and Atticus were concerned that a party-wall adjoining Cicero's beloved 'Palaestra' (where he exercised and enjoyed learned conversations) should be repaired and not be a danger to Pomponia and young Quintus.[90] But we know little of Terentia's contacts with them. Cicero and Terentia were firm allies, but the intimacies of the relationship between the two were not confided to Atticus. It took a crisis to compel correspondence from husband to wife and to give him the opportunity to describe emotions.

6 Living through disaster

We now enter a period which brought the pain of separation and threw the major responsibility of keeping the family going on to Terentia and Tullia, as well as an important political role, especially behind the scenes.

Cicero's departure

Cicero's popularity with the majority of his fellow-citizens did not last long. The scandal about the sacrilege at the sacrifice to the Good Goddess in 62 and the consequent trial and acquittal of Clodius broke the fragile alliance of senators and *equites* on which Cicero had prided himself. He chose not to join Pompey, M. Crassus and Caesar in a plan of joint action for political advantage which they initiated in 60. During Caesar's consulship of 59, Cicero was sidelined. His extended holiday that spring was a response to his political exclusion and the growing danger from his enemy P. Clodius Pulcher. When he returned to Rome in June, he kept out of political debate, but was so busy with advocacy and court work that he had to dictate a letter to Atticus, to whom he normally wrote in his own hand, while taking a walk to refresh his voice.[1] The letters focus on Cicero's observation of politics. He gives a vivid description of how the audience at the Games of Apollo applied the lines of a tragedy to Pompey and encored passages such as 'By our suffering you are Great', but we do not know if he was present, or if Terentia and Tullia were.[2] Since Piso was quaestor, it seems likely he would go to the games with his wife, and perhaps to the gladiatorial show put on by an individual at about the same time. Cicero makes no mention of his family at this time, although Clodius' threats are a constant theme and Cicero was anxious for Atticus' return. Because Atticus did come back to Rome, there is another gap in the letters between about September 59 and March 58.[3]

By then, Clodius had become tribune and promulgated a law outlawing anyone who had killed citizens without trial. Cicero went into mourning, as did *equites* and the Senate.[4] Terentia and the rest of the family must have done the same. She and Tullia will have put on black or dirty clothes and left their hair loose, a dramatic sign of grief and an appeal for help.[5] He consulted his most powerful friends. Hortensius and others, *in his own house*, advised him to flee, Cicero later thought out of malice.[6] Pompey led him to think he would protect him and then let him down.[7] Cicero sent his son-in-law Piso to plead with Pompey at his Alban villa, and then went himself, but Pompey, it was said, slipped out to avoid seeing him.[8] He and Piso had a fruitless interview with the consul L. Piso.[9] He thought of killing himself and afterwards regretted that he had not.[10] It was the tears of his family (*mei*) which prevented him (*QF* 1.4/4.4, Thessalonica, c. 5 Aug. 58). He decided it was best to go quietly. Later, Cicero's public narration of this decision underlined his reluctance to cause violent dissension in the state:

> I saved the commonwealth by going away, judges; by my pain and grief I deflected from you and your children slaughter, devastation, fire and rapine, and all by myself I saved the commonwealth twice, once by my glory [63 BC], a second time by my suffering. For I shall never deny that in this I was a human being. I cannot boast that I was not pained by the loss of my excellent brother, dearest children, most loyal wife, the sight of you, my country, my rank. If I had not suffered, what benefit would I have conferred on you, in leaving for your sake things I held cheap?
>
> (*Sest.* 49)

He sacrificed himself for the good of his country:

> When I had judged the situation, I wept for the separation from my unhappy wife, the loneliness of my dearest children, the ruin of my loving and excellent brother[11] (who was abroad), the sudden ruin of a well-established family; but I put all these things second to the lives of my fellow-citizens, and I preferred that the commonwealth should fall stricken at the departure of one man rather than perish by the destruction of all . . . To take on such mental agony, for one man to suffer while the city still stands the things which happen to the conquered when a city is captured, and to see oneself torn from the embrace of one's family, the house taken stone from stone, one's fortunes plundered, . . . to undergo all this for the sake of preserving your fellow-citizens – and that when you are present and sorrowing, not such a philosopher as those who care for nothing, but loving your own people and things as common humanity demands – that is glorious and godlike fame. For a man who with equanimity for the sake of the commonwealth abandons things which he never thought dear and pleasant demonstrates no remarkable benevolence towards the commonwealth; but a man who leaves for the sake of the commonwealth things from which he is agonisingly torn truly loves his country, whose survival he puts before his love of home and family.
>
> (*Dom.* 96, 98)

58 *Living through disaster*

Such was the slant he could put on events in retrospect. After dedicating in the Temple of Capitoline Jupiter a small statue of Minerva, which he had kept in his house,[12] surely accompanied by Terentia and Tullia, Cicero left Rome. According to Plutarch, he quitted the city discreetly at midnight and on foot, but escorted by friends.[13] Perhaps Terentia and Tullia said goodbye to him at home, as Ovid's wife later did when her husband was banished.[14]

Wife and daughter of an exile

In social terms, it was disgraceful to be the wife of an exile, and Terentia might have been acutely embarrassed, although Cicero assured her (p. 64) that there was nothing to be ashamed of if they had done no wrong. Ovid nearly seventy years later wrote that his wife might blush when people called her an exile's wife and think it a disgrace to appear to be married to him.[15] Cicero's enemies continued to taunt him even after his restoration.[16] Women may also have been catty about Terentia and Tullia.

The legal consequences of exile were more serious. Cicero had earlier argued that Roman citizens who went into voluntary exile to avoid punishment did not lose their citizenship, unless they chose to become citizens of the state in which they lived. Exile was not a punishment in Roman law, but a refuge.[17] After his own exile or, as he would call it, his 'calamity' or 'disaster', he was more specific: such people, condemned on a capital charge, chose to take a new citizenship not because their Roman citizenship had been taken from them but because they were interdicted from shelter, fire and water. When they took the citizenship of the place where they were living abroad, they ceased to be Roman citizens.[18] Cicero had not become a naturalised citizen of Thessalonica.

A standard modern view is as follows.[19] Interdiction from fire and water was pronounced by the Senate or a high magistrate when a man charged with a crime went into voluntary exile before trial or sentence. It was assumed he had adopted another country. He became an outlaw and no Roman could shelter him. He could not return, on pain of death, and he lost citizenship and property. The decree would run something like this: 'It appears that he is in exile and it is decided that his property should be sold and he himself interdicted from fire and water'.[20] Interdiction was not the legal penalty for the offence with which the man was charged, but the consequence of his own actions in avoiding the penalty, which was, in theory, death.[21]

If he lost citizenship, this had consequences for his marriage and family. Now Cicero had not been summoned to answer the charge of having illegally executed Roman citizens. The second Clodian law accused him but gave him no opportunity to answer the charges.[22] So he was not on the same footing as most exiles but more like the victims of the Sullan proscriptions, interdicted by a law, not after a judicial procedure and their own withdrawal.[23] He would avoid using the word *ex(s)ul* of himself. When, on his return, Clodius pretended to assume that he had become naturalised in a foreign city, he implied that Cicero was an exile who had given up his Roman status. Cicero could deny this and remind people that the Senate in 57 had described him as a citizen who had deserved well of the commonwealth.[24] Because Clodius' action was controversial and because it was overturned, there could be argument about Cicero's legal status during his absence from Rome.

According to a later legal handbook:

> Since someone who is interdicted from fire and water [under the Cornelian law for some crime][25] loses his Roman citizenship, it follows that his removal from the Roman citizen body releases his children from his power just as though he had died; for it is contrary to reason that a man whose status is that of a foreigner should have a Roman citizen in his power . . .
> The agnatic tie is broken by status-loss . . . Status-loss is the exchange of one status for another and happens in three ways, namely in the first, the second – also called intermediate – or the third degree . . . Second degree or intermediate status-loss means loss of citizenship but not liberty, as where a man is interdicted from fire and water . . . The agnatic tie is destroyed not only by first or second degree status-loss but even by the third.
> (Gaius 1.128, 158–63, tr. Gordon and Robinson 1988, with modifications)

So the man under the interdict lost citizenship, but not liberty. His children were no longer in his power. They lost their special rights of succession as agnates to his estate. (Gaius' text comes from a section on inheritance.) Because he was no longer a citizen, he was no longer validly married to his Roman wife.

A Roman who became a prisoner of war or a slave underwent first-degree status-loss. Horace vividly describes what this meant for the family of the heroic Regulus, a general who was captured by the Carthaginians and returned to Rome to negotiate on their behalf, but persuaded the Senate not to make peace and so returned to torture and death at Carthage. His wife tried to embrace him, but he avoided her kiss (because she was no longer his wife) and moved his little children away, looking at the ground, because he had undergone status-loss. Then he hastened away, 'a noble exile'.[26] Cicero's opponents taunted him with not behaving as well as Regulus.[27]

If Cicero was, after the second Clodian bill was passed, a non-citizen, then Terentia was not his legal wife (*uxor iusta*). But she went on behaving as if she were. The legal position may have been that she was a woman not married according to Roman law, but united to a man in a relationship to which they both agreed and treated as a marriage, although they lacked legal capacity.[28] There would be nothing to stop her following him into exile, living with him and being accepted in local society. All the same, Cicero's status-loss made their legal position very dangerous.

60 *Living through disaster*

Clodius' initial bill (the law on citizen status, reaffirming the right of appeal), passed after Cicero left, among other things interdicted from fire and water anyone who had executed a citizen without trial.[29] This meant that nobody could shelter the outlaw. Then Clodius passed a second law, 'about the exile of Cicero', confiscating his property and banishing him for ever on pain of death to 400 (or possibly 500) Roman miles from Italy.[30] No one was to shelter him; anyone who did was liable to death, exile and confiscation of property. This might have affected Terentia or Tullia. His own possessions and land were to be sold to the benefit of the state. His Palatine house and his villas were to be destroyed and a monument put up on the Palatine site.[31] The destruction of his house symbolised the annihilation of his deeds and lineage: Cicero was to be regarded as a despot who had plotted against the People, a traitor to his country. His fate was that of legendary figures who had tried to make themselves kings.

Keeping the home fires burning

Cicero's swift departure must have left his affairs in disarray. He left Terentia in charge of his new house and scattered villas and presumably commissioned her to administer his revenues from various sources, including land, and to see to necessary expenditure, including upkeep of buildings and maintenance of slaves. She was responsible for Marcus' education, the morale and good behaviour of the staff and, to some extent, Tullia's welfare.

When we try to reconstruct what happened to Terentia and Tullia in 58/7, nearly all the evidence comes from Cicero himself, who was far away at the time and romanticised the facts later in his speeches. In public, it was necessary to stress the efforts of fellow-senators, Quintus, Piso and the major proponents of recall.

> For the mourning-clothes and grief of my unhappy wife and the sorrow of my excellent daughter and my small son's yearning for me and his childish tears were restricted to their unavoidable journeys and for the most part hidden in the darkness of the house.
>
> (*Red. Pop.* 8)

This was all very proper as a statement to the assembly. But Terentia and Tullia did not spend all their time shut up in their shady houses. They put on their black clothes and left their hair dishevelled in order to show themselves outside in the classic form of protest, and they visited the houses of others in order to work for Cicero's return.

After Cicero left, the Council of the Plebs passed both Clodius' bills. Terentia and Tullia now knew where they stood. It must, even so, have been a terrible shock when Clodius' supporters came to burn down the Palatine house and loot the contents. The villas at Tusculum and Formiae were also plundered and burned, and the rest of the property put on sale.[32] Cicero put it later in terms of desecration: 'the *Lares* of our household were tormented' (*Leg.* 2.42). Perhaps it was Terentia who reported to Cicero the shocking sight of columns being removed to the house of one consul's mother-in-law in Rome and even trees from the villa being taken to the other consul's villa at Tusculum. Furniture and silverware were, naturally, pilfered.[33] She and her household escaped, perhaps warned before the mob arrived, and she took refuge (probably with her half-sister Fabia) in the house of the Vestal Virgins about five minutes' walk away.[34] The sacrosanctity of the Vestals would protect her. Tullia was presumably living with her husband, Piso. Most of the household staff must have been scattered, perhaps to those villas which had not been touched. It is not clear if Terentia stayed with the Vestals for the whole period of Cicero's absence. She may have gone on to reside with Tullia, but if she stayed with the Vestals, it will have helped highlight her protest.

The view from Greece

Cicero's emotions were one of the problems with which Terentia and Tullia (and Quintus and Atticus) had to cope. So they are an important part of the narrative. Ancient critics found him wanting: why could he not bear misfortune philosophically?[35] Cicero was at times suicidal, at first unable to do much practical thinking, and inclined to rehash grievances. The family needed to write and boost his morale.

The news of the promulgation of Clodius' second bill caught up with him as he travelled.[36] He journeyed by a circuitous route through southern Italy and eventually sailed for Greece from Brundisium. Friends who were prepared to break the law received him kindly. He thought it too dangerous to accept Atticus' offer of hospitality at Buthrotum, but went on to Thessalonica and remained there from May to November, deeply depressed.[37] He commends his family to Atticus or asks him to watch over Terentia and the children and he relays his wife's thanks for Atticus' good offices: 'Terentia thanks you often and most warmly'.[38]

He reminds Atticus of what he has lost: 'rank, glory, children, fortune, brother'.[39] We would expect his wife to appear in such a list (but he may be thinking that she might join him). Again, he hopes to be restored to his brother and children,[40] but 'I am missing not just my possessions nor my family, but myself.'[41] We do not know what Terentia had advised, but Cicero was prepared to blame Atticus for his advice, despite his sympathy,[42] and it seems possible that he might, in some moods, have felt that she too had caused him to make the wrong decision:

> since I was betrayed, led on, ensnared by guile, so that I neglected all my defences, let down and abandoned the whole of Italy which was eager and ready to protect me and handed myself and my family over to my enemies.
>
> (*A* 3.15/60.7, Thessalonica, 17 Aug. 58)[43]

It would not be surprising if Terentia had attended the meetings in their house at which Hortensius and others counselled Cicero not to make a fight of it. A few years later, in a family crisis affecting her son Brutus and son-in-law Cassius, Servilia took a leading role in a meeting to which Cicero was invited as an adviser. Cassius' wife Junia Tertia and Brutus' wife and cousin Porcia were also present.[44] But there is no hint of blame in his letters to Terentia, and Cicero could also blame himself. It was his consulship which had robbed him of his 'brother, children, country, fortune', he tells Quintus.[45] The brothers did not meet as Quintus travelled through Greece on his way back from Asia. Cicero explained that he could not bear his brother to see him as a ghost of his former self.[46] He also blamed himself for ruining his brother and the rest of the family and not being in Rome to defend Quintus if he were prosecuted.[47] But he loves and misses him. He says more about Terentia when writing to Quintus, so perhaps the lack of emphasis on her when writing to Atticus comes from a sense of delicacy. To praise his other main helper too often to Atticus might hurt his feelings and, moreover, a Roman did not parade his love for his wife even to intimate friends. He lists all his family, in the appropriate order: first Quintus himself, then the elder child, then young Marcus and young Quintus (who for the last three years had been in the care of his mother and two uncles) and finally, as a climax, his wife. He was missing a man who was more than a brother. When he describes how he misses Tullia, we have a flash of detail: 'And then at the same time I am missing my daughter. What dutiful love she shows, what good behaviour, what character. She is the image of me in face, conversation and feelings' (*QF* 1.3/3.3).

It is hard to get the right nuances here without making Cicero sound even more self-centred than he was. 'Dutiful love', *pietas*, was not just filial duty from child to parent, but reciprocal affection between family members, which resulted in people doing their duty by each other and included, when appropriate, extremes of self-sacrifice and warm feeling.[48] Good behaviour, *modestia*, was the discreet and well-mannered behaviour proper to a specific age and sex: here the unassuming and chaste deportment of a young married woman and daughter. Character, *ingenium*, describes her inborn moral character and intellectual ability. Then Cicero suggests that she closely resembles him and is a sort of soul-mate. It sounds as if it was accepted in the family that Tullia had features which reminded them of her father – a common characteristic of children, and of course physical resemblance to the father was a conventional piece of evidence which guaranteed the mother's sexual fidelity. Cicero puts into his own mouth in a dialogue the remark that children's looks, character, deportment and gestures usually come from their parents (*Div.* 2.94). This seems to come from observation. If Cicero can remind his brother that Tullia is like him in mind and conversation, it suggests that her father found her a bright and interesting companion and for a moment we seem to have evidence of a lively personality as well as a model daughter.

> I am missing my sweet and adorable son. Like a hard-hearted beast, I let him go from my arms, a boy who understood more than I would have liked, for the poor little thing realised what was going on. I am missing your son, the picture of you, whom my Cicero loved as a brother and respected as an elder brother. And I did not allow that poor wretched woman, my loyal wife, to come with me, but left her in Rome to take care of what is left after our shared calamity and of our shared children.
> (QF 1.3/3.3)

In the same letter to Quintus, thinking of what he has lost, Cicero says he was 'blessed in my brother, children, wife, wealth, the way I obtained my money, status, authority, reputation, influence' (QF 1.3/3.6). He knows he need not commend 'my daughter and yours and our Cicero'. Their orphan status grieves Quintus as much as it does him. 'But as long as you live they will not be fatherless . . . Please watch over Terentia too' (QF 1.3/3.10).

Correspondence with Terentia

There are four letters from Cicero in exile to Terentia and the children. The first was sent from Brundisium on 29 April, as he was leaving Italy.

> I write to you less often than I could because, although my whole life is wretched, when I either write to you or read your letters, I am so overcome by tears that I cannot bear it. I wish I had not clung on to life so much. Then we would not have seen any evil in our lives, or not much. But if fortune has kept us for any hope of retrieving any comfort, my mistake was not so serious; but if these evils are unalterable, then I want to see you as soon as possible, my life, and to die in your arms, since neither the gods, whom you have worshipped with the utmost purity, nor human beings, whom I have always served, have repaid us with gratitude . . . How lost and crushed I am! What now? Should I ask you to come, a woman who is sick and exhausted in body and spirit? Should I not ask you? Should I then be without you? I think this is what I shall do. If there is any hope of my return, do you strengthen it and push things on; but if, as I fear, all is up, come to me, by whatever means you can. Be sure of this one thing: if I have you, I shall not feel I have completely perished. But what will happen to my little Tullia?[49] Now you see to that; I have no counsel to give. But certainly, however things turn out, the poor girl's marriage and fair fame must be safeguarded. What else? What will happen to my Cicero? May he always be in my embrace. I cannot write more now; grief prevents me.
> (F 14.4/6.1, 3, Brundisium, 29 April 58)[50]

Among these fond messages, Cicero keeps Terentia up to date on practical matters, making sure she knows they owe a debt of gratitude to his host in

Brundisium and which of his humbler friends are staying with him (F 14.4/ 6.2, 6).[51] He assures her that she must not worry about him manumitting slaves (in an attempt to avoid their being confiscated). Although it seems that he had freed his own slaves informally, on the understanding that their freedom would not come into effect if he managed to retain ownership, he had told 'her' slaves (probably those in her dowry) that she would act according to their deserts (a certain Orpheus was the only one who stood out for doing his duty) (F 14.4/6.4).[52] Later, Cicero agreed to act in accordance with the advice of friends who had been consulted by his wife (F 14.1/8.3, despatched from Dyrrachium, 25 Nov. 58). This 'minor matter' is in the context of what had been going on in Rome. 'I do not know what you are doing, whether you have been able to hold on to anything or, as I fear, have been stripped of everything' (F 14.4/6.4). Naturally, there had not yet been time for Cicero to hear the news of the destruction of the house and two villas. Tullia's husband looked like being loyal (F 14.4/6.4). Cicero tried to encourage his wife, insisting that it was their virtue, not a moral fault, which had ruined them. He would try to be strong, because their children wanted him to live (F 14.4/6.5). 'See to your health, as well as you can, and be sure that I am more upset by your wretchedness than by my own. My Terentia, most faithful and excellent wife, and my dearest little daughter, and our remaining hope, Cicero, farewell' (F 14.4/6.6).

In this and the other letters of his exile, we can see Cicero not only displaying genuine emotions but consciously or unconsciously playing the role both of the conscientious and considerate Roman husband and of the distraught lover. There is also a fascinating mixture of sentiment and concern for practicalities, which he happily delegates to his wife. Meanwhile, Terentia was left to live as honourably as possible (F 14.4/6.5). We can see from Cicero's letters to her that she was supporting him courageously when she wrote to him.[53] The second letter in the extant sequence to Terentia was not written until 5 October, when Cicero had been in Thessalonica for months. Terentia had apparently complained that he was sending her only short notes.

> Please don't think I send letters of any length to anyone, except when anyone sends me a good deal of information, to which I think I ought to reply. I have nothing to write and writing is the hardest thing for me to do at this time. When I write to you and to our little Tullia I cannot do it without weeping many tears. For I see that you are very wretched, you whom I wanted always to be happy. I ought to have seen to that, and if I had not been so cowardly, I would have seen to it.
>
> (F 14.2/7.1)

He had written to Piso to thank him for his efforts and encourage him to continue (F 14.2/7.2). He did so, and Cicero praised him publicly after his return.[54] Terentia, for her part, was as diligent in looking after family interests, children and property as Cicero felt he ought to have been, and showed herself practical and energetic. With true consideration for Cicero's feelings, she had not told him the most shocking things which had happened to her:

> I see that you are doing everything most bravely and lovingly. I am not surprised, but I grieve for the misfortune which makes my sufferings be relieved by such terrible sufferings of your own. For that loyal man, P. Valerius, has written to me how you were taken from the Temple of Vesta to the *Tabula Valeria*. I wept when I read about it. Ah, light of my life, my darling, to whom everyone used to go for help, to think that you are now so tormented, brought low in tears and mourning-clothes, and that I am responsible for this happening, because I saved others to destroy us!
>
> (F 14.2/7.2)

Cicero refers to this incident elsewhere as if it involved physical insult, if not injury, to his wife. He held Clodius responsible:

> What offence had my poor wretched wife committed against you, when you tormented her, dragged her away, lacerated her with every form of cruelty? What had my daughter done, whose unceasing tears and gloomy mourning-clothes made you rejoice, when they attracted the attention and concern of everyone else? What had my little son done, whom nobody saw except worn out and in tears, all the time I was away? What had he done to make you want to kill him by treachery on so many occasions?
>
> (*Dom.* 59)

> My wife was tormented, plots were laid against the lives of my children, my son-in-law, a Piso son-in-law, was spurned with a kick when he knelt in supplication to a consul Piso.
>
> (*Sest.* 54, cf.145; *Mil.* 87)

He accuses Clodia, the tribune's sister, of having acted cruelly to his family during his absence (*Cael.* 50). It is hard to be sure how much violence was involved. Did the consul actually kick his kinsman?[55] Was Terentia manhandled and her hair torn or body wounded? Were there attempts on Marcus' life? It seems odd that the letters do not say more about such physical dangers. But the oratorical passages repeat some of the strong language which Cicero used in his letter when he received the news.

Terentia was certainly in the front line. It seems that she was forced to leave her sanctuary and face an interview with Clodius at the *Tabula Valeria*, a wall-painting near the tribunes' headquarters at the Porcian Basilica.[56] We do not know the subject on which Clodius wanted to question her, but it was presumably about property. Cicero uses 'tormented' to describe Clodius' treatment of his 'fortunes' in the same breath as referring to the incident when Terentia was 'dragged away' (*Sest.* 145).⁵⁷ The description is much like that of the later eulogy to the anonymous wife of the proscribed man (p. 18).

Terentia had written to Cicero about their house, 'that is, the site'. Cicero wanted it restored to him, if he were recalled from banishment. But he worried about Terentia paying for expenses with her own resources, since she might lose them if he could not make a comeback. She could let other people pay. He also worried about her health, since she was taking on so much work, which only she could do (*F* 14.2/7.3, Thessalonica, 5 Oct. 58). It is clear that she was interceding with many different people and keeping Cicero informed of any progress. He needed to write to thank various people whom she named, just as he kept her informed of the good offices of people who helped him abroad (e.g., *F* 14.1/8.3, despatched from Dyrrachium, 25 Nov. 58; 14.3/9.3–4, Dyrrachium, 29 Nov. 58). She went around dressed in mourning. This, in Cicero's version, attracted general pity from all except inveterate enemies. Although he told the People later that the sorrow of his wife, daughter and son was less visible than that of his brother who was active in the Forum, because they only went out when it was essential and were mostly indoors (*Red. Pop.* 8), Terentia and Tullia could still receive visitors and visit their equals. Perhaps a visit to Clodia to ask for her intervention underlies the charge of her cruelty. She was, after all, Clodius' sister, a neighbour and widow of an ex-consul. It would have been obvious also to approach Julia, the daughter of Caesar and wife of Pompey; Aurelia, Caesar's mother; Tertia, Crassus' wife; Caesar's new wife, the daughter of Piso (Caesar was now in Gaul and could not be approached directly, except by letter); perhaps Servilia, a political lady, half-sister of Cato, once mistress of Caesar and wife of a consul of 62. In 51, writing to congratulate C. Claudius Marcellus on his election to the consulship, Cicero mentions that Marcellus' mother Junia, 'a serious and excellent woman', had supported his status and well-being to a degree that he would not have been able to ask from a woman: this seems to be a reference to the time of Cicero's exile.⁵⁸ Terentia and Tullia could also try feminine diplomacy directly on influential men: for instance, perhaps P. Cornelius Lentulus (nicknamed Spinther), consul-elect for 57, and Pompey. We are specifically told that Lentulus protected the family.⁵⁹ A younger man, M. Juventius Laterensis (praetor 51), defended Cicero's wife and children in his absence. L. Cornelius Balbus, the Spanish friend of Pompey and Caesar, relieved all the family with all possible attentions (*officium*): tears, consolation and action. C. Rabirius Postumus, the banker, offered Cicero effective aid on the night of his departure and staunchly helped Cicero's children and wife during his absence.⁶⁰ These, at least, were in close touch with Terentia. Cicero, in later years, ends letters to Terentia with a wish for her good health (where to Atticus he makes a variety of personal and often affectionate remarks). The closure to this letter is emotional, though brief: 'Farewell, my darlings, farewell' (*F* 14.2/7.4; cf. pp. 64, 69).

A glimmer of hope appeared and Cicero resolved not to let down the friends who were working for his recall. He wrote to Atticus of 'the sad and grieving prayers of my excellent and only brother, the promises of Sestius and the rest, the hope of that unfortunate woman Terentia and the pleas of my unhappy Tulliola and your steadfast letter' (*A* 3.19/64.2, Thessalonica, 15 Sept.). He remembered the charm and dignity of his old life and imagined the possibility of celebrating his return in Atticus' beautiful house with his family (*A* 3.20/65.1, Thessalonica, 5 Oct. 58). 'My Pomponius, fight to let me live with you and my family [*mei*] . . . I am overwhelmed with grief and longing for all those things which were always dearer to me than I am myself' (*A* 3.22/67.3, despatched from Dyrrachium, 25 Nov. 58). Cicero was beginning to see results from all the lobbying which Atticus and others had been doing in Rome and his mind was beginning to work on the terms of the bill which eight of the tribunes were supporting. His cousin, C.Visellius Varro, had been helpful in drafting one version.[61]

The third letter to Terentia was written partly in mid-November at Thessalonica and partly after he moved to Dyrrachium/Durazzo, to be nearer the action. It was sent on 25 November and begins with impassioned self-blame:

> Letters from many people and everyone's talk tell me of your incredible courage[62] and fortitude and how you are tireless in your mental and physical labours. How wretched I am! To think that you, gifted with such courage, loyalty, integrity and kindliness, should fall into such troubles because of me, and that our little Tullia, from whom her father had such pleasure, should feel such grief from him! For what should I say about Cicero? As soon as he began to have understanding, he felt bitter pain and suffering.
> (*F* 14.1/8.1, despatched from Dyrrachium, 25 Nov. 58)

Terentia had told him she thought their sufferings were decreed by fate, but Cicero blames himself for having been led into the wrong decision by false or foolish friends. He would try not to let her down. There was some hope, though it was more difficult to get back home than it had been to leave (*F* 14.1/8.2). But he hoped to return to her arms, regaining his family and himself (a formulation which recurs repeatedly), a reward for their *pietas* (perhaps towards Rome; *F* 14.1/8.3). He praises Piso's conduct, clearly expecting that Tullia would read the letter, although the body of the text is addressed to her mother. There appears to have been some misunderstanding between Terentia and Quintus in their work for Cicero's recall: 'I did not mean to criticise you about Quintus, but I wanted you to be as close as possible, especially as you are so few' (*F* 14.1/8.4). This shows that some

68 *Living through disaster*

of the correspondence from Cicero is lost. Terentia had written that she intended to sell some of her own property:

> As for what you say, my dear Terentia, about your intention of selling a village,[63] what, I beg you (poor wretch that I am!), what will happen? If the same fate overwhelms both of us, what will happen to our poor boy? I cannot write any more for weeping, nor will I make you weep too. I will write only this: if our friends are loyal, money will not be lacking;[64] if they are not, you cannot do everything with your money. I adjure you by our wretched fortunes, see to it that we do not ruin our ruined boy. If he has anything to stop him being a pauper, he will need only average ability and average fortune to achieve the rest.
> (F 14.1/8.5)

Cicero could hope that Marcus would still have a political career. Tullia could be looked after by her husband. (It must be assumed that Piso had received all her dowry, which, if she married in 63, had probably been transferred in three annual instalments in 62–60.) But Cicero clearly hoped that Terentia could keep her own fortune intact, for the eventual benefit of their children. Suzanne Dixon (1986: 98–9) rightly highlights both Terentia's control of her own fortune and the assumption of her devotion to her husband's cause and the welfare of their children. Cicero's 'frantic' outburst may be 'emotional blackmail', as she suggests, but I think his own emotion is genuine and he may be perceptive in supposing that she too would be upset. The letter ends with practicalities: he asks Terentia to send couriers and informs her (F 14.1/8.6–7) that he has moved to Dyrrachium, a friendly city and near Italy (in fact within the forbidden zone), though he might move (perhaps to Atticus' estate; cf. A 3.19/64.1, Thessalonica, 15 Sept. 58).

On 29 November, Cicero had received three letters from the courier Aristocritus and nearly made them illegible with his tears:

> I am overcome by grief, my dear Terentia. But my own sufferings do not torture me more than yours and those of all the rest of you. But I am more wretched than you, very wretched as you are, because this disaster is common to both of us, but the blame is all mine ... I am overcome by pain and shame: I'm ashamed because I did not show manly courage and due care for my excellent wife and sweet children.[65] For, night and day, I see before my eyes your mourning and grief and the shakiness of your health ... As long as you have hope, I shall not fail, lest everything should seem to have been ruined by my fault.
> (F 14.3/9.1–2, Dyrrachium, 29 Nov. 58)

There was now hope that the incoming tribunes would press for Cicero's recall, so he was anxious that Terentia and Quintus should arrange for frequent couriers, who would normally be their own (or his) slaves (F 14.3/

9.3–4). He also expected that Terentia's letters on political developments would be well informed and valuable (*F* 14.3/9.5). He gives Terentia credit for taking on a great share of the burden of working for him and in writing to her he tactfully does not mention Atticus, who was also tireless on his behalf and with whom Terentia was in close contact. Terentia had suggested that she should join her husband, but he thought she should stay in Rome, since he realised that she had shouldered a large share of the work.

> If you succeed in what you are trying to do, it is for me to come to you; if not – but I need not say the rest … Take care of your health and be sure that you are and have always been the dearest thing in the world to me. Farewell, my Terentia. I imagine I see you and so I am made weak with tears. Farewell.
>
> (*F* 14.3/9.5)

Despite the illness from which she suffered at least during two periods of this traumatic year (*F* 14.4/6.3, Brundisium, 29 April 58; 14.3/9.2) and her grief and worry, Terentia was clearly one of the most active of Cicero's supporters. Tullia wore mourning, to advertise the family's wrongs, and it seems that she interceded for her father (*A* 3.19/64.2, Thessalonica, 15 Sept. 58). Her youth will have been a useful tool. She went with Piso to go down on her knees to the consul, who repelled his kinsman and his relative by marriage with arrogant and cruel words (*Red. Sen.*17). Her husband is praised for his loyalty, courage and an authority unexpected in such a young man (*Red. Pop.* 7; cf. *Red. Sen.* 38) and was clearly sending Cicero reports (*A* 3.22/67.1, despatched from Dyrrachium, 25 Nov. 58). He had even given up the post in Pontus and Bithynia to which he had been appointed, in order to stay in Rome and work for Cicero's recall. In 55, attacking L. Piso (cos. 58) in the Senate, Cicero proclaimed that, if he had had free choice of any man in Rome for Tullia's husband, he would have chosen Piso Frugi above all (*Pis. frag.* xiii). Cicero was beginning to see results from all the lobbying.

Cicero prayed that he would be able to enjoy his son-in-law's company with his wife and children (*F* 14.3/9.3), but Piso died before his return. 'He was not allowed to reap the reward for his devotion [*pietas*] from the Roman People or from me' (*Sest.* 68). The blow must have been a bitter one for Tullia, still childless and deprived of her father. We are not informed about the practical results of her becoming a widow at the age of twenty. She will have got her dowry back and no doubt her husband will have named her in his will as a sign of his approbation, leaving her perhaps a legacy of clothes, jewellery, a dressing-set and similar luxuries which he had given to her or provided for her use.[66] It may have been difficult for Piso to bequeath real estate to her, since that would in practice go to her father and he was at the moment not entitled to hold land under Roman law. Besides, Piso himself, if his father was still alive, may have had no houses and farms to leave.[67]

The beginning of the end

Cicero responded to a setback early in 57 with a desperate note to Atticus: 'From your letter and from the facts themselves I see we are completely ruined. I beseech you, in matters where my family needs you, not to fail us in our wretchedness' (*A* 3.27/72, Dyrrachium[?], early Feb. 57). A tribunician bill for Cicero's recall had been met by violence on 23 January and in the rioting Quintus had narrowly escaped with his life. He had been hurled from the rostrum and had to be rescued by his slaves and freedmen.[68] The Tiber was full of dead bodies, the sewers were blocked, the blood in the Forum had to be mopped up with sponges.[69] This is the last letter of the series, for Atticus seems to have joined Cicero in Greece. They may have stayed at Buthrotum for most of the time. With Atticus away, it was left to Terentia, Tullia, Quintus and friends to work for Cicero's recall. Naturally, nothing certain can be said about the activity of Terentia and Tullia during these months of sustained effort, when Pompey declared his support; Caesar withdrew his objections in return for a promise from Quintus; the consul Lentulus was constant in his efforts; and the tribunes Milo and Sestius used their own toughs against Clodius' gangs.[70]

7   Restoration

Finally, the hard work paid off. By May, Terentia and the family will have seen signs that the tide had turned. The Senate passed a resolution commending Cicero to Roman officials and foreign kings abroad, thanking those who had helped him and summoning everyone who wanted the commonwealth to be secure to come to Rome.[1] That the Senate equated support of Cicero with patriotism was a glory for Cicero's descendants (*Red. Sen.* 25). There were demonstrations of support at various games.[2] The great actor Aesopus, who is likely to have been in touch with Terentia and Quintus, worked on the audience. Surely Terentia and Tullia attended all the theatrical performances and the gladiatorial games, and perhaps not wearing mourning. In July, when men of the property-owning classes came from the Italian towns to vote in the consular elections and attend the festival in honour of Apollo – and some in response to the Senate's appeal – a bill for Cicero's recall was promulgated. Voters from all over Italy turned out. Terentia may have offered hospitality to those who usually stayed with Cicero or came to dine. Her continued presence in Rome was important. On 4 August 57 the bill was passed in the Centuriate Assembly.[3]

Tullia was already on the road to Brundisium, about 360 Roman miles from Rome. Horace, some twenty years later, with a large party, took fifteen days for roughly the same journey.[4] (Fast couriers could do it in seven days [Ch. 5, n. 5].) Tullia, despite her longing to see her father, would probably choose shorter stages and perhaps rest for a day or two at her father's villas or those of friends.[5] It remained a major undertaking.[6] Horace gives satirical descriptions of the discomforts of the journey to Brundisium even for upper-class travellers: noise, delays, bad or scarce water, long hauls up hills, tiredness, the scorching wind of the Apulian Mountains, gritty bread, ruts, rain.[7] Tullia may have been sheltered from some of this, but even those who could usually find a friend to put them up had to suffer from rough roads, weather (probably hot, with a possibility of thunder-storms and heavy downpours), dust and fatigue (Figure 7.1).[8] There might be danger too: highwaymen notoriously attacked travellers, even on the Appian Way just outside Rome. Tullia would take a considerable armed bodyguard, as well as servants and baggage.[9] Someone would also have to take care of

72 *Restoration*

Figure 7.1 A Roman road in Italy, lined with shops (the entrance to Lucus Feroniae, July 1994; Treggiari)

administrative details such as the supply, feeding and stabling of horses. She may have left Rome before the promulgation of the bill (which had to happen at least seventeen days before the vote). Terentia could send news of the promulgation after her. Perhaps Cicero and she also sent messengers back and forth. The timing and stage-management of the vote and the synchronisation of two journeys were immaculately performed.

The welcome

Cicero took ship at Dyrrachium the day the vote took place, and landed at Brundisium on 5 August.

> There was my Tulliola waiting for me. It was her birthday, which happened to be the birthday both of the colony of Brundisium and of your neighbour the goddess Salus [Well-being]. This was noticed by the crowd and celebrated with a great deal of congratulation from the people of Brundisium.
>
> (*A* 4.1/73.4, Rome, C. 10 Sept. 57)

In a speech the following year, Cicero reminded the judges that Tullia was still grieving for her husband when she came to meet him (*Sest.* 131).[10] Cicero stayed in Brundisium until he heard from Quintus, on 11 August, that the bill had become law. Then he and, presumably, Tullia travelled through

Italy, greeted by deputations from the towns they passed (*A* 4.1/73.4; *Sest.* 131; cf. *Red. Pop.* 4). Cicero tells us that *patres familias* came with their wives and children as if to a festival, everywhere he went. Tullia must have been fully involved. Terentia probably went some distance out of the city to greet him and join his procession. At the outskirts of Rome, a huge crowd of all ranks came to meet him; at the Capene Gate, the plebs were crowding the steps of the temples to cheer him. The cheers went on as he went on to the Forum and Capitoline (to sacrifice) and then home. It is said that the welcome lasted all day.[11] Next day, he gave a speech of thanks in the Senate for the benefits conferred on him, his brother and his issue (*liberi*, which includes Tullia): the emphasis on male members of the family is in accordance with etiquette, for it was not proper to name women in a public speech (*Red. Sen.* 1, 27). A few days later, he thanked the People:

> For, Quirites, although nothing is more to be wished by a human being than a prosperous, equable and unceasing fortune with a favourable course of life without mishaps, yet, if everything had been tranquil and peaceful for me, I would have missed an incredible and almost divine pleasure of happiness which I now enjoy thanks to you. What sweeter thing is given to the human race by nature than his own children [*liberi*] to each of us? To me, both because of my kindness for them and because of their own excellent character, my children are dearer than my life: yet I did not feel as much delight in acknowledging them as babies as I now feel in having them restored to me.
>
> (*Red. Pop.* 2)[12]

He regularly spoke of his restoration as his restoration to his family or of his family to him.[13] It was a new birth for him and his children and brother (*Red. Sen.* 27; cf. *A* 4.1/73.8, Rome, c. 10 Sept. 57). Being remade a citizen meant being born again, and as a consular.[14] He alludes to the suffering inflicted on him and the family (*mei*; *Dom.* 69; *Har. resp.* 4) and the pain he suffered from the separation (*Dom.* 145).

Cicero had already been sure that for his restoration to be complete, he needed to get back his house and possessions.[15] He now hoped to rebuild on the 'outstanding site'.[16] It was decided that he should get the site back and be paid compensation of 2,000,000 sesterces for the house and 500,000 for the Tusculan and 250,000 for the Formian villas, figures which he and others thought stingy.[17] So the house was given back to Cicero and his children (*Har. resp.* 16). There were severe money worries, but the rebuilding of the Palatine house and the villa at Formiae was begun. Cicero put his Tusculan villa on the market, but failed to sell it.[18]

74 *Restoration*

Readjustment

There are hints that the re-entry into family life had not been easy. 'My finances are in disarray, as you know. Besides, there are some domestic matters which I will not trust to writing. I love my brother Quintus as I ought'.[19] 'The other things which worry me are more secret. My brother and daughter love me' (*A* 4/2.74.7). It would not be surprising if both Terentia and Cicero found it difficult to adjust.[20] She had been caught up in hard work, needing to make decisions and act on her own initiative. She did not, like her daughter, have a month or so of travelling in the same gilded carriage in which some private conversation was possible and even the constant interruptions from cheering crowds might have cemented her unity with Cicero. As the tension unwound, she may have felt purposeless and unwanted. Now Cicero was back and plunging into politics; there were financial worries; his safety and her security were still under threat. Cicero wrote to Atticus on 23 November 57:

> On 3 November the builders were driven out by armed men from our building-site, the portico of Catulus was wrecked . . . , my brother Quintus' house [next door] was first battered by stones thrown from our site and then set alight by hurled firebrands by order of Clodius, with the city looking on. There was much protest and groaning from almost everyone.
>
> (*A* 4.3/75.2, Rome)

On the 11th, Cicero himself was attacked by Clodian gangs on the Sacred Way, but he retreated into a nearby house and his guard defended him.[21] Violence continued, with hot political battles, until Pompey, Crassus and Caesar re-established their alliance and took a firmer grip of Roman politics in April.

If there was some friction between Cicero and his wife (and perhaps even his small son) in late 57, it was probably transient.[22] It remains striking that Cicero hinted at it to Atticus: we have seen how discreet he usually was about his wife. In January, Cicero assured Quintus of the good health of both their families. Building work continued on both Palatine houses.[23] We are not told where Cicero was living while the work went on. (Quintus, himself away on public business, rented a house somewhere for his household and let the house on the *Carinae*, while hoping to move back into his Palatine house after 1 July.[24]) But the scholar Licinius Tyrannio was teaching in Cicero's house and one of his pupils was young Q. Cicero, whose education was going well.[25] Perhaps Cicero too was in temporary accommodation, but he was making a show to keep up his standing and his house was as full as ever:[26]

> I am building in three places [the Palatine site, Tusculum and Formiae], I am smartening up the rest. I am living rather more expensively than

I used to; it was necessary. If I had you here, you would have to give place for a little while to the builders.

(*QF* 2.5/9.1, Rome, March 56)

It was around this time that Cicero acquired another splendid villa, at Cumae. It was on the banks of the Lucrine Lake and had a view of the sea, a garden, a grove and a colonnade.[27] Cicero is said to have possessed a valuable table of citrus wood from Mauretania, which cost half a million sesterces. It was still extant in Pliny's day. This may be too much to swallow,[28] but, if he did own such a table, it might be at this time that he acquired it.

Tullia's new engagement and marriage – and divorce

Tullia was still a widow. She and her mother should have been looking around for a new husband ever since her return to Rome. We do not know exactly when Piso had died, but a year's mourning was conventional. That did not stop thinking about suitable men, exploration of possibilities or even a new wedding. It was not always easy to find a good match, especially when a father's political standing was not as clear as it had been. All the family must have been engaged in the search in the autumn and winter of 57/6. We hear nothing until Cicero tells Quintus in mid-March that he hopes he has fixed things with Crassipes, but that the bridegroom was going out of Rome. He mentions also Tullia's fondness for her uncle (*QF* 2.4/8.2).

Furius Crassipes was young, wealthy, a patrician and a prospective senator. He was to hold the quaestorship, perhaps in 54, which would make him about twenty-six now.[29] His *gens*, the Furii, had been distinguished in the early Republic, but had held no consulship for generations. The Crassipedes could show a praetor in the second century and an aedile in the 80s. But we do not even know the *praenomen* of Tullia's husband. His immediate family is unknown. He possessed the great attraction of a house and park on the outskirts of Rome,[30] but he failed to distinguish himself, which may be why some sources forget that Tullia had a second husband (Asc. 5C; Plut. *Cic.* 41.5).

The engagement came on 4 April, when Cicero was playing a dangerous game, trying to drive a wedge between Pompey and Caesar. The next day Cicero successfully proposed a motion in the Senate that one of Caesar's laws of 59 should be re-examined on the 15th.

> I sent you a letter [now lost] before, in which I wrote that our Tullia was betrothed to Crassipes on 4 April . . . On 6 April I gave a betrothal party for Crassipes. Your Quintus and mine, that excellent boy, was unable to come to this party because he was slightly unwell. On 8 April I went to see Quintus and saw him completely recovered and he talked to me a great deal and very sympathetically about the disagreements of our women [Terentia and Pomponia]. What more would you like to know?

> It was as jolly as could be. But Pomponia also complained about you. We will talk about this when we are together . . . That day I dined at Crassipes'.
>
> (*QF* 2.6/10.1, 2, 3, en route to Anagnia, 9 Apr. 56)[31]

We must hope that Terentia and Tullia were included in these celebrations. Cicero's egocentric remarks emphasise the importance of the connection between the two men, who would now become *adfines* (relations by marriage). The father- and son-in-law relationship was an important one in social and political life.[32] No doubt Cicero's friends and acquaintances offered him their congratulations. We know P. Cornelius Lentulus did, although he was away governing Cilicia. Cicero replied with thanks and the (conventional) hope that the union would bring him pleasure (*F* 1.7/18.11, Rome, late June or July 56; cf. *F* 2.15/96.2, quoted on p. 95).

The wedding and marriage are not directly mentioned in the correspondence. Patricia Clark (1991) has even argued forcefully that the marriage never took place. But our knowledge of Tullia's life from the glorious moment when she met her father at Brundisium until his departure for Cilicia in 51 is scanty, simply because Cicero and Atticus were both in Italy and there is a major gap in the correspondence. It is not credible that a young widow would have been left on the shelf for six years and that her father would start working hard for her remarriage only when he had to leave Rome. Cicero occasionally mentions Crassipes and one allusion seems decisive. When M. Licinius Crassus and Cicero were reconciled in November 55, Crassus left for Syria 'almost from my home, for . . . he dined with me at my son-in-law Crassipes' house in the suburbs' (*F* 1.9/20.20, to P. Cornelius Lentulus Spinther, Rome, Dec. 54).[33]

The two men seem to have got on well. Crassipes gave Cicero a welcome-home dinner after he had been at Antium in the summer of 56.[34] In late autumn 54, Cicero knew that heavy rain had washed away Crassipes' promenade.[35] The latter's house and park outside Rome on the Appian Way seem to have enhanced Cicero's lifestyle. Of course, it had even more effect on Tullia. Her social circle should also have improved, since to the connections of her first husband she could now add the patrician kin and friends of her second. As a young matron of perhaps twenty-two, with an up-and-coming husband and a consular father who after April 56 was committed to throwing his influence and oratorical talent behind the most powerful men in Rome, she could expect a position of distinction, which she had been brought up to appreciate. How the young couple got on in private we cannot know. There is no trace in our evidence of any pregnancy. If there had been a child, however short-lived, we might expect to hear, especially if there had been one during Quintus' absence on campaign in Gaul, when Cicero conscientiously kept him up to date with family matters.[36]

The marriage must have ended in divorce, for Tullia was free to marry again in July 51, when Crassipes was still alive. Since it was undesirable to leave a young woman unmarried, the divorce had probably taken place shortly before this. It may have been by mutual consent, because of their lack of success at procreation. In any case, Cicero remained on polite terms with his ex-son-in-law, although he may have been reluctant to ask him for favours.[37] This would not exclude a reason for divorce discreditable to Crassipes, that he committed serious faults or divorced Tullia unilaterally for no fault of her own (since Cicero later was able to remain on similar terms with Dolabella, who had shown great lack of consideration for Tullia and whose infidelity was an open scandal). Some support for this possibility might be found in the fact that the timing of the divorce was apparently awkward for Tullia. She must have known since 52 that Cicero would have to go abroad to govern a province, under Pompey's new law. It would have been easier for her if the divorce had occurred earlier, so that Cicero could have taken the lead in the search for a new husband. There seems no likelihood that she divorced in order to marry someone else with whom she had fallen in love, although such behaviour is not unexampled. Cicero the very next year was entertained by a juicy piece of scandal: 'Paulla Valeria, the sister of Triarius, made a divorce without giving a reason, on the day her husband was going to come back from his province; she is going to marry D. Brutus' (*F* 8.7/92.2, from Caelius, Rome, mid-Apr. 50).[38]

Visits, parties, entertainment

After the dinner at Crassipes' house on 8 April, Cicero went on a trip, via a friend's house at Anagnia and on to Quintus' villa at Laterium, then to Arpinum for five days, then his villa at Pompeii, and a brief stop at Cumae on the way back. He planned to reach Rome on 6 May. He does not say whether Terentia or Tullia accompanied him, but it seems likely neither did, since he was travelling fast to check properties. He wrote to Atticus, asking him to see to the house and to set a guard upon it, since there was still danger of violence from Clodius' gangs.[39] Perhaps Terentia was away somewhere with Tullia: it would have been sensible to get away from the builders and it was a good time of year for Antium. During this time, Pompey had met Caesar at Luca/Lucca, and Pompey told Quintus to make Cicero back them. For a time, he avoided the Senate.

In mid-summer, there was a proper family holiday at the seaside. Cicero wrote from Antium asking Atticus to pay them ('us' here is a real plural and cannot mean Cicero alone) a visit and to bring his new wife Pilia, 'as is fair and as Tullia wants' (*A* 4.4a/78.2, Antium, c. 20 June[?] 56). Pilia and Atticus had married on 12 February. Perhaps Terentia and Tullia went to dinner, as Cicero did.[40] Pilia was, or became, a particular friend of Tullia, who was probably closer to her in age than Terentia. Antium was especially delightful because it was cool and because Tyrannio and others had arranged the library.[41] The builders were still busy on the Rome house and at least one of the villas was uncomfortable because it remained unfinished, perhaps even the following year.⁴² It was lucky for the family that they had the house in Antium. Still, Cicero was able to renew the invitation to Atticus and Pilia, who apparently had not come to Antium, and ask them to dinner in Rome on 2 July: 'Our whole household sends greetings' (A 4.12/81). It looks as if Cicero's marriage was back to its normal routine: his mind was much engaged with politics and literature, but he found time to share some evening engagements with his wife.

The marriage of Tullia and Crassipes probably took place soon after the engagement, once the political situation was settled and after the stay in Antium. Crassipes wanted to give Cicero and perhaps his future wife and mother-in-law a welcome-home dinner at his house in the suburbs as they returned to Rome on 1 July (A 4.5/80.4, Antium, soon after 20 June[?] 56; 4.12/81, Antium, end of June[?] 56). Perhaps the wedding followed soon after.

Letters are scanty for the rest of the year and early 55. In the spring of next year, Cicero was again in the south, at his new villa at Cumae.⁴³ A promenade and Laconian baths were under construction in Rome and Atticus was keeping an eye on the works, of which Terentia's servant, the steward Philotimus, was in charge. Cicero was enjoying a collection of books he had recently bought, as well as the local seafood.⁴⁴ On 27 April, Cicero stayed with his friend Paetus at Naples en route to his villa at Pompeii.⁴⁵ Short stays away from Rome later in the year were enlivened by the presence of Atticus' scholarly freedman Dionysius. Cicero once says that Dionysius was the only companion he had taken, but that need not exclude the presence of Terentia.⁴⁶ Nor does he say if she was accompanying him to Milo's wedding in Rome on 18 November.⁴⁷ Cicero was studying hard and writing.

The following year, domestic life followed a similar pattern. Quintus left to join Caesar in Gaul in late April or early May and Atticus went to Epirus in May, so we glean some details about the family. Cicero was at Cumae and Pompeii in May and had been teaching Marcus during his holiday.⁴⁸ This passing mention suggests that it was usual for Marcus and Terentia, and perhaps Tullia, to join him on these trips. Cicero was looking after some piece of business for Pilia and expected that this would win Tullia's approval (A 4.16/89.4, Rome, c. 1 July 54). He kept quiet at a trial because his daughter was worried that if he spoke he would offend Clodius. She was unwell. He made the effort to be in Rome to attend the theatre, where he was cheered. Again, we do not know if Terentia went too.⁴⁹ Cicero was feeling confident about his position in the state and looking forward to being free of financial worries.⁵⁰ He was once more working very hard as an advocate, even in an August heatwave.⁵¹ In a notable speech defending Cn. Plancius,⁵² who had protected him in 58, he claims that his love for his children 'than whom nothing can be more pleasant to me' drove him to defend Plancius, through whom he had been preserved for them. Whenever he looked at them, he remembered Plancius (*Planc.* 69).⁵³

Domestic affairs were going well; the boys got on with everyone and were studying hard; building at the country-houses was progressing.[54] Cicero escaped to Arpinum to enjoy the cool of the river and inspected Quintus' estates in the neighbourhood. His account gives a good impression of how he must have been with his own property: interested in both farming and improving the country-houses with such additions as fishponds, aviaries, conduits, baths, columns, colonnades, promenades, palaestras, groves, ivy, stucco, paving and statues.[55] Since Cicero wanted to invite Pomponia to bring young Quintus there, it must be assumed that Terentia was in residence, and perhaps had been there during the hot weather in July and August (QF 3.1/21.1-8, Arpinum and Rome, Sept. 54). When they returned to Rome, the two boys were being educated together and it seems that Pomponia and young Quintus were living in Cicero's house until November.[56] The work on both the Palatine houses was almost finished.[57] Despite worries about politics, Cicero claims that his domestic life is happy: he finds pleasure in literary work, oratory, his house and his estates (A 4.18/92.2, Rome, between 24 Oct. and 2 Nov. 54). But to Quintus he could admit:

> I am tortured, my sweetest brother, I am tortured, because there is no commonwealth and no courts and at this time of life, when we ought to be in the full bloom of senatorial dignity, we are either tossed up and down by toil in the Forum or kept going by reading and writing at home.
> (QF 3.5/25.4, Tusculum, end of Oct. or beginning of Nov. 54)

Yet, 'Literature and our studies and leisure and my villas delight me, and especially our boys' (QF 3.7/27.2, Rome, Dec. 54).

In public, when taunted because he was no longer speaking out with his old freedom, he could argue that his sacrifice in 58 had earned him the right to think of his own welfare and that of his family, as long as he did not fail in his duty to the commonwealth (*Planc.* 91–2).

The household

Domestic life during the next two years, 53 and 52, is sparsely documented, though Cicero continued his usual routine, speaking in the courts, writing letters to political contacts and recommending people. There is a gap in the letters to Atticus (partly since Atticus and Cicero were both mostly in Rome, but it is likely that some letters have been lost) between late November 54 and 5 or 6 May 51, and our collection of the letters to Quintus has no letters after 54. Cicero was at Cumae in April, very worried about his secretary, Tiro, whom he had left seriously ill at Formiae, and receiving a visit from Pompey.[58] Quintus' congratulations when he received the news of Tiro's manumission may perhaps suggest the feelings of the rest of the family:

> By my hope of seeing you, my Cicero, my Tulliola and your son, I am delighted, my Marcus, at what you have done about Tiro. He did not deserve his lot in life and you have decided to make him our friend, not a slave. Believe me, when I read your letter and his, I jumped for joy, and I both thank and congratulate you.
> (F 16.16/44.1, Q. Cicero to M. Cicero, Transalpine Gaul, end of May or beginning of June 53)

Tiro was an important figure in the household from this time on. He was a young man whose education Cicero had at least supervised. He was now perhaps twenty, a generation younger than Cicero, several years older than young Quintus.[59] It seems likely that he, like the free boys of the household, and like the younger Crassus' slave Apollonius,[60] was given rich educational opportunities to study and discuss with people like Diodotus the Stoic, Licinius Tyrannio and Pomponius Dionysius, as well as Cicero himself and his cultivated peers.[61] He first appears in the correspondence in 54, when he had the job of composing political reports for Quintus.[62] Cicero always writes to him affectionately and familiarly.[63] It is hard to distinguish the tone he uses towards him from that he uses to his own family: 'I thought I could bear missing you a little more easily, but really I cannot bear it'; 'Again and again farewell'; 'As you love me – or as you know I love you – so be sure to look after your health'.[64] Cicero was inclined to become fond of the young men he taught, like M. Caelius Rufus, and even of his educated slaves, like the reader Sositheus, who died untimely.[65] We may guess that Tiro had been born in the household and had been known to the family all his life. He had literary pursuits of his own and was an important assistant in his patron's literary work. He corresponded with Atticus,[66] Quintus and young Marcus and when he was ill in 50 all the male Cicerones addressed him jointly.[67] Terentia, Cicero assures him, valued him highly (F 16.9/127.2, to Tiro, Brundisium, 26 Nov. 50). His must have been a familiar and kindly presence to her and Tullia.[68] We probably owe the survival of at least the *Ad Familiares* collection to him: it includes a book of letters addressed to him. He also preserved Cicero's memory by writing his *Life*.[69] Terentia's relationship with him contrasts with that of Pomponia and Statius, Quintus' favourite freedman.

Separation

Terentia and Cicero were about to be semi-detached again. The routine of family life was interrupted when, thanks to a change in the timetable for appointment of governors, Cicero was sent to Cilicia as proconsul. Because of the new system, he could expect to be away for a year, but it was accepted that husbands and wives were often separated for much longer: governors and legates could be away for several years and commanders-in-chief for five or six.[70] A marriage continued in being despite such breaks.[71]

Cicero set off, with Quintus, as a general under his command, and young Quintus and young Marcus, who would further their education by visiting the famous Greek cities, staying at foreign courts and observing the business of administration. Mothers would expect to lose their sons to the demands of public life in their teens. Cicero said an emotional goodbye to Atticus at Tusculum, where he had probably been staying ever since he was invested with military command, which meant he could not be in Rome itself.[72] Quintus' wife, Atticus' sister, was one of the subjects of their conversation, but we are not told why they were worried about her. Then Cicero went to Arpinum, where Quintus joined him and they had a long talk about Atticus and Pomponia. Cicero tells Atticus that Quintus did not show any annoyance with his wife. The next day, Cicero went to stay the night at Aquinum/ Aquino and Quintus to his villa at Arx/Rocca d'Arce (the *Arcanum*), where Cicero joined him for lunch. It was a holiday, probably the festival of the household gods on 1 May. It was therefore expected that the owners would invite the staff to a meal:

> When we arrived there, Quintus said, very kindly, 'Pomponia, you invite the women and I'll fetch the boys in.' Nothing could have been sweeter, as I thought at least, than his words, intention and expression. But she, in our hearing, said, 'I myself am a guest here.' I think this was because Statius [Quintus' confidential freedman] had gone ahead of us to see to the lunch for us. Then Quintus said, 'You see. This is what I have to put up with every day.'
>
> (A 5.1/94.3)

Cicero was upset by the tone of Pomponia's response and by her facial expression. The family went to recline on the dining-couches without her.[73] Quintus sent her food from the table, but she sent it back. As he told his brother when he rejoined him down at Aquinum next day, she refused to sleep with him that night, their last night together before an absence of over a year and a half, and her attitude when she left was unaltered. This vivid scene is significant for the storminess of the marriage of Quintus and Pomponia, which would eventually end in divorce.[74] It is also significant for suggesting points of tension in any upper-class marriage: the division of responsibilities; the lack of privacy in a slave household; the separations imposed by a husband's career; wives' possible jealousy of trusted slaves and freedmen; wives' need to be supreme at least in household management (the 'last straw' as well as the pretext for Pomponia's outburst). Cicero is determined to defend Quintus to his brother-in-law (who, by the time he received the letter, may well have heard Pomponia's side of things). It is clear that Pomponia had behaved badly in front of the servants and Cicero. But it is also apparent that she was not just bad-tempered but upset, and that Quintus, who had kept the moral high ground, was upset too. The incident, trivial as it may have been, is assessed in the context of high expectations

Figure 7.2 Italian hill country (valley of the Turano, looking downstream from Roccasinibalda towards Rieti; Treggiari)

of courtesy and love between wife and husband. If Terentia was present, she may well have sided with her husband against Pomponia, with whom she had not been getting on well a few years before (*QF* 2.6/10.2, en route to Anagnia, 9 April 56). We would expect her to be present, since, like Pomponia, she was soon to say goodbye to her husband. Cicero was not accustomed to such tantrums from his own wife, or he could not have expressed his shock to Atticus.

Travelling about twenty-five Roman miles per day via Minturnae, his villa at Cumae, the Trebulan territory, Beneventum, Venusia and Tarentum, and seeing friends en route, Cicero reached Brundisium on 22 May.[75] It is possible that Terentia went with him all or part of the way. If so, she may have been spared the rumour that Caelius heard in the Forum on 24 May: that Cicero had been assassinated by an old political enemy on his journey south.[76]

Since Tullia was no longer married, it is probable that she too set Cicero on his way or accompanied him to Brundisium. Then she and her mother might return up the Appian Way and spend some days of relaxation at a coastal villa or at Arpinum. There would be no need for them to be in Rome in the heat of summer, especially in July and August, when the old house on the banks of the Liris would be the most desirable of their residences. The hills were best in summer (Figure 7.2).

8   Finding the right man

The major family preoccupation of the eighteen months of Cicero's absence was the search for a new husband for Tullia. The letters give us a reflected image of what Tullia and Terentia did in Rome. If we first see what the letters tell us of what Cicero knew and planned, we shall be able to reconstruct, in part, the actions and experiences of Tullia and her mother.

Drawing up a list

After Cicero's departure, the most important task facing Terentia and Tullia was to get Tullia married again. They were to act on their own initiative in ratifying an engagement, as it was not practical for Cicero, so far away, to give his explicit consent as *pater familias*. Since Tullia was now a mature woman (nearly twenty-seven when her father left), her own views would be decisive. Some idea of the complexity of the task can be gathered from the one-sided and piecemeal information which Cicero received and relayed back to Atticus from the far-flung cities and camps of Asia Minor. No correspondence with Terentia survives until after the engagement had taken place.

   Cicero, on leaving the neighbourhood of Rome, had given two important commissions to Atticus: to see that his year in Cilicia was not extended and to look for a new husband for Tullia. Unfortunately, Atticus was about to leave for Epirus. The first mention of the second task is made obscure by a defective text, but it is already clear that there was a shortage of candidates, though they had several in mind. One man whose name we do not know seemed a possibility to Atticus, but Cicero thought Tullia could not be persuaded to accept him. Another was Ser. Sulpicius Rufus, a patrician and son of the homonymous consul of 51, who might be approached through Brutus' mother Servilia, a friend of Atticus (A 5.4/97.1, Beneventum, 12 May 51; cf. Nep. *Att.* 11.4). Three other possibilities occurred to various people: a candidate supported by a woman called Pontidia; a very proper young man called Ti. Claudius Nero; and an up-and-coming but controversial married man, P. Cornelius Dolabella. The chronological sequence is made complicated because our only direct witness is Cicero himself, though we can sometimes reconstruct from him what others had said; because the main actors in the drama were scattered; and because communication between them took months.

When a woman re-entered the marriage market after being widowed or divorced, there would be a limited number of prospective suitors or men whom she and her family thought eligible. Tullia had been married twice and produced no children (at least, none who lived long enough to be recorded in our sources). Her previous marriage had ended in divorce: we do not know the grounds which gossip assigned. On the credit side, her father was Rome's greatest orator, one of the most distinguished consulars, and aligned with both Pompey and Caesar. But his political success had been slight in the 50s, he was in an awkward position with the dynasts: too eminent and proud to act as a mere agent or mouthpiece, too powerless to take an independent line as a senior statesman should. When it came to a struggle between Pompey and Caesar (which was foreseen in 51/50), his position would be difficult, so he was not the ideal father-in-law for an aspiring politician. He had, however, much to offer: his central position in cultured society; his houses; comparative wealth (which any Roman would expect him to increase greatly in Cilicia); the fact that he had only two children, so that Tullia's dowry might be substantial. Tullia too, if her father is to be believed, had intelligence and charm; we do not know about beauty, though if she resembled her father, she might have been handsome.

She might, then, be a bride worth considering for a man at the outset of a political career (from his mid-twenties on) or for an older man who had lost his wife or divorced, perhaps a man with children by a prior marriage. It all depended on how many unmarried men there were at the given moment – or men who intended to become unmarried. Moving in various circles, Tullia and Terentia could get a sense of who some of these were. From their point of view, a man of senatorial or wealthy equestrian family was required. His birth (patrician, plebeian noble, descended from senators who had not reached high office or equestrian), the standing of his father and grand-father (consul as against praetor, praetor against mere quaestor, special achievements against mere office-holding), his connections (uncles, cousins, siblings; his mother's family), any previous marriage and children, ability and education, financial resources, character, looks, and personality: all must be weighed. As Atticus says (A 5.4/97.1), it was sometimes difficult to rank candidates. Since young men often married in their late twenties, a high proportion of those who might have been suitable were probably engaged or already married to their first wives. We might expect a pool of men in their thirties whose first wife had died or who had divorced rapidly, and also a number of more elderly widowers or divorcees. But the search seems at first to have been directed at young men, and Cicero seems to have at once formed the opinion that there was a shortage of eligible men, *inopia* (A 5.4/97.1; the text is partly corrupt, but this word is secure).

It was not always easy to contact the right parties. Cicero thought it would be difficult to get to Sulpicius through Servilia when both he and Atticus were away. Many people were to be engaged in the search. It was natural that Cicero should rely especially on Atticus among his men friends, because they were in each other's confidence, Atticus knew Tullia well and he had an unrivalled circle of acquaintance among nobles and *equites*. We later find Cicero keeping his ear to the ground on Atticus' behalf, when the latter was looking for a husband for his very young daughter (*A* 13.28/299.4, Tusculum, 26 May 45). We hear also of P. Sestius, the tribune of 57 for whose support Cicero was grateful but whom he found prickly as a friend,[1] and of M. Caelius Rufus, whom, like Sestius, Cicero had defended in a notorious trial, but who was an attractive character with a wide circle among the young. Men might be match-makers, especially on behalf of kin or friends. According to Nepos, it was Cicero who had negotiated the match between his friend Atticus' sister and his own brother.[2] In 37, one of the three men who ruled Rome, M. Antonius, masterminded the alliance of his colleague's lieutenant, the new man and great general M. Agrippa, and the young daughter of Atticus, who had done him great service in dangerous times. Maecenas, confidential friend and skilled diplomat, is attested as the intermediary between the young Caesar (Octavian) and Scribonia.[3] One advantage of the mediation of third parties might be that the principals were not committed until a satisfactory bargain was arranged. They would not lose face if the match fell through, they could claim ignorance if questioned; a number of practical matters (such as financial arrangements) could be explored; enquiries could be tentative.[4] We see this already in the letter just cited (*A* 5.4/97.1). The man whose name came up in discusssion and whom Cicero was sure Tullia would not like could be quietly dropped. Presumably no feelers had been put out in his direction and he was spared any gossip.

Women, however, were often the protagonists in match-making. Here we know of Pontidia, Servilia and Postumia, Ser. Sulpicius' mother. Women in senatorial circles would have met Terentia and Tullia (at least since her first marriage) both at women's events and at mixed parties which included wives. They might also be on the lookout for matches for their unmarried sons, nephews or brothers.[5] Naturally, in Cicero's absence, Terentia was probably the most important intermediary of all. There are other examples of mother's participation in the choice of a daughter's husband.[6] It is unthinkable that Terentia would not have had a crucial role in the matter, even had Cicero not been away.

Cicero later claims that, because he was going to be so far away, he told 'his family' (*mei*) to take a decision without consulting him (*F* 3.12/75.2, to Ap. Claudius Pulcher, Side, 3 or 4 Aug. 50; quoted below p. 94). There is no reason to doubt that he gave Terentia and Tullia these instructions. That did not stop him writing to them about his views as the situation changed.

Tullia was, it is generally thought, a daughter-in-power (*filia familias*). There is no evidence that Cicero had emancipated her and made her

86 *Finding the right man*

independent.[7] If this is right, her father's consent was legally necessary for her marriage.[8] Cicero would therefore be giving his approval in advance for whomever Tullia and her mother chose. This was sensible, in view of his absence. His retrospective acceptance of the marriage would also validate it.

Running affairs in Rome

Cicero's financial affairs needed to be handled by someone on the spot. He probably appointed C. Camillus, a close friend and financial and legal expert, to act as his business representative in Rome.[9] Cicero wrote to him from Brundisium when he was dissatisfied with the way Philotimus was handling a delicate matter.[10] He sometimes worked in conjunction with Atticus, who had also been handling multifarious interests for Cicero since 65 and continued to do so, although he was often away from Rome.[11]

It seems likely that Terentia had a general mandate to administer her husband's property, as well as her wifely responsibility to conserve it, as guardian (*custos*).[12] Since Philotimus had apparently worked as Cicero's steward, with special responsibility for the Palatine house since 59,[13] she had probably had a great deal to do with the administration of her husband's property for many years. At latest, this is likely to have started when Cicero went to Sicily as quaestor in 75. Whatever the legal set-up, Terentia, with her freedman in a key position, naturally knew a great deal and carried a lot of weight.

The view from Cilicia

The Cicerones sailed to Actium in Greece, regaled on splendid food at stopping-points by members of Atticus' staff, and then went overland to Athens, arriving on 24 June.[14] Cicero had had no news from home by 27 June, by mischance or perhaps because Terentia had not been able to send couriers (*A* 5.10/103.4, Athens, 27 June 51; her freedman Philotimus was supposed to co-ordinate mail when he was in Rome, but only some of Cicero's correspondence was carried by his own couriers).[15] An exchange of letters between Rome and Cilicia took about three months at best.[16] After enjoying philosophical society for ten days, they all set sail, with staff, in several ships,[17] and eventually reached Ephesus on 22 July. Cicero reminded Atticus discreetly (he could not always trust the courier) about 'that domestic worry', a match for Tullia.[18] Caelius in his report about political news was triumphant about the election of his friend P. Cornelius Dolabella as a member of the board of fifteen priests in charge of sacrifices.[19] Meanwhile, Cicero had entered the province of Cilicia at Laodicea on 31 July and set off along the main road to the theatre of war in the East, holding assizes as he went. He longed for his normal occupations in the full glare of public life in Rome: 'I am missing the sunlight, the Forum, the city, my house, you.'[20] 'You', which is plural, may include Atticus' family and Cicero's family, as well as Atticus himself. Young Quintus and Marcus were left with King Deiotarus of Galatia while their fathers were campaigning.[21] Life at a Hellenised Celtic court must have been educational and fun. Despite his busy life as governor and general, Cicero continued to think about Tullia, 'my domestic concern which is my biggest care'. His friend Sestius had told him about a conversation he had had with Atticus about it, and Cicero asked Atticus to work hard on it and let him know what could be done and what his own views were (*A* 5.17/110.4, 15 Aug.[?] 51). But Atticus went off to Epirus for the winter and could no longer do much (e.g., *A* 5.21/114.1, Laodicea, 13 Feb. 50). Cicero fought a successful campaign, left Quintus in charge of the army in winter quarters, and travelled back westwards to Laodicea, settling civil matters and holding assizes again from mid-February until 1 May 50.

The short-list

During the winter of 50, as far as Cicero knew, he had only two candidates to consider. He alludes to both discreetly, since the post was insecure. Writing to Atticus, Cicero said that he agreed with him in thinking Postumia's son the top candidate for Tullia, since Pontidia was not behaving as if she was in earnest (*A* 5.21/114.14, Laodicea, 13 Feb. 50). It may have been a letter from Terentia which had made this assessment of Pontidia, but she then perhaps retracted it. In the meantime, Atticus had supported Pontidia's candidate, which would have meant Cicero 'going back to his old bunch of people [*grex*]'. There is a known M. Pontidius from Arpinum, who practised advocacy in Rome,[22] so 'his old bunch' might mean the governing class of Arpinum and its locality. When the point about Pontidia's earnestness was cleared up, Cicero decided he much preferred him to the man supported by Servilia, and wrote to communicate the opinion he shared with Atticus to Terentia and Tullia (*A* 6.1/115.10, Laodicea, 20 Feb. 50, with SB *A* iii.244). It is unsatisfactory that we cannot identify the favoured candidate. Shackleton Bailey takes it that the 'old bunch' means the *equites* and therefore the man was 'a mere *eques*'.[23] This would not preclude his being already on the senatorial ladder as a new man, perhaps about to stand for the quaestorship. Cicero used the same metaphor of *grex*, a herd or flock and hence a group of people, in court, addressing Ser. Sulpicius Rufus (cos. 51):

> Your nobility, though of the highest, . . . is not very clear to the people and the voters. For your father was of equestrian station and your grandfather not well known for any outstanding achievement . . . So I am in the habit of counting you in our category [*in nostrum numerum adgregare*], because you have, by virtue and hard work, succeeded in being thought worthy of high office although you are the son of a Roman *eques*.
>
> (*Mur.* 15)

88 *Finding the right man*

The 'old bunch' might then mean the upwardly mobile sons of *equites*. *Equites* in general seem too big a group. In looking for a dependable husband for a woman who had been married before, fathers might lower their sights to a husband not active in public service. A cultured, wealthy, well-born *eques*, rather like Atticus himself, might qualify. Even Augustus considered such men when looking for a third husband for his daughter, the mother of his heirs.[24] So we might think of a more restricted category within the *equites*: the governing class of Arpinum or a nearby town, new men aiming at a senatorial career, or men who had something else in common with Cicero. Cicero belonged to a number of social groups. He himself uses the same expression ('*grex*') for 'a group of persons having common interests, aims etc., a circle, set or similar' to describe Scipio's circle of friends.[25] Such a circle of friends with intellectual interests would include senators and *equites*.

The other man, canvassed by Servilia and by Postumia, the wife of Ser. Sulpicius, was the younger Ser. Sulpicius. Since he was a patrician and son of a consul (in office that very year), he might be expected to have trumped anyone from the 'old bunch', although Cicero had in 63 been able to portray his father as the equivalent of a new man. His father, a contemporary and old friend of Cicero, was an eminent jurist with philosophical interests, whom Cicero later praised for making the law an art and on whose patriotism he pronounced a posthumous public eulogy.[26] He had missed winning the consulship for 62 and had to wait a long time before he finally got it for 51. His wife was possibly behind this late success. She was patrician like him, 'of a family verging to extinction. She married a patrician in manifest need of support.'[27] But there was some scandal attached to her reputation,[28] although this did not stop Cicero holding discussions with her at his villa at Cumae, and in 45 Cicero wanted Atticus to consult her on a point of family history.[29] Nothing is known against the young man, whom presumably Cicero knew well, although the evidence in the letters does not start until 51. He later disgraced himself in Cicero's eyes by joining Caesar's army in 49, on his father's orders, but Cicero did not refuse to meet him a short time after and by 46 was expressing to his father warm appreciation of his intellectual gifts and his friendship.[30] One would expect Cicero to have found him a congenial son-in-law, one who shared his dedication to oratory.[31] Instead, Sulpicius was to marry a fellow-patrician, Valeria, the sister of M. Valerius Messalla Corvinus (who would be a fellow-student of young Marcus in Athens and, like him, join the tyrannicides and then change sides and flourish under Augustus). Sulpicius and Valeria became the parents of the poet Sulpicia, who was at the heart of a group of poets later in the century.[32]

In the midst of all his preoccupations, Cicero did not forget to send his love to Atticus' baby daughter and enjoy a running joke about her much like one they had had about Tullia in her childhood:

> I am delighted that you say your little daughter is a pleasure to you in Rome. Although I have never seen her I still love her and know for certain that she is lovable.
>
> (*A* 5.19/112.2, 21 Sept. 51)

> I am pleased that your little daughter so carefully gave you instructions to send her love. I am pleased that Pilia did too. But your daughter is even more attentive since she is fond of someone she has never seen. So give them both my love.
>
> (*A* 6.1/115.22, Laodicea, 20 Feb. 50)[33]

Meanwhile, the marriage market in Rome had suddenly changed. Caelius wrote to warn Cicero that his friend Dolabella had applied for permission to prosecute Ap. Claudius, Cicero's predecessor in Cilicia, with whom he had struggled to keep on good terms in spite of his disapproval of his record of oppression and extortion.

> It occurs to me that, between the application and the formal laying of the charge, Dolabella's wife left him. I remember the job you gave me when you left; I do not think you will have forgotten what I wrote to you. It is not the right time to say more; I can give you one piece of advice, if you do not dislike the idea, that at this time you give away nothing about what you want and wait and see how he comes out of this trial. It would cause bad feeling against you if it got out ... I urge you to refrain from committing yourself about Dolabella. Handling things like that will be better for the matter I'm talking about and for your status and reputation for fairness.
>
> (*F* 8.6/88.2, 5, Rome, Feb. 50)

If it were known that a marriage alliance was being made between Cicero and Dolabella, there would be publicity because of the trial. Cicero's efforts not to be seen to condemn Appius' governorship would be compromised. Even if negotiations about a marriage were secret, Caelius was sure that Dolabella could not be trusted to hold his tongue. He would see that if it were known he was going to marry Cicero's daughter, it would be thought that Cicero was against Ap. Claudius. In any case, he was an indiscreet man, and even if he knew that gossip would damage him, he still would not be capable of keeping quiet. Caelius advised Cicero to wait until after the trial if he were interested in pursuing the possibility of a match with Dolabella (*F* 8.6/88.2).

Before Cicero could have received Caelius' letters about Dolabella's likely divorce, he wrote a witty letter to his equestrian friend Volumnius Eutrapelus, asking him to foster Dolabella's friendly feelings towards him (*F* 7.32/113.3, Laodicea[?], Feb. or March 50[?]). We do not know why

Eutrapelus and Dolabella were connected at this time, though Dolabella's joining Caesar in 49 and Eutrapelus' friendship with Antony, attested for 43 BC but probably dating to at least the time when Eutrapelus' freedwoman Cytheris was flaunted round Italy as Antony's mistress, suggest that both may already have belonged to Caesar's circle.[34] This may be why Cicero thought of Dolabella as someone with whom he wanted to maintain friendly relations.

Cicero must have realised that decisions could be made only by those on the spot. His job was to keep some irons in the fire. Some time between mid-February (*A* 6.1/115.10, Laodicea, 20 Feb. 50), when he had written to Terentia supporting Pontidia's candidate, and April, Cicero had had a visit from Ti. Claudius Nero at Laodicea, which caused him to send off a letter recommending Nero's interests to one of the eastern governors.[35] He also wrote to Terentia and Tullia to tell them that Nero was a suitor to Tullia, and apparently expressing his own approval of the match (*A* 6.6/121.1, Side, c. 3 Aug. 50). Both these candidacies were to be overtaken by events. The second letter to Rome arrived only after Tullia's engagement to another man, about the end of May.[36]

Nero was a most suitable candidate, 'a nobly born, talented and self-controlled young man', as Cicero said in the formal recommendation to the governor, claiming to like him more than any other noble. The Claudii Nerones, though less eminent than the family of the Claudii Pulchri to which Clodius and his brother Appius belonged,[37] were patricians who boasted C. Claudius Nero (cos. 207), who had defeated Hasdrubal at the Metaurus. But there were no consulships after 202, only a number of praetorships. Young Nero's father served against the pirates in 67, probably as an ex-praetor.[38] He was still active in 63,[39] but perhaps chose not to attempt the consulship or died without finding an opportunity to stand. Cicero will have known him relatively well: they were fellow-senators and close in age. He knew the son, or of him, by 54, when Nero applied to be chosen as the prosecutor of Gabinius.[40] The younger Nero's talent is illustrated by his subsequent career. He went on to serve under Caesar, to be quaestor in 48 and to attempt to take a principled line in the dissensions of 44–39. He reached the praetorship in 42 and died a natural death in 33. Failing to get Tullia, he eventually married a relation, Livia Drusilla, perhaps in 43.[41] They divorced in 39, so that Livia could marry the young Caesar, the future Emperor Augustus. Their elder son, another Ti. Claudius Nero, would in AD 14 become the second emperor.

Caelius' letter about Dolabella reached Cicero in early May and Cicero assured Caelius that his advice confirmed Cicero's own decision about keeping on the right side of Ap. Claudius, 'a man at the peak of his age, resources, honours, ability, children, relations, connections by marriage, friends'.[42] He said nothing directly about Dolabella. He had in fact written to Claudius promising his support in the trial.[43] In this letter, he calls Dolabella rash for attacking Claudius. Both Caelius and Claudius had reported to him some 'silly and childish talk' by Dolabella, who must have declared an intention of becoming a suitor to Tullia. But Cicero claims that he would have been more likely to break off his previous connection with Dolabella (whom he had defended on two capital charges[44]) than to form a new link.[45] Cicero had sensible reasons for keeping in with Claudius, an influential consular, whose daughters were married to Pompey's elder son and to M. Brutus, both friends of his.

Letters to Atticus in the spring (A 6.2/116–6.3/117) have nothing on a match for Tullia, since Atticus was in Greece. But when travelling east again, probably in mid-June, Cicero sent another appeal:

> Seeing that you have got back to Rome, I hope, safe and sound, please as usual see to everything which you see matters to me, especially about my Tullia. I wrote to tell Terentia what I would like concerning a match for her when you were in Greece.
> (A 6.4/118.2, en route, mid-[?] June 50)

This probably refers to the letter to Terentia about Pontidia's candidate. On 5 April, Ap. Claudius was able to write to inform Cicero that he had been acquitted, and from his camp Cicero, on perhaps 26 June, sent effusive congratulations (F 3.11/74).

The view from Rome

Now that the evidence has been set out, let us reconstruct Tullia's part in this decision. She and her mother had been told to do what they thought best. At about twenty-seven, Tullia must have been keenly aware of the importance of making a satisfactory match, which would give her children, position and conjugal affection. Through her previous husbands and her father as well as her women friends, she must have known, more or less well, all the young men of senatorial family in their twenties and thirties. Many of them would be currently married. Others might be ruled out as enemies of her father or of unsavoury reputation, or simply because she disliked them. Senior senators who required a wife would be obvious. She would also know of some rich and important *equites*, perhaps with connections with Arpinum or nearby towns.

Her initial list, like her father's, probably included Ser. Sulpicius Rufus, a desirable possibility. But there was a problem with making an approach – apparently nothing could be done by Terentia and Tullia directly – and the matter was still hanging fire at the end of 51. By then, Pontidia's candidate had put in an appearance. We cannot guess what Tullia thought of him, but Terentia apparently changed her mind about him and wrote to tell her husband so. In April, Terentia will have received Cicero's letter of 20 February supporting Pontidia's candidate. It was too late. Since Nero was abroad, he had made no direct contact with Tullia. Cicero's April letter recommended Nero arrived after the engagement, probably in June. So up to February, everything was vague and no strong possibility had presented itself.

In or before February 50, Tullia must have known that Dolabella's wife – usually identified with Fabia, another patrician, a kinswoman of Terentia's relative the Vestal Virgin[46] – had left him. She is the subject of one of Cicero's ungallant jokes. It is transmitted as an example of Humorous Rebuttal, in the form of a pretended agreement. 'When Fabia wife of Dolabella said she was thirty years old, he said, "It is true. She's been telling me that now for twenty years."'[47] If we press this, then Fabia at some time during the marriage claimed to be thirty and was thought to be older, so she may have been older than Dolabella. There must have been a son of this marriage, for in the young Caesar's train at Alexandria in 30 there was a young man called Dolabella, who was kind to Cleopatra.[48] There are other probable references to this man. He in turn fathered a son, P. Dolabella, consul in AD 10, and the family continued.[49] Presumably this son lived with Fabia after the divorce.

It was at this point in mid-winter that Dolabella's indiscreet talk gave rise to rumours that he was a favoured suitor. Anything Cicero, in reaction to this, risked writing about his views on Dolabella will not have reached Terentia until late May. It seems that the letters of Terentia and Tullia during the period after Dolabella's wife left him in February had not informed Cicero of any preliminary negotiations. There may have been a short interval before Fabia sent notice of divorce or the two of them arranged a consensual divorce. But Dolabella might have presented himself as a suitor before these details had been finalised. It may be that Dolabella had intended to court Tullia even before his wife left him. What did Tullia know about it? Was she encouraging him even before his divorce? A few years later, we find young Quintus flattered by the alleged overtures of a married woman on the point of divorce.[50] So people might be even less shocked by a man making such a move than Cicero was at what he was told about a woman.

P. Cornelius Dolabella was a patrician and probably an elder son, since his father held the same first name.[51] Nine members of the family are known from among republican office-holders: their appearances are sporadic and their exact family relationships mostly unknown.[52] Their fortunes revived with Sulla's: one Cn. Dolabella was consul and another urban praetor in 81.[53] Tullia's suitor's father was probably the man who held the urban praetorship in 69 or thereabouts, was judge in one of Cicero's civil cases and went on to be governor of Asia.[54] He probably died soon after this posting. The grandfather was probably L. Dolabella (son of a Publius and grandson of a Lucius), an ex-praetor who won a triumph in 98.[55] Tullia's husband's political career is known from 49, when he was a legate in Caesar's army. He held the tribunate in 47, having become a plebeian, presumably by adoption. He held neither quaestorship nor praetorship, but Caesar chose him to hold the consulship in 44.[56] The ancient source which makes him twenty-five when he became consul and so born in 69 is to be rejected.[57] But he had held neither of the qualifying offices and must have been under the minimum age (forty for a patrician). It is remarkable that Caesar showed such exceptional favour to a man who was 'avid, pretentious and arrogant, with no sign of competence'.[58] He was perhaps thirty or thirty-one in 44.[59] This would mean he had been born in about 74, which would make him perhaps a year or two younger than Tullia. But the age gap would not be felt to be great. On the other hand, if he had been born in 69, he would have been only about nineteen in 50, which would make him a very awkward match for Tullia.[60] It would also mean that he had married Fabia at a precociously early age, soon after taking the adult toga. This is not impossible – his fellow-patrician Julius Caesar had married Cornelia, daughter of Cinna, when he was sixteen, in 84/3, but he needed to be married if he was to become priest of Jupiter[61] – but it does not seem likely that Dolabella had married so young. Nor, if we look at his political career, does it seem likely that a boy in his teens would have been twice prosecuted, elected to a priesthood and undertaken two prosecutions of his own. All suit better an ambitious young man in his twenties. Nor would it be sensible for Caelius to talk of vices which 'have been shaken off as he has grown older' if he were not yet twenty.[62]

What made Tullia accept Dolabella? Because of Cicero's verdict when he met the young couple, it is easy to assume that it was his charm. Caelius hints at it. Caesar, hoping to get Cicero to come back to Rome and join his side, wrote in the following year that he found Dolabella delightful (*iucundus*), ascribing to him humanity (*humanitas*), good feeling and goodwill towards himself, which would make him persuade Cicero (*A* 9.16/185.3, copied into letter from Formiae, 26 Mar. 49). Here again (despite the fact that Caesar is being polite), we get a hint that Dolabella had an attractive personality. This might go far to explain the peculiar favour in which Caesar later held him, which has led to speculation that Dolabella might have been Caesar's natural son.[63] With women, the womaniser is by definition successful. But Tullia might have had other motives. 'Dolabella's motives were mercenary, snobbish the women'.[64] Dolabella was a patrician noble, with a praetorian father, whose fortune he had presumably inherited. But Tullia had already had two well-born husbands: the first a plebeian noble with excellent connections, the second a patrician. It would matter that Dolabella was not socially inferior to either: she could boast that all three were of the first rank, *primarii*, as Sulpicius Rufus was to say.[65] But he cannot have looked a better catch, from the snobbish point of view, than Ti. Claudius Nero (though Tullia may not have realised that the latter was in the running). His father's and grandfather's praetorships would have made him outshine Crassipes, but he does not seem to have had a powerful family network of living kin. Caelius uses the word *optimus* of Dolabella, an 'excellent man' (p. 95). He is probably thinking of ability as well as birth. At this stage, Dolabella must have looked promising, like other erratic young men. He was an energetic politician, unlike Crassipes. But there were several strikes against him: he had made enemies and it was not clear that he would get away to a good start on the senatorial ladder. Snobbery does not seem an adequate explanation of Tullia's decision. Syme suggests that 'Cicero's consort might appear obdurate against blandishments' and that Tullia, at the ripe age of about twenty-seven and after two marriages (she 'had already run through two husbands'), should not have been susceptible to Dolabella's charm, but hints that they nevertheless succumbed.[66] His remark about Terentia rests on a stereotypical view of her as a hard and ambitious woman. His view of Tullia suggests she lacked feeling, that Piso's death was her fault and that she could be impervious to love because of her age and previous experience. This opinion deserves no respect. Personal feelings, in practice, formed part of the balance-sheet. Tullia needed someone to give her children and companionship, as well as social standing. Cicero's opinion that there was a shortage of good candidates had turned out to be right. Negotiations were conducted discreetly and expeditiously. Tullia, with her mother's backing, agreed to marry Dolabella and the engagement was celebrated in late May or early June.[67]

Dolabella

Cicero left his province at Tarsus at the end of his term in July and on 3 August stopped at Side in Pamphylia. There he received his postbag. It included a letter from Ap. Claudius congratulating him on the match which had been made between Tullia and Dolabella. Even Cicero had difficulty composing a reply: he pretends it is the most difficult case he had ever had to plead.

> I would wish that what was done by my family without my knowledge will turn out happily for me and my Tullia, as you have been kind and friendly enough to hope . . . I must not use gloomy language about an event on which you yourself call down good omens, but I am still distressed. One thing I am not afraid of is that you should not fully understand that what was done was done by others. I had given them instructions that they should not refer matters back to me, since I was going to be so far away, but do what they thought right. Someone might say, 'What would you have done if you had been here?' I would have approved the marriage, but about its timing I would have done nothing that you did not want, nothing without consulting you.
> (F 3.12/75.2–3, Side, 3 or 4 Aug. 50)

From a subsequent letter, we learn that Ap. Claudius had visited Cicero's house and met his family to talk to them about Cicero's hope of being awarded a public thanksgiving for his victories. Cicero expressed the wish that Claudius could value all his family as Cicero valued his: no doubt the reference is chiefly to his relations by marriage, the Pompeii and Brutus' family, balancing Cicero's son-in-law (*F* 3.31/76.1, Rhodes[?], Aug. 50). Cicero is careful, in writing to Claudius, not to express any misgivings about the choice of bridegroom, who was now a member of his own family.[68]

There was also a letter from Caelius, which survives:

> I congratulate you on your marriage alliance with a definitely excellent [*optimus*] man – that's what I think of him. As for the other things, which up to now have let him down, they have been shaken off as he has grown older, and any which remain will, I am sure, swiftly be removed by your company and moral authority [*auctoritas*] and by Tullia's goodness [*pudor*]. For he is not aggressive in his vices nor slow to understand what is better. And then, the most important thing, I am very fond of him.
>
> (*F* 8.13/94.1, Rome, early June 50)

Cicero replied to Caelius:

> I am delighted that you express approval of Dolabella and are fond of him. As for those things which you hope will be moderated by my dear Tullia's good sense [*prudentia*], I know what they correspond to in your [earlier, lost] letter. What would you think if you read the one I sent to Appius at that time [*F* 3.10/73], after reading yours? Oh well, that's life. May the gods approve of what has been done! I hope I shall find him a pleasant son-in-law – your social skills will be a great help in bringing that about.
>
> (*F* 2.15/96.2, Side, 3 or 4 Aug. 50)

And he let Atticus know his reactions:

> While I'm in my province polishing up Appius' record as governor, all of a sudden I've been turned into his prosecutor's father-in-law. 'May the gods approve it', say you. So be it, and I'm sure you hope so. But believe me, it's the last thing I expected. I had sent the women reliable messengers to tell them about Tiberius Nero, who had negotiated with me direct. They reached Rome after the engagement had been celebrated. But I hope this match is better. I understand that the women are really delighted with the young man's attentiveness and charm. Spare your criticism of other things.
>
> (*A* 6.6/121.1, Side, c. 3 Aug. 50)

The vices which even Caelius admits must have included sexual irregularities. Perhaps Fabia was not prepared to tolerate them. Years later, after the marriage broke up and Dolabella's political choices put him beyond forgiveness for his former father-in-law, Cicero revealed that he had been hopelessly vicious from the start. News had reached Rome that, while governing Syria, he had seized and tortured to death C. Trebonius, one of the assassins of Caesar.

> Cruelty was his delight from boyhood; the depravity of his lusts was such that he always rejoiced in the fact that not even an enemy could taunt him with them without compromising his own modesty. And this man, ye gods, once belonged to my family [literally 'was once mine' – *meus*]. For his vices were hidden and I did not investigate them. Perhaps I would not be a stranger to him even now, unless he had been discovered to be an enemy to us, to the walls of his fatherland, to this city, to our household gods, to the altars and hearths of all of us, in short to nature and humanity.
>
> (*Phil.* 11.9–10)

Such accusations of boyhood vice are a piece of rhetorical invention, adding verisimilitude to an attack on an opponent's character, whether in the law-court or in politics. Cicero needed to claim that the alleged vices were hidden, or else his tolerance of Dolabella as a son-in-law would have been culpable. The charge of cruelty fits the context, in which Dolabella had just been declared a public enemy for his conduct. The vices which were too degrading to be described would be sexual. Cicero 'passed over' similar depravity in Antony, but only after having accused him of having prostituted himself to male lovers for gain and having had a notorious liaison with Curio.[69] Presumably homosexual relationships are meant here too. But accusations of unchastity with men (*impudicitia*) were routinely made against any young man; particularly, Cicero claimed, if he were good-looking.[70] Cicero perhaps hints at such youthful misbehaviour here because the natural sequel of youthful sexual incontinence, seduction of women of his own class, was easily associated with Dolabella.

Cicero's return

Cicero must have received letters from Terentia and Tullia at Side but no reply survives, so we do not know what he wrote to them on receiving news of the engagement. Instead, we have the affectionate letter he wrote from Athens:

> If you and Tullia are well, my darling [*lux nostra*], I and our sweet Cicero are well.
> ... As we disembarked, Acastus [a courier and member of the household staff] met me with letters. He had made the journey with great energy and reached Athens on the twenty-first day. I received your letter, from which I understood that you were afraid that earlier ones had not

been delivered to me. They have all been delivered to me and you have written everything to me most carefully. I was very grateful for that. Nor was I surprised that the letter Acastus brought was short. For now you are expecting me in person, or rather us in person. We are anxious to come to you as soon as possible, even though I understand to what sort of country we are coming. For I have been informed by the letters from many friends, which Acastus brought, that matters are heading towards war, so that I shall not be able to conceal what I think when I come. But since we must submit to fortune, we shall see to it that we come quickly, so that we may discuss the whole thing more easily. Please, as long as it is not bad for your health, come as far as possible to meet us.

(F 14.5/119.1, 16 Oct. 50)

Cicero here explicitly mentions that Terentia and he will be having political discussions and planning for what he should do. This side of their life is not often mentioned: it was probably routine. He also asked her to take care of some business to do with an inheritance from a certain Precius: she is to see that Atticus or, failing him, Camillus looks after his interests until he comes (F 14.5/119.2). Contemporary letters to Atticus show that Cicero was determined that Philotimus should not get his hands on this money and that he had written both to Philotimus and to Terentia (a lost letter) that he wanted to keep it for the expenses of a triumph.[71]

Atticus returned to Italy and was met by Pilia, perhaps at Brundisium. Cicero was pleased to hear what she said about Tullia's marriage (A 6.8/122.1, Ephesus, 1 Oct. 50). This seems to mean more than the usual good wishes and congratulations: perhaps Pilia found some reassuring things to say about Dolabella. Cicero also tried to find out how Atticus reacted to him, asking him to write to him about Tullia, 'that is, about Dolabella' (A 6.9/123.4). We are not told that the wedding had taken place. If Shackleton Bailey's conjectural reconstruction of a corrupt passage in a letter from Caelius is accepted, then Tullia postponed the wedding until her father's return. Shackleton Bailey's translation of this conjectural text reads: 'You know that they are marking time at home (?). You are holding things up (?)' (F 8.12/98.4, dispatched on 23 September from Rome). But we cannot put much weight on this. The return journey stretched to nearly four months.[72] Cicero was anxious to get back to Rome before the end of December because he had hopes of a triumph, which might be easier to get while the friendly consuls of 50 were in office.[73] But he was not hurrying and there is no hint that he wanted to return for a wedding. He would probably have seen his presence as less important than getting his daughter established, to maximise her chances of childbearing.[74] There is a clinching piece of evidence. It was customary for a dowry to be transferred to the husband in three annual instalments, starting one year after the beginning of the marriage. We find out later that the due date for the first payment of Tullia's dowry was

1 July 49. Therefore, the wedding must have taken place on 1 July 50, at a suitable interval from the engagement. If Atticus returned to Rome in mid-June, as Cicero expected, then he and Pilia may have attended.

When Cicero reached Brundisium, he was met by Terentia, just as he had asked, which was clever of her as his estimate of his arrival-time had been wrong (F 14.5/119.2, to Terentia, Athens, 16 Oct. 50). His pleasure comes through in his report to Tiro: 'next day, 24 November, we reached Brundisium at the fourth hour after sunrise, and at the same time Terentia, who is very fond of you, entered the town' (F 16.9/127.1, Brundisium, 26 Nov. 50). She brought news of Atticus, who had been ill. 'Terentia, who came to the gates of Brundisium at the same time as I reached the harbour and who met me in the forum, told me that L. Pontius had said to her in the territory of Trebula that your fever had left you' (A 7.2/125.2, Brundisium, 25 Nov. 50). Terentia's behaviour contrasted with that of her sister-in-law Pomponia, who (as Atticus told Cicero) failed to travel even as far as their villa near Arx to wait for her husband.[75] Terentia, Cicero and Marcus, perhaps still with the Quinti, reached Aec(u)lanum on 6 December and stayed at Pontius' house near Trebula, though Cicero uses the first-person singular to express this (A 7.3/126.1, near Trebula, 9 Dec. 50). It was perhaps there that Tullia and Dolabella met them, probably intending to accompany them for the rest of the journey to Rome.

> What else is there to report? Oh yes, I find my son-in-law charming [*suavis*], as do Tullia and Terentia. He has as much talent [*ingenium*] and good manners [*humanitas*] as you like. We must put up with the other things you know about . . . But we'll talk about this when we are together: it will be a long conversation.
>
> (A 7.3/126.12)

Cicero could find one advantage about Dolabella: apart from Pontidia's candidate,[76] Dolabella was the only one of the possible suitors who would not need to persuade Cicero to borrow money for him. But it is unlikely that his opinion of Dolabella's financial solidity was correct.

Cicero and the others may have broken the journey again at their villa at Pompeii, as Cicero had on the outward trip.[77] By about 10 December, they were probably at the villa at Cumae, where Cicero had a two-hour interview with Pompey.[78] The next stopping place was Formiae, from where Cicero intended to go to Tarracina on 29 December and then stay with someone in the Pomptine Marshes and at Pompey's splendid Alban villa in the hills near Rome, before entering Rome on his birthday, 3 January.[79] While at Formiae, Cicero heard that Dolabella was named as co-heir to a woman's estate, on condition that he changed his name to hers and became a Livius. Cicero was doubtful whether it was right for a young man of noble birth to change his name because of a woman's will. It would depend on how much the inheritance was worth.[80] We do not know the sequel, but we see

Cicero already taking a sympathetic interest in Dolabella's affairs. Cicero changed his mind about entering Rome, since he wished to retain his military command in case he could secure a triumph. In the event, he did not return to the city and his house until the autumn of 47. Tullia and Terentia probably did enter the city.

9 Public and private quarrels

We now come to a period in which friendships, families and marriages shattered under the strain of civil war. Pompey broke with his former father-in-law Caesar. Senators had to decide which side to take. Their conduct was scrutinised by their peers. Families might be split by conflicting loyalties. We shall see the gradual breakdown of Terentia's long-established marriage. It was not inevitable: the relationship during these difficult years had its ups and downs and the friction we can occasionally observe may not have been the reason for the eventual divorce. Tullia's marriage, in contrast, showed difficulties within a year. She was exposed to the embarrassing consequences of Dolabella's reckless extravagance and then (Cicero thought) to a catastrophic drop in her standard of living. There may also have been sexual betrayal.

Terentia and Tullia, moving in Roman society in the late 50s, will have been involved in the sort of political talk that Caelius had relayed to Cicero. They probably had a pretty good idea of which way Dolabella would jump. There is nothing to suggest, however, that their choice of Dolabella was influenced by the thought that he might be on the other side from Cicero and so provide a certain amount of insurance for the family.[1] Cicero had already indicated to Atticus that he would feel obliged to side with Pompey, despite his ties to Caesar and although he was disillusioned with the *optimates*.[2] Terentia will have been well aware of his consistent public support for Pompey (and private reservations) over nearly twenty years. It is hard to guess what her personal views were, and Tullia's. They were probably nuanced, and their ideas of what their husbands ought to do probably fluctuated as did those of Cicero, Caelius and all the rest who were caught up in this dangerous situation as it changed and developed from day to day.

The beginning of the civil wars: November 50 to June 49

Terentia and Tullia in Rome

The period Cicero spent in Italy after his return is richly documented in the correspondence, including letters to Terentia. The end of the year saw everyone preoccupied with the probability of war. Cicero's talk with Pompey convinced him there was no hope of peace.[3] Between 27 December and 18 January 49, there are no letters to Atticus: Cicero went up to somewhere near Rome on 4 January and was pleased by the ceremonial greeting he received.[4] The women, with Dolabella, may have gone straight on to Rome and home. The Senate passed an emergency decree on 7 January and Cicero wrote to Tiro, who was still ill at Patrae (in a letter 'from all the family'): 'I have come upon a very fire of civil discord, or rather war. I wanted to cure it'.[5] On receiving the news from Rome, Caesar crossed the Rubicon and marched down the Adriatic coast. When word of his progress reached Rome on the 17th, Pompey evacuated the city. There were scenes of panic. Cicero, who still held a military command, was given some responsibilities to raise troops for the Pompeians on the west coast. He wrote to Atticus next day to say he was leaving before daybreak and then probably went back to Formiae, which was his base for the next few months.[6] His mind was in a turmoil about what course of action he should take in the civil war.[7]

Both Terentia and Tullia stayed in Rome. Terentia was at the Palatine house, as she must have wished to be after over two months' travelling; Tullia seems to have stayed with her rather than at Dolabella's. Her husband probably went to join Caesar soon after his return to Rome. We do not know what sort of establishment he maintained in Rome at this time or later, though it would have been usual for a married man to possess a house.[8] In an uncertain situation, in winter, Rome was the obvious choice for any woman.

There was a complication: Tullia was pregnant. This may have been the first time she succeeded in conceiving. Her condition is not mentioned until Cicero eventually notified Atticus of the baby's birth on 19 May. But close family must have been aware of it all along and her well-being must have been of concern. She carried the child for at least 196 days. (Full term is 266-plus.) So she must have conceived in October and was now approaching the end of the first trimester (when there is risk of miscarriage and morning-sickness is often a problem). According to an ancient specialist, all excess was to be avoided: too much emotion, vigorous exercise, sitting on hard sedan-chairs (others were permissible), being driven in a carriage, and many other things which might provoke miscarriage. Let us hope she had had a well-upholstered sedan-chair and smooth-moving bearers. From the fortieth day after conception for about four months, the pregnant woman might take passive exercise in a litter or sedan-chair, and then in a carriage, walk, exercise her voice, take active exercise such as dancing, punching a leather ball, playing ball and taking massages. In the seventh month, she was to give up carriage-exercise and the other more energetic pursuits because of the risk of going into labour.[9] Probably Tullia had professional advice, something like this, from doctors and midwives. Alexio was Cicero's personal doctor up to his death, by a sudden illness, in 44,[10] but we do not know if he was already performing that function in 49, nor if he was a member of the household in Rome. Since Cicero was careful of his health, he probably always had a slave or freed doctor in his train when he travelled, and it is likely that Terentia or he kept others in Rome to attend on the family and his staff, as well as having access to free professionals. Atticus had a doctor in his household.[11] Midwives were often slaves or freedwomen and on domestic staffs of the rich at least in the late first century, but they might also be independent workers.[12] Apart from these experts, Tullia will have had the advice and sympathy of her mother and of those servants who had acquired some knowledge of pregnancy and childbirth. Unfortunately, we know nothing of women slaves belonging to any of the family (with the possible exception of some ex-slaves on one inscription (Ch. 4, n. 1)) nor whether slaves were bred in the household. It would be surprising if they were not. Many owners preferred home-bred slaves. Atticus employed no others for specialised domestic work.[13]

Atticus also stayed in Rome, keeping inside his house.[14] But to stay in Rome, waiting for the Caesarians, was a political statement. There might also be physical danger. Cicero soon had doubts:

> **Tullius to his Terentia and Father to his sweetest daughter; Cicero to his Mother and sister: fondest greetings**
>
> I think you must reflect again and again carefully about what you should do, my darlings [*animae meae*], whether you ought to be in Rome or with me or in some safe place. This is not just something I need to plan, but you too.
>
> The considerations which occur to me are these: you can be safe in Rome through Dolabella and your being there can be a help to us if any violence and plundering break out; but then again I am concerned, because I see that all the good men are away from Rome and have their women[15] with them. Besides the region in which I am contains towns friendly to us and also our estates, so that you could be with me a lot, and, when you are not, you could be comfortable in our own properties. I really cannot decide so far which of the two would be the better plan. Please observe what other ladies of your rank are doing and take care that you are not prevented from leaving when you want to do so. I would like you to reflect on this again and again carefully both between yourselves and with friends. You [plural] will tell Philotimus to see that the house has fortifications and a garrison. And please set up reliable couriers so that I may have some letter from you every day. But most of all take care to be in good health, if you want us to be the same.
>
> (F 14.18/144, Formiae, 22 Jan. 49)

It is striking that Cicero left the decision to them and expected them to organise elaborate precautions . He also asked Atticus what he thought.[16] He was much preoccupied by his own honour and that of his wife and daughter. Like Hector in the *Iliad*, he wondered what the Trojans and the

Trojan women in their trailing robes would think of him.[17] What other women thought of Terentia and Tullia mattered to them and to him. He wrote to them again in much the same terms as before:

> You too now need to plan, not just I, what you should do. If he [Caesar] is going to come to Rome in an orderly way, you can rightly be at home for the present. But if, in his madness, he is going to give over the city to be looted, I am afraid that Dolabella himself cannot give us enough help. And I am afraid that we may now be cut off, so that you are not allowed to go out when you want to. It remains for you to reflect, as you yourselves are best placed to do, whether ladies like you are in Rome. For if they are not, you must consider whether you can honourably be there. As things stand at present, provided we are allowed to hold this area, you can perfectly well be with me or on our estates. It is also to be feared that in a short time there will be hunger in the city. I would like you to reflect on these matters with Pomponius [Atticus], with Camillus, anyone you choose; in sum, to be of brave spirit.
> (F 14.14/145, Minturnae, 23 Jan. 49)

He adds a swift political comment, an affectionate ending and request for letters and a greeting from the Quinti and a certain Rufus (probably the quaestor he had worked with in Cilicia). He was genuinely afraid that the temples and homes abandoned by Pompey might be desecrated and plundered by Caesar – even fired.[18] He thought of sending young Marcus and young Quintus to Greece, out of the way,[19] and worried about the women's physical safety: 'But about Tullia and Terentia, when I imagine the arrival of barbarians [Caesar's Gallic troops] in the city, I am afraid of all sorts of things' (A 7.13/136.3, Minturnae, 23 Jan. 49). He again asks Atticus to think about what honour requires and returns to the same point in the next letter,[20] and again:

> About our women, among whom is your sister, please consider whether it is sufficiently honourable for us that they should be in Rome when the rest of the same standing have left.[21] I have written to them and to you yourself about this before. I would like you to urge them to leave, especially as we have those estates on the coast of which I am in command which will allow them to be comfortable considering the circumstances. For if we give offence because of our son-in-law (though I ought not to be held responsible for that [his joining Caesar]), the offence is increased by our women of all others remaining in Rome.
> (A 7.14/138.3, Cales, 25 Jan. 49)

Tullia was still thought of as attached to Cicero rather than to Dolabella. But Terentia's behaviour reflected directly on her husband, because it was expected she would identify with his interests.

Terentia was in charge at the Palatine house: she forwarded letters from Atticus to her husband, who was moving around a great deal, as the headings of the daily letters to Atticus testify.[22] She probably sent a daily courier with letters from herself and a variety of correspondents. Caesar and Pompey were negotiating and Cicero saw the hope of a return to Rome.[23] Atticus had replied to Cicero's appeals by advising that they should stay in Rome and Cicero wrote to them approving this (*A* 7.16/140.3). But the women had already decided to go and Cicero expected them to join him at Formiae. He heard, however, that people in the city were more nervous than before.[24] Temporarily encouraged by news from Rome (some of which Terentia, Tullia and perhaps Pomponia may have given him directly, along with letters) he wrote next day before daylight to thank Atticus for all he had done for them:

> On 2 February our women arrived at Formiae and told me of your attentions towards them, full of your sweet devotion. I want them to stay in the Formian villa until we know whether we are to have a shameful peace or a wretched war, and the Cicerones together with them. I myself with my brother am setting out for Capua on the 3rd, the date of this letter, to go to the consuls, since we have been ordered to report on the 5th.
> (*A* 7.18/142.1, Formiae, 3 Feb. 49; cf. 7.20/144.2, Capua, 5 Feb. 49)

Terentia and Tullia at Formiae

Dolabella was keeping Cicero better informed about Caesar's success than were the Pompeians he met in Capua and elsewhere.[25] He and Caelius, with whom Cicero had been keeping in touch,[26] reported that Caesar was satisfied with Cicero's behaviour in continuing to work for peace.[27] By now, he was afraid there might be a massacre when the Caesarians entered Rome. Nevertheless, the plan was that Terentia would return on the 13th (*A* 7.22/146.1, Formiae, 9 February 49). It sounds as if her assessment of the risk from the Caesarians and the danger of hostile gossip from the Pompeians did not agree with Cicero's. By evening, an optimistic letter from her freedman Philotimus in Rome suggested that the Pompeians looked stronger and this made Cicero afraid that to send the women back to Rome would cause hostile talk. People would say that (despite the current euphoria) he had given up on the Pompeians and that the return of the women of the family was the preliminary to his own (which would mean that he was prepared to acquiesce in Caesar's take-over of the city; *A* 7.23/147.2, Formiae, 10 Feb. 49). The women remained at Formiae, but it was not certain that they would stay long (*A* 7.26/150.3, Formiae, 13 Feb.? 49).

The letters of these weeks are mostly on what Cicero could glean of the intentions of Pompey (whose conduct he thought deeply dishonourable) and Caesar: there is little on his private life, except the difficulty of deciding

Public and private quarrels 105

on an honourable course of action. He wrote daily to Atticus in Rome and Atticus wrote almost as regularly to him.[28] Cicero agonised about what he should do, when he disapproved of Pompey's management of the war and saw many 'good men' staying comfortably at home, either in Rome like Atticus, or in suburban or nearby villas, while he and others who supported Pompey were wandering around Italy in poverty with their wives and children, leaving their houses in the city prey to looting and fire.[29] At this point, he did not think that it would be useful to the state for him to leave Italy if Pompey did so, nor expedient for his children, nor right and honourable (*A* 8.2/152.3, 4, Formiae, 17 Feb. 49). But, in response to a direct order from Pompey that Cicero should join him in Apulia, the four male Cicerones set out on 17 February. They reached Teanum Sidicinum, but then, receiving a report that Caesar was marching to Capua and would that night reach Aesernia, not far to the north of them, they were afraid that their route was already cut and so proceeded only a little further, to Cicero's lodge at Cales, to await news.[30] Letters from Pompey, who looked as if he would evacuate Italy from Brundisium, and news of troop movements convinced Cicero, Quintus and their friends that they had no hope of getting through.[31] From Cales, Cicero wrote a worried letter to Atticus. If he went to join Pompey now, it would have to be by ship from the west coast, a depressing prospect in mid-winter, while Pompey would go via the Adriatic. Should he go with Quintus (which would infuriate Caesar, since Quintus had been one of his generals) or without his brother and with young Marcus? What would Caesar do to his property, when the People might approve of his violating it?[32] Cicero was afraid of a replay of what Clodius had done in 58. The Cicerones then returned to Formiae on 19 February, and he wrote to Atticus again that evening. First thing in the morning, he sealed the letter ready for despatch, when one of the praetors arrived at his house with further news. Despite his worries, Cicero was able to joke with Atticus and to think about Tiro's welfare.[33]

What were the women suffering? First Terentia and Pomponia saw their husbands and sons – and Tullia her father, brother, uncle and cousin – setting off for the war. They had no idea when or whether they would return. Then they all came back, with no firm intentions. Cicero at least was tense and preoccupied, busy with correspondence (often late in the evening and before dawn) and a constant crowd of callers,[34] and conversation with another ex-consul, M'. Aemilius Lepidus, with whom he spent most of the day,[35] trying to make sense of a swiftly changing situation. Cicero talked to the local people, from both town and country, but found them interested only in their farms, villas and money.[36] These seem to be people who would pay respectful calls on him in order to find out what was going on, as they did even in ordinary times before the fourth hour (after dawn). Then there would be the local gentry, people like C. Arrius and Sebosus.[37]

So the house must have been full of many kinds of men, including social equals who would need to be invited to meals and some who would need to stay the night. Some of the senators' wives and local women must have called on Terentia and Tullia. Their duties as hostesses were heavy and their lives public. Cicero's remarks about women of rank leaving Rome and about wives wandering around Italy with their husbands suggest that Junia Tertia may well have been at Formiae with Cassius and other (unidentifiable) senators' wives with their husbands.

The suspense would continue. Cicero kept a ship ready at the nearby port of Caieta/Gaeta for instant embarkation, as well as one at Brundisium.[38] He suffered from eye-trouble[39] and insomnia.[40] It must have been a difficult time for the family. Cicero knew it and apologised later about 'the annoyances and worries with which I made you wretched, which I am very sorry for, and Tulliola, who is sweeter to me than my life' (*F* 14.7/155.1, aboard ship, Caieta, 7 June 49). This was the first period of more than a few days which the foursome had been able to spend together in one place since father and son had gone off to Cilicia. But it was not a time for the relaxed enjoyment of the intimate family circle. Tullia must have worried about Dolabella; they all worried about Cicero's course of action – his honour and his safety.

Cicero, who still did not know what Pompey was doing, was now considering a retreat to Arpinum, whence he might reach the Adriatic and so join Pompey[41] or (when he thought the route was blocked)[42] so as to avoid a possible meeting with Caesar. He was ready to offer as an excuse the need to mark Marcus' coming of age in his home town.[43] It was out of concern for his wife and daughter and the two young men that he had hesitated about whether to risk joining Pompey, but they all wanted him to do so and thought his staying was shameful and unworthy of him, while Quintus was ready to do whatever his elder brother thought best.[44] When he posed a set of ethical questions to Atticus, he asked whether a man who had conferred great benefits on his country and had suffered because of it (he is thinking of his record as consul and the exile which parted him from those he loved) should be allowed to think of himself and his family (*A* 9. 4/173.2, Formiae, 12 March 49). A letter from Atticus relieved Cicero's conscience and made all of them feel better: Cicero thought he could remain at Formiae.[45]

Cicero told Atticus that after his years of hard work, his age made leisure attractive and he was made softer by the pleasure of life at home (*A* 9.10/177.3, Formiae, 18 March 49). It was natural that he did not want to go on his travels again. He was, after all, fifty-seven. And he saw less prospect of a happy return even than when he was exiled.[46] But this suggests how pleasant he was finding life with his family. We can picture the family at dinner together after nightfall on 13 March (actually mid-January by the true calendar), when a letter arrived from Atticus (*A* 9.8/175.1, Formiae, 14 March 49).

Tullia's former husband Crassipes arrived from Brundisium and called on her father to give him news of Pompey and the threatening talk current in his camp.[47] Cicero does not tell us if he and Tullia met. Caesar besieged Pompey in Brundisium and Dolabella wrote with the news from there.[48]

The situation developed enough for Terentia and Tullia to decide to return to Rome. After Pompey sailed for Greece (17 March) and Caesar took the city, he marched towards Rome, spending the night of 27 March at Sinuessa and visiting Formiae on the 28th. He had an interview with Cicero, who refused to go to Rome to take part in senatorial debates, unless he could speak against the war. Cicero commented critically on those who accompanied Caesar.[49] It is not clear if the interview took place at Cicero's villa or if Dolabella was one of the Caesarians in the town. But, since Dolabella had been with Caesar at Brundisium and, in a letter which Cicero had received on the 26th Caesar had praised him as a delightful companion and said he relied on him to convince Cicero to come to Rome,[50] it seems likely that Dolabella came to see his father-in-law and his wife at their house and perhaps stayed the night. If Caesar called on Cicero, it will have caused a certain amount of extra upheaval, even if he did not dine. When Caesar, as dictator, dined with Philippus in December 45, he had a guard of two thousand troops, who took up a good deal of space. But the next day, when he was Cicero's guest (perhaps at the villa near Cumae, perhaps at the one inherited from Cluvius at Puteoli),[51] the soldiers had tents and Caesar and his companions were accommodated in three dining-rooms, with a substantial meal for the slaves and less grand freedmen, and an elegant dinner for the more eminent people. 'But he wasn't the sort of guest to whom you say, "Please come again on your way back."'[52]

After seeing Caesar, Cicero set out at once for Arpinum.[53] He wanted to be there on the 31st 'and then to wander around my little villas, which I do not hope ever to see again' (he was thinking of joining Pompey).[54] Cicero gave Marcus the white toga of manhood, an event which meant his coming of age as a citizen and which was usually a major celebration. It would normally have taken place at Rome, where Marcus would have been presented to his fellow-citizens in the Forum, but that was impossible; his second home-city, Arpinum, was the best substitute, and the Arpinates were pleased. The ceremony took place on 1 April, the feast of Venus Verticordia. The Liberalia, on 17 March, would have been more traditional,[55] but Cicero had obviously put political duties first and could not be in Arpinum then.

Terentia and Tullia in Rome once more

The women, whose share in the transition to manhood would have been limited, did not go up to Arpinum. It seems that Tullia and perhaps Terentia had left Formiae for Rome about the same time as Cicero left for Arpinum,[56] for Tullia met Atticus, who had time to mention their conversation to Cicero in a letter which reached him by 4 April. 'What Tullia told you about the young men is true' (*A* 10.1a/191.1, Laterium, 4 Apr. 49). The 'young men' probably refers to her brother and cousin[57] (rather than a bunch of Caesarians with whom she might recently have been in touch) and their views on what action to take. If we suppose that Tullia left Formiae on the 28th, she should have reached Rome on the 30th (breaking the journey twice). She probably had Dolabella's escort. This would ease the journey considerably. If Caesar held his political interviews in the morning, they could leave with him early enough in the day to reach a convenient stopping place in good time. Armed guards would protect them from a dangerous countryside. The roads were full of troops being levied for the civil war and the mood was pessimistic.[58] Tullia was now five to six months pregnant, so travelling was a serious undertaking. There is no hint of any anxiety in the letters. Tullia talked to Atticus about various things, including Cicero's difficult relationship with Atticus' freedman Dionysius, warning her father that he was on his way to see him (*A* 10.2/192.2, Laterium or Arcanum, 5 or 6 Apr. 49).

Cicero, who still had not decided his ultimate destination, was tearing himself away from everything he held dear.[59] On 3 April, he had already gone as far as Quintus' villa at Laterium, near Arpinum;[60] on the 5th he was at his brother's other villa, at Arx,[61] a more 'hidden' place than Minturnae, where he had initially decided to stay.[62] Then he went on to Cumae.[63]

That Tullia, Pomponia and perhaps Terentia had gone back to Rome must have caused gossip. If Terentia did not go with the others, she was certainly there by 14 April (A 10.4/195.12). The timing was significant: Cicero and presumably Quintus had just seen Caesar, who had invited them to co-operate. Caesar had had public notices put up in Formiae advertising a meeting of the Senate on 1 April.[64] Many senators had returned. Atticus too was still in Rome, though thinking of going to Epirus.[65] Caesar was now in undisputed control of Italy and about to take the war overseas, although he held out hope of peace. The elder Cicerones had not decided exactly where to go, but intended to leave Italy when it was possible. But for them to allow their wives to go to Rome must have been seen as a partial endorsement of Caesar. It allowed them to hedge their bets, using wives as an apparent guarantee of their behaviour and exploiting the assumption that in politics wives were attached to husbands. For Tullia, it was natural: her husband was one of Caesar's men and for the moment he was not on campaign, though about to command a fleet in the Adriatic.[66] Rome was now safe from the perils Cicero had imagined earlier.[67]

Cicero was still planning to leave Italy as soon as he could. So when the women left, they expected a long period of physical detachment. But Tullia, who had previously thought it was honourable for Cicero to go, now repeatedly begged him to wait and see what happened in Spain, where Caesar had gone to fight the Pompeians, and added that Atticus agreed with her (*A* 10.8/199.1, Cumae, 2 May 49). Atticus was being very kind to Tullia:

> The most important thing I have ever had to write is that you have never, out of all your very many favours, done anything more welcome to me than your charming and assiduous attention to my Tullia. She herself has been delighted by it, and I am just as much delighted. Her courage [*virtus*] is wonderful. How well she bears public disaster and family

tangles! How courageous was her spirit [*animus*] when we parted! There is affection, there is the greatest sympathy. Yet she wants us to do right and to be of good repute. But I say less than I might on this subject, in case I start to feel for myself.

(*A* 10.8/199.9–10)

Tullia also passed on her reading of Atticus' intentions (that she thought he did not intend to leave yet) to her father (*A* 10.8/199.10). Meanwhile, rumours of Cicero's leaving Italy had reached M. Antonius, who had been left in charge of Italy by Caesar. He wrote to assure Cicero that he did not believe this and to urge him to stay: 'I cannot believe that you are going to cross the sea, since you value Dolabella and your Tullia, that excellent lady, so highly and are valued so highly by all of us' (*A* 10.8A/199A.1, place uncertain, 1 May 49).

Tullia's presence in Rome helped Cicero to mask his intentions: she may well have knowingly deceived people. M. Caelius Rufus wrote in similar terms, asking Cicero not to sacrifice his fortunes, his only son and all his family. It would have been easier had only his own life been at stake. The family's tears and advice to wait for news from Spain sapped his resolution (*A* 10.9/200.2, Cumae, 3 May 49). The tears must have been chiefly Terentia's and Tullia's (known from letters), although the boys wept over Caelius' letter.[68] Caelius wrote:

> By your fortunes, Cicero, by your children, I beg and beseech you not to take a dangerous decision about your welfare and safety ... If you love yourself, your only son, your house, your remaining hopes, if we and that excellent man your son-in-law have any influence with you, whose fortune you ought not to be willing to wreck by forcing us to hate or abandon that cause on the victory of which our welfare depends, or to feel an impious wish against your welfare ... Take thought again and again, Cicero, lest you ruin yourself and all your family.
> (*A* 10.9A/200A.1, 2, 5 = *F* 8.16/153.1, 2, 5, Liguria[?], c. 16 Apr. 49)

Cicero assured Antonius that he was thinking of his son-in-law.[69] To Caelius, he wrote a discreet and disingenuous letter, dealing with the specific arguments:

> I am not afraid of those things which you loyally and affectionately put forward as fearful. For, in this upheaval of the world, there is no bitter suffering which does not (it is clear) hang over everybody. I would gladly buy out the commonwealth at the cost of my private and family troubles, even by those very ones of which you warn me to beware. To my son, whom I am glad that you hold in affection, if any commonwealth exists in future, I shall leave a sufficiently rich inheritance in the memory of my name; but if there is none, his fate will be the same as that of the other

citizens. As to your request that I think of my son-in-law, an excellent[70] young man whom I hold in great affection, can you doubt that I am tormented by anxiety for him, when you know how highly I value him and my Tullia? I am even more anxious because amid our common miseries I delighted myself with this little hope at least, that my Dolabella, or rather our Dolabella, would be free of those inconveniences which he contracted by his liberality. I would like you to enquire what days[71] he bore while he was in the city, how bitter they were to him, how dishonourable to me myself as his father-in-law . . . We pray you, wherever in the world we are, that you watch over us and our children as our friendship and your loyalty demand.

(F 2.16/154.4–5, 7, Cumae, 2 or 3 May 49)

Ideally, the bond between father-in-law and son-in-law was supposed to be strong.[72] Dolabella, as one of the family, might now correctly be called 'mine', *meus*, by Cicero, who often qualifies Terentia and Tullia with this adjective (e.g., F 14.3/9.1, to Terentia, Dyrrachium, 29 Nov. 58; A 11.6/ 217.4, Brundisium, 27 Nov. 48). He also called him 'our Dolabella' when writing to Tiro, though here the usage might be that appropriate to a common friend.[73] But he does not use the word often, although he was eventually to repent that he had ever regarded Dolabella as 'his' (*Phil.* 11.10; pp. 96, 140). The letter to Caelius indicates that Dolabella had by now left for the war in Spain. While he was in Rome he had been dunned by his creditors. This is the first sign of difficulties in the marriage. Both Dolabella's absence and continuing financial difficulties would justify Tullia's return to a comfortable life in her father's villa.

Terentia and Tullia at Cumae

On 7 May, Cicero thanked Atticus warmly for a letter which had given great pleasure to Tullia (A 10.13/205.1, Cumae). This proves that she and, almost certainly, Terentia had joined him at the villa at Cumae. Atticus, who had been in close touch with them in Rome, would not need to be informed of the precise date of their arrival (though a modern family man might have reassured his friend that his pregnant daughter and aging wife had managed the journey comfortably). On 2 May, Cicero had mentioned that Tullia was writing to him (A 10.8/199.1, Cumae), but if she had reached Cumae by the 7th, she must have already left Rome or been on the point of doing so, for Cicero seems to regard Rome to Cumae (138 Roman miles) as a five-day journey.[74] They might have travelled via Cicero's houses at Formiae and Minturnae (a lodge, which he owned at least from 51),[75] and probably journeyed by litter. Cicero did not give them his full attention: plans for a secret departure were once more in train. To divert suspicion, he went to his villa at Pompeii on 12 May, meaning to stay there while the ship was equipped for sea, but well-meaning centurions who wanted him to take over a command caused him to flee back to Cumae the next day before dawn.[76] During his absence, Q. Hortensius Hortalus, a young man of whose undutiful behaviour to his father Cicero had strongly disapproved and who was now appointed to command Caesar's fleet in the Tyrrhenian Sea but to whom he was polite for his father's sake,[77] made a detour to pay a call on Terentia (*A* 10.16/208.5). He spoke of Cicero in laudatory terms. Such regard for etiquette made Cicero rank him a little above his fellow-Caesarian, M. Antonius, who was going round Italy flaunting his mistress, an actress, but had not attempted to pay his respects.[78] This brief mention shows how Terentia, like Cicero, would expect to receive calls from people of rank who visited the neighbourhood.

By now, it was only rough weather that was holding up Cicero.[79] He expected to sail at any moment and hoped Atticus was going to Epirus. Then he was delayed again by lack of a wind.

On the 19th Tullia went into labour and gave birth to a boy, nearly two months premature. The journey or anxiety had perhaps contributed to this. As has been said, the experts thought travelling in a carriage was dangerous during this phase of pregnancy. 'Seven-months' babies were not usually expected to survive, although a few did.[80] 'I must rejoice that she has given birth safely; but the child is extremely weak' (*A* 10.18/210.1, Cumae, 19 May 49). Cicero uses the neuter of his grandson, literally 'what was born': although people may still refer to unborn or young babies as 'it', the phrase suggests that he could not regard him as a person likely to live. The baby is never mentioned again: we assume he lived only a short time. This ending of her pregnancy must have been a bitter disappointment to Tullia, and to her mother.

Terentia was probably present during the labour, along with the midwife and other women (servants). Three helpers were recommended. Their function was to support the woman in labour when she sat on the birthing-stool and to give calm encouragement.[81] A male doctor will have been within earshot. Cicero and other male relatives will not have been in the room.

Despite the fact that Tullia had just given birth and must have been anxious about the child, Cicero prepared to set out to Formiae immediately, perhaps the same day.[82] This is the last letter he managed to send to Atticus before he left Italy: it was dangerous to write any more about his intentions. But he did not leave Italy until 7 June, when he embarked on a ship in the harbour of Caieta, and at once, before writing to a list of friends to commend his wife and daughter to them,[83] wrote a humorous and affectionate letter to Terentia. He claims that he vomited up black bile on the night after he left them, and with it the anxiety with which he had been making her and Tullia wretched. He was feeling so much better that he claims some god must have cured him, and he asks her to make an offering to that god, as she usually does (*F* 14.7/155.1, aboard ship, Caieta, 7 June 49). Terentia and Tullia had probably managed to join Cicero at Formiae while he was waiting there, so as to have time for another farewell.

I would exhort you to be braver in spirit, did I not know that you are braver than any man. And yet I hope that things are in such a way that you are comfortable there and that I at long last will defend the commonwealth with men like ourselves. Please first of all look after your health; then, if you think fit, use those villas which are as far away as possible from the troops. It may be a good idea for you to use the farm at Arpinum with the staff of city slaves if the price of grain goes up.

Our charming Cicero sends you his dearest love. Again and again, fare well.

(F 14.7/155.2–3)

So Cicero and his son, and presumably his brother and nephew, set sail and went to join Pompey in Greece. Cicero later claimed that in taking this decision he was yielding to, or rather obeying, his family (*mei*; A 11.9/220.2, Brundisium, 3. Jan. 47). But this seems not to have been true of Quintus, and Tullia, at least, had not consistently advocated it: she had recently been asking him to await the outcome of the war in Spain. No doubt others, like Cicero himself, could change their minds from day to day, with changing circumstances. Tullia could well have thought in early May that, having waited so long, her father might have planned to wait until she had presented him with his first grandchild. Or, when the child was not expected to live, he might have stayed to comfort her and her mother and to see how she did.

During Cicero's absence in Greece, June 49 to October 48

Terentia's responsibilities

For some time mother and daughter probably remained at Formiae. Then they might go up to Arpinum to enjoy the cooler climate there. But they would probably return to Rome for the winter. During Cicero's absence, it is clear from the scanty correspondence that Terentia was responsible for the financial affairs of the family, but Cicero was critical of how things were done, particularly by his wife's servant Philotimus, and also relied heavily on Atticus. There was also C. Camillus, his business representative. The way things were handled was complicated. For instance, even before Cicero left Italy, we find him writing to Atticus about the Oppii, rich bankers from Velia, who might have dealings with Terentia. She was in Rome and: the figure she gave him (whatever it was) made sense (A 7.13/136.5, 23 Jan. 49; 7.13a/137.1, 24 Jan. 49; both from Minturnae). Subsequently, after Terentia went to Formiae, Cicero commissioned Atticus to decide what to do, perhaps to take out a loan: 'About the Oppii, I have nothing to suggest. You will do what seems best to do. You will talk to Philotimus, and what is more you will have Terentia on the 13th' (A 7.22/146.2, Formiae, 9 Feb. 49). Clearly Philotimus knew about the accounts, but Terentia's input would be more important. (She did not, however, return to Rome.) A few days later,

Cicero knew that Terentia had written directly to Atticus: 'About the 20,000 sesterces, Terentia has written back to you' (*A* 7.26/150.3, Formiae, 13 Feb.[?] 49). This may be the amount to be borrowed. Perhaps it was intended to defray the expenses of Cicero's journey, for he wrote again: 'I have written to Philotimus about getting [my] travel-money either from the Mint (for nobody is paying debts) or from the Oppii, your neighbours' (*A* 8.7/155.3, Formiae, 21 Feb. 49). There is a later mention of Atticus and Philotimus consulting about the best way to handle the business with the Oppii and this again seems to refer to travel-money, since Cicero goes straight on to say he would regard 'Epirus' (which seems to mean Atticus' estates there) as his own property (which would mean receiving hospitality and perhaps funds there), but would probably not be going that way.[84] So it seems at this point to have been left to Atticus and Philotimus to obtain the money.[85] These texts argue (up to a point) against the later allegation (p. 114) that it was Terentia's fault that Cicero was short of funds for his journey to Greece. She was in some way involved in the negotiation,[86] but she was not alone it that and she seems to have been doing her best, especially if she was borrowing money on her own recognisances to lend or give to Cicero. More important, it demonstrates the complexity of Cicero's arrangements and the diffusion of responsibility: it would be easy for him to blame any of his assistants if things went wrong.

One thing which presumably went right was the paying of the first instalment of Tullia's dowry to Dolabella on 1 July.

Supplying Cicero at war

We have no letters from the rest of the year 49, after Cicero's departure. He must have had some explaining to do when he reached Pompey. There is an anecdote that the latter asked him where his son-in-law Dolabella was. He replied neatly, 'With your father-in-law.'[87] He made himself unpopular among the Pompeians, was often unwell and played no active role in the war. As 48 begins, we find him in Epirus, worried about his financial position. He had run into problems in 49, when money was tight for everyone because of the war. Caesar's measures to deal with debt,[88] though moderate, did not please him at all and must have reduced his income.[89] He was 'very hard up indeed'.[90] Cicero had thought he had left his affairs in good shape, in the care of Terentia's steward Philotimus, although he had showed his irritation with the man often enough.[91] Cicero had distrusted his honesty as early as the summer of 50,[92] but had left the matter to Atticus[93] and Terentia[94] to sort out, and had had good intentions of being less negligent when he returned from Cilicia. He knew, in theory, how to deal with a steward: you checked each item of expenditure and, if you approved them, you approved the total.[95] He does not seem to have lived up to these good intentions in 49.

Although he had been able to keep, man and provision the ship in which he made his getaway, the arrangements for keeping him in funds seem to have been inadequate. According to Plutarch, Terentia was blamed for this retrospectively when Cicero and she divorced: 'he was neglected by her during the war, so that he was sent away lacking even necessities for the journey'.[96] Since Terentia was with Cicero at Cumae and Formiae, and not in control of his finances in Rome, she was as handicapped as he was himself at the time he set out. The responsibility then presumably belonged to Philotimus and Atticus, as suggested above. In 48, when Cicero was in Greece, Philotimus was still Cicero's steward, but Cicero did not know where he was. He asked Atticus to rescue him. He had thought he had left everything in good shape, because he trusted someone 'whom you know I have for a long time trusted too much' (*A* 11.1/211.1–2, second[?] week in Jan. 48). This seems to refer to Philotimus,[97] although it might conceivably mean Terentia.[98] There was certainly a cash-flow problem, which he relied chiefly on Atticus to solve, since with his international contacts he could arrange to draw on the savings of Cicero's governorship, which were held in Asia.[99] As for his own everyday expenses in Epirus, he had to accept clothes and spending money (20,000 sesterces) from Atticus' agents there.[100] Although Terentia was now probably in Rome, it is unfair to blame her for this, since Cicero was in the habit of receiving hospitality from Atticus' agents when he passed through the area where Atticus had estates. It was a convenient arrangement. But we cannot tell exactly how Cicero expected the job of managing his very considerable assets and the major payments he had to make to be divided up between Atticus, Camillus, Terentia, her confidential freedman Philotimus and lesser members of the slave or freed staff.

Tullia's difficulties

This uncertainty about his resources affected Tullia, for it was time for Cicero to think about how he would pay the second instalment of the dowry on 1 July 48. But worse problems seemed to be threatening:

> You mention the dowry in your letter. By all the gods I call upon you to take up the whole matter and protect her, who is made wretched by my fault and negligence, by means of my resources, if I have any, or by your funds, if it is not a nuisance to you. I beg you not to allow her to be in need of everything, as you write she is. On what expenses are the profits from my estates going? Those 60,000 sesterces you mention – nobody ever told me they were deducted from the dowry; I would never have allowed it. But these are trivial examples of the wrongs which have been done to me; I am prevented by pain and tears from writing to you about them.
>
> (*A* 11.2/212.2, Epirus, middle of March 48)[101]

The 60,000 sesterces are a mystery. Presumably, Cicero thought they had been deducted by Philotimus (possibly on Terentia's instructions) from the first payment of dowry to Dolabella's agents on 1 July 49.[102] If this was money Cicero had promised, his honour would be compromised. If Terentia had promised part of the dowry from her own resources[103] and then kept back 60,000, it would be more comprehensible. The problem does not seem to have been only about the shortfall in the dowry. Tullia was actually in want. It seems that Dolabella was not maintaining her. In later times at least, it was *expected* that a husband would maintain his wife by using the income from her dowry, though he was not legally compelled to do so.[104] It seems likely, as Suzanne Dixon has argued,[105] that since 49 Cicero himself had been making his daughter an allowance for living expenses.[106] Such arrangements were sometimes made through contracts between a wife's family and her husband, as the later jurists tell us. If we suppose that Tullia lived mostly in a house belonging to Dolabella (possibly rent free),[107] then 60,000 might actually represent this allowance. Marcus, who had to rent a house, was later allowed 80,000 when he was a student in Athens (p. 139).

Cicero was also afraid that the house in Rome was threatened in some way and that he was a special target.[108] But Dolabella, probably under Caesar's instructions, wrote him a reassuring letter of 'scrupulously respectful and courteous tone'.[109] He was able to tell him that Tullia was well, though Terentia had not been, but was now better. Addressing Cicero affectionately, he found it his obligation as a member of the family (*pie*) to suggest that he (Cicero) had done enough for duty and his friendship with Pompey (who had now lost Spain and was besieged in his camp) and that he could honourably leave him, perhaps retire to Athens or some other quiet place, and hope that Caesar would protect his status. Despite the siege, Dolabella's messenger got through and was ordered to bring back a reply.[110] None survives. A few weeks later, Cicero wrote to Atticus in Rome. Atticus had asked what Cicero wanted done about the second dowry instalment. Both alternatives were dangerous: to hand over such a large sum at a difficult time; or to break off the relationship with Dolabella when his interest with Caesar might be vital. Atticus had certainly mentioned the possibility of a rupture, if he did not recommend it. Cicero left a decision to Atticus and to Tullia's wishes and judgement. Atticus had apparently told Cicero that he was not a special target, but Cicero was still worried about matters which he could have avoided, but which would be made less serious by Atticus' careful administration. 'Take care especially, as you say in your letter, in all things and make provision that she about whom you know I am most wretched lacks nothing' (A 11.3/213.3, Pompey's camp at Dyrrachium, 13 June 48). Another cautious letter, when Cicero says he was ill with anxiety, delegated the management of his affairs to Atticus and left the decision about the dowry to him (A 11.4a/214, Dyrrachium, mid-June 48). In the end, the second instalment was paid and the idea of divorce shelved for the moment.

One of the items about which Atticus was concerned was the sale of some estates, which had not gone through; Cicero was also hoping to buy a farm at Frusino near Arpinum. He asks Atticus to arrange for Tullia's maintenance. Still harping on what had gone wrong, he wishes he had talked to Atticus instead of writing – he means in the winter and spring of 49.[111] The same day he wrote to Terentia. It is a short and chilly letter, even if we take into account the need for discretion when his letters had to pass through a war zone:

> *To his family, greetings*[112]
>
> We do not often have anyone to whom we may give a letter and we have nothing we want to write about. From the last letter I have received from you [singular], I learned that it has not been possible to sell any farm. So please consider [plural] how the one whom you [plural] know I want to pay may be paid. You say our daughter is thanking you. I am not surprised that you deserve that she should thank you as you deserve. Do push Pollex [a courier] off as soon as possible if he has not already set out.
> Take care of your health.
> (*F* 14.6/158, Pompey's camp, 15 July 48)

Terentia was given the responsibility of raising money on Cicero's behalf, from which he could pay Dolabella. Terentia had clearly helped Tullia in some way, perhaps by contributing to the second instalment of the dowry or perhaps by paying debts.[113] There is no irony in Cicero's lack of surprise: he knew Terentia loved her daughter and would do her duty by her.[114] But he might have felt sore about her generosity, when he had made a muddle of his resources.

Pompey forced Caesar to abandon the siege and the war now moved to Thessaly, where Caesar defeated Pompey at Pharsalus on 9 August. Marcus did well as a cavalry officer: he could ride and throw the javelin well and was considered tough.[115] He must have trained hard in Rome and Cilicia and Galatia, but we hear nothing of it. Caesar promised an amnesty to Pompeians who asked for mercy. Cicero had not been in the battle but had been left behind at Dyrrachium. He refused to take command of the Pompeians there and went first to Patrae (where he had friends). During this period, Terentia and he must have discussed the results of the Pompeian defeat by letter. Perhaps Marcus' record gave her some satisfaction. Dolabella, on Caesar's behalf, had asked Cicero to return to Italy.[116] At Patrae, he and Quintus quarrelled: the Quinti decided to make a separate peace with Caesar.[117] Cicero and Marcus reached Brundisium about the middle of October and probably rented a house there. As Cicero claimed later to his friend M. Marius, he wanted to be with his own people and things.[118] But there was to be no reunion yet with his wife and daughter. Cicero and Marcus could not return to Rome because the war was still on. Although they had friends in Brundisium, the bustling port would not be a congenial residence.

The function of Dolabella as an intermediary points up the impact of civil war on family life. Terentia and Tullia could worry about the safety of Cicero and Dolabella at the front. Terentia might pray for victory for her husband's side and Tullia be torn between hopes for her husband's success and the boost a Caesarian victory would give to his future career and hopes for her father and old friends who were with Pompey. There could be no entirely happy outcome. Since the headquarters of both sides were in Greece, the women could do little to ensure safety for the husband who turned out to be on the losing side. Terentia probably took care to maintain contact with Caesar's consular colleague, P. Servilius Isauricus (who might be approached through his wife Junia and mother-in-law Servilia) and, after Pharsalus, when, probably in October, Caesar was named dictator for twelve months, with his Master of the Horse and deputy in Italy, M. Antonius.

10 Three divorces, a wedding, a funeral and a baby

It was a sad homecoming to Italy. For those who had stayed behind, the situation was no happier. Terentia and Tullia had spent the last year waiting for news from the war, in a Rome thinly populated by men of rank, relying on the companionship of Atticus and Pilia. Terentia had the familiar burden of keeping the family property going. Just as Terentia had been a semi-detached wife during Cicero's exile and governorship, so now both were living apart from their husbands. Terentia, as the wife of a Pompeian, had to worry that her property might be confiscated (*A* 11.9/220.3, Brundisium, 3 Jan. 47). Tullia, although her husband came back safe in the autumn of 48, was to be troubled by his behaviour in Italy the following year.

During Cicero's stay at Brundisium, October 48 to September 47

For now, contact was through letters. Pompey had been defeated and was later killed, Cicero was heartsore about the loss of many old friends and worried about what Caesar would do to him. The most painful of his griefs was the bitter quarrel which had arisen between him and the Quinti. In October 48 Cicero and Marcus landed at Brundisium, with no wife, mother or sister to greet them. Since the calendar was about three months ahead of the real season, the heat and dust of summer might well help deter Terentia and Tullia from undertaking the journey. The extant correspondence resumes in early November. Cicero had apparently written to Terentia to inform her of their safe arrival. He was clearly depressed, especially by the quarrel with Quintus.

> You write that you are glad we have returned safely to Italy: I hope you will always be glad of it. But disturbed by mental agony and the great injuries done me by <my family>[1] [possibly the Quinti], I am afraid we have adopted a plan which we shall have difficulty disentangling. So, help me, as far as you can; but I have no idea what you can do. It is no good you getting on the road at this time. The journey is a

long one and the road unsafe, and I do not know what good you can do if you come.
Farewell.

(F 14.12/159, Brundisium, 4 Nov. 48)

Allowance must again be made in the letters of this period for the uncertainties of the mail. Cicero was constantly worried about how to arrange for his letters to be delivered. His own resources were not what they had been and travel in time of civil war was much more difficult. He can hardly ever have been sure that the messenger was trustworthy or would get through. So his letters needed to be discreet. This letter is not overtly affectionate, in contrast to the letters of exile when he was exceptionally emotional, but it reads like an appeal for help, even though he discouraged Terentia from joining him, as she had no doubt offered to do. This was very sensible and considerate in view of the danger and discomfort she would have suffered: she had had rheumatism as a young woman and was now no longer young.[2] It may be that this letter reflects a cooling of his love for his wife. But there are no words of love for Marcus or Tullia either. He had difficulty writing even to Atticus, let alone others; his sickness was physical as well as mental.[3] The major factor is his depression, which made it impossible for him to take decisions, and this affected his relationship not only with Terentia but with Tullia.[4]

By the end of the month, he could write more in his usual style to Atticus about his options and public life. There is a quick, but warmer, note to Terentia:

> In my own sufferings, I am tortured by the illness of our Tullia. There is no need for me to write more to you about her; for I know she is equally of great concern to you. You write that you want me to move closer. I see that it ought to be done and I would have done it already, but many things have prevented me, which have not even now been sorted out. But I am expecting a letter from Pomponius [Atticus], which I should like you to see get delivered to me as soon as possible. Take care that you are well.
>
> (F 14.19/160, Brundisium, 27 Nov. 48)

To Atticus, he wrote about how upset he was to hear that Tullia was ill and weak, but thanked him for taking care of her (A 11.6/217.4, Brundisium, 27 Nov. 48). Tullia and Atticus were presumably in Rome, but Terentia could have been at a villa, from which she would send a bunch of letters. She might have moved closer to Cicero.

By 10 December at the latest, Dolabella must have been back in Rome to enter upon his tribunate. At some point before this, emulating P. Clodius, he had arranged his transition to the *plebs* by getting himself adopted by a plebeian Cornelius Lentulus, so that his name was now (Cornelius)

Lentulus.⁵ Soon after, Cicero wrote to Terentia again, expressing his concern that Dolabella, as well as Tullia, was ill, and asking her to take care of her own health and Tullia's (*F* 14.9/161, Brundisium, 17[?] Dec. 48). This puts Terentia almost certainly in Rome. It also makes one wonder if Tullia and Dolabella were living in Cicero's house. A few days later, a note with the same request accompanied two friends, who had called on him and would report to Terentia about his state of mind (*F* 14.17/162, 23[?] Dec. 48).

Atticus was to work to protect Cicero's reputation for honourable conduct, and Cicero also needed him to stay in Rome because he was being pressed for money, apparently by Tullia's creditors. 'I turn it over to you: find a way out. Just see to it that nothing can get in her way at this time.' He could write no more for weeping, except to thank Atticus for his affection for Tullia (*A* 11.7/218.6, Brundisium, 17 Dec. 48). His fifty-ninth birthday was a sad one, after more revelations about young Quintus' hostility.

> I am oppressed by everything and can scarcely bear it, or rather cannot bear it at all. The culmination of all these miseries is that I shall leave that poor wretched girl despoiled of her father, her paternal inheritance, her whole fortune. So I should indeed like to see you, as you promise. I have no one else to whom I may commend her, since I understand that the same things are being planned for her mother as for me. But if you do not find me, let this recommendation be enough and soften her uncle's heart towards her as much as you can.
> (*A* 11.9/220.3, Brundisium, 3 Jan. 47)

Cicero was expecting confiscation of property. Since his children were presumably in his paternal power, they legally had no property: anything Cicero allowed them to use would be confiscated along with the rest of his property. Terentia's dowry would also be at risk. If her own property was threatened with confiscation, they and the children stood to lose everything. As often, Cicero's fears turned out to be exaggerated, but he might have considered the possibility of transferring one or more of his beloved villas to his daughter (whom he would have had to emancipate, so that she could own them legally). For after her death, when he temporarily felt he did not want possessions, he talked of having no one to whom he could pass them on.⁶ The idea might have looked attractive also in late 46 and early 45, after her divorce.

Although Cicero wrote to Terentia with concern for her, he had little to say. But he tells her, the day after his franker letter to Atticus,

> If you are well, it is good; I am well.
> Although the times are such that there is no reason why I should look forward to a letter from you or write to you myself, yet somehow or other I both look forward to letters from you and write to you when I have someone who will carry a letter.

Volumnia should have been more obliging to you than she was and she could have done what she did do more carefully and cautiously. But there are other things which we are looking after and which give us more pain: these are wearing me out, as those [the Quinti] who forced me out of my own opinion [in 49] wanted. Take care of your health. Farewell.

(*F* 14.16/163, Brundisium, 4 Jan. 47).

This is a fascinating letter for the light it casts on the social interaction of a senator's wife with a woman of the *demi-monde*. For Volumnia must be Volumnia Cytheris, the mistress of M. Antonius. Terentia will have approached her in an attempt to safeguard her property, as Shackleton Bailey suggests (SB *F* i.502), and perhaps to get a better deal for Cicero. Cytheris was the freedwoman of Cicero's friend P. Volumnius Eutrapelus and had been a mime-actress, taking part in farces in which nudity was expected of the female lead. Cicero had perhaps met her already.[7] He had strongly disapproved of the way she accompanied Antonius on an official tour in 49 and still more of the fact that Antonius' mother was expected to put up with her company.[8] If Julia had to travel with Cytheris as if she were her daughter-in-law, it cannot have been social suicide for Terentia to pay a call on her. It should have been a good way to approach the susceptible Antonius.

The lack of caution with which Cicero claims Volumnia had operated makes it possible to suggest that Terentia's intervention is linked with something Antonius did for Cicero that December and which Cicero felt could have been handled more tactfully:

> I have almost been ordered to leave Italy. For Antonius sent me a copy of a letter from Caesar in which he said he had heard that Cato and L. Metellus had returned to Italy with the intention of being openly in Rome. He did not like that . . . Everyone was banned from Italy except those whose case he had heard personally . . . So Antonius wrote to ask me to forgive him and to say that he had to obey the letter. Then I sent L. Lamia to him to prove that Caesar had told Dolabella to write to me telling me to come to Italy as soon as possible and that I had come because of that letter. Antonius then published a decree making an exception of [D.] Laelius and me and publishing our names. I wish he had not: he could have made an exception of a category without naming names.
>
> (*A* 11.7/218.2, Brundisium, 17 Dec. 48)

The edict could have exempted men who had already returned with Caesar's permission, while making it clear that Cato and Metellus were excluded from Italy. It is highly likely that Terentia had helped Cicero in this.

After 19 January 47, there is a gap in the extant correspondence until March. We learn that Terentia was still responsible for getting funds to

Cicero for him to live on. But Atticus was also involved. Cicero writes to his friend to see to the payment of 30,000 sesterces to P. Sallustius, about which he has also written to Terentia. He had borrowed this sum from Cn. Sallustius (probably a brother) and had been using it for his expenses, but it had almost all been spent. The debt was to be settled with funds which Cicero had in Rome. Then Terentia should send her husband more money for his day-to-day expenses in Brundisium. He did not want to borrow there again, as he did not know that ready cash was available in Rome to cover the loan (*A* 11.11/222.2, Brundisium, 8 Mar. 47).[9]

The political and social misconduct of Dolabella made everything worse. He was now tribune and his legislative programme was reminiscent of the policies of Cicero's old enemy Clodius. He was 'distinguishing himself', pressing for abolition of debts and remission of rents on houses.[10] This resulted in armed violence in the city, which Antonius, as Master of the Horse, eventually suppressed with his troops.[11] Cicero was ashamed to show his face with such a son-in-law (*A* 11.14/225.2, Brundisium, April 47). Dolabella's actions added to Cicero's misery about his own position, 'and other things which I cannot write for weeping': Tullia's situation (*A* 11.15/226.3, Brundisium, 14 May 47). Plutarch dates to this period, as the motive for Antonius turning against Dolabella, an alleged affair between Dolabella and Antonius' wife, his cousin Antonia. Cicero's public position later (when he had not publicly broken with Dolabella) was that this was a mere pretext which Antonius put forward for a cruel divorce of an innocent wife, when he had already decided whom to marry next.[12] If Plutarch was merely inventing a plausible context,[13] then neither alleged adultery nor Antonius' divorce is closely dated. We can only put the remarriage to Fulvia some time between 47 and 45 and the divorce shortly before.[14]

Relations between Terentia and Cicero were now further complicated by the former decision to make her will.[15] As a woman, she must have gone through a legal procedure (*coemptio*) in order to have the right to make a will and she would need her guardian's consent.[16] These formalities would present no obstacle to Terentia. As a well-organised woman, she had no doubt drawn up a will several times earlier in her lifetime, for instance on her marriage and the birth of her children or on Tullia's marriage. The political situation (and, some think, illness)[17] made it urgent to do so again. She will have drafted it with advice from friends and perhaps her guardian. It would be witnessed by seven adult male citizens. No doubt it included manumissions and legacies to friends or dependants, as well as the vital appointment of a *heres*, heir and executor. It would obviously be dangerous to appoint Cicero if he was threatened by confiscation. And she could not appoint Marcus, a son in paternal power, for property he inherited would belong to his father. So the solution appears to be to choose a friend, and to leave legacies to the children, perhaps on condition that they were out of paternal power. (This would happen on Cicero's death or if he emancipated them.) The political situation seems to have posed problems which necessitated the best legal advice. What Terentia thought best for the children would not easily coincide with Cicero's views. We are hampered because Cicero's letters which mention it did not have to explain things which Atticus knew and we do not. On 3 June, he asked Atticus, if he thought it right and that it was something he could take on, to talk to Camillus and then for both of them to give Terentia some advice about her will. 'The times warn her to see to satisfying those whom she should.[18] There is a report from Philotimus that she is doing some things wickedly. It is scarcely credible, but certainly, if anything can be done, precautions should be taken' (A 11.16/227.5, Brundisium, 12 or 13 June 47). Cicero was probably primarily concerned with the interests of the children. 'Wickedly' must be his interpretation of what Philotimus (in a letter from the East) had said she was doing. But he had learned to be cautious about accepting Philotimus' statements of fact.[19] It was a delicate matter for Atticus and Camillus to intervene, as it would have been for the husband to do it directly. But their expertise in finance and law could be useful. There is no mention of the will, quite properly, in a short note to Terentia despatched the previous day, in which he expressed concern for her health, since he had been informed by letter and word of mouth that she had developed a sudden fever. He thanked her for letting him know about a letter from Caesar[20] and urged her to keep him informed of new developments (F 14.8/164, Brundisium, 2 June 47). She was still working on his behalf. A short follow-up note a few days later wished her recovered strength and asked her to take all necessary steps and keep him informed (F 14.121/165, Brundisium).

Tullia came to stay with Cicero in Brundisium, not just to comfort him. The journey was a long one, but she and Terentia had each managed it on previous occasions. It was now late spring by the true calendar, so travelling conditions must have been reasonably good. Plutarch claims, unconvincingly, that Terentia did not provide her daughter ('a young girl', an obvious exaggeration) with a proper escort or travelling money.[21] Her husband was still in Rome as tribune. Cicero wrote to inform Terentia of her arrival:

> Our Tullia came to me on 12 June. Her outstanding courage [*virtus*] and extraordinary kindliness [*humanitas*] gives me even more grievous pain that by our negligence it has been brought about that her lot is far other than her love [*pietas*] and deserts [*dignitas*] demanded.
> (F 14.11/166, Brundisium, 14 June 47)

He told his wife he was thinking of sending young Marcus to Caesar[22] and promised to tell her if he left Italy. The lack of previous consultation with the boy's mother seems high-handed, but Marcus was of age. Again Cicero expresses concern about her health. Tullia told Cicero of the kindness Atticus had been showing her, but her presence was not the tonic it usually was:

I have not been able to take from her courage, kindliness and love the pleasure I ought to have taken from such an extraordinary daughter. Instead, I have been overcome by unbelievable pain at the realisation that such a human being is condemned to such a wretched lot, and that this happens through no sin of her own, but by my grievous fault.

(*A* 11.17/228, Brundisium, 12 or 13 June 47)

At least part of Tullia's suffering must have been due to Dolabella, whose indebtedness and neglect of her comfort had an impact on her life and of whose political excesses she presumably disapproved. There were other transgressions. Cicero's early reaction to Tullia's presence was to decide that it would be best if she did not stay to grieve together with him, but went back as soon as she was willing (*A* 11.17a/229.1, Brundisium, 14 June 47). The text as emended includes 'to her mother'. It sounds as if Tullia might have been staying with her mother before she came to Brundisium. If so, there are two possible explanations. The first is that the young couple was living with Terentia in the Palatine house. The alternative is that Tullia had separated from Dolabella. In any event, her stay with her father was to be prolonged. This in itself suggests that the marriage was going badly. We do not have to wait long for explicit evidence about it.

A brief note to Terentia sent on 19 June, apart from the usual courtesies about her health, included some information:

We had decided, as I wrote to you earlier, to send Cicero to meet Caesar, but we changed the plan since we got no news of his coming. About the other matters, although there is nothing new, you can find out what we would like and what we think at this time needs to be done from Sicca.[23] I am still keeping Tullia with me.

(*F* 14.15/167, Brundisium)

Cicero continued to blame himself for the mess he had got into by leaving Italy in 49 and then by going back. His political career was in ruins, and this affected the standing of his wife and daughter, and his political decisions and his general negligence of financial matters had completely changed the financial situation and expectations of the family. But the disaster suffered by Tullia, her failed marriage with Dolabella, was not his responsibility. Although it might be considered partly Cicero's fault that he had not seen her married before he left (compulsorily) for Cilicia, Tullia and her mother had chosen Dolabella. It was a poor choice, for reasons which Cicero had seen clearly at the time. Dolabella's track record was bad and he did not change his ways. But Cicero was meticulous in avoiding any flavour of 'I told you so'. He did not exculpate all his family for his own anguish: 'we have brought it all on ourselves by those mistakes and sufferings of mind and body, which I wish those nearest to me [possibly the Quinti] had chosen to heal [rather than making worse]' (*A* 11.25/231.1, Brundisium,

5 July 47). He reminds Atticus about the will and then goes on at once to Tullia's problem:

> Her good nature [*facilitas*] distresses and torments me. I think no human being like her has ever lived.[24] If I can do anything on her behalf, I want you to advise me. I see there is still the same difficulty . . . [text doubtful]. But this gives me more anxiety than everything else. In paying the second instalment [due 1 July 48] we were blind. I wish we had done something else; but the opportunity has passed. I beg you, if from out of the ruin something can be got together, collected and kept safe, from silverware, textiles (of which I have quite a lot), furniture, see to it. It seems to me now that the end is in sight and that there will be no negotiation of peace and that the present set-up will perish even without an enemy. About this too, if you think fit, talk to Terentia at a favourable moment. I cannot write everything.
>
> (*A* 11.25/231.3, Brundisium, 5 July 47)

Politics, in his opinion, were dangerously unsettled and the Caesarians might lose their grip. Perhaps Dolabella was on his way into the political wilderness. Certainly he seems to have been neglecting his moral duties as a husband. For Cicero thought that Tullia was threatened by actual want (as in 48) and it is for this reason that he thought of selling valuables. On the 9th, Cicero summoned up the energy to write two letters, to Terentia and to Atticus, about divorce. The details of his thinking are spelled out in the letter to Atticus, which allows him to be brief and discreet in the letter to his wife:

> I have written to Pomponius [Atticus] what I want decided should be done, later than I should have done. If you have talked to him, you will understand what I want to happen. It is not necessary to write more openly, since I have written to him. I would like you to write to me on that matter and about other matters as soon as possible.
>
> (*F* 14.10/168)

The letter to Atticus mentioned that Camillus had written, saying that Atticus had spoken to him, and that he himself was expecting one from Atticus, although he thought Atticus probably had no information about the will: 'if it is other than it should be, I do not see that it can be altered' (*A* 11.23/232.1, 9 July 47). The date at which the third instalment of Tullia's dowry should have been transferred to Dolabella had just passed. So Tullia's problem called for extended treatment.

> I beg you to think about this poor wretched woman, both the point about which I wrote to you recently, that something should be collected to ward off poverty, and also about the will itself. I wish I had done

something about the other matter [divorce] before, but we were afraid of everything. Indeed the best choice in that appalling situation would have been divorce. We would have done something like men, whether I alleged his policy of the cancellation of debts or the way he breaks into other men's houses at night or Metella or all the evils. The money would not have been lost and we would have shown that we felt manly resentment. I remember your letters of course, but also what the time was like; even so, anything would have been better. Now it looks as if he is giving a warning. For we have heard about the statue of Clodius. To think that my son-in-law of all people should be doing this or cancelling debts! So it seems best to me (and you agree) that notice of divorce should be sent to him. He will perhaps ask for the third instalment. Consider therefore whether notice should be sent when he raises the matter or before.

(*A* 11.23/232.3, Brundisium, 9 July 47)

It is odd that Cicero does not say that Tullia wanted a divorce, but it sounds as if there has been a row with Dolabella which triggered her departure. We have no details on the alleged house-breaking, but Cicero is hinting at rape or seduction. Metella was an aristocratic woman with whom Dolabella was having an affair. She is presumably the wife of the younger Spinther, to be identified as Caecilia Metella, the daughter of Celer (cos. 60) and of the notorious Clodia.[25] Two years later, Cicero was agog to know if a rumour that Spinther was divorcing his wife was correct. It was.[26] She was younger than Tullia; her name was linked with a number of men.[27] She may have helped inspire Dolabella's idea of putting up a statue to her uncle, Clodius, which was a public slap in the face for Cicero, the man Clodius had exiled.

It is this paragraph that Atticus was to communicate, in part, to Terentia. Tullia had probably remained in her father's paternal power, and this would mean that theoretically he could unilaterally bring about a divorce.[28] But, as we have seen, he had earlier left the decision about whether there should be a divorce to her (*A* 11.3/213.1, Pompey's camp at Dyrrachium, 13 June 48). It would, however, no doubt be more comfortable for Tullia, once the decision had been made, for her *pater familias* to make the announcement to Dolabella. In the present circumstances, this means that Tullia, after talking with her father, would decide in principle to divorce. Atticus, in Rome, and Terentia, who might have been somewhere like Tusculum, but anyway closer to Rome than Cicero, would decide the moment for the decision to be put into effect. They would handle the details of timing and finding a messenger, probably a freedman. It is interesting that the decision needed to be made, in effect, by the whole family, in consultation with at least one close friend. (We cannot tell whom Tullia might have consulted among her contemporary men or women friends.) But Cicero immediately got cold feet and told Terentia so:

As to what I wrote in my previous letter about sending notice of divorce, I do not know what power he has at this time and how excited the mob is. If we need to fear his anger, you will remain quiet. Still, perhaps he will raise the matter. You will judge how the whole thing stands and you will do what seems least wretched in these very wretched circumstances.

(*F* 14.13/169, Brundisium, 10 July 47)

Cicero wrote again to Atticus, reminding him he needed to take some precautionary measures (he who had never done so in the past!), no doubt to safeguard his children, in the light of Terentia's plans (*A* 11.19/233.2, Brundisium, 22 July 47). Atticus wrote both to Cicero and to Tullia, advising them not to move against Dolabella. They must have heeded this advice, for nothing was done.[29] Tullia was still in limbo, legally married but not living with her husband and presumably estranged from him. Cicero was saddened by his inability to resent an injury, or even to grieve at it, without risking reprisals by his son-in-law (*A* 11.24/234.1, Brundisium, 6 Aug. 47). He wrote the rest of the letter in his own hand, to keep it confidential. He asked Atticus again to see about the will, as he 'wished' (this verb is plausibly conjectured by Shackleton Bailey) had been done when Terentia first began to enquire about it. She had not consulted either Atticus or Cicero, but now that they had had a talk, Atticus might advise her to entrust it to someone whose fortune was not threatened by the civil war. Cicero himself would choose Atticus for this trust, 'if she [Tullia] would like it', but he had so far hidden his worries from her. 'About the second matter [the selling of valuables], I do know that nothing can be sold at present, but they can be set aside and hidden so that they will escape the ruin which threatens.' Atticus had written that Cicero's property and his own and Terentia's would be available. Cicero believed that Atticus' would be, but not that his and Terentia's could be saved. But he criticised what Terentia herself was doing. 'I omit innumerable other things.' He had a complaint about Terentia's handling of money. Atticus had asked her by letter to exchange 12,000 sesterces, what was left of the money. She sent a written draft for 10,000 and said this was the balance.[30] This was a paltry bit of cheese-paring, but Cicero uses it as evidence of what she might have done with a big sum (*A* 11.24/234.2–3). The passage is eloquent for Cicero's changed attitude towards his wife. In the past he had trusted her to handle his property as well as her own and had even admitted his own negligence and lack of clarity about money matters. Now he could not even give her the benefit of the doubt or conceal his annoyance from Atticus, as conventional etiquette on marital reticence demanded. It is entirely possible that Terentia was being scrupulous in her accounting, especially when we remember the theoretical separation of the property of husband and wife, which made it so difficult to keep accounts straight when they had some life in common, even when they were not in the same house.[31] Cicero might have owed her 2000 sesterces.

Short notes to Terentia on 11 and 12 August tell her, first, that he had not heard anything of Caesar's arrival or the letter which Philotimus was said to be carrying, and, second, that he had received a letter from Caesar, who was said to be arriving sooner than expected (he was still in Asia).[32] Cicero would let her know when he had decided whether to wait for Caesar in Brundisium or go to meet him. Terentia was still helping Cicero. He asked her to send the couriers back as soon as possible and told her that he had had an encouraging letter from Caesar (*F* 14.24/170, 11 Aug. 47; 14.23/171, 12 Aug. 47; both Brundisium). Caesar (writing from Egypt) forgave Cicero and restored him to his position.[33] Cicero continued to ask Atticus to do what he could about the will. On the subject of the cash he needed, he repeated that Terentia had said that she had sent the balance, and said that he would draw on money which Atticus had written about, if he needed to (*A* 11.21/236.1, Brundisium, 25 Aug. 47). Cicero was regretfully expecting that Caesar would come to Rome via Brundisium, which meant that he would have to wait there, which was a pity as the climate was bad and affected his health and Tullia's (*A* 11.22/237.2, 1[?] Sept. 47, Brundisium). Although the whole town had been loyal to Cicero and they had friends there,[34] too many enemies were coming and going through the port in these months. So living there was uncomfortable. But he was expecting Tullia to remain with him. Another note to Terentia promised to send word of his intentions when the couriers returned – he expected them any day – and expressed his unfailing wishes for her health, as all these letters from Brundisium do (*F* 14.22/172, 1 Sept. 47).

Events then moved more rapidly, with a gap in the letters. Caesar landed at Tarentum and Cicero went to meet him. Caesar treated him warmly.[35] Cicero soon got on the road to Rome.

October 47 to February 45

The last extant letter to Terentia is notorious:

> We think we shall reach the villa at Tusculum either on the 7th or the next day. Let everything there be ready. For perhaps there will be several people with us and, I think, we shall stay there some considerable time. If there is no basin in the baths, let there be one; in the same way those other things which are necessary for life and health.[36] Farewell. The Kalends of October, from the territory of Venusia.
>
> (*F* 14.20/173, 1 Oct. 47)

It is short and to the point, with no endearments. If it was written during a rest-stop in open country, that may partly explain the brevity.[37] But a Victorian scholar held that 'a gentleman would write a more civil letter to his housekeeper'.[38] Cicero does not say, as he had done after his exile, that he is looking forward to seeing her. He does not even mention that Tullia was travelling with him, as she probably was. It is fair to see this note as evidence that Cicero had lost his old feelings for his wife. But he still trusted her to administer the staffing, supplying and maintenance of the Tusculan villa, and so presumably of the house and all the other villas. He did not doubt that she, in her usual capable way, would make the arrangements he vaguely specified. If Terentia was awaiting him at Tusculum, there was no open breach between them at this point.

The niggling suspicions about her administration of property may have been a symptom rather than the prime cause of the estrangement. It is quite improper to take Cicero's point of view as a realistic assessment of Terentia's conduct, any more than we can think that we have an objective picture from Cicero of his brother's actions in this same period. Cicero was not in a normal frame of mind.[39] And, in general, it must be an error to accept the portrait that one divorcing partner paints of the other.

It would not be unparalleled for a man who had gone through a gruelling time to think at the age of fifty-nine of making a fresh start.[40] Besides, Roman divorces quite often seem to occur at the end of a separation, such as the husband's foreign posting.[41] But, considering what perplexity he was in about Tullia's marriage, it was hardly sensible to break up his own marriage. Divorces could be arranged relatively easily, since the will of one partner was sufficient. The complications, if any, were in the sorting out of dowry and in damage to reputation or the feelings of children. There was a divorce between Cicero and Terentia, probably late in 47 or early 46.[42] Contemporaries blamed Cicero, so it seems unlikely that Terentia took the initiative, though a bilateral agreement is possible. The reaction of Tullia and Marcus can only be conjectured.

To divorce a wife of long standing who had given a man children was regarded as disgraceful. Antonius, in reply to Cicero's invectives against him in 44, among other things, charged Cicero with having cast out the wife with whom he had grown old; Dio makes the Antonian Fufius Calenus (cos. 47) focus on the fact that she was the mother of his two children.[43] Plutarch says that among the troubles which Cicero brought on himself was his choosing to divorce Terentia, because (Plutarch states these as facts, not as Cicero's allegations) he was neglected by her during the war, so that he went abroad ill-provided and when he returned found her inconsiderate, for she did not go to join him (as we have seen, he told her not to); failed to provide properly for Tullia's journey; and incurred so many debts that she emptied the house in Rome.[44] This last detail could be based on the sale or removal of valuables to safety which Cicero had himself ordered. We have also seen that Cicero was always trying to obtain ready money, sometimes by selling things.[45]

Modern scholars, outdoing Plutarch, often accuse Terentia of avarice and of trying to safeguard her own property at his expense or of being complicit with the dishonest Philotimus, of 'petty embezzlement' and even 'fraudulence'.[46] Balsdon thinks these suspicions are 'fantastic obsessions' of Cicero. Crook defends her against the assumption by editors that Cicero was right to think she was robbing him. 'She was just independent of mind and purpose, and did not always do things exactly as Cicero wanted or take his word for everything.' But how could she have robbed him, when the property of married people was in theory separate? Perhaps because, although they did not have a joint account, they had a 'joint accountant', Philotimus.[47] This certainly suggests why Cicero could think she had robbed him. A political dimension has been suggested. Cicero himself in a letter to Plancius mysteriously accused her of treachery.[48] This may be another of his imaginary fears. Others emphasise Terentia's alleged selfishness and heartlessness.[49] The idea that she was a difficult woman who controlled Cicero goes back to Plutarch.[50]

Terentia, on her part, might fairly have resented Cicero's fecklessness with money and his failure as a politician.[51] She has found some defenders. Luise Neubauer (1909) championed her effectively against her critics. Claassen (1996) dismisses the allegations of sharp practice. There was some reason for Terentia to feel exhausted by Cicero's demands. She may also have thought he threatened her children. By a divorce from Cicero, she would safeguard her property from the threat of confiscation and could live peacefully under Caesar. Perhaps she already owned a house in Rome. It is likely that Cicero took the initiative to divorce and that the reasons by which he defended his action were flimsy. Terentia deserved better of him, but she may have seen some advantages in ceasing to be attached to him and his political fate. As a *vidua* (the word is used both for a divorcée and for a widow: a woman who had been married but now was not), she could act independently and concern herself with her children.

It is not clear where Tullia went in the autumn of 47; perhaps back to her mother. Dolabella went abroad with Caesar after his tribunate ended in December 47.[52] Cicero, on his return, seems to have made Tusculum his base, though he was sometimes in Rome, and to have buried himself in his books.[53] The extant correspondence with Atticus does not resume until spring 46.[54] Cicero was dining out with the conquerors and expecting news about Caesar from Dolabella on his return from Africa (where Caesar had defeated the Pompeians at Thapsus).[55]

On 12 June, he sent Tiro to meet Dolabella, who was to come and stay with him the next day, and Atticus on the 14th. Atticus was thinking about Tullia's problem: whether to divorce. Her options were open (*A* 12.5c/241, Tusculum, 12 June[?] 46). About this time, Cicero was training Dolabella and his fellow-Caesarian A. Hirtius in oratory, while they improved his knowledge of haute cuisine.[56] This gave him some protection.[57] Dolabella also had other intellectual interests.[58] It is possible that Tullia was one of this cultured circle at the villa and that it was there she met her husband. There was some reconciliation, for she conceived a child, who was to be born some time in January 45. If she carried the child to term, he will have been conceived in May at the earliest or mid-June at the latest.[59] Since Dolabella did not come back to the neighbourhood of Rome until mid-June, we can conjecture that Dolabella and Tullia met under her father's auspices at his favourite Tusculan villa and that she had decided against divorce. Their reunion was blessed with startling promptitude.

By summer 46, Tiro was looking after at least some of Cicero's financial affairs.[60] Cicero wrote to him from Tusculum about readying the dining-room in Rome for a planned dinner-party, which would include a certain Tertia.[61] If Cicero would not invite a woman unless he had a hostess,[62] then this means either that Terentia was still the *mater familias* or that Tullia could act as his hostess. Tertia, who is probably Junia Tertia, Cassius' wife, would not accept an invitation if Publilius were invited. He is probably the brother of Cicero's ward Publilia, who was to be his second wife. So this party may fall in the run-up to Cicero's second marriage: he was probably already divorced from Terentia, and Tullia would be the hostess for her contemporary Junia. The latter's attitude may illustrate the bad feeling caused by his divorce. This was not Cicero's only dinner-party in Rome. He had plenty of callers and dinner-guests.[63] Dolabella was with him again, perhaps at Tusculum, and was accompanying him to Rome.[64]

These scattered facts about Cicero's life are all we have to go on in guessing the date of his divorce and second marriage, and Tullia's divorce. On the whole, the conventional view that Cicero and Terentia divorced early in 46 seems likely. It is reasonable to put the divorce of Tullia and Dolabella after Dolabella's second visit and before he went to Spain in November.[65] The motives, on Tullia's side, will be those rehearsed in 47: Dolabella's infidelities, debts and radicalism. He could accuse her of having left him to be with her father, and probably with not having lived with him even when he was in Italy. We do not know if the divorce was consensual.[66] To divorce a pregnant wife might seem perverse by modern standards (and it caused some scandal to Romans), but the pregnant divorcée is almost a commonplace in Roman society.[67] The important thing was that there should be no doubt about paternity. No scandal attaches to Tullia, except for incredible allegations about her relationship with her father, part of the political invective typical of the period (below p. 159).

We do not know what Tullia felt about the end of her marriage.[68] She had been close to deciding on divorce on several occasions and it may be that the brief rapprochement with her husband had shown her that their problems were insurmountable. Whatever the formal position – whether she divorced Dolabella, whether the divorce was consensual or whether he divorced her – she was probably content with it. Perhaps she hoped to find happiness in the love of her father, mother and friends, and in the child who was to come. It would have been legally possible for her to remarry once it was clear that she was carrying Dolabella's child, but there is no suggestion that another marriage was thought of in the few months that remained to her.

Probably some time in summer or autumn 46, Cicero received a consolatory letter from L. Lucceius, mostly about politics, but with some reference to Cicero's domestic problems, which he promised to bear philosophically.[69]

132 *Three divorces, a wedding, a funeral and a baby*

The reference may be to the divorces. Late in the year, Cicero was at his villa at Astura and offered the top floor of his Rome house to Atticus' secretary, since it was not being used.[70] This might suggest a reduction in the household since Terentia had left. After a brief tour of his villas, Cicero was anxious to get back to Tullia, who may have been staying with Pilia and Atticus in Rome.[71] Cicero was already thinking of remarriage for himself and wrote to Atticus about two candidates. The preceding sentence mentions that Postumia, Sulpicius' wife, had been to see Caesonius at his house and Caesonius had written to tell Cicero. Although Caesonius is probably the M. Caesonius who had been praetor with Cicero, he is not attested as an intimate friend, but nevertheless perhaps Postumia was match-making again. Cicero goes on:

> About the daughter of Pompeius Magnus, I wrote back to you to say that I had no idea of doing anything about her at present. But as to the other one whom you mention in your letter, I think you know her personally: I have never seen anything uglier. But I am nearly with you, so we shall talk about this.
> (*A* 12.11/249, 29 Nov.[?; by the sun] 46, but the letter might be considerably earlier)[72]

Pompey's daughter by Mucia, Pompeia, had been married to Faustus Sulla, son of the dictator and Caecilia Metella and twin brother to Milo's wife, Fausta. She had been with her husband during the war in North Africa (after her father's death) along with her two children. When he was killed, she fell into Caesar's hands and he treated her and the children kindly and sent them to her brother in Spain.[73] She was probably still abroad at the time of this letter, and returned to Rome on the defeat of the Pompeians in Spain in the spring of 45.[74] She would have made a suitable wife for Cicero, by birth and connections, as far as we can judge. We can only guess about the identity of the second woman. Another source tells us that Hirtius suggested he might marry his sister, but Cicero (it is said) politely replied that he could not concentrate on a wife as well as on philosophy. The idea of a match with Hirtia fits well with the context of 46, when Cicero was seeing a good deal of Hirtius, but the response perhaps was shaped by the source, which is arguing against marriage, especially for the philosopher.[75] The story is found in a Christian tract and derives – and is probably directly quoted – from Seneca's treatise *On marriage* (below p. 149). Hirtia may have been the 'ugly' woman. Her brother, who had served under Caesar since about 54 (along with Q. Cicero for some of the time), was to hold the consulship of 43. He was a new man, perhaps from Ferentinum, on the *Via Latina* on the way to Arpinum,[76] and was sufficiently distinguished to connect himself by marriage with Cicero. It may be preferable to think that there were at least three possibilities being discussed: Pompeia (mentioned by Atticus, but not in Rome), Hirtia (put forward by her brother) and the second woman mentioned by Atticus. Pompeia and (probably) Hirtia were of child-bearing age.[77]

We get a glimpse of Tullia operating to help her father but also to bestow a favour on someone outside the family, by exploiting a female network. Cicero's friend M. Fabius Gallus wanted to buy the house next to Cicero's in Rome, which belonged to a certain Crassus (or Cassius)[78] but was tenanted by his sister (or half-sister) Licinia. Cicero, who had to go out of town, asked Tullia to do what she could to facilitate the sale.

> When I got back, I asked my Tullia what she had done. She said she had taken the matter up with Licinia, but I don't think Crassus sees much of his sister, and she had said that she didn't dare move house in the absence of her husband [Dexius] (who has gone to Spain) and without his knowledge.
> (F 7.23/209.4, to Fabius Gallus, Rome, Dec. 46)

This was not one of Tullia's successes, but it nicely illustrates negotiation between women and some unsurprising limits which applied to another lone *mater familias*, Licinia. The text also provides an example of a husband who was on active service and did not have a house of his own available to him and his wife in Rome, which might have been Dolabella's situation.

Cicero had his mind on what should have been a more important matter. We do not really know when he married again, though December 46 has been suggested.[79] It came between November 46 (but only if A 12.11/249 belongs to November) and Tullia's death in February 45.[80] Cicero received felicitations from Cn. Plancius on his new marriage. Plancius (who had protected Cicero during his exile) was a Pompeian living in exile in Corcyra: as when he wrote to other exiles, Cicero is tactfully gloomy about the situation at Rome:

> I know that your congratulations and best wishes on what I have done are sincere. But at such a wretched time I would not have made any new plans had I not found on my return that my domestic affairs were no better than those of the commonwealth. There were those to whom my welfare and fortunes should have been very dear because of the undying benefits I had conferred on them. But I saw that because of their wickedness there was no safety for me within my house-walls, no place free of plots. So I thought I should defend myself by the loyalty of new relationships against the treachery [*perfidia*] of old ones.
> (F 4.14/240.3, cf. 1, to Plancius, Rome, winter of 46/5[?])

Cicero's suspicions of treachery are unconvincing and his sharing of them with Plancius is unworthy if he means to blame Terentia, as 'the treachery of old' relationships suggests.[81] The reference to 'benefits' fits political 'friends' better than his wife. So he probably means that she was having too much to do with people indebted to Cicero who were now merely pretending to support his full restoration and that therefore there was plotting and treachery in the house.

His new wife was named Publilia, a girl young enough to be his granddaughter. Scholars guess she was fourteen or fifteen.[82] She is often said to have been his ward.[83] This would suggest that he was a friend of her dead father, but the sources do not make the position entirely clear: 'The girl was extremely rich and Cicero had been left as heir in trust and looked after her property' (Plut. *Cic.* 41.3); 'You took as your second wife a virgin, though you were an old man, so that you could pay your debts out of her property' (Dio 46.18.3, speech of Calenus). Plutarch's text might refer to a trust, *fideicommissum*, by which her father left property to Cicero on the understanding that he would turn it over to her. The reason for this would be that the father was in the top property class and forbidden by law from making a woman his heir.[84] Such trusts were unenforceable in law at this period. Moral obloquy could be poured on men who disregarded their obligations. The Dio text fits guardianship better than trusteeship: the implication might be that Cicero, as guardian, authorised dowry which he could use as husband and also, by becoming Publilia's husband, avoided rendering account of his financial decisions as guardian. But the invective is meant to make Cicero's behaviour suspicious, not to supply historical fact, so it should not be pressed. Plutarch's first sentence is more factual and might derive from Tiro and so deserve some credence.

Her father was probably an M. Publilius.[85] The Publilii had held high office centuries back, but produced nobody of political importance in Cicero's time. She had a mother still living, whose name is unknown, and there was a man called Publilius who was probably her brother (but could be an uncle). He was invited to the sealing of Cicero's will.[86] Terentia apparently contradicted Cicero's story of the reasons for their divorce and said that he wanted to marry again (as Cicero's second marriage tended to confirm) and had fallen for Publilia's beauty. Tiro, in his writings, defended Cicero against this discreditable charge and argued that he had a sound reason: he married Publilia for her wealth, in order to pay his debts.[87] This citation of Tiro immediately precedes the sentence quoted above and is followed by the further statement that because Cicero owed 'tens of thousands', he was persuaded by his friends and family to marry the girl despite his age and to free himself from his creditors by means of her property. Although Cicero needed to repay Terentia's dowry and could use Publilia's for the time being to do so, he does not seem to have been in particular financial difficulty at this point and was expecting to get Tullia's dowry back. But still, allegations of gold-digging would stick. There was a good deal of criticism too about his choosing, at sixty, a virgin bride. He retorted coarsely, 'She'll be a grown-up woman tomorrow'.[88] When an old man married a very young wife, unfavourable comment was likely. When Pompey in 52, at the age of about fifty-four, married Cornelia (daughter of the polyonymous, well-born and well-reputed Q. Caecilius Metellus Pius Scipio Nasica), who was the young, beautiful and learned (but still agreeable) widow of P. Crassus, some people said she would have been a better match for one of his sons.[89] Cicero reached sixty in January 46.[90] As for political motives, Publilia may have had Caesarian connections:[91] Cicero hints that she helped him strengthen his position. There may well be something in Terentia's view that he was attracted to her personally – at least for a short time. We have seen that he weighed the attractions of other candidates, but at that time Publilia was not even in the running. Perhaps he met her for the first time – or for the first time since his return to Rome – late in 46 and was strongly attracted to her youth and beauty, so that he was ready to disregard the inevitable gossip about his infatuation, mercenary motives and decrepitude. He may also have hoped for more children.

Publilia's mother and Publilius were presumably influenced above all by Cicero's status and possessions. Perhaps they thought he would be kind to Publilia in a fatherly way.

In 46/5 Cicero was 'picking up the threads of his old life', deep in reading and writing about philosophical and rhetorical topics.[92] The outcome of the war was still dubious. He was writing supportive, sometimes humorous letters to a number of Pompeians who had not returned to Rome and taking a kindly interest in their families. In the winter, he was staying in Rome, waiting for Tullia's baby to be born. He wrote to a former Cilician officer of his, telling him nothing about the baby, but saying that, although Tullia seemed to have regained her strength, he was still kept in Rome because he needed to get Dolabella's agents to pay the first instalment of the dowry.[93] The etiquette of what it was proper to mention is not what we might have expected, especially in a letter which has kind remarks about the correspondent's small son.[94] Tullia's child was also a son and was born safely, some time in January. Asconius (5C) tells us the birth took place at Dolabella's house, but he does not mention the divorce, so he may be making an assumption. It is more likely that the baby was born at Cicero's house.[95] The later legal rules required a pregnant divorcée to notify her ex-husband of her pregnancy within thirty days of the divorce. He then had three options: to repudiate the child; to send guards to watch over his ex-wife (this suggests she would not be in his house), keeping his options open; or to do nothing (which would mean he would be obliged to acknowledge the child).[96] There seems to be no need in the present context for any such suspicions or precautions. Tullia's pregnancy would have been obvious before the divorce if it took place shortly before Dolabella left. The baby was called after Dolabella and presumably recognised, by letter, as Dolabella's younger son. Tullia, probably some weeks later, was taken to the villa at Tusculum to convalesce. She died there in February, no doubt of complications. We do not know where she was cremated (perhaps in Rome) or where the ashes were deposited. She was perhaps thirty-two.

March 45 to December 44

There are no letters to Atticus in December, January (both Cicero and Atticus were in Rome) and February. The correspondence resumes on 7 March, when Cicero had hidden himself away at Astura. So we have no details on Tullia's illness and death. Cicero grieved long and sincerely.

> In wanting me to recreate myself from this grief, you are my constant friend as ever. You can bear witness that I have not failed myself. When I was at your house I read everything that anyone has ever written on how to diminish grief. But all consolation is defeated by pain. I have, however, done something which no one ever did before me. I have consoled myself through writing. I will send you the book, if the clerks have copied it. I can tell you that there is no consolation like it. I write for days at a time, not that I get any good by it, but for the moment I am distracted – not, of course, enough (for intense feeling presses on me), but I find release and I do my utmost to repair not my mind but my countenance itself, if I can. When I do this, I sometimes think I am doing wrong [*peccare*] and sometimes that I would be doing wrong if I did not do it. The solitude helps me a little, but it would be much better for me if you were here. This is the only reason I have to leave here, for it is all right considering the bad circumstances. But that too gives me pain. You cannot be the same towards me. For the things you loved have perished.
> (*A* 12.14/251.3, Astura, 8 March 45)

He was unable to stop memories crowding in on his mind.[97] The last thing which made life worth living had gone.[98] He found some comfort in planning to build a shrine to her memory.[99] He saw this as something he owed to her. It was to be a shrine (*fanum*), intended to attract visitors, not a tomb, and was to secure a deification (*apotheosis*).[100] In the end, after weeks of discussion of possible sites, the scheme came to nothing.[101]

Cicero's friends sent letters of consolation, of which one from Ser. Sulpicius Rufus (father of one of the potential suitors of 51) survives.[102] He claimed to be deeply grieved himself, but attempted to offer comfort by reminding Cicero that the loss of a child should make little difference to one who had already lost things equally dear: country, honour, status, offices. But Cicero might be thinking of what *she* had lost.[103] People who died at the present time were lucky.

> What could she look for, what hope, what solace for her heart? That she might live her life married to some first-class young man? Did you have the chance of choosing a son-in-law from the present generation of young men worthy of your status, to whose good faith you would think it safe to entrust your children? Or so that she might give birth to children whom she might rejoice to see flourishing, who would be able

> to hold property handed down by their parent, who might seek offices in due order and enjoy their freedom in public life and in the affairs of their friends?
>
> (F 4.5/248.3)

After thinking about the destruction of cities and the shattering effect of the civil wars on the Empire, he reminds the grieving father that Tullia had to die some time:

> Remember . . . that she lived as long as she needed to. She lived while the commonwealth was alive; she saw you, her father, praetor, consul and augur; she was married to first-class young men; she enjoyed almost all good things; when the commonwealth died, she departed from life . . . If those in the underworld have any sensation, she, with that love [*amor*] she bore you and her affection [*pietas*] for all her family, would not want you to do this [mourn extravagantly].
>
> (F 4.5/248.5, 6)

Sulpicius, who may not have known Tullia well, thinks of her vicarious happiness in the public life of her father or the success and prosperity of the children she might have had in more settled times. Her happiness in marriage, as far as he could assess it, would depend entirely on the status of her husband. It would of course have been inappropriate to allude to the fact that she was divorced from two of her husbands, but he steers clear of any personal remark, apart from the reference to her affection for her family. Cicero was able to turn the philosophical arguments back against him: he was especially unfortunate because, unlike famous fathers who had lost sons (he had been studying the literature of consolation), he could not console himself with public life.[104]

> The one solace I had left has been snatched from me. My thoughts were not distracted by the affairs of my friends nor by taking care of the commonwealth; it did not please me to do anything in the Forum; I could not bear to look at the Senate-house; I thought – and I was right – that I had lost all the fruits of my hard work and good fortune. But when I realised that I shared this with you and some others and when I broke myself in and forced myself to bear this tolerantly, I had a person with whom I could take refuge, with whom I could find repose, in whose conversation and sweetness [*suavitas*] I laid aside all cares and pains.
>
> But now with this deep wound, even those things which seemed to have healed have broken open again. For then, when I came back miserable from public life, a home welcomed me and cheered me. But now when I grieve, I cannot take refuge from my home in public life and find repose in its good things. So I am absent both from home and

Forum, because my home cannot now console me for the grief I feel about the commonwealth, nor can the commonwealth console me for my private grief.

(F 4.6/249/.2–3, Atticus' villa near Nomentum, mid-April 45)

The egocentrism of this passage is dictated by Cicero's need to respond to what Sulpicius had said: we cannot 'exclude with assurance more altruistic feelings, perhaps more embarrassing to express'.[105] Sulpicius was not an intimate friend like Atticus, to whom Cicero could reveal his deeper affections. But the sketch of Tullia, as far as it goes, is consistent with the accounts of the pleasure Cicero took in her company which he gave to Atticus when she was alive, of the sweetness of her nature and the strength he derived from her support and advice. It gives us a partial picture of her relationship with her father, not the full account of her life and character which we would like to have. Lacey's summing-up, 'Few daughters have had a finer epitaph',[106] seems over-generous: although most Roman tombstones would conventionally express little more than recognition of a woman's dutiful affection for her family, while listing her name and perhaps those of husband or children, some give as much sense of her individuality as this and others go much further on her life, virtues and actions, though the *Eulogy of 'Turia'* was unique.

By March, Cicero was able to take care of routine business. Some of this concerned Terentia. She had been criticising the way Cicero had handled the ceremony of the sealing of his will. She did not like his choice of witnesses and perhaps felt she should have been invited to the ceremony. Cicero defends himself and criticises her own procedure. His mind had been on more important matters than which seven men should have the honour of setting their seals to the document and whom it would be polite to ask to the party. This seems to be a very recent will, made necessary by the birth of his grandson and the death of his daughter. If the baby had been his son's child and young Marcus and the baby had been in Cicero's paternal power, they would have had an automatic claim on his estate. But as the child was his daughter's, he had no claim. So it was important that Cicero mention him and arrange for him to inherit something. Cicero was prepared to let anyone, including Terentia, see the contents of the will: they would see that he could not have paid the child more honour than he had.[107] Terentia may also have changed her will from the one which had been discussed earlier. Her ex-husband seems to hint that Terentia should also name the grandson in her will.

Cicero was conscientious, if prickly, in his treatment of Terentia and was anxious that her dowry should be duly returned to her as his duty (*officium*) required. Some people thought that this would also facilitate some advantage to young Marcus which his mother might confer, but Cicero did not rely on this. Atticus would deal with the dowry.[108] This matter recurs.[109] Cicero wanted to have a clear conscience.[110] Atticus tried to get Cicero to take more part in the matter, perhaps by seeing Terentia, but he shrank from this and left the job to Atticus: 'Those are the wounds which I cannot handle without groaning with pain'.[111] The reference to his pain suggests that the breakdown of his marriage (however much he blamed his wife) grieved him. He was genuinely anxious to pay Terentia.[112] Cicero was still trying to repay her out of money paid by his own debtors (who included Dolabella) in the last letter we have to Atticus.[113] A payment was due to be made on 1 January 43: Cicero urged his agents to see to it.[114] Presumably this payment was made. The letters to fellow-politicians written in 43 contain little that is personal. Cicero's family disappears from the record in the last months of his life.

Terentia too did her duty. Marcus' allowance came from the rent of some flats (which in 44 yielded 80,000 sesterces) on the Aventine Hill and the Argiletum (the road running through the Subura to the Forum), which Terentia had apparently made over to Cicero out of her dowry.[115] This transfer was perhaps made for the sake of her son, although when he first mentions the property Cicero implies it is his own (as it would be in law, since Marcus was a son-in-power). Unless Terentia alone had been responsible for the divorce or it had been written into their original marriage contract, Cicero would have no right to claim a fraction (later it was one-sixth) of the dowry for each of the children, and by the time we hear of this property Tullia was dead. It seems probable that the transfer was part of an amicable arrangement. In fact, Terentia was taking seriously her duty to contribute to the prosperity of her surviving child. Just as Cicero took it for granted that his property was held as if in trust for his children,[116] so it was natural for a mother to endow a child even during her lifetime.

Tullia's baby was known as Lentulus (his father's new name). Cicero wrote to Atticus: 'I should like you some time, when it is convenient to you, to visit baby Lentulus and choose slaves, as you think fit, from the staff and assign them to him'.[117] It sounds as if the baby was at Cicero's villa at Tusculum (rather than in his house in Rome, where it would have been easy for Atticus to drop in), for it appears the baby is in the same place as the household slaves, who seem to be Cicero's own, perhaps including those who had loved and served Tullia.[118] A wet-nurse (unless Tullia suckled him herself as long as she could) and other staff must have been found for him at birth. These are extra attendants of some sort, perhaps a doctor or a male *paedagogus*, for instance, or child companions, and possibly they are to be transferred to the baby's ownership.[119] In any case, we see Cicero taking a close interest in the baby's welfare. There is a follow-up letter thanking Atticus for visiting him and asking him to assign whichever servants and as many of them as he decides.[120] Unhappily, this is the last mention of the child, who probably died in infancy.

Dolabella and Cicero continued on friendly terms.[121] There was some natural sympathy between them. Cicero made one of his appalling jokes about Dolabella, who was a short man, perhaps when seeing him off on campaign in 47 or 46: 'Who has tied my son-in-law to that sword?'[122] Their normal relations had included such favours as Dolabella's obtaining Roman citizenship from Caesar for a friend of Cicero and helping a Pompeian secure a pardon.[123] They were both friends of the scholarly but disreputable Nicias of Cos.[124] After Dolabella went to Spain in 46, Cicero sent him a letter of recommendation for clients of his own, in which he referred politely to the affection Dolabella had always shown to him.[125] After the divorce, Cicero continued to send him letters full of gossip and jokes and to assure him of his affection.[126] Cicero also wrote a letter to Dolabella,[127] who was expected back from Spain after Caesar's victory, talking of his suffering over Tullia's death and telling him his arrival would be a comfort, though he would miss Cicero's cheerfulness and charm.[128] When Dolabella arrived at Tusculum, they had a long and affectionate talk.[129] He even wanted Cicero to dedicate a book to him.[130] Other visits were planned.[131] Dolabella was a useful ally among Caesar's followers.[132] When Dolabella became consul in place of the murdered Caesar, Cicero soon found his administration worth praising to Atticus and to his face.[133] But their private relationship was soured by Dolabella's dishonourable failure to pay back the dowry. In late 44, Cicero was ready to shame him publicly and to show the world that his estrangement was on patriotic as well as personal grounds.[134] For Dolabella had abandoned the Ciceronian line of defence of the commonwealth. He went off to the East as governor of Syria and on the way tortured and murdered the tyrannicide C. Trebonius. The Senate and Cicero repudiated him: his vices were revealed and he had become an enemy of his country. Cicero was ashamed that he had once belonged to his family.[135] Dolabella was besieged at Laodicea by Cassius and committed suicide in 43.

As *pater familias*, Cicero could, with his daughter's consent, claim back the dowry he had given.[136] Dolabella was expected to pay it back by instalments. It is hardly surprising to see that he suffered no penalties for his misconduct such as the law would (later at least) have allowed Tullia's *pater familias* to claim, for instance immediate repayment of the whole dowry.[137] The matter was settled informally. Cicero could not afford to offend his ex-son-in-law. But the gentleman's agreement did not work well. Cicero expected payments.[138] We do not know that any came through.[139] In 44 the new consul was in debt to Cicero for an instalment due on 1 January and, as far as we know, never paid it.[140] Cicero's attitude went from irritation to indignation.

When Tullia died, Cicero could not bear to be with his new wife. Gossip alleged that she seemed pleased at the death of her stepdaughter.[141] Her relationship with Tullia, so much older than herself and so much loved by Cicero, could not have been easy. She may have felt some relief and, in his oversensitive state, Cicero saw that she could not enter fully into his grief. In the midst of all Cicero's preoccupations at Astura (including the departure of Marcus for a student-life in Athens), Publilia decided she ought to come and see him. They had been apart for well over a month.

Three divorces, a wedding, a funeral and a baby 141

I am writing this in my own hand. Please see what ought to be done. Publilia has written to me that her mother has <talked>[142] to Publilius <and> will come to me with him <to talk to me> and that she will come with them, if I permit. She beseeches me at length and like a suppliant to allow her to come and to write back to her. You see what a nuisance it is. I have written back that I am grieving even more now than when I said to her that I wanted to be alone. So, I said, I did not want her to come to me at this time. I thought if I did not reply that she would come with her mother. Now I think she will not. For it was clear that the letter was not her own. I want to avoid what I see will happen, that they [Publilius and the mother] will come to me, and the only way of avoiding it is for me <to get out of here>. I do not want to, but I shall have to. So what I am asking you to do now is to find out how long I can stay here without being caught. You will do it 'with restraint', as you say in your letter.

(*A* 12.32/271.1, Astura, 28 Mar. 45)

But Atticus could not get firm information, so Cicero decided to leave Astura and go to Atticus' villa outside Rome on the *Via Nomentana*, at Ficulea.[143] Later he returned to Astura (2–15 May) and then went to Tusculum (17 May–21 June), Arpinum (22 June–6[?] July), Tusculum (7 July onwards). Some time during this period, he seems to have sent notice of divorce to Publilia.[144] This, and perhaps the death of his grandson, will have made a new will necessary. Cicero thought of seeing to it in Rome on 15 July, but then decided to postpone it for a couple of days.[145] He may also have had to discuss other arrangements about Publilia. He later wrote to Atticus from Astura saying he did not want to return to Rome before 5 September, but that Atticus could deal with Publilius in his absence. He wondered what people were saying about his divorce and reckoned it had been only an ephemeral piece of scandal (*A* 13.34/350, Astura, c. 26 Aug. 45). The following year, while Publilius was behaving evasively with Atticus, Cicero's old friend Caerellia came to Pompeii as an envoy from him and his mother, to ask Cicero something, perhaps to take Publilia back. He replied that it was impossible and he did not wish it.[146] She did not seem upset by the failure of her mission. Nor was Cicero. He had treated his young wife cruelly: no excuse is possible.

Another woman was apparently making overtures to Atticus with a view to marrying Cicero, who happened to have praised her in the hearing of her three sons and of Attica. Atticus had apparently twitted him with being too attractive, but Cicero reckoned old age should protect him from enterprising women.[147] Cicero had apparently received Publilia's dowry as a down-payment on the marriage (not delayed until the first wedding anniversary or paid in instalments). He was therefore morally obliged to pay it back with the least possible delay. We find he paid 200,000 sesterces of what was still outstanding to Publilius and was paying the remainder by a draft, perhaps post-dated.[148] Cicero was anxious to get this cleared up quickly, as he was leaving Italy – or so he thought (*A* 16.6/414.2, Vibo, 25 July 44). Fortunately, Cicero's cash flow must have been much improved by inheritances, including a substantial one from Cluvius in August 45,[149] but there was a continuing problem with getting his debtors (including Dolabella) to pay on time. So Publilia's brief and mistaken marriage was over.

11 Death and survival

Terentia

After the business of reorganising family property as a result of the divorce, we hear very little of Terentia's life. She must have had somewhere to live. Possibly she already owned a suitable house in Rome. Like Cicero, she might see her capital increased. When the banker M. Cluvius of Puteoli died, leaving Cicero, Caesar and others as heirs to his substantial fortune, he left Terentia a sizeable legacy, 50,000 sesterces. This legacy and expenses for his tomb were to be paid for out of the share left to T. Hordeonius, one of the co-heirs and executors, not from Cicero's share. Cicero found out these facts from Balbus (*A* 13.46/338.3, Tusculum, 12 Aug. 45). It is interesting to see a friend of Cicero deciding to benefit Terentia also.[1] Cluvius must have known her and perhaps made the bequest because of the divorce. The inheritance from Cluvius alerts us to the fact that she may have received other legacies from clients or friends of Cicero of which we know nothing. It would have been a suitable recognition for favours she may have done them as hostess or intermediary. Other bequests may have come to her quite independently of Cicero's contacts.

There is another suggestive item. The *Suda*, an encyclopedia in Greek composed in the late tenth century AD but based on scholarship in earlier compilations, preserves the information that a distinguished grammarian owed his Roman citizenship to Terentia. He was a Phoenician called Diocles, captured in war (probably that between Caesar and Pompey), who became the slave of a freedman of Caesar in Rome and was taught by Licinius Tyrannio of Amisus, who had, among other things, been the tutor of young Q. Cicero. Once he was trained, his owner gave him as a present to Terentia, 'the wife of Cicero'. (Our authority could have been mistaken on the identity of the wife, but the dates probably fit.) There is no hint of why he did this. Terentia then freed him. Diocles taught a school, taking the name of his teacher Tyrannio, and wrote learned works.[2] Terentia no doubt took a share of the profits of the school. It is unsurprising to us that Cicero had learned freedmen (Tiro, perhaps the poet Laurea) and employed the learned freedmen of others (M. Pomponius Dionysius, the elder Tyrannio).[3] But it is a surprise that Terentia was the patroness of Terentius Tyrannio. Many modern scholars have supposed that she was incapable of sympathising with her husband's literary interests.[4] Elizabeth Rawson more justly says, 'there is no indication that she cared for poetry or philosophy'.[5] But this is an argument from silence. Terentia is not said to have been highly educated like Cornelia, wife of the cultivated P. Crassus and later of Pompey, but she was probably at the normal level for a woman of at least equestrian family, and she had been exposed to some literary society in her own home and when she dined out with her husband (even though she did not share the evening meal with him all the time). For what it is worth, Jerome and perhaps Seneca thought she had drunk in philosophy from Cicero (below p. 149). If a freedman of Caesar gave her a scholar as a present, he must have thought the gift would be welcome. This suggests he thought Terentia had some literary interests. It also suggests that she was worth courting, even by a dependant of the dictator. It is a pity that we cannot date the gift precisely, whether Caesar was still alive and whether Terentia was still the wife of Cicero.[6]

Terentia was a spectator of the shocking political events of 44/3. As a woman who had been concerned with politics all her adult life, she must have been keenly interested, especially as she had a son who aimed at a political career. Marcus was now in Athens studying rhetoric and philosophy. In late summer 44 Cicero had thought of going on a private visit to Athens, to see Marcus and attend the Eleusinian Mysteries, with the additional cover of the legateship granted him by Dolabella.[7] But he came back in order to lead what he saw as the fight for the Republic, against the consul Antonius.[8] The series of speeches in which he attacked Antonius and tried to strengthen the resolution of the Senate, and the huge number of letters in which he co-ordinated the support of the generals, made any reconciliation with Antonius impossible when fortunes changed. For Antonius, on the run after his defeat at Mutina, made a deal with the Pontifex Maximus, M. Aemilius Lepidus, governor of Narbonese Gaul and Nearer Spain; won over C. Asinius Pollio, governor of Farther Spain, and L. Munatius Plancus, governor of Transalpine Gaul; and then made an alliance with Caesar's heir, the former Octavius, now C. Julius Caesar (I call him the young Caesar). Plancus and Pollio, whose correspondence with Cicero is extant, as is that of Lepidus, held consulships in 42 and 40, respectively, and survived as eminent men into the principate of the young Caesar, honoured, for example, by Horatian odes.[9] Lepidus, Antonius and Caesar became a Commission of Three, triumvirs, for the setting up of the commonwealth. Their powers were conferred by a law, passed on 27 November 43. Their title echoed that of Sulla as dictator. Following the precedent of Sulla and ignoring the example of clemency set by Caesar when he was dictator, they also drew up lists of their enemies, who were outlawed, to be killed on sight and have their property confiscated. Cicero was one of the more important senators, among more than two or three hundred, to be put on the list of the proscribed.[10] He had set himself up as a senior stateman, an idealist of calm authority, as the idealising portraits of him show (Figure 11.1). Now he was up against the reality of brute force. Quintus and their two sons were also listed. The intention was to wipe out the male line of the Cicerones and to confiscate their wealth. The family would be extinct. The proscription list went up in Rome on 27 November. Cicero had time to escape overseas. Instead, he was killed, at Formiae, on 7 December.

It was an anxious time even if your own family were not condemned to death. Even Atticus went into hiding at P. Volumnius' house, until Antonius assured him of his safety.[11] Prominent women needed protection: Atticus helped Servilia, the mother of Brutus and mother-in-law of Cassius, just as he had earlier protected Antonius' wife Fulvia.[12] Anyone who sheltered a proscribed man was also liable to be killed.[13] There were murders in the city and the houses of the proscribed were looted. Amid the stories of violence, betrayal and heroism, it is hard to separate fact from fiction, but it is clear that the proscriptions made an indelible impression on those who lived through them and on succeeding generations. Terentia and Publilia, especially if they remained in the city, must have suffered anxiety, fear and revulsion. Troops guarded the gates of Rome and searched for victims, some of whom hid in sewers, dung-heaps or wells. Headless corpses lay in the streets. A praetor who had been holding elections in the Forum was cut down after fleeing to a shop when he heard the soldiers were after him. One wife who had tried and failed to save her husband turned herself in to the triumvirs, who ignored her, so she starved herself to death.[14]

The fate of the Cicerones

Tales clustered round the memory of the proscriptions, and in years to come the rhetorical schools found them a fertile context for deliberative speeches. The Elder Seneca, who wrote memoirs about the practice-speeches which distinguished orators of the time of Augustus composed – following the pattern set by Cicero himself with his younger friends Hirtius, Pansa, Dolabella and the rest[15] – presents one imaginary court case defended by the alleged assassin of Cicero.[16] He gives seven themes in his book on deliberative speeches in a historical setting. Five are about Greek history or legend: 'Agamemnon debates whether he should sacrifice Iphigeneia'. The two Roman themes are both about Cicero, whose own writings could be exploited as a model: 'Cicero deliberates whether to ask Antonius for mercy'; 'Cicero deliberates whether to burn his writings, because Antonius promises him his life if he does so'.[17] The second scenario is a flight of fancy, as Seneca himself says.[18] All the orators on the second theme advised Cicero not to trust Antonius, as did most of those on the first, except a few hostile to Cicero's reputation. Seneca then passes to the historians. Livy (writing under Augustus Caesar, the former triumvir) made it clear that Cicero had no time to ask for mercy. He left Rome as the triumvirs approached and first went

146 *Death and survival*

Figure 11.1 Cicero in later life: idealised portrait bust (Mattei bust from the Wellington Museum, Apsley House, London; English Heritage Photographic Library)

Death and survival 147

to Tusculum, then cross-country to his villa at Formiae, with the idea of taking ship from the port of Caieta (as he had in 49). He put to sea several times, but sometimes the winds were against him, sometimes the sea too rough. So he went back, with the words 'I will die in my country, which I have so often saved'. Like other famous last words, these are suspect. The soldiers caught him. Cicero refused to let his slaves fight to defend him and stuck his head out of the litter so that he could be decapitated. The killers cut off his hands too (in other versions his right hand only) and fastened them, either side of his head, to the speakers' platform in Rome.[19] Other historians, Aufidius Bassus and Cremutius Cordus, agreed that Cicero had faced death bravely.[20] Seneca cites, among others, Livy's 'obituary' of Cicero:

> He lived sixty-three years, so that, if he had not died by violence, his death could have seemed not even untimely. His genius was happy both in his works and the rewards of his works; he himself long enjoyed prosperous fortune; but in the long course of happiness he was from time to time struck by severe wounds, his exile, the ruin of the side which he had defended, the death of his daughter, his sad and premature death. Of all these adversities he bore none as a man ought except his death, which in truth to one making a true estimate might have seemed less undeserved because he suffered nothing crueller from his victorious enemy than he would have inflicted had he achieved the same fortune. If anyone, however, weighs his virtues against his faults, he was a great and memorable man. To express his praise would take a Cicero as eulogist.
>
> (Sen. *Suas*. 6.22)

It is striking that Livy, in summing up Cicero's life and in particular his political career, not even explicitly mentioning his status as a new man and his remarkable achievement of the consulship,[21] puts Tullia's death, along with the exile and the defeat of the Pompeians, as one of the three great misfortunes which befell him.

Velleius Paterculus, in the time of Augustus' successor, put the blame for Cicero's death and mutilation on Antonius and paid tribute to Cicero's patriotism, service to his fellow-citizens and brilliance as an orator.[22] Plutarch, writing about a century later, gives suspiciously full details.[23] Like Livy, he says Cicero went to Tusculum. Quintus was with him. When they heard about the proscriptions, they decided to go to Astura and take ship from there. They were carried along in litters, stopping often to lament. Then Quintus reflected that he needed money for the journey and so went to his house, perhaps his villa at Arx. After some further hesitation, Cicero sailed from Astura to Caieta and so reached the villa at Formiae. The household slaves attempted to rescue him by making him get in his litter and go down to the ship again. When the assassins arrived, they were told by a young freedman of Quintus, who had been educated by Cicero, where he had gone.

148 *Death and survival*

The details of his death are the same as in Livy, with the vivid addition that, after ordering his slaves to put down the litter, Cicero rested his chin on his hand in a characteristic pose, gazing at the assassins, his face wasted by anxiety and his hair unkempt and dirty. (He was probably careful of his appearance normally: Dio makes Calenus claim his hair was combed and scented, his cloaks of fine weave, his togas long.)[24] There was a story in some historians that Antonius handed over the traitorous freedman to Pomponia, who tortured him horribly to death, but Plutarch found nothing at all about such a man in Tiro's life of Cicero. Appian's narrative is similar to Plutarch's, with a different traitor. He also points out that Marcus was safely in Greece and tells an improving story about the Quinti, that each begged the assassins to kill him first: they obliged by dividing into two groups and killing them simultaneously.[25] Dio has young Quintus hiding his father and refusing to say where he was in spite of being tortured and Quintus coming out and surrendering to spare his son further pain. He also has an extra story about the treatment of Cicero's head: that Antonius' wife Fulvia (the widow of Clodius and then of Curio) held it in her hands, spat on it and pierced the tongue with her hairpins.[26]

Cicero died on 7 December.[27] His body was cremated by a friend from the neighbourhood, not by Atticus or either of his divorced wives, who were not anywhere near.[28] They must have heard the shocking news as soon as the pieces of Cicero's body arrived in Rome. Terentia at least must have grieved for the father of her son and become even more anxious about young Marcus.

Cicero's property was confiscated. The Palatine house passed to L. Marcius Censorinus (cos. 39), who had tried to defend Caesar against his assassins and now supported Antonius.[29] The villa near Cumae (on the way to Puteoli) went to Antistius Vetus, during whose tenure a little while after Cicero's death hot springs were discovered on the property.[30] If this is C. Antistius Vetus (cos. suffect 30), as is generally thought, he too had been a Caesarian. But he joined the Liberators[31] and was legate to Brutus in 43, so can hardly have bought the villa at a knockdown price in 43 or 42. Perhaps he acquired it respectably from its original buyer in the 30s, when he had come to serve the young Caesar. We do not know what, if anything, Marcus was able to keep or rescue. More might have been preserved for him if Cicero had transferred one or two of his precious villas to Terentia in part repayment of her dowry. He had preferred to keep them all.

Terentia and the triumvirs

The population of Rome, men and women, did not rejoice as it was ordered to do in the triumph of Lepidus which came hard on the heels of the proscriptions. Nor was the sale of confiscated property as profitable as the triumvirs desired. They therefore published an edict, demanding that 1400 of the richest women should submit a valuation of their property and pay whatever percentage was demanded, for the expenses of the civil war. The women petitioned Fulvia, who repulsed them, and Julia, Antonius' mother, and Octavia, young Caesar's sister, who received them kindly. Then they approached the triumvirs in the Forum and Hortensia, daughter of a famous orator, made an eloquent speech.[32] The women were driven away by the lictors, until the crowd protested and the triumvirs were forced to say they would consider the matter. Next day, they reduced the number of women liable to the tax to 400 and imposed contributions on men as well. Clearly both Terentia and Publilia would fall into the class of 1400 richest women in Rome and probably into the 400. Terentia at least should have been an important member of the delegations. She will have known Hortensia since the days when Cicero overtook Hortensius as Rome's greatest orator.

We do not know when Marcus came back to Italy, but it was after Philippi in 42 and after further service under Domitius Ahenobarbus and Sex. Pompeius,[33] which may have lasted until 36. The boy who had gone away, aged nineteen, to study in Athens, received the news of his father's murder when he was twenty-two and fought in a bitter civil war, then returned as a military man. We can imagine a joyful reunion. Terentia would still feel responsible for exercising a mother's authority and for helping him. No doubt it came naturally to her to advise him on the administration of whatever part of Cicero's property he was able to reclaim.

New alliances

Years later, at Messalla's house, a minor poet called Sextilius Ena was asked to recite. He invited Asinius Pollio, an orator and historian; Cornelius Severus, another poet, was also present. Sextilius decided to recite a poem on the subject of the proscriptions. He began, 'I must weep for Cicero and the silence of the Latin tongue'. Pollio was so offended that he left, telling his host Messalla that he could not stay and listen to someone who thought he was dumb.[34] Was Publilia present at this recitation? There may be a reason why she could have been in Messalla's house, other than as an invited guest.

The ascetic monk Jerome (c. AD 347–420), who had been an enthusiastic reader of Cicero, drawing on Seneca's treatise *On marriage*, produces a puzzling and tantalisingly brief reference to Terentia in the context of a diatribe against marriage. (The next wife named is Socrates' Xanthippe, allegedly a shrew.)

> Cicero, when he was asked by Hirtius to marry his sister, after the divorce from Terentia, completely steered clear of doing so, saying he could not concentrate equally on philosophy and a wife. She, meanwhile, that noble wife and one who had drunk wisdom from Tullian springs,[35] married Sallust his enemy and thirdly Messalla Corvinus, and so rolled gradually down the steps of eloquence.
>
> (Jerome *Against Iovinianus* 1.48=316A)

150   *Death and survival*

Is it credible that Terentia married C. Sallustius Crispus, the historian (?86–35)? He had opposed Cicero as tribune in 52, attacking him as a bandit and dagger-man, which would be enough to qualify him as an enemy for such a source.[36] After being expelled from the Senate by the censors of 50, he joined Caesar, attained a praetorship for 46 and governed Africa. On his return, perhaps in 45, but in any case before March 44, he was charged with extortion, avoided being tried and retired from public life to write history. His monograph on the Catilinarian conspiracy (c. 42/1) used Cicero as a principal source and gives the consul his due. If Terentia married him, it would fit neatly into the period immediately after Sallust's return from Africa.[37] Sallust was a wealthy man (probably thanks to his time in Africa) and, as he would not be standing for office, did not need, though he may have liked, a good dowry. Terentia's social position would have been an advantage for a new man from Amiternum in the Sabine country, as her knowledge of politics would have helped the historian. Terentia must long have been acquainted with Cicero's friend Cn. Sallustius, who must be a member of the same family as the historian, but not necessarily on good terms with him.[38] She had also had dealings with P. Sallustius (perhaps the former's brother), on Cicero's behalf. But her age is against this scenario. If she married Cicero in 80 or 79 at, say, eighteen, then she was born around 98. So, if the date of Sallust's birth is rightly put in 86, then she would have been about twelve years older. That is not impossible,[39] and some authorities have accepted it,[40] but judicious modern opinion is against it.[41] For Terentia to have married Sallust is, therefore, conceivable but unlikely.[42]

Publilia would make a better fit. Syme thinks she must have been born by 60 at latest, which would make her fourteen at the time of her marriage to Cicero. She could have been only twelve, though that seems improbable. I would prefer to guess she was born around 62. She could have married Sallust late in 45, having left a proper interval after the divorce from Cicero (which would make it clear she was not pregnant by him). But if Caerellia's mission was to see if Cicero wanted to remarry her, then we must postpone a possible marriage to Sallust until some time after the first week in May 44.[43] She might have been between sixteen and eighteen, in either case highly eligible. This marriage seems quite possible.[44] If Publilia had some Caesarian connection, she was an even more desirable match for Sallust.

The second husband mentioned by Jerome is M. Valerius Messalla Corvinus, a patrician and also a literary man (64 BC–AD 8). He was a contemporary of Marcus: they were fellow-students in Athens. It is hardly conceivable that Terentia married him, *pace* Carcopino (1957), who attributes the match to her intelligence and force of character. Like Marcus, he joined the Liberators. After Philippi, he surrendered to Antonius, and by 36 had begun to work with the young Caesar, whose side, as consul, he took in the campaign against Antonius and Cleopatra in 31.[45] Cicero had praised his skill as an orator.[46] He had two sons: the elder, Messallinus (cos. 3), probably born in 36; the younger, M. Aurelius Cotta Maximus (cos. AD 20), probably born about 14. The mother of the elder may have been a Calpurnia, 'by a marriage contracted c. 40', but the most that we can be sure of is that Messalla had a wife when the elder son was born; the mother of the younger, because of his name, must be an Aurelia.[47] It is conceivable that Publilia was married to him, in c. 37/6 (which would mean a divorce from Sallust, if she had him as her second husband, and would make her the mother of the elder son) or after the death or divorce of the mother of Messallinus, or after the death or divorce of Aurelia. But we must remain sceptical: 'The problem . . . serves to set in harsh relief how little is known'.[48]

It is attested that Vibius Rufus, who became suffect consul in AD 16, was married to the wife of Cicero and he is said to have thought that this would have a good effect on his oratory. (He had also collected a chair which Caesar had used in the Senate and on which he had been sitting on the Ides of March.) He was in fact well known as an orator and is frequently mentioned by the Elder Seneca.[49] The marriage might be doubted, but is supported by the evidence of a large family tomb from the territory of Tusculum with three inscriptions which attest a freedman: M. Publilius Strato, freedman of Publilia and of C. Vibius Rufus.[50] Joint ownership of a slave by two people of opposite sex who are not close kin strongly suggests that they are married to each other. Almost certainly the same M. Publilius Strato is found in AD 33 making a dedication to the *Lares Augusti*, along with two others, one of them C. Vibius Philippus, who will be another freedman of Vibius Rufus.[51] Vibius, a new man, could have been born in about 42 (his consulship would be late, when he was about sixty), so the age gap between him and Publilia ('who cannot have been born later than 60') would not be unthinkable for a woman at perhaps her third or fourth marriage. All this is documented by Syme, the first to adduce the inscriptions.[52] Rufus probably had a son, C. Vibius Rufinus, a friend of the poet Ovid, who reached the consulship (possibly in AD 21 or 22) and the proconsulship of Asia.[53] Syme thinks he was no more than thirty-five in AD 16, so born not before 20 BC. He concludes he was unlikely to be Publilia's child. But the date does not rule out Publilia, who would still have been of childbearing age in 20, probably aged around forty.[54] We might suppose the marriage to have taken place not long before. That would, if Syme is right on Vibius' date of birth, make him quite young for an upper-class bridegroom. But nothing prevents us pushing back his birth a few years. The age gap would then be less striking. Admittedly, Publilia might still be described as 'an old and much married lady', like the Cornificia disparaged by her first husband, Cicero.[55]

So we have the intriguing possibility that Publilia, after her disastrous first marriage, went on to marry the middle-aged Sallust and to divorce or be divorced or widowed; to marry her ex-stepson's fellow-student, only slightly older than herself, and again to divorce; and then to marry her junior, perhaps in the late 20s, and possibly to remain with him until his or her death. But this speculation depends on a series of guesses, a house of cards in which we should have no trust.

152 *Death and survival*

Terentia's long unattached life

If we dismiss Jerome's evidence on Terentia, then she presumably did not remarry after the divorce, but remained a *vidua*. If she was in her fifties at the time of the divorce, this is not surprising. Younger women who were widowed might also refrain from remarriage: Aurelia, mother of Caesar, Servilia, mother of Brutus (after two marriages), and Clodia, widow of Metellus Celer (at least for a long time), are contemporary examples.

We hear nothing directly of her personal life after Cicero's death, except that two writers of the first century AD claim she lived to the great age of 103. Valerius Maximus gives a brief list of women who lived to an advanced age: Livia, wife of Rutilius, to 97; Terentia to 103; Clodia, wife of Aufilius, to 115, with fifteen children predeceasing her.[56] Pliny copies these three (but spells Clodia's husband Ofilius) and adds the noble Statilia in the reign of Claudius.[57] Terentia's age is accepted as fact by reputable scholars.[58] All three women have distinguished husbands, known to fame. Rutilius is identified with the consul of 105 and his wife as a sister of M. Livius Drusus, tribune in 122.[59] A. Of(f)ilius was an *eques* and jurist, who may have been co-heir to Cluvius and to whom Cicero at one point owed money and whose juristic opinion he valued.[60] All these women, then, are highly placed, which lends some credence to the tradition of their longevity, although Clodia's 115 years are suspect.

One other senatorial lady, a generation younger than Terentia, is known to have had a long life: Junia Tertia, the daughter of Servilia, sister-in-law of Porcia and wife of C. Cassius Longinus, the leader of the conspiracy against Caesar. It was probably she who had scorned to dine with Publilius (p. 131). Her husband committed suicide at the first Battle of Philippi in October 42. She lived on for sixty-three years, without remarrying, until AD 22. Her fortune was large (something must have been done to preserve it through the civil wars), but she left nothing to the emperor. The *imagines* of twenty-four noble families were carried at her funeral, but not those of her brother Brutus and her husband Cassius.[61] For Tacitus, she represented a late survivor of the Republic. Terentia had died years before, before Augustus (AD 14). If she was born in 98, then, if she lived to 103, she died in about AD 6. But Publilia could have lived to see, or at least hear about, Junia's funeral, as well as Terentia's.

Terentia lived to know of the deaths of Fulvia and Antonius; the supremacy of the young Caesar and his transformation into Augustus (in 27, when she was already about seventy-one); the vicissitudes of his family, and the adoption of his successor, the former husband of Atticus' granddaughter (in AD 4, when she may have been 101). She could have read Horace's poems addressed to friends of Cicero and Vergil's epic on Rome (neither of which mentioned Cicero). At eighty-one, she could have attended some of the ceremonies of the Secular Games in 17.

Terentia almost certainly outlived Marcus. Remarkably little is known of him. He returned to Rome after the amnesty in 39, was elected to a priesthood and held a suffect consulship in 30, as the young Caesar's colleague, when Antonius had been defeated.[62] He went on to govern Syria[63] and rose to the top of the senatorial ladder by being proconsul of Asia. He was allegedly a heavy drinker, who once threw a two-handled goblet at M. Agrippa,[64] and owed the consulship to his father's reputation.[65] If it is true that Marcus was at a party with Agrippa, this shows he was moving in important circles, probably in the 30s or 20s. Agrippa became engaged to Atticus' daughter Caecilia (perhaps in 37) and subsequently married her, but they divorced in 28.[66] Atticus died on 31 March 32.[67] It would be appropriate if Marcus got to know Agrippa quite well through his father's old friend. We do not know whom he married (it is unlikely that he never married) or the date of his death, and he apparently left no son.[68] It is possible that he gave Terentia a granddaughter – or more than one.

Longevity is also attributed to Tiro, who, if he lived to 99, will have outlived Terentia.[69] Part of Tiro's literary output was devoted to the preservation of Cicero's memory. In law, he was a client of Marcus, to whom he had specific obligations. But social ties would subsist with his dead patron's ex-wife. Those of Cicero's letters which were addressed to Atticus and therefore in his archives were probably first organised under Atticus' supervision. His biographer Nepos, as a visitor to the house, was able to consult eleven papyrus rolls of letters.[70] The collection was later expanded and eventually became generally available, possibly in Nero's time.[71] There is no provable involvement of Tiro or the family in this process. But what happened to the rest of the letters suggests that both Tiro and Terentia were at least partly responsible for their collection and preservation.[72] Tiro, as secretary, will often have supervised the copying of official or political letters of which Cicero needed to retain a copy. He had also been making a small collection of letters for possible publication.[73] He was therefore in a good position to act as editor, soliciting copies of some letters from some of Cicero's surviving friends or their heirs and finding others in the archives which now belonged to Marcus. One book of *Letters to Friends* (*Ad Familiares* 16) consists of letters Cicero or other members of the family wrote to Tiro or about him. (Tiro is the only addressee of freed status in the extant correspondence.) This is the strongest proof that Tiro had an important hand in the collection and arrangement of the letters. The correspondence with Quintus may, by agnatic succession, have passed to Marcus as the closest surviving relative of the Quinti. This too may have been collected by Tiro. Finally there are the family letters of the fourteenth roll of *Ad Familiares*. Tiro would hardly have kept copies of the scrappy notes from Brundisium and the territory of Venusia in 48/7. We must owe these, in some way, to Terentia, their recipient. She may have left them in the house in Rome, but that was confiscated. How well did the contents survive? It does not seem likely that Tiro would have had the opportunity to take quantities of papers to his own villa at Puteoli to preserve them in 43. Terentia may have kept them herself, by inadvertence or for the sake of the love-letters from exile. If so, she must deliberately have handed over the originals or copies to her son or Tiro.

It seems we must assume some involvement of Terentia in the preservation of the memory of her ex-husband, the father of her son. The memory of Cicero would be important to the advancement of young Marcus. He, at least, needed to know the tradition to which he belonged. The interesting thing is that he and Tiro thought everything obtainable was worth preserving. The last letter to Terentia is not a model of style, family affection or lofty virtue: Marcus would have no motive in referring to it in public or even letting friends see it. But it was thought worthwhile to preserve anything which Cicero had written. It is like the way families preserved masks of all the male ancestors, however unflattering. Terentia at least co-operated in this pious task.

12 Conclusions

Terentia

Character

Terentia has, on the whole, had a bad press from modern scholars.[1] Cicero's critics blame him without exonerating her. Biographers of Cicero tend to like him and to sympathise with him against his wife. Here is an extreme example:

> While he enjoyed vigorous health and prosperous fortunes, he tolerated with a calm mind the arrogance [*alterezza*] of his wife Terentia, whose character led her to domineer [*spadroneggiare*] in the household, in such a way that, while she meddled in the public business of her husband, she completely neglected domestic interests and let them be overturned in financial disorder.
>
> (Ciaceri 1930: 294)

Among recent biographers in English, Mitchell concludes that Cicero's suspicions that Terentia was defrauding him were justified, that she was 'generally unsympathetic' to him during this stay in Brundisium and, above all, was 'niggardly' to Tullia.[2] Shackleton Bailey seems inclined to accept the justice of Cicero's suspicions of her financial probity and adds the belief that she worked to undermine his position with Caesar.[3] Rawson is properly cautious: 'the rights and wrongs of this unhappy business are irrecoverable'.[4] Political historians, if they mention her at all, often take a view dictated by what Cicero said when relations had soured. Syme, who gives some credence to the idea that Terentia feared that Cicero wanted to marry Clodia, portrays her as 'obdurate against blandishments . . . snobbish' and 'harsh and coriaceous'.[5] Stockton thinks, 'She was not the most self-effacing of wives nor the softest-tongued, and the marriage fell a good way short of being idyllic'. But he realises that money may only have been 'the ostensible reason' for the divorce.[6] Even social historians are severe on her administration of property.[7] Some attempt to look at the marriage from her point of view:

More than nine hundred of Cicero's letters survive, including twenty-four to his wife Terentia, but there is nothing in them to suggest that she shared his literary or political confidences; she evidently tolerated him for the egotist that he was and, until in the end he became obsessed with the idea that she was stealing his money and he divorced her, she kept a home for him.

(Balsdon 1962: 46)[8]

Warde Fowler (1908: 150–2) is more sympathetic:

> an ordinary lady, of no particular ability or interest, who may stand as representative of the quieter type of married woman. She lived with her husband about thirty years, and until towards the end of that period, a long one for the age, we find nothing substantial against her. If we had nothing but Cicero's letters to her, more than twenty in number, and his allusions to her in other letters, we should conclude that she was a faithful and on the whole a sensible wife. But more than once he writes of her delicate health,[9] and as the poor lady had at various times a great deal of trouble to go through, it is quite possible that as she grew older she became short in her temper, or trying in other ways to a husband so excitable and vacillating. We find stories of her in Plutarch and elsewhere which represent her as shrewish, too careful of her own money, and so on; but facts are of more account than the gossip of the day, and there is not a sign in the letters that Cicero disliked or mistrusted her until the year 47. Had there really been cause for mistrust it would have slipped out in some letter to Atticus. Then, after his absence during the war, he seems to have believed that she had neglected himself and his interests . . . I suspect that Terentia was quite as much sinned against as sinning.

In reaching a verdict, most writers look at the alleged reasons for the divorce and in particular at the history of Cicero's criticism of her financial dealings late in the marriage and at Plutarch's report of Cicero's alleged reasons.[10] This is plainly a procedure which would not stand up in a court of law. It can never be right to listen to only one side in a divorce or dispute. In assessing a marriage, rather than the justification for the decision of one or both parties to divorce (as if either Cicero or Terentia had to sue for divorce in a modern court), we should look at the whole relationship over time. This might well reveal a better marriage and a warmer, more generous woman than this handful of quotations suggests. We still have the insuperable problem that our information comes from Cicero and that his perception of Terentia was incomplete and partial. If the historian should judge no man happy until he is dead,[11] that is when the whole life may be reviewed, then perhaps we should not assess a marriage until it is ended by death or divorce. We cannot call Terentia's marriage entirely happy. But it is also true that when a marriage has ended in divorce, that fact must not cast doubt on the possibility that happiness and concord may have predominated over the years. It will be worth reviewing rapidly the evidence which has been discussed.

A wife is what a wife does

It is impossible to speak with confidence of Terentia's inner life, though some attempt it: 'Terentia's character was not at all spiritual. She remained insensible to her husband's literary glory' (Ciaceri 1930: 380). That is pure guesswork. We have no evidence about Terentia's interest in Cicero's genius as a writer. There is indeed no evidence to suggest that 'she shared his literary confidences' in the extant letters. She had no need to correspond about her interest in seeing his latest book, as some of his male friends or the philosophical Caerellia might.[12] During his exile, when the letters are fullest, Cicero was composing nothing except other letters. Nor was his stay at Brundisium fertile. There is no reason why literature should crop up in the extant letters to her. We do not know what they talked about when they were together. We might guess she was interested in the matter of the speeches, in the approach he chose to take. His working day was of course dedicated to reading and writing with his male servants and assistants. His pattern was to work extremely hard, whether in Rome, when he was preparing briefs or political speeches, or during his brief holidays in the country, when he marked out blocks of his leisure-time for the composition of particular treatises.[13] Even late in life he might be up before a summer daybreak, writing philosophy and a letter.[14] Though Seneca might cast Terentia in the role of philosophical pupil (p. 149) and Sidonius in the fifth century affirm that she held a light while he wrote,[15] we have no contemporary evidence of such involvement. But there would sometimes be time for Terentia at dinner and normally at bedtime, the one privileged time for wives, curtain-lectures and conversation. Cicero valued elegant diction in women and thought they acquired it in a cultured home.[16] He would not have tolerated its absence or a less than adequate literary education in his wife. He would have expected her to be a polite hostess if the conversation or entertainment at dinner were literary. At least once he used Greek when writing to her.[17] It was a conventional idea that women were educated by their husbands after marriage: to the extent that they lived in a cultivated household, surrounded by their children's tutors, resident intellectuals and literary friends, they must have continued to absorb a good deal, even though the husbands did not give them tuition.[18] There is no reason to suppose that Terentia read deeply in history or philosophy – like Cornelia, mother of the Gracchi, or Cornelia, wife of Pompey – or that she was a wit, musician and dancer versed in more frivolous Greek and Latin literature, like Sempronia, but she could surely fit into her society without appearing rustic.[19] If she helped preserve the letters, she had some regard for Cicero's writings. She was herself an adequate correspondent.

Balsdon also seems to miss the discussion of politics which exists. It is less prominent than in the much richer collection of letters to Atticus, but it occurs. Cicero writes in 58, mentioning that Terentia is optimistic about the tribunes for 57, but adding that they will also need Pompey's help, and Crassus may be dangerous (F 14.2/7.2, Thessalonica, 5 Oct. 58). He was writing to those Terentia mentioned to him, thanking them and telling them that his wife had written to him about their *officium*. He hoped the tribunes would act early in 57, or if the matter went stale, it would be all up. So she must write immediately to tell him how it went, explaining how the whole business was developing and giving her predictions (F 14.2/7.4; 14.3/9.3–5, Dyrrachium, 29 Nov. 58). He says that he hopes for the support of all the tribunes, P. Cornelius Lentulus (nicknamed Spinther), the consul elect, Pompey and Caesar (F 14.1/8.2, to Terentia, Dyrrachium, 25 Nov. 58). It is clear that Terentia was seeing important people, including the tribunes; that she was acting as liaison with her husband; and that she was capable of writing full, careful and literate reports on politics. The subjects she wrote about so carefully when he was in Cilicia no doubt included political developments and, like his friends' letters, the likelihood of war (F 14.5/ 119.1, Athens, 16 Oct. 50). He shared with her his perception of the effect of the actions of Labienus and Calpurnius Piso, and asked her to let him know what was going on in Rome (F 14.14/145.2, Minturnae, 23 Jan. 49).

Cicero expected Terentia to be well informed and able to judge for herself how the political situation would affect their family fortunes. He frequently asks for her input (*consilium*) and leaves final decisions to her because she is on the spot.[20] We know from other sources that *consilium* was part of the wife's role.[21] She got prompt information and let him know (F 14.8/164, Brundisium, 2 June 47). She made suggestions for action (e.g., F 14.3/9.5, Dyrrachium, 29 Nov. 58; 14.19/160, Brundisium, 27 Nov. 48). He sometimes did what she told him (F 14.2/7.4, Thessalonica, 5 Oct. 58; 14.23/9.3). Delicate judgements and predictions of the future were entrusted to her (e.g., F 14.13/169, Brundisium, 10 July 47; cf. A 11.25/231.3, Brundisium, 5 July 47). She urged him to be of good spirits as he left for exile (F 14.4/6.5, Brundisium, 29 Apr. 58). Like any Roman man, or Servilia,[22] she consulted a council of friends, perhaps in 58 those whom Cicero was accustomed to summon (F 14.1/8.3, despatched from Dyrrachium, 25 Nov. 58).

They worked as a team. Plutarch tells us that Terentia was disinclined to tolerate interference from Cicero in her own sphere of operations, the household, but preferred 'to take a share in his political concerns'.[23] This is confirmed by the letters, which, however, only show what went on when the two were separated. We can imagine that Terentia discussed with Cicero whether he should undertake the prosecution of Verres. Q. Cicero, in his handbook on electioneering, did not advise his brother to deploy his wife's talents as a canvasser, but it is hard to imagine that she did not have a role. She was involved in the consulship and the suppression of the Catilinarians (pp. 44–8). Along with the children, she was part of the decision that Cicero should avoid confrontation in 58 (p. 57). In 49, she was involved in all the discussions about whether Cicero should join Pompey (pp. 110–11). She was a leading player in the effort for Cicero's recall in 58 to 57 and played a part in the conciliation of Caesar in 48/7 (pp. 118–28). His brave and fatal fight for the Republic in 44/3 was undertaken when he no longer had to consider the interests, fears and cautious counsels of his wife and daughter.

Not only did Terentia look after the day-to-day running of the household, but she was often left in full control. Full parental responsibility might fall to her. It was her job to see that Marcus was kept from destitution in 58, so that he might still hope for a political career (*F* 14.1/8.5). Similarly with Tullia in 49–47, much of the burden fell on her. She worked at the top level in Cicero's finances as well as her own.

Terentia fulfilled her major role in marriage by presenting Cicero with two children, widely spaced though they were. This was to intensify the social disapproval which greeted their divorce. Few scholars attempt to comment on the secrets of the marriage-bed. It has, however, been confidently stated that 'Cicero could not have been an ardent lover'. This view is presumably based on Cicero's remark that he had not been very interested in *demi-mondaines* even as a young man, let alone in old age.[24] Boissier is surely right when he argues for the austerity of Cicero's youth, when he was apprenticed to oratory, an occupation which left little time for amusements or even for the conversation of friends, as he said when defending Caelius' way of life in the courts.[25] But he was no ascetic. If he had been like Laelius or the younger Cato, who allegedly had not experienced sexual intercourse before their marriages,[26] we might expect such a remarkable fact to be recorded. He was an emotional and energetic man. He can throw in an observation on sexual turn-offs in a serious comment to Atticus about the disgust he felt at Pompey's behaviour at the beginning of the civil war: 'Just as in erotic contexts anything done dirtily, unattractively or in an unseemly manner makes one hostile, so the slovenliness and degradation of his flight turned me from my love' (*A* 9.10/177.2, Formiae, 18 March 49). He delighted in double entendres in both speeches and private jesting.[27] If he could be witty, he did not mind being coarse (p. 134). But contemporaries could find little support for stories of illicit behaviour.[28] His fondness for Tullia gave some basis for allegations of incest, but they should be ignored.[29] They belong to the political orator's fund of invective, which allowed Cicero and others to suggest incest between his enemy Clodius and two of his sisters. If the taunt was actually thrown at Cicero by contemporaries (the evidence is later), they must have done it because they knew it would hurt. The allegation allowed the pungent characterisation of Tullia as the mistress in relation to her own mother: *filia matris paelex*.[30] Cicero's friendship with Caerellia allowed his enemies to suggest he was having a disgusting affair with a woman as much older than him as he was older than Publilia. (This would make her at least a centenarian.) Letters to her survived into late antiquity, but apparently gave no secure grounds for supposing adultery.[31] Antonian propaganda apparently also alleged that Cicero pimped his wife, presumably Terentia.[32] The basis for this is perhaps Terentia's negotiations in her husband's interest with many different men, especially in 58/7 and 48/7. But none of this invective carries conviction. That Cicero did not make the gossips suspect extramarital affairs or flings with slaves or courtesans (though if casual they would be too trifling to show up in invective) gives us no grounds for saying he lacked ardour towards Terentia (the letters from exile go some way to suggesting the opposite, after twenty years of marriage) or Publilia (the rumours and his own joke are against it).

The most noticeable feature of the letters to family is the warm affection which, in their good times, Cicero showed for all of his close kin. The children are delightful or very sweet, *suavissimi*;[33] along with Terentia they are 'my darlings', *mea desideria*.[34] Terentia is 'my Terentia', his 'excellent wife', *uxor optima*; 'most faithful and excellent wife', *fidissima et optima uxor*; 'the light of my life', *lux mea*; 'my light, my darling', *mea lux, meum desiderium*; 'my life', *mea vita*; or 'my sweetest and most longed-for Terentia', *mea suavissima et optatissima Terentia*.[35] Terentia and Tullia are his two 'souls', *animae*, or 'my dearest souls', *meae carissimae animae*.[36] Cicero in 58 knew Terentia loved him and assured her of his love for her.[37] The letters from exile are in part love-letters, which appeal for Terentia's continued love and support, insist that she is the most important thing in his life and look forward to a joyful reunion.[38] Hints in his letters suggest that Terentia's replies of the same period reciprocated the emotion.[39]

It is striking that the virtues which Cicero attributes to his female relatives are those which he praises in men. He found himself wanting in 'manly courage', *virtus*,[40] but, though it is rarely ascribed to women, he found it in Terentia.[41] She was also brave, *fortis*, 'braver than any man'.[42] Terentia showed loyalty and good faith, *fides*, an important conjugal virtue.[43] Cicero also praises her integrity or uprightness, *probitas*, and kindliness, *humanitas*.[44] He considered that both he and his wife had shown *pietas*, which meant they deserved the happiness of his restoration to his family: this is perhaps self-sacrificing love of country.[45] Terentia was also scrupulous in her religious observance.[46] Everyone went to her for help.[47]

It would be wrong to assume that the marriage was always one of undiluted happiness until shortly before the divorce. There is a trace of coldness from Terentia to her husband after his exile (p. 74). But it is not mentioned again and perhaps was a mood which passed swiftly. Similarly, Cicero's unease about Terentia's financial dealings seems to have been ephemeral until the last year of their marriage (pp. 97, 112–16, 122–3, 127–8). The one letter from 50 is as affectionate as those from exile, though less emotional (pp. 96–7). Only in retrospect was it apparent that the marriage was breaking down in 48/7. Not until the last did Cicero's usual courtesy fail.

Idealised prescriptions stressed partnership of husband and wife and the sharing of property, an idea in stark contrast with the law's insistence on separation of property in the interests of the blood-kin of each partner.

At one time we see Terentia thinking of using her fortune for the sake of the partnership; later we see the children's economic well-being as an object of both husband and wife (pp. 116, 139). Equity and faith were the ideals against which Cicero measured himself and Terentia. He took seriously his duty to make wife and daughter happy and not to neglect their interests.[48] Even after the divorce, he thought of his duty to Terentia (pp. 138–9). She, as far as we can see, always acted with good faith towards him.

Publilia

The only piece of evidence for Publilia's character is that she wrote to Cicero asking to be allowed to join him. It may not have been her own letter or decision, but she was prepared to act properly as his wife. Abandoned by her elderly husband, whom she had had no opportunity to get to know, she necessarily and properly depended on the guidance of her mother and her male relative (brother or uncle). She may provoke our compassion in her difficult and probably painful situation.

Tullia

Scholars usually accept Tullia at Cicero's estimate: 'His darling Tullia was as faithful and affectionate as ever'; 'the ever-faithful Tullia'; 'She must have had great patience with her father, as well as the understanding that her similarity to him gave and that Terentia clearly lacked'; 'a daughter to whom he had always been exceptionally attached and on whom he had come to depend heavily for comfort and companionship'.[49] He never utters any criticism of her. He plainly delighted in her company and conversation (pp. 62, 124, 137). After her death, when he wanted to commemorate her with a shrine, Cicero justified the deification of humans such as Hercules and Pollux. He promised in his *Consolatio* to himself, which is now lost except for a few fragments, that he would consecrate her as 'the best and most learned of all women'.[50] So perhaps some of their conversation was on literary topics. We can surely assume that, in the exchange of conversation which Cicero enjoyed so much with Tullia, politics had an important place. We find him listening when she asked him to wait to get the news of Caesar's campaign in Spain in 49 (p. 108), and he could say he deferred to the views of Terentia, Tullia and young Marcus in deciding to join Pompey that year (p. 112).

The warmth with which she is always mentioned in the correspondence, with Atticus and Quintus as well as with her mother, is striking.[51] Tullia, in her natal family, was surrounded by love. Her character is largely painted by her father. *Virtus*, 'manly courage', is often found in her.[52] Like her mother, she was 'braver than any man'.[53] She showed 'kindliness', *humanitas*,[54] and 'dutiful love', *pietas*.[55] Cicero praises her character and inborn abilities, *ingenium*, and good behaviour, *modestia*.[56] Her good nature, *facilitas*, seems to have been shown especially in forgiving Dolabella (p. 125). It would have been against the rules of etiquette for an outsider, or even Quintus or Atticus, to praise Terentia to him, except in the most banal polite terms, but Caelius could permit himself some compliments on Tullia (p. 95).

Tullia seems to have loved her father generously and unreservedly. Her *facilitas* perhaps stopped her criticising his negligence in securing her comfort when she married Dolabella. We have no hint of any reluctance to go along with plans he made for her. Perhaps she did achieve the vicarious satisfaction in her father's successes that was attributed to her (p. 137). She must certainly have rejoiced in his return from exile. He stresses her ability to sympathise with him. She visited him in his misery at Brundisium and made a home for him after they both divorced.

Home life

Cicero regarded his home life as a refuge from the showy and illusory friendships of political life (pp. 50, 137) and his exhausting and often frustrated work. The idealisation of the wife and children who greet a man as he returns home from work occurs in the poets.[57] Just as the idealised farmer's wife was a helpmate essential to the success of the farm, so Cicero's women were engaged in his work and not protected from it as we sometimes imagine the stereotypical upper-class Victorian wives and daughters were.

Cicero's treatises were composed when he could do little in public life. It may be worth asking whether the great surge of writing on rhetoric and philosophy which he undertook between 46 and 44, some of it well known to be a response to Tullia's death, also went to fill the space left by Terentia.[58]

The relationship between father and daughter and husband and wife rested on consent, achieved through consultation and affection and social expectations. Cicero could not have relied on Terentia during his exile without it, nor deployed Tullia in suitable matches. Terentia could have divorced her husband at any time if she found the marriage no longer congenial. The heavy husband or *pater familias* is strikingly absent from the world of these letters. Neither Cicero nor his brother Quintus mentions paternal power when a son is being disobliging, nor, during a terrible quarrel described by Cicero, could Quintus constrain Pomponia to come to dinner or share his bed when she was feeling cross (pp. 81–2). The limits for the good wife or daughter were imposed by upbringing and conscience rather than a dominant male.

Mother and daughter seem to have done their duty by each other. It is hard to get any sense of their feeling for each other, but that does not mean it was not affectionate. Terentia's concern for Marcus may be reflected in the transfer of the properties which secured him an income (p. 139). Her dutifulness towards Tullia also translated into action (p. 116). Cicero never questions her devotion to them.

Similarly, we cannot tell much about what Tullia's first two marriages meant to her. She was forgiving to Dolabella, or the reconciliation of 46 would not have taken place. Unlike Pomponia, she did not refuse to sleep with him.

Both Terentia (e.g., *A* 12.37/276.3, Astura, 4 May 45) and Tullia seem to have got on well with Atticus, and Tullia had a particular friendship with his wife. Terentia's closeness to her husband's closest friend should be a credit to her. There were no quarrels with Tiro, as far as we know: this is unlike the temperamental Pomponia's difficult relationship with her husband's favourite freedman. At least in 56, the neighbours, Pomponia and Terentia, were not getting on (p. 75), but that is no indication that Terentia was naturally quarrelsome. Pomponia seems to have been a difficult woman. We can only guess about Tullia's affection for Marcus (who was only a toddler when she was first married). Quintus was fond of his niece, but again we are uninformed on his relations with his sister-in-law or those of his son with Terentia and Tullia, though Terentia at least saw a good deal of young Quintus. The terrible split of 48 between the brothers and young Quintus' volatile behaviour later must have affected relations between the Quinti and Terentia and Tullia. Perhaps they had a hand in patching up the quarrel.[59]

The family, inevitably, had ups and downs. A lacunose record may make transient difficulties and feelings sound more lasting than they were. Discretion, etiquette and convention may prevent the expression of feeling and loyalties which nevertheless ran deep. This may help explain why Cicero (quite properly by modern standards, in my view) avoided discussing his wife with his best friend and why he (quite improperly in my view, at least for Dolabella) kept Tullia's ex-husbands in his social circle. We must not, however, judge Cicero according to our morality. By the standards of his day, he did well to remain married to the wife of his youth for over thirty years. His love for his daughter was no doubt exceptional. But he let them both down by failing to ensure their security and well-being (as he admits during his exile), by his financial inefficiency and by divorcing the mother of his children. A man 'diminished his house by divorce', says Tacitus.[60] Cicero's lack of loyalty and consideration towards Publilia was scandalous. On the other side, no valid criticisms were brought by contemporaries against Tullia and we have attached no weight to those made by political enemies or her own husband against the conduct of Terentia. She kept faith with Cicero when she might have divorced him as an outlaw in 58/7.

The nature of our evidence makes it impossible to know Terentia and Tullia and still more Publilia, as we feel we partly know Atticus and Cicero himself. We do not have their letters or descriptions by Cicero of their own interests, appearance, daily life or thoughts and affections which did not concern him. Their personalities are only partly revealed. But we can find out something of the lives they lived. Some features are specific to their choices or those of their husbands, much is shaped by their peculiar chances and circumstances. But they partly exemplify a larger group. They show us something of the social and moral expectations of their class, the normal routine of living, the course of marriage, the reasons for divorce, the experience of childbirth and the rearing of children, and the impact of extraordinary events, violence and civil war on the most privileged of Roman women. They show us too how affection and duty were balanced between the natal family of parent, child and sibling, the extended family and the later ties of marriage, and how a woman might remain strongly attached to her parents and yet both semi-detached and semi-attached in her marriage.

Chronology

Showing the major events in family life, a selection of Cicero's literary works and political landmarks (all dates BC).

106	3 Jan.: Cicero born
c. 102 (or 104)	Brother Quintus born
90s	Cicero educated in house of L. Licinius Crassus (cos. 95)
?91	Cicero presented to Q. Mucius Scaevola the Augur (cos. 117) for forensic training
91–89	War with the Allies. Cicero served under Sulla and under Strabo (89)
88	Sulla marched on Rome
87–82	Domination of Cinna and Cinnans
84	*On invention* (rhetorical textbook)
82–?80	Dictatorship of Sulla
81	Cicero's first speech: *On behalf of Quinctius*
80	*Defence of Sextus Roscius of Ameria*
?80 or 79	Marriage of Terentia and Cicero
mid-79	Cicero went to Greece (six months in Athens) and Asia Minor (Rhodes) for further oratorical and philosophical training
?78	5 Aug.: Tullia born
77	middle of the year: Cicero returned to Rome
75	Cicero quaestor at Lilybaeum (Marsala) in Sicily
70	*Prosecution of Verres*
69	Cicero plebeian aedile
68	Extant letters to Atticus begin. ?Quintus quaestor
67	Tullia engaged to C. Calpurnius Piso Frugi. Younger Quintus born ?at end of year. Cicero elected at head of poll for praetorship (Asc. 85C)
66	Cicero praetor in charge of the extortion court
65	Son Marcus born (on or about 17 July). Quintus plebeian aedile
64	Cicero's consular candidacy

63	Cicero consul. ?Tullia married C. Piso Frugi (quaestor 58). 8, 9 Nov., 3, 4 Dec.: *Against Catiline* i–iv
62	*Defence of Sulla.* Cicero bought a house on Palatine. Quintus praetor
61–58	Quintus governing Asia
59–50	Domination of Rome by Pompeius, Crassus and Caesar (off and on)
59	Caesar consul
59	*His consulship* (*Consulatus suus*) (poem, circulated soon after Dec. 60 [A 2.3.4])
58	Tribunate of P. Clodius Pulcher
58/7	Cicero's exile. Tullia's husband Piso Frugi died
57	5 Aug.: Cicero landed at Brundisium and was met by Tullia.
57	*After his return, in the Senate* and *After his return, to the People*. 29 Sept.: *On his house*
57/6	Quintus legate to Pompey
56	*Defence of Sestius, Invective against Vatinius, On the reply of the haruspices, Defence of Caelius, Defence of Balbus*. Feb.: Atticus married Pilia. April: Tullia engaged to Furius Crassipes
?56–?51	?Tullia the wife of Furius Crassipes
55	*Invective against Piso, On the orator, On his own sufferings* (*De temporibus suis*)
54–52	Quintus legate to Caesar
54	*Defence of Plancius, Defence of Rabirius Postumus*
53/2	Cicero elected augur
52	*On the laws* (begun, ?'published' posthumously)
51	May: Cicero left for Cilicia, his proconsular province
51/50	Cicero governor of Cilicia, accompanied by Marcus and the Quinti
50	1 July: Tullia married P. Cornelius Dolabella. 24 Nov.: Cicero reached Brundisium and was met by Terentia
49	Outbreak of civil war between Pompeius and Caesar
49	Cicero served under Pompey in Italy and Greece
48	Battle of Pharsalus: Pompeius defeated. Oct.: Cicero returned to Italy and lived at Brundisium
47	Sept.: Caesar forgave Cicero and allowed him to return to Rome
46	Terentia and Cicero divorced. Tullia and Dolabella divorced
45	Feb.: Tullia died, shortly after birth of her son. 1 Apr.: Marcus went to Athens
45	*On the ends of good and evil* (begun by 29 May), *Tusculan Disputations*
44	15 March: Murder of Caesar
44	*Philippics* 1–4, *Cato the Elder On old age, Laelius On friendship, On duties*

43   *Philippics* 5–14
43   August: Triumvirate of M. Antonius, Lepidus and Octavian
43   7 Dec.: Cicero died in proscriptions

Ages

The chart indicates the age reached on a person's birthday in the given year.

Year	Cicero, born 106	Terentia, if born 98	Tullia, if born 78	Marcus, born 65
105	1	–	–	–
104	2	–	–	–
103	3	–	–	–
102	4	–	–	–
101	5	–	–	–
100	6	–	–	–
99	7	–	–	–
98	8	–	–	–
97	9	1	–	–
96	10	2	–	–
95	11	3	–	–
94	12	4	–	–
93	13	5	–	–
92	14	6	–	–
91	15	7	–	–
90	16	8	–	–
89	17	9	–	–
88	18	10	–	–
87	19	11	–	–
86	20	12	–	–
85	21	13	–	–
84	22	14	–	–
83	23	15	–	–
82	24	16	–	–
81	25	17	–	–
80	26	18	–	–
79	27	19	–	–
78	28	20	–	–

Ages   169

Year	Cicero, born 106	Terentia, if born 98	Tullia, if born 78	Marcus, born 65
77	29	21	1	–
76	30	22	2	–
75	31	23	3	–
74	32	24	4	–
73	33	25	5	–
72	34	26	6	–
71	35	27	7	–
70	36	28	8	–
69	37	29	9	–
68	38	30	10	–
67	39	31	11	–
66	40	32	12	–
65	41	33	13	
64	42	34	14	1
63	43	35	15	2
62	44	36	16	3
61	45	37	17	4
60	46	38	18	5
59	47	39	19	6
58	48	40	20	7
57	49	41	21	8
56	50	42	22	9
55	51	43	23	10
54	52	44	24	11
53	53	45	25	12
52	54	46	26	13
51	55	47	27	14
50	56	48	28	15
49	57	49	29	16
48	58	50	30	17
47	59	51	31	18
46	60	52	32	19
45	61	53	–	20
44	62	54	–	21
43	63	55	–	22
42	–	56	–	23

Glossary

Cognomen surname, denoting an individual and usually a branch of a *gens*: e.g., 'Cicero'
Commercium right to make contracts valid in Roman law
Consular ex-consul, of the rank of ex-consul, of the consul(s)
Conubium right of intermarriage
Dignitas dignity, status, worth
Dominus master, owner of slaves
Emancipatio emancipation, release of a son or daughter from paternal power by the *pater familias*
Equites cavalrymen (knights), members of the second order in the state, below senators. Singular *eques*
E(x)sul an exile, a banished man
Familia family, household (including slaves). Plural *familiae*
Filia familias daughter in paternal power, daughter of a household. Plural *filiae familiarum*
Filius familias son in paternal power, son of a household. Plural *filii familiarum*
Gens clan: e.g., the Tullii
Imagines portraits of ancestors
Imperare to order, to rule
Imperium military command; empire
Imperium populi Romani the rule/empire of the Roman People
Ius gentium the law of all races
Lanifica (feminine singular adjective) wool-making, spinning
Latins the people of the plain of Latium, the ethnic group to which Romans belonged
Liberi issue, offspring
Manus control of a husband over a wife and her property
Mater familias wife of a *pater familias*, mother of a household
Mile, Roman 1000 paces, 1.45km, about 95 yards less than an English mile
Mulier woman, esp. sexually experienced woman. Plural *mulieres*
Municipium country town in Italy
Nobilis known, known man, 'noble'. Plural *nobiles*

Nomen gentile clan name: e.g., Tullius, Tullia
Novus homo new man
Optimates the best people
Ordo order. Plural *ordines*
Patronus/patrona patron of client; ex-owner of ex-slave
Pater familias father of a household; independent man with power over his children. Plural *patres familiarum*
Patria potestas paternal power
Patrician (noun and adjective) belonging to a restricted group of aristocratic families by descent in the male line. By end of Republic, only fourteen clans survived
Pietas dutiful love (of those to whom love is due: family, country, gods, etc.)
Plebeian (noun and adjective) non-patrician
Plebs the common people, the non-patricians as a body
Pontifex Maximus High Priest
Populares those who try to please the People. Singular (noun and adjective) *popularis*
Populus (Romanus) the (Roman) People
praenomen forename: e.g., Marcus
Principate the period of the emperors 27 BC–AD 235
Provocatio right of appeal
Pudicitia chastity
Republic the period of republican government 509–43 BC
Salutatio formal morning-call
Salutatores those making a formal morning-call
Senatus the Senate
Stola the dress of a Roman married woman
Verecundia restraint, modesty
Via Latina the Latin Way
Vidua a divorcée or a widow
Villa country-house
Virtus manliness, manly courage, virtue

Notes

1 The rank into which they were born

1 Notes will be kept as few and succinct as possible. Where I have not cited sources or convenient authorities, the curious reader will normally find a wealth of information in *The Oxford Classical Dictionary*³. For this paragraph, for instance, one might look up Lucretius, consul, Epicurean. For agreed facts, particularly on individuals' families and careers, I acknowledge a debt to the standard handbooks and commentaries.
2 Dates are BC, unless indicated as AD.
3 Cf. Richardson 2003.
4 *QF* 2.16/20.4, Rome, late Aug. 54.
5 Gaius (second century AD) 1.9–12.
6 Cf. the view attributed to Cecil Rhodes (Augarde 1991: 180).
7 Modifications to this rule, introduced probably in the second century, are an excellent demonstration of the fact that Roman citizenship was by then clearly more desirable than that of other Italian groups (Cherry 1989: 244–66).
8 *Rep.* 1.43: 'grades of status' (*gradus dignitatis*). For intense class-consciousness see the lively chapter by Balsdon 1979: 18–29.
9 I use the definition adopted by most scholars. See especially Wiseman 1971.
10 Cf. Brunt 1971: 67–8. The scholarly controversy about the exact definition of the group (Brunt 1982; Shackleton Bailey 1986; Badian 1990) need not concern us here. Direct descendants of consuls, like Terentia's son, certainly counted as *nobiles*.
11 The ancient distinction between patrician and plebeian families was of limited *political* importance after a plebiscite of 367 required that at least one of the two consuls of each year had to be a plebeian. We talk of a mixed plebeio-patrician nobility. Only plebeians could vote in the Council of the *Plebs*, whose decrees from 287 were recognised as laws. Patricians retained a social *cachet*.
12 Cicero and his brother read Lucretius (*QF* 2.10 [9]/14.3, mid-Feb. 54). Nepos admired Lucretius (*Att.* 12.4). One could conjecture that Atticus read him and also that he and Cicero knew him personally.
13 Griffin 1985: 155. Cf. *Sest.* 116; *Fin.* 2.12. *Ordo*: Val. Max. 5.2.1, 8.3.3.
14 Griffin 1985.
15 Fowler 1908: 247–61 for Cicero's time; Balsdon 1969: 206–12 for an overview.
16 See D'Arms 2003: 49–78 for an evocative account of seaside life and culture; Griffin 1985: 89–103 on swimming and other amusements, for women as well as men; cf. Balsdon 1969: 220–1. Cicero sees swimming as the obvious pastime at Baiae (*F* 9.2/177.5, to Varro, Rome, c. 22 Apr. 46).

17 *A* 14.15/369.3, Puteoli, 1 May 44; 14.16/370.1, Puteoli, 2 May 44; 14.17/371.1, Pompeii, 3 May 44; 14.19/372.6.
18 *LTUR* (ii: 72, 85, 104) lists three women owners of houses in Rome at this period: Caecilia Metella in the 80s (*SRosc.* 27), Clodia Metelli in the 50s (*Cael.* 18, 36, 38, probably the same house in *Mil.* 75), Fulvia in the 40s (App. *BC* 4.29). There is plenty of evidence of women owners in the Principate, especially from inscriptions on water-pipes. Clodia also had a suburban property on the Tiber (*Cael.* 36, 38; *A* 12.38a/279.2, Astura, 7 May 45, etc.; SB *A* v.412–13). Clodia probably inherited her villa at Baiae from her husband (*Cael.* 38). Servilia acquired one at Naples (*A* 14.21/375.3, Puteoli, 11 May 44).
19 Jewels or silver toilet-sets could be turned into cash. If the husband's status were imperilled, it could easily be proved that they were not part of his property and so not subject to confiscation.
20 There is a rich bibliography on Roman houses. Treggiari 1999: 33 lists some of the principal items. As background to Terentia and Tullia the following are especially useful: E. Rawson 1976; Wiseman 1987a; Wallace-Hadrill 1994b; Tatum 1999: 159–62. It is unfortunately impossible to supply a plan or illustrations of a typical upper-class house in Rome at this date. Only basements sometimes survive. Houses at Pompeii or Herculaneum give only a partial idea. The specialised accounts of Wiseman 1987a and Wallace-Hadrill 1994b suggest brilliantly what these palaces must have been like.
21 Vitr. 6.5; Treggiari 1999: 41.
22 George 1997. An elaborate toilette took time, even if we allow for male exaggeration (*Mil.* 28).
23 Hor. *Epp.* 1.1.87. The bed would not usually be used for sleeping. See further Treggiari 1994: 316–19. Loom: Asc. 11C.
24 E.g., Pomponia (*A* 1.5/1.3, Rome, Nov. 68); Valeria Paulla (*F* 11.8/360.1, to D. Brutus, Rome, late Jan. 43).
25 See especially Purcell 1994; Horsfall 2003.
26 *Dig.* 9.2.52.2, where P. Alfenus Varus (cos. suffect 39 BC) discusses possible suits for damages.
27 Treggiari 1979; Joshel 1992b; Dixon 2001b, 2001d.
28 *QF* 2.5/9.2, Rome, end of March 56; *Flacc.* 18; *Pis.* 9. The whole state could be 'the dregs of Romulus' (*A* 2.1/21.8, Antium[?], c. 3 June[?] 60).
29 *QF* 2.5/9.2; Sall. *Cat.* 50.1.
30 E.g., *Cat.* 4.17, *Dom.* 13, 54, 89–90.
31 Cicero once refers to a freed labourer, who ran away, along with an educated freedman (who is named) (*A* 7.2/125.8, Brundisium, 25 Nov.[?] 50). He does not much mind about the first man's dereliction of duty. A more general reference to labourers, contrasted with luxury slaves, is in *SRosc.* 120. On urban staff in the late first century BC/early first century AD, see Treggiari 1975; Griffin 1976: 95–6, 105 = 1985: 14–15, 31.
32 *On the Republic* (written 54; Scipio, C. Laelius and others, set in 129); *Cato the Elder on old age* (44; M. Porcius Cato, Scipio and Laelius in 150); *Laelius on friendship* (44; Laelius and his sons-in-law Q. Mucius Scaevola and C. Fannius in 129).
33 Griffin 1975.
34 *Sest.* 96 (56 BC). Cf. *Rep.* 3.23: 'when certain men, because of their wealth or birth or other resources, control the commonwealth, it is a faction but they are called *optimates*'. See Brunt 1971: 92–5.
35 For the horror of war see, e.g., Ovid *Fasti* 6.487–90; Orosius 5.18, on the battle of 11 June 90, when the consul P. Rutilius and his army were slaughtered by the Marsi and Marius' troops saw bodies and weapons floating down

the bloodstained River Tolenus. Marius then counter-attacked and killed 8000 Marsi.
36 *De or.* 3.2.10.
37 This was the view of the winners (*SRosc.* 131, 140–1).
38 *Cat.* 2.20. For the verdict cf. *Parad.* 6.2.46. For the language cf. *Har. resp.* 54–5; *Phil.* 2.117, 14.7.
39 To study what a person knows, her mental map (e.g., the historical figures or geographical features of which she is aware) and what is most prominent in her thought and feeling at any given time, we would ideally need a substantial sample of writing. Even that would give only a partial notion. For Terentia, I argue from Cicero's writings and from probability.

2 The world into which they were born

1 For demography, see Saller 1994; Parkin 1992; Sallares 2002; Harlow and Laurence 2002.
2 Hor. *Epp.* 1.7.7 for parents' fears for children's health in August in Rome.
3 See Bradley 2005 for what this meant to parents.
4 Parkin 1992: 105–11.
5 Cf. *Dom.* 62 for Piso's removal of marble columns from Cicero's house to his mother-in-law's. Piso's wife's father was probably P. Rutilius Nudus (Syme 1955a: 137) who may have got as far as the praetorship (*MRR* iii.183). The Rutilii were related to C. Julius Caesar through his mother Aurelia. Münzer: 1999: 300 conjectures that Piso's wife Rutilia and Aurelia influenced Caesar's choice of Piso's daughter Calpurnia as his wife.
6 See Gardner 1995 and, more generally, Gardner 1986. For a general introduction to Roman law, Crook 1967.
7 Marshall 1990.
8 For a full treatment of emancipation, see Gardner 1998: 6–113.
9 Delia 1991: 208–9 argues against this view.
10 On guardianship Gardner 1993: 89–97.
11 Dixon 1985a; Crook 1986: 65–7.
12 E.g., Setälä 2002.
13 Treggiari 1979; Kampen 1981; Günther 1987; Joshel 1992b; Dixon 2001b, 2001c: 113–32.
14 They had to be qualified by shared Roman citizenship (or the equivalent) and age, and could not be closely related.
15 Brief surveys of the institution of marriage in Evans Grubbs 1994: 361–78; Treggiari 2003. Dixon 1985b gives a stimulating account. For fuller treatment, Gardner 1986: 31–116; Treggiari 1991.
16 Treggiari 1991: 441–58 or 2005c: 136–7.
17 *Leg.* 3.10, 28–32.
18 Val. Max. 6.3.7. Two aristocratic women who poisoned their husbands c. 154 were, it is said, strangled at the orders of their kin to avoid public trial (Val. Max. 6.3.8). In these instances I am interested not in what really happened but what readers liked to believe happened.
19 Val. Max. 6.3.10: going out bare-headed; 11: talking to a 'vulgar' freedwoman; 12: going to the games without husband's knowledge. For the need to have respectable companions or servants, see, e.g., *Dig.* 47.10.15.15; Macrob. 2.5.6. Older married women and kinswomen are sometimes known to have acted rather like chaperones, but there is no Latin noun expressing this.
20 *ILLRP* 793.
21 Treggiari 1991: 105–6 (in potential brides), 218–20, 233–7 (in wives). *Pudicitia* in men denotes abstention from the passive role in homosexual

intercourse (*Cael.* 42; Williams 1999: 97–100, 174). For *virtus*, see McDonnell 2006.
22 Livy 1.57–9; Joshel 1992a.
23 Livy 3.44–8. See 3.44.2–3 for upbringing. Wiseman 1979: 106–7 gives Cicero's references. See also Joshel 1992a.
24 *Verr.* 2.1.63–72.
25 *Verr.* 2.1.63–4. Since Cicero calls her *mulier* (just after drawing the distinction between *virgines* and *mulieres*), she may have been previously married.
26 *Verr.* 2.1.65, 68.
27 *Laud. Tur.*
28 Dixon 1991; Treggiari 1991: 229–61.
29 Dixon 1997: 161.
30 Cf. *Cael.* 20. Women also went out without their husbands (*QF* 3.1/21.19, Rome, Sept. 54). On the daily life of Roman women, it is still worth consulting Balsdon 1962. Cf. Treggiari 1991: 414–27. On women at dinners, Bradley 1998; Roller 2003, arguing that women reclined (like men) and a wife would share a couch with her husband. Unmarried girls did not stay for the drinking (*convivium*) which followed (Varro ap. Nonius 372 Lindsay).
31 Wiseman 1974a: 130–7.
32 Griffin 1985: 155; Treggiari 2005c: 130–1, 138.
33 Berg 2002; Shumka 2000.
34 Bradley 1991: 13–75; Barrett 1996: 6–7; Hemelrijk 1999.
35 *De or.* 3.45.
36 Sall. *Cat.* 25.2, 5.
37 Rawson 2005: 145.
38 There seems no reason to doubt that this applied in the late Republic. Cf. Watson 1967: 39. The strongest evidence is that one of Cicero's contemporaries, the jurist Ser. Sulpicius Rufus, referred to underage brides (*Dig.* 12.4.8).
39 Shaw 1987: 39, 43–4; Saller 1994: 25–41.
40 Treggiari 1991: 401–2; Harlow and Laurence 2002: 81.
41 Soranus *Gyn.* 1.20 (writing early second century AD); Parkin 1992: 123; cf. Treggiari 1991: 39–43.
42 Harlow and Laurence 2002: 13–15, 56–8, for a full account.
43 Barrett 2002: 10.
44 *A* 13.21a/327.4, Arpinum, 30 June or 1 July 45; Nep. *Att.* 12.2.
45 Treggiari 1991: 153–4; Harlow and Laurence 2002: 58–60.
46 Treggiari 1991: 401–2.
47 On literary texts see Potter 1999.
48 Many of the women, however, are depicted as courtesans.
49 Potter 1999: 20–9; Treggiari 2002: 17–19.
50 E.g., Joshel 1992b: 3–15; Dixon 2001c: *passim*.

3 Cicero: from *eques* to consul

1 The following are especially helpful on family, personalities and 'private' life: Balsdon 1964; Shackleton Bailey 1971; Rawson 1983; Bradley 1991: 177–204. Haskell 1942 remains a lively read.
2 *A* 11.9/220.3, Brundisium, 3 Jan. 47; 13.42/354.2, Tusculum, end of Dec. 45 attest day and month (cf. Plut. *Cic.* 2.1). The year is given by Gell. 15.28.3; Euseb. *Chron.* on 106; and can be worked out from the fact that he held his consulship in the first year he was eligible. Place: *Leg.* 2.3. Marius too came from a village (Plut. *Mar.* 3.1; Coarelli 1993: 238).
3 Respectively, *Leg.* 1.1, 15, *Leg.* 2.1, 6; cf. *A* 2.11/32.2, Formiae, c. 23 Apr. 59; *Planc.* 22; *Am.* 68.

4 *Leg.* 2.3; *A* 2.16/36.4, Formiae, 29 Apr./1 May 59; *Leg ag.* 3.8; *F* 14.7/155.3, to Terentia, aboard ship, Caieta, 7 June 49.
5 *QF* 3.1/21.1, Arpinum, Sept. 54; *Tusc.* 5.74.
6 *Leg.* 2.4; *A* 2.15/35.3, Formiae, c. 28 Apr. 59: 'into my ancestral mountains and to my cradle'. I adopt the conjecture that the line is from Cicero's *Marius* (Skutsch 1985: 770). For objections, SB *A* i.381.
7 *Leg.* 2.5.
8 See Rawson 1983: 1–4 for a first-hand description of the town. For the town and villa, Coarelli 1993: 232–7.
9 *Phil.* 12.20, cf. *A* 16.8/418.2, Puteoli 2/3 Nov. 44; *F* 11.5/353.1, to D. Brutus, Rome, 9 Dec. [or shortly after] 44.
10 Syme 1986b: 2 = *RP* vi.210.
11 *Cic.* 1.1.
12 Wiseman 1974b: 153–64 = 1987a: 207–18.
13 *Brut.* 62; *Tusc.* 1.38; cf. Wiseman 1974b: 158 = 1987b: 212.
14 Cf. Dio 46.4.2–5.3. Fullers trampled the cloth in a mixture of stale urine with water and fuller's earth. Their establishments, like tanneries, needed to be isolated.
15 Nisbet 1961: 194.
16 *De or.* 2.265.
17 *Brut.* 168.
18 *Leg.* 3.36.
19 He had failed to win office at Arpinum, but was tribune at Rome in 119 and consul for the first time in 107. He married a patrician Julia.
20 It is not surprising to find another M. Gratidius as an army subordinate to C. Marius in 88. He was unfortunately murdered when sent to take over an army from Sulla (Val. Max. 9.7 *Roman Soldiers* 1). Cicero's great-uncle, M. Gratidius, would not have given up a son for adoption if he had not had at least one left. This officer should be his elder son. A third M. Gratidius turns up as legate to Q. Cicero in Asia in 61–59, full of family affection. He will have been the son of Marius' officer and a second cousin to M. and Q. Cicero. He must have previously held an elected office and was on the senatorial ladder (*QF* 1.1/1.10, ?Rome, end of 60/beginning of 59; *Flacc.* 49; cf. Wiseman 1971: 234).
21 Sall. *Hist.* 1.30, 36–7, with bibliography in McGushin 1992: *ad loc.*; Wiseman 1971: 55. For the murder, see Asc. 84C; *Comm. Pet.* 10; Val. Max. 9.2.1; on Gratidianus' 'meteoric' career, Dyck 1996: 598–600. Gratidianus' mother had tried to dissuade him from a political career.
22 *Off.* 3.80–1; cf. Pliny *NH* 33.132, 34.27. Cicero found his oratory appropriate for popular assemblies (*Brut.* 223). Cf. E. Rawson 1991: 20–1, who argues that Gratidianus' court case against Aculeo (*De Or.* 1.178) marks a split with the Cicerones.
23 Carney 1960.
24 *Red. Pop.* 19–20, confirmed by *Parad.* 16. Cicero, on his own way into exile, dreamed that Marius comforted him (*Div.* 1.59, 2.136–41). But his verdict on Marius is mixed. See, e.g., *A* 9.10/177.3, Formiae, 18 Mar. 49; *Off.* 3.79; *Tusc.* 5.56 for the bad side. The great Marius' son was about four years older than Cicero and as a student became a friend of Atticus (Nep. *Att.* 1, 2.2). Made consul, well below the normal age, by the Marians in the fight against Sulla (it is said against the wishes of his mother Julia), he perished bravely and his memory was cherished by the Italians (Vell. 2.27). Cicero does not write of the relationship but must have known him (Horsfall 1989: 61; E. Rawson 1991: 19–20). He alludes to his exile (*De Or.* 3.8).
25 It was well known in 45 (*A* 12.49/292.2, Tusculum, 20 May). A friend,

M. Marius, who lived on the Bay of Naples in the 50s and 40s, may have been a kinsman (Balsdon 1964: 188; SB *F* i.323–4).
26 *De Or.* 2.2–3.
27 *A* 1.5/1.1, Rome, Nov. 68; *Fin.* 5.1. See also *Fin.* 5.5–6, 15, 71, 75–6, 86, 95; *Verr.* 2.3.170, 4.25, 137, 145.
28 *Cic.* 1.1, 2.1.
29 E.g., *Red. Pop.* 5.
30 A view once expressed by Terentia (*F* 14.1/8.1, dispatched from Dyrrachium, 25 Nov. 58).
31 Nicolet 1974: 910 n.2 assumes Helvia was Arpinate.
32 It is usually thought that he was a Visellius by adoption, a son of a Terentius Varro from Reate, whose *cognomen* and tribe he kept. But that is odd, as C. Aculeo had at least one other son. So perhaps he was adopted by a Varro, and Visellius is C. Aculeo's *nomen*. See Taylor 1960: 282 (*contra* 266; Wiseman 1971: 275; Shackleton Bailey 1991: 86). For his ability as an orator and jurist, see *Brut.* 264.
33 *A* 3.23/68.4, Dyrrachium, 29 Nov. 58.
34 *Lig.* 21; *QF* 1.1.10.
35 Balsdon 1964: 172; Shackleton Bailey 1971: 4–5.
36 Cf. Dixon 1997.
37 *De Or.* 2.2.
38 *De Or.* 2.1–3; cf. Fantham 2004: 27–8. Q. Cicero and the sons of Aculeo all benefited from this instruction. Atticus too may have frequented Crassus' house.
39 *Leg.* 1.13; *Am.* 1.
40 Nep. *Att.* 1.4 with Horsfall 1989: 59; *Prov. Cons.* 40.
41 *Lig.* 21; *Div.* 1.72; *Phil.* 12.27; Plut. *Cic.* 3.1; Mitchell 1979: 9.
42 *Brut.* 313–15; Plut. *Cic.* 3.4
43 *Planc.* 67; *Phil.* 6.17: 'a me ortus'. Cf. Tac. *Ann.* 11.21.
44 Syme 1980: 422 = *RP* iii.1236.
45 Syme 1987: 320 = *RP* vi.234.
46 Sumner 1971: 258, arguing forcefully for 76/5 for Tullia's birth against 78/7.
47 Tyrrell and Purser 1885–1933: i.43; Strachan-Davidson 1900: 77; Lacey 1978: 17 [early autumn]; Syme 1978b: 292 = *RP* iii.1085; Mitchell 1979: 99.
48 Shackleton Bailey 1971: 22: 'not long before his eastern tour'; Rawson 1983: 25: 79 BC; 'in about 79' (Harlow and Laurence 2002: 95).
49 Groebe (in *RE* viiA: 1329) and Balsdon (1964: 173) put Tullia's birth in 79. (Drumann and Groebe 1919: vi.614 had put it in 79/8.) Gardner (1986: 38) reckons she was engaged at twelve (in late 67), so she must think she was born in 79.
50 Alexander 1990 no. 126.
51 Alexander 1990 no. 129.
52 Alexander 1990 no. 132.
53 E.g., Rawson 1983: 25–6.
54 Plut. *Sulla* 22.1; App. BC 1.77.
55 Plut. *Pomp.* 66.3; Wiseman 1974a: 180; below, p. 132.
56 Pp. 98, 71–2, 97; *A* 6.8/122.1, Ephesus, 1 Oct. 50; cf. 4.19/93.1, Rome, end of Nov. 54.
57 *Sest.* 7; probably by sea.
58 *F* 6.12/226.3, to Ampius Balbus, Rome, ?Aug./Sept. 46.
59 Cf. p. 18 on 'Turia'.
60 Shackleton Bailey 1971: 12 suggests 'a physical or nervous breakdown'.
61 *Brut.* 315.

62 *Fin.* 5.1–5.
63 I rule out 79 and 77, if we suppose Terentia travelled to and from the East with Cicero, as then she would have been heavily pregnant for the journey. I would like to suppose that the young couple were together for much of the pregnancy, and the birth and early life of their daughter.

4 Terentia: the young wife

1 *CIL* vi 27261 (cf. 34178): (a) 'TERENTIA T—/ M. TERENTIO —/ TULLIAE —/ M. TERENTIO —/
(b) M. TERENTIO M. F. CL —/
(c) M. TVLLIO CICER—/ TULLIAE TU—/ TULLIAE GAIAE L. P—/ TULLIAE M. L. P—.

(a) Terentia T— to Marcus Terentius —, to Tullia —, to Marcus Terentius —, (b) to Marcus Terentius son of Marcus Cl—, (c) to Marcus Tullius – ?of Cicer(o) —, to Tullia Tu—, to Tullia freedwoman of a woman P—, to Tullia freedwoman of Marcus P—.

The inscription was wrongly thought in the fifteenth century to be to Cicero's own daughter, but the two freedwomen in part (c) strongly suggest that all those commemorated were ex-slaves or their descendants. Only one is definitely freeborn, the man in (b), who may be son of a freed M. Terentius. We thus have:

- Terentia T— (perhaps a *cognomen*; she is dedicating the monument, at least part (a), to the others who are named);
- M. Terentius?;
- Tullia?;
- M. Terentius?;
- M. Terentius M. f. Cl? (perhaps a *cognomen*, possibly his tribe: Claudia or Clustumina?);
- M. Tullius Cicer(?onis l.), ?freedman of Cicero (this suggests that some of these may have been freed by Cicero's wife and perhaps daughter directly, though others might be freed by their freed slaves and some be children of freed slaves);
- Tullia Tu(?che), (possibly freeborn, though Tuche/Tyche is a typical slave name);
- Tullia, freedwoman of a woman, P? (possibly freed by Tullia or by a freedwoman of Cicero);
- Tullia, freedwoman of Marcus, P? (possibly freed by Cicero, but more likely by a freedman of Cicero, if the preference was to give Cicero's *cognomen* when he was the manumitter).

If Cicero's daughter were one of the patrons, she would have to have been emancipated by her father, so that she was the legal owner, rather than just enjoying the services of the slaves as part of her *peculium*, the property a daughter-in-power was allowed to administer by her father. There is no other evidence for this.

2 Asc. 91C. It must be a half-sister. 'Sister', *soror*, can mean a cousin (or half-cousin) by a paternal uncle, but such cousins would bear the same name. See Shackleton Bailey 1977a: 306.
3 Syme 1978b: 292 = *RP* iii.1085.
4 Plut. *Cato min.* 19.3; *MRR* ii.107–8; Alexander 1990 no. 167.
5 Sall. *Cat.* 15.1.
6 Treggiari 1991: 161–70.

7 Cf. Treggiari 1994.
8 *F* 9.26/197.2, to Papirius Paetus, Rome, shortly before 17 Nov. [true calendar] 46.
9 *Dig.* 26.7.13.2, 27.3.1.5, 50.16.194.
10 *Cic.* 8.2.
11 I agree with Saller 1994: 214 that Plutarch intends us to understand that this was the full value of the dowry.
12 *A* 16.1/409.5, Puteoli, 8 July 44.
13 *A* 15.29/408.2, Formiae, 6 July 44.
14 Cf. Carp 1981: 193.
15 *Cael.* 18; *A* 12.32/271.2, Astura, 28 March 45; 16.1/409.5, Puteoli, 8 July 44.
16 Plut. *Cic.* 8.3.
17 Verg. *Aen.* 8.361; *Har. resp.* 49; Suet. *Gr.* 15.1.
18 *Har. resp.* 31.
19 *A* 6.1/115.2, Laodicea, 20 Feb. 50; *Quinct.* 93; *Cael.* 9; *Phil.* 2.68.
20 *F* 16.26/351.2, Q. Cicero to Tiro, 44[?].
21 Columella 12 preface 1–10.
22 Treggiari 1991: 221, 227, 244, 257, 424–6; Engels 2003.
23 Pearce 1974.
24 *Frugalitas* (*Epp.* 4.19.1–2).
25 Treggiari 1991: 166, 220, 243–4; Dixon 2001d: 117–19.
26 Asc. 43C.
27 Livy 1.57.9; Suet. *Aug.* 73.
28 Small *et al.* 2003: 55.
29 For the exploitation of similar, though less mountainous, land in medieval times, see Dyer 2000; Short 2000.
30 *A* 12.32/271.2, Astura, 28 March 45; 15.17/394.1, Astura, 14 June 44; 15.20/397.4, Tusculum, 20 June 44.
31 *A* 12.32/271.2; cf. *A* 14.7/361.2, Formiae, 15 Apr. 44; 14.11/365.2, Puteoli[?], 21 Apr. 44; 15.15/393.4, Astura, 13[?] June 44.
32 *A* 16.1/409.5, Puteoli, 8 July 44; *A* 12.32/271.2, Astura, 28 March 45.
33 Nep. *Att.* 13.6, with Horsfall 1989: 90.
34 Treggiari 1994: 317.
35 Rives 1992.
36 E.g., Cicero supposed Atticus to have sacrificed to a nymph on his estate (*A* 1.13/13.1, Rome, 25 Jan. 61).
37 For alfresco meals, cf. Horace's sacrifice of a kid to a spring on his farm (*Odes* 3.13) or the later hunting mosaics which show sacrifice of the quarry which was subsequently eaten (e.g., *The Small Hunt* at Piazza Armerina [Dunbabin 1999: 133, pl. 137; cf. 142]).
38 *QF* 1.3/3.9, Thessalonica, 13 June 58.
39 Bradley 1998: 36–8, 51–2.
40 *F* 9.26/197.2, to Papirius Paetus, Rome, shortly before 17 Nov. [true calendar] 46.
41 Treggiari 2005b: 16–18, 28–32. Add *Off.* 1.12, 32, 54; *Fin.* 3.57, 62, 65, 68; 4.17.
42 *Mur.* 23; *A* 12.1/248.1, Arpinum, 27 Nov. [by the sun] 46. The Romans expected both kissing and embracing between adult family members. See, e.g., *Mur.* 88 (mother kissing son on his election to the consulship); *Font.* 46 (male embraced by mother and sister); *Phil.* 3.18 (young Quintus in the arms of father and uncle); *Flacc.* 95; *Dom.* 98 (mutual embracing in the family). Ancient custom allegedly prescribed that women kiss their own and their husbands' kin down to cousins' children (e.g. Polyb. 6.2).
43 This was a theme of the philosophical schools, but Cicero's descriptions are

180 Notes to pages 37–41

vivid enough to be, partly at least, from his own observation: e.g., *Fin.* 5.42, 48, 55, 61.
44 *QF* 1.3/3.3, Thessalonica, 13 June 58.
45 Val. Max. 7.1.1; Stat. *Silv.* 4.8.27; cf. Ovid *Met.* 481–2, 659.
46 *Comm. Pet.* 17, 44; cf. *De Or.* 1. 87, 2.182; Plut. *Rules for politicians* tr. Russell 1993: 144.
47 *De Or.* 1.1–2; *Brut.* 318, 321; Plut. *Cic.* 7.1–2.
48 *Arch.* 13; *Sulla* 26; *Div.* 2.142.
49 *A* 2.20/40.6, Rome, c. mid-July 59; *Acad.* 2.115; *Brut.* 309; *Tusc.* 5.113.
50 *F* 13.16/316.4, to Caesar, Rome[?], winter of 46/5.
51 *A* 15.1/377.1, Puteoli, 17 May 44; 15.2/379.4, district of Vescia, 18 May 44; 15.3/380.2, Arpinum, 22 May 44.
52 Treggiari 1977a.
53 Cf. *De or.* 1.136.
54 Terentia and the children did not necessarily dine with Cicero every evening when they were all at home. See Bradley 1998: 36–8, 51–2. Grand houses had several dining-rooms.
55 *Div.* 1.90.
56 *De Or.* 1.173, 1.184, 1.199–200.
57 *Sulla* 26; *Comm. Pet.* 44, 47, 49, 50.
58 *Comm. Pet.* 44.
59 *De Or.* 1.1.
60 Cf. *Dig.* 24.1.31.8; Hor. *Odes* 3.8.

5 **The life of mother and daughter**

1 Atticus later adopted the name of his maternal uncle and became Q. Caecilius (*A* 3.20/65.1, Thessalonica, 5 Oct. 58).
2 Letters on politics, which need not concern us, are particularly well represented from Cicero's last burst of activity after the murder of Caesar and before his own death at the end of 43.
3 I do not specify the addressee in citations of *F* 14.
4 Shackleton Bailey's Indices of Persons (Roman and Italian) in the *Onomastica* (1992, 1995, 1996) give the specific references. Treggiari 2002: 124–8 shows his lists for Tullia from the speeches and letters only, adding his own numbering for the latter. In Treggiari 2002: 49–73 I attempted a case-study based on those references as an illustration of research methods. Claassen 1996: 214–15 reviews the references to Terentia in the correspondence. It is rewarding to read all the letters chronologically, seeing the material on family life in as much of its historical context as possible. I have now done this several times since 1962. A classic description of what the experience means is given by Shackleton Bailey 1994.
5 Cugusi 1979: xxv–xxix has a useful list of the time letters normally took. Less than a day was enough for letters from Rome to Antium or Tusculum, one or two for Formiae, two for Arpinum, three or four for Cumae or Pompeii, seven to nine for Brundisium.
6 *A* 13.21a/327.4, Arpinum, 30 June or 1 July 45.
7 Calpurnii Pisones, remoter kin, appear among office-holders from the third century. The great-grandfather was L. Calpurnius L. f. C. n. Piso Frugi, the author of the first law on extortion (*Verr.* 2. 3.195, 4.56, etc.). As consul in 133 (*A* 1.19/19.4, Rome, shortly before 17 July 65), colleague of P. Mucius Scaevola (the father of Cicero's teacher, the consul of 95) he fought a successful campaign against the slave rebellion in Sicily. He opposed C. Gracchus (*Tusc.* 3.48, etc.). He was an active orator and wrote unadorned *Annals* (*Brut.*

106, etc.), quoted by Cicero in the 40s (*F* 9.22/189.2, to Papirius Paetus, between 46 and 44). The grandfather, another Lucius, praetor ?113 or 112, a man of ostentatious integrity, was killed in Spain in 111 (*Verr.* 2.4.56–7), probably in his father's lifetime (Münzer 1999: 377–9). The father, as praetor in 74, vetoed many of the edicts of his colleague Verres, kept track of his departures from his own edict and was a refuge for the oppressed (*Verr.* 2.1.119, 2.4.56). He was probably the L. Piso who protected the Achaeans (*Div. Caec.* 64; Alexander 1990 no. 174). Cicero calls him his friend in 69/8 (*Caec.* 35). Cicero consistently underlines the uprightness of three generations. The wives of the Pisones Frugi are unknown.

8 *Font.* 39; *Fin.* 2.90.
9 *Tusc.* 3.16.
10 A Calpurnius by birth and a Pupius by adoption, who was to be consul in 61; see further Asc. 15C; SB *A* i.303.
11 He offered Cicero a favour (*A* 1.1/10.2, Rome, shortly before 17 July 65).
12 Menstrual blood, which was thought to have magic properties, inspired disgust in at least some men (Pliny *NH* 7.64–7, 11.44, 28.77–86). But doctors understood, in part, the link between menstruation and the ability to conceive (Soranus *Gyn.*1.19). They recommended moderate exercise, relaxation, a daily bath, etc. to make the first menstruation easy; later the woman should do what she found comfortable (Soranus *Gyn.* 1.25–6). Roman women, like others until the twentieth century, used cloths or rags to absorb the flow (Plut. *Quaest. conv.* 2.2). These would be washed and reused.
13 Cf. Tert. *virg. vel.* 11.
14 *Dig.* 38.10.8, Pomponius, citing Cicero's contemporary Ser. Sulpicius Rufus.
15 *A* 1.6/2.2, Rome, shortly after 23 Nov. 68; Asconius (82C) must be wrong to put the death in 63.
16 In giving the place from which Cicero sent a letter, we write, for brevity, 'Tusculum' although Cicero would have said 'at my *Tusculanum*'.
17 First mentioned *A* 1.5/1.7, Rome, Nov. 68; Shatzman 1975: 404–5.
18 *A* 1.5/1.7; 1.6/2.2, Rome, shortly after 23 Nov. 68; 1.7/3, Rome, before 13 Feb. 67; 1.8/4.2, Rome, after 13 Feb. 67; 1.9/5.2, Rome, March or Apr. 67; 1.10/6.3, Tusculum, c. May 67; 1.11/7.3, Rome, Aug. 67; 1.3/8.2, Rome, end of 67; 1.4/9.3, Rome, first half of 66; 1.1/10.5, Rome, shortly before 17 July 65. By 45, there were two 'gymnasia', spaces for walking and talking, surrounded by colonnades. The upper one was called the Lyceum (and contained a library, *Div.* 2.8) and the lower the Academia, after two of the Athenian philosophical schools (SB *A* i.282, citing *Tusc.* 2.9 [add 4.7]; *Div.* 1.8). Like eighteenth-century shrubberies and landscaped grounds, these would make attractive places for the women of the family to walk, though that was not their declared purpose.
19 *A* 1.10/6.4; 1.11/7.3; 1.4/9.3; 1.20/20.7, Rome, after 12 May 60; 2.1/21.12, Antium[?], c. 3[?] June 60.
20 *A* 1.4/9.3.
21 *A* 2.1/21.1, 11, Antium[?], c. 3[?] June 60; Shatzman 1975: 405.
22 Details on venues in Balsdon 1969: 252–61. Rome had no permanent stone theatre until 55. Women's attendance at gladiatorial shows was accepted (Ovid *Ars* 1.164–75).
23 Servius *Commentary on Vergil Eclogues* 8.105.
24 Plut. *Cic.* 20.1–2; Dio 37.35.4. Cf. Scullard 1981: 199–201.
25 *A* 12.2/260.1.1, Astura, 17 March 45.
26 Ovid *Fasti* 1.79–88.
27 *Leg. ag.* 1.
28 *Div.* 1.18.

Notes to pages 45–51

29 *Cat.* 3.15.
30 *Cat.* 3.18–21; *Div.* 1.20–1; Dio 37.34; cf. Rawson 1983: 81; Vasaly 1993: 81–7.
31 *Cat.* 3.29.
32 *Cat.* 3.23.
33 Griffin 1985: 155; Treggiari 2005c: 130–1, 138; Schultz 2006: 28–33.
34 Plut. *Cic.*19.3, 20.1–2. See Wiseman 1974a: 130–7.
35 *Div.* 1.18.
36 Cf. the consul of 186, who approached a respectable woman for information through his mother-in-law (Livy 39.11.4–7).
37 *A* 2.1/21.3.
38 *Cat.* 1.9–10, cf. 4.2; *Sulla* 52; Sall. *Cat.* 28.1–3; Plut. *Cic.* 16.2; App. *BC* 2.3; Dio 37.32.4–33.1.
39 Normally nobody was turned away by his doorkeeper or because he was still asleep (*Planc.* 66).
40 Sall. *Cat.* 55; Plut. *Cic.* 22.1–2.
41 Plut. *Cic.* 22.3–5.
42 Treggiari 2005b: 32–3.
43 Alexander 1990 nos. 226–34.
44 *Phil.* 2.95, 113, cf. 35, 92; 3.10, 16; 5.11–12.
45 Cf. *Phil.* 2.17: 'He says that I did not give up the body of his stepfather for burial'. Cicero implicitly denies this. Plutarch says all the bodies were handed over. I owe the reference to Van der Blom 2003: 296.
46 A high-born woman, but whose father L. Cornelius Scipio Asiaticus (cos. 83) had been proscribed by Sulla.
47 *F* 5.6/4.1, to P. Sestius, Rome, mid- or late Dec. 62.
48 A loan which might be an embarrassment if Antonius were prosecuted for extortion (*A* 1.12/12.1–2).
49 *A* 1.13/13.6, Rome, 25 Jan. 61; 1.14/14.7, Rome, 13 Feb. 61.
50 *A* 1.9/5.2, Rome, March or April 67; 1.12/12.2, Rome, 1 Jan. 61; 1.16/16.15, Rome, beginning of July 61; Wiseman 1974a: 138–46.
51 *A* 1.12/12.3, Rome, 1 Jan. 61; 1.13/13.3, Rome, 25 Jan. 61.
52 Wiseman 1974a: 140.
53 Possibly between May and October (Berry 1996: 14).
54 *F* 5.6/4.2, to P. Sestius, Rome, mid- or late Dec. 62; *A* 1.13/13.6, Rome, 25 Jan. 61; 1.16/16.10, Rome, beginning of July 61; Plut. *Cic.* 8.3. For the propriety of a consul having a grand house and the need to have one big enough for entertaining guests and for receiving crowds of all sorts of people, see *Off.* 1.139.
55 The ready money came partly from loans; one, of 2,000,000, from his client P. Sulla, then being tried for involvement in the conspiracy of 63. This naturally attracted criticism (Gell. 12.12; Berry 1996: 30–3, 39–42).
56 Papi 1998.
57 *A* 1.4/14.1, Rome, 13 Feb. 61; 1.19/19.1, Rome, 15 Mar. 60.
58 *A* 1.14/14.3; 1.16/16.5, 11.
59 *A* 1.16/16.18.
60 *A* 2.1/21.11, Antium[?], c. 3[?] June 60.
61 *A* 2.3/23.2, Rome[?], shortly after mid- or late Dec. 60; 2.4/24.7, Antium, early Apr. 59; 2.7/27.5, Antium, Apr. 59.
62 *A* 2.2/22.3, Antium, mid- or late Dec. 60; 2.3/23.4, Rome[?], shortly after 2.2/22.
63 Scullard 1981: 58–60; Lott 2004: 30–7; Schultz 2006: 129.
64 *A* 2.1/21.1, Antium[?], c. 3[?] June 60.
65 *A* 1.20/20.1, Rome, after 12 May; Shatzman 1975: 405; *Acad.* 2.9; D'Arms

2003: 189. If [Sall.] *Inv.* 3–4 is correct, Cicero may have owned it and been remodelling it by 62.
66 *A* 16.6/414.2, Vibo, 25 July 44, Shackleton Bailey's translation; see Fowler 1908: 247–62.
67 [Sall.] *Inv.* 3; this may be P. Crassus (cos. 97), who committed suicide in 87, father of the consul of 70.
68 *A* 4.5/80.2, Antium, late June 56, with SB *A* ii.185–6. Catulus is probably the consul of 102, who died in 87; Cicero actually bought the villa from a much less eminent man, a certain Vettius.
69 ([Sall.] *Inv.* 3; *A* 1.16/16.10, Rome, beginning of July 61; *A* 2.8/28.2, Antium, 16[?] Apr. 59.
70 Plut. *Pomp.* 40.5.
71 *Or.* 32; Hor. *Odes* 3.29.12.
72 But fishing was a Roman sport (Balsdon 1969: 221–2).
73 *A* 2.7/27.4, Antium, shortly after 2.6/26.
74 Cicero mentions walking beside the sea (*A* 14.13/1, Puteoli, 26 Apr. 44) and the pleasure of walking and talking (*A* 2.3/23.4, Rome[?], Dec. 60; 4.10.1, Cumae, 22 Apr. 55; *F* 2.212/95.2, to Caelius, camp on the River Pyramus, 20[?] June 50). Walking was part of Cicero's exercise regime (*A* 2.23/43.1, Rome, Aug.[?] 59; above p. 37).
75 *A* 2.7/27.5, Antium, early Apr. 59; 2.9/29.4, Antium, 16 or 17 Apr. 59; 2.12/30.4, Tres Tabernae, 19 Apr. 59; 2.15/35.4, Formiae, c. 28 Apr. 59.
76 Antium was a citizen colony and now a popular resort.
77 *A* 2.8/28.2, Antium, 16[?] Apr. 59.
78 *A* 2.9/29.4, Antium, 16 or 17[?] April.
79 *A* 2.10/31, Forum Appii, 20 April.
80 Plaut. *Poen.* 17–35; Ovid *Am.* 3.2, *Ars* 1.89–100, 135–63, *Tr.* 2.283–4; Juv. 11.201–2. Women, married and unmarried, watched mime (Ovid *Ars* 1.501, *Tr.* 2.497–516), but perhaps Cicero would have discouraged his wife and daughter from attending such daring shows.
81 *A* 2.12/30.2, 4.
82 *A* 2.10/31, with SB *A* i.377.
83 He expected Tiro to ride a horse or mule on the journey from Brundisium to Rome (*F* 16.9/127.3, Brundisium, 26 Nov. 50). For his own use of a *raeda*, see *A* 5.17/110.1, en route between Synnada and Philomelium, 15 Aug.[?] 51; *Mil.* 28. During his triumphal journey through Italy in 57, he used a gilded chariot (*Red. Sen.* 28, a reference I owe to R. Kaster). A horse was the solution if speed were necessary, the road bad or hilly, etc. (Apuleius *Florida* 34–5). See Balsdon 1969: 213–16.
84 Perhaps we should not argue from the silence of the sources that no Roman woman rode.
85 *A* 2.11/32.1, c. 23 April; *A* 2.14/34.2, Formiae, c. 26 Apr. 59; 2.15/35.3, Formiae, c. 28 Apr. 59.
86 *A* 2.16/36.1, Formiae, 29 Apr. or 1 May 59.
87 It was not convenient if he wanted to combine a visit to Cicero with his long journey to Buthrotum. (*A* 2.11/32.2, Formiae, c. 23 Apr. 59).
88 *Leg.* 1.1–4, 2.1–5.
89 *A* 2.24/44, esp. 3; *Vat.* 26.
90 *A* 2.4/24.7; 2.6/26.2; 2.7/27.5; all Antium, early April 59.

6 Living through disaster

1 *A* 2.22/42.3; 2.23/43.1, 3, both Rome, Aug.[?] 59.
2 *A* 2.19/39.3, Rome between 7 and 14 July 59.

184 *Notes to pages 56–61*

3 The surviving correspondence with Quintus opens in late 60/early 59 with a tract on provincial governorship, meant for wider circulation (*QF* 1.1/1). *QF* 1.2/2 (Rome, between 25 Oct. and 10 Dec. 59) is all on business or politics.
4 Tatum 1999: 154. For mourning as a protest, see Lintott 1999: 16–20. For a detailed calendar of events see Kaster 2006: 393–408.
5 Cf., e.g., Livy 1.26.2, 26.9.7.
6 *A* 3.8/53.4, 29 May 58; *QF* 1.3/3.8, 13 June 58; *A* 3.10/55.2, 17 June 58; 3.13/59.2, 5 Aug. 58; 3.15/60.2, 17 Aug. 58, all from Thessalonica; *Dom.* 28, *Sest.* 41.
7 *QF* 1.3/3.9, 1.4/4.4, c. 5 Aug., both from Thessalonica; App. *BC* 2.15, Dio 38.14.7–17.4.
8 Plut. *Cic.* 31.2–3; Seager 1979: 104–5.
9 *Pis.* 12–13.
10 E.g., *A* 3.3/47, en route, c. 24[?] Mar. 58; *QF* 1.3/3.3, 6.
11 Cf. *Sest.* 49.
12 *A* 7.3/126.3, near Trebula, 9 Dec. 50; *F* 12.25/373.1, to Cornificius, c. 20 March 43; *Leg.* 2.42; Plut. *Cic.* 31.5, Dio 38.17.4.
13 *Cic.* 31.5; cf. App. *BC* 2.15.
14 Ovid *Tr.* 1.3.15–100.
15 *Tr.* 4.46–56. Strictly, Ovid was 'relegated' (sent to a specific place outside Italy), not exiled, and so did not lose his rights as a citizen (*Tr.* 5.11.9–10, 15–22).
16 Mitchell 1991: 142.
17 *Caec.* 100, 69 BC.
18 *Dom.* 78; cf. *Balb.* 31.
19 Berger 1953 s. *Caput, Interdicere aqua et igni.* For full and convincing discussion see Strachan-Davidson 1912: ii.16–74.
20 Livy 25.4.9.
21 The Sullan laws, which codified previous practice, established standing courts for capital charges.
22 *Dom.* 83–5. Friends too had continued to put him down in their wills.
23 Strachan-Davidson 1912: ii.31–2.
24 *Har. resp.* 17; *Dom.* 26, 85; *Sest.* 128; *Pis.* 34, with Strachan-Davidson 1912: ii.53–4.
25 The bracketed portion may be a gloss. Gaius telescopes the legal position: the interdiction was not the Sullan punishment but the practical consequence.
26 *Odes* 3.5.41–8.
27 *Sest.* 127.
28 Such a 'wife' was sometimes later called *uxor iniusta* (Treggiari 1991: 49–51).
29 Tatum 1999: 153–6; Moreau 1987: 472–83.
30 *A* 3.4/49.1, Vibo[?], 3 April 58.
31 Claassen 1992 regards this as a sentence of *relegatio*.
32 *Red. Sen.* 18; *Dom.* 62; *Pis.* 26; *Leg.* 2.42; Plut. *Cic.* 33.1.
33 *Dom.* 60, 62; *Pis.* 26.
34 P. 31; Rawson 1983: 116.
35 Plut. *Cic.* 32.4–5; Dio 38.18–29; Mitchell 1991: 141–3; Claassen 1992.
36 *A* 3.1/46, place unknown, c. 22 March 58.
37 On the emotional impact of exile and on *F* 14.4/6, *A* 3.7/52, *QF* 1.3/3, see the rich and judicious discussion of Hutchinson 1998: 25–48. Claassen 1992 gives a thorough account of Cicero's reactions to his banishment.
38 *A* 3.6/51, near Tarentum, 17 Apr. 58; *A* 3.19/64.3, Thessalonica, 15 Sept. 58; *A* 3.5/50, Thurii, 6 Apr., cf. 3.8/53.4, Thessalonica, 29 May 58; 3.9/54.3, Thessalonica, 13 June 58.
39 *A* 3.10/55.2, Thessalonica, 17 June 58.

40 *A* 3.15/60.4, Thessalonica, 17 Aug. 58.
41 *A* 3.15/60.2.
42 E.g., *A* 3.15/60.4, 7.
43 Cf., e.g., 3.19/64.3, Thessalonica, 15 Sept. 58; *QF* 1.4/4.1, Thessalonica, c. 5 Aug. 58.
44 *A* 15.11/389.1–3, Antium[?], c. 7 June 44.
45 *QF* 1.3/3.1, Thessalonica, 13 June 58.
46 *QF* 1.3/3.1, cf. *A* 3.9/54.1, both written at Thessalonica, 13 June 58.
47 *QF* 1.3/3.2, cf. 1.4/4.4, Thessalonica, about 5 Aug.
48 Saller 1994: 105–14.
49 This might be taken in close connection with her mother's proposed departure to join Cicero in lifelong exile. Marcus presumably would have accompanied his mother for a time.
50 See Hutchinson 1998: 28–33 for a brilliant discussion of the 'tact and emotional skill' deployed in this letter. 'The grief . . . is inextricably interwoven with the relationship, which Cicero is partly writing to sustain' (33).
51 Here he mentions the loyal Clodius Philhetaerus, sent back to Rome because of an eye complaint; he praises Sallustius and Pescennius (the latter, he hopes, will be attentive to Terentia); Sicca was less satisfactory and has left him. Later, he planned to cut down his followers (*A* 3.19/64.1, Thessalonica, 15 Sept. 58).
52 Dixon 1986: 95–102.
53 Carcopino 1947: i.235 justly remarks on her moral energy ('*énergie morale*') and says she took on the sweet character of a consoler ('*elle prend la douce figure d'une consolatrice*'). Most of what he says on the emotion in these letters is sympathetic (235–7). Rawson 1983: 119 thinks Terentia may have 'had little sympathy with failure and depression'.
54 *Red. Sen.* 38; *Red. Pop.* 7; *Sest.* 68.
55 Kaster 2006: 179–80 on *Sest.* 26 documents supplication and rejection and shows how shocking a kick was.
56 *Vat.* 21; Richardson 1992: 376; *LTUR* v.16; *contra* Dixon 1986: 97; Moreau 1987: 477.
57 See Shackleton Bailey 1985: 149 for a conjectural emendation, which would mean his children were 'tormented'.
58 *F* 15.7/99, between Iconium and Cybistra, early Sept. 51; cf. 15.8/100, written to Marcellus at the same time and place as the previous letter; 15.2/118.1, to Marcellus, Tarsus, late July 50.
59 *F* 14.1/8.2, despatched from Dyrrachium, 25 Nov. 58; *Sest.* 144.
60 *Planc.* 73; *Balb.* 58; *Rab. Post.* 47.
61 *A* 3.23/68.4, Dyrrachium, 29 Nov. 58.
62 The Latin word *virtus* was used primarily for 'manliness' and attributed to men.
63 Or a 'street of houses'.
64 Cf. *A* 3.20/65.2 for Atticus' promised support and Nep. *Att.* 4.4 for a gift of 250,000 sesterces.
65 *Virtus* was demanded of Roman men in all difficulties, and hard work and due attention, *diligentia*, was a particular virtue of the good *pater familias* in administration of the household, business and family affairs. Both in moral courage and in practical ability to look after his family, Cicero has been found wanting.
66 Cf. Treggiari 1991: 388–91; Pölönen 2002: 174–5.
67 For substantial bequests to wives at this time, cf. *Caec.* 11–12: Caesennia inherited the usufruct of her husband's entire property; her son left his wife a quantity of silver; *Top.* 16–17: hypothetical examples. A wife might also be heir or co-heir (Treggiari 1991: 383–6).

68 *Sest.* 76; cf. Plut. *Cic.* 33.3.
69 *Sest.* 75–7.
70 Stockton 1971: 190–3; Mitchell 1991: 152–6.

7 Restoration

1 *Red. Sen.* 24, 28; *Pis.* 34.
2 *Sest.*115–27.
3 Mitchell 1991: 154–6; Kaster 2006: 401.
4 Hor. *Sat.* 1.5, via Aricia, Forum Appi, Anxur, Fundi, Sinuessa, Capua, Caudium, Beneventum, then a short cut by mule-track via Trivicum, Canusium, Egnatia. Cato the Elder had managed it in five days (Plut. *Cato mai.* 14.4). See also Friedländer 1907: i.281.
5 Praetors regarded twenty Roman miles a day as reasonable for litigants, because it allowed for those who had to walk (*Dig.* 2.11.1, 50.16.3 pr.).
6 Cicero called it 'a journey of so many days' when describing how Cytheris undertook it to greet Antonius on his return in 48 (*Phil.* 2.61).
7 *Sat.* 1.5; *Epp.* 1.18.52–3.
8 If she stayed on the Appian Way, she might have broken the journey at Lanuvium (where Cicero had a lodge at least from 45, using it when going between Tusculum and Astura); Tarracina (where Cicero had not succeeded in acquiring a lodge but had a host [F 7.23/209.3, to Fabius Gallus, Rome, Dec. 46]); Formiae (where she could use the villa); Minturnae (where Cicero had a lodge from 51); Cales (where Cicero had a lodge in 49) and/or Pontius' house in the territory of Trebula (where Cicero stayed in 51 and 50 and Terentia by herself in 50; the territory bordered the Appian Way between Saticula and Suessula [SB A iii.191]); Capua (a major centre, but Cicero never indicates where he stayed when there); Beneventum (which was one day's march from Capua for Caesar [A 9.15a/184.2, from Matius and Trebatius to Cicero, March 49]), perhaps Aec(u)lanum (fifteen Roman miles from Beneventum where Cicero at least once received a letter and at least once seems to have stayed [A 7.3/126.1, in the territory of Trebula, 9 Dec. 50; 16.2/412.4, Puteoli, 11 July 44]); Venusia (where Cicero lodged [A 5.5/98.1, Venusia, 15 May 51] and which was on his usual route [A 16.5/410.3, Puteoli, 9 July 44]); Tarentum; Brundisium (forty-five Roman miles further on, a long day's journey but one which Cicero did in 58 and 51, perhaps because there was nowhere to stay and the ground was flat [SB A iii.201]). For Cicero's lodges, which he may have owned earlier, cf. Shatzman 1975: 406–7, SB A iv.308. They were useful not just for a night's lodging, but for a siesta to break the journey (A 13.34/350, Astura, c. 26 Aug. 45). At Brundisium, Tullia could expect to stay with Cicero's staunch friends the Laenii Flacci, as they both did after they met (*Sest.* 131).
9 A 7.1/132.1, Formiae, 27 Dec. 50; Asc. 31C, 50C; Lintott 1999: 23, 83–5, 120.
10 Carcopino 1947: i.256–7 unfairly finds Cicero unfeeling for not having mentioned Piso's death in the letters. It had happened during a gap in the correspondence.
11 A 4.1/73.5; *Sest.* 131; cf. *Pis.* 51–2; App. *BC* 2.16. Perhaps they went to the house on the Carinae (Kaster 2006: 371–2).
12 For Cicero's exploitation of love of family in speeches, see Treggiari 2005b: 16–29; for his representation of himself as a family man, 29–34.
13 *Red. Sen.* 1, 8; F 1.9/20.4, to Spinther, Rome, Dec. 54; *Red. Sen.* 1; *Red. Pop.* 2, 5; F 3.10/73.10, to Ap. Claudius, Laodicea, early Apr. 50.
14 *Red. Pop.* 5. Cf. SB A ii.64 for references to rebirth.

15 *A* 3.15/60.6, Thessalonica, 17 Aug. 58, 3.20/65.1, 5 Oct. 58.
16 *A* 4.1/73.7, Rome, c. 10 Sept. 57.
17 *A* 4/2.74.2–5, Rome, beginning of Oct. 57; *F* 1.9/20.4, to Spinther, Rome, Dec. 54.
18 *A* 4.2/74.7, Rome, beginning of Oct. 57.
19 *A* 4.1/73.8, Rome, c. 10 Sept. 57. Weinstock 1934: 712 thinks of a breakdown in understanding between Pomponia and Terentia.
20 For a different view, see Claassen 1996: 211.
21 *A* 4.3/75.3.
22 Cf. Neubauer 1909: 216.
23 *QF* 2.2/6.4, Rome, 17 Jan. 56; 2.2/6.2; 2.4/8.2, Rome, mid-March 56.
24 *QF* 2.3/7.7 Rome, 12–15 Feb. 56.
25 *QF* 2.4/8.2, Rome, mid-March 56.
26 *QF* 2.5/9.4.
27 *QF* 2.5.4; D'Arms 2003: 189.
28 Pliny *NH* 13.29; Shatzman 1975: 415.
29 The date is disputed. The old view was that it was 51. See *SB F* 1.477–8. Crassipes as quaestor served in Bithynia. Marriage a couple of years before the quaestorship seems *a priori* more likely.
30 *LTUR Suburbium* 277.
31 After dining with Crassipes on the 8th, Cicero had been to see Pompey, who showed no sign of annoyance with his attack on Caesar. The engagement celebrations did not stop his intense political activity.
32 Treggiari 1991: 109, 366. Add Ovid *Met.* 481, 659.
33 Crook 1990: 164 supposes Crassipes was not present.
34 *A* 4.5/80.4, Antium, soon after 20 June[?] 56; 4.12/81, Antium, end of June[?] 56.
35 *QF* 3.5/25.8, Tusculum, end of October or beginning of November 54.
36 May–December 54, *QF* 2.13/17–3.7/27.
37 *A* 7.1/124.8, Athens, 16 Oct. 50; 9.11/178.3, Formiae, 20 Mar. 49.
38 The second marriage seems to have been a success: the couple were still married after Brutus had conspired against Caesar (*F* 11.8/360.1, to D. Brutus, Rome, end of Jan. 43).
39 *A* 4.7/77.3, Arpinum, c. 13 April 56.
40 *QF* 2.3/7.7, Rome, 12–15 Feb. 56.
41 *A* 4.8/79, Antium, soon after 4.4a/78.2.
42 *A* 4.5/80.4, Antium, soon after 4.8/79; *QF* 2.9/12.2, 3, Cumae[?], 55[?].
43 *A* 4.6/83, Cumae, about 19 Mar. 55.
44 *A* 4.10/84.1–2, Cumae, 22 Apr. 55.
45 *A* 4.9/85.2, Naples, 27 Apr. 55.
46 When Quintus, after an improvement in his relations with his wife, took her away to his estates near Arpinum, he was also accompanied by a scholar (*A* 1.6/2.2, shortly after 23 Nov. 68). The Romans' ideas of 'quality time' with family are peculiar to them.
47 *A* 4.11/86.2, Tusculum[?], 26 June 55; 4.13/87.1, Tusculum, 15 or 16 Nov. 55.
48 *QF* 2.13/17.1, Cumae or Pompeii, May 54.
49 *A* 4.15/90.4,6, Rome, 27 July 54.
50 *QF* 2.15/19.2–3, Rome, end of July 54.
51 *QF* 2.16/20.1, Rome, late Aug.; cf. *QF* 3.3/23.1, Rome, 21 Oct. 54.
52 Alexander 1990 no. 293.
53 Crassus had previously used almost the same formula about Cicero, referring to his wife rather than children (*A* 1.14/14.3, Rome, 13 Feb. 61).
54 *QF* 3.3/23.1.

188   *Notes to pages 79–86*

55 *Sen.* 24–5, 51–60 suggests an informed interest in farming.
56 *QF* 3.7/27.9, Rome, end of Nov. 54.
57 *QF* 3.3/23.1, Rome, 21 Oct. 54.
58 *F* 16.13–15, 10/40–3, to Tiro, Cumae, 10–17 Apr. 53.
59 Gell. 13.9; cf. *F* 16.10.43/2; 16.3/122.1; SB *A* iii.231, *F* i.344–5.
60 *F* 13.16/316.4, Cicero to Caesar, Rome[?], winter 46/5.
61 Treggiari 1977a: 26–8.
62 *QF* 3.1/21.10, Arpinum and Rome, Sept. 54.
63 E.g., *F* 16.18/219.
64 *F* 16.1/120.1, between Patrae and Alyzia, 3 Nov. 50; *F* 16.6/125.2, Actium, 7 Nov. 50; 16.2/121, Alyzia, 5 Nov. 50, all to Tiro.
65 *A* 1.12/12.4, Rome, 1 Jan. 61. Cf. *Sen.* 26, 28–9 on the delights of young companions.
66 *A* 5.20/113.9, 6.7/120.2.
67 Though the letters were written by Cicero (*F* 16.1/120, 16.3/122–16.6/125), Quintus also wrote separately later (*F* 16.8/147).
68 I see no sign of resentment between Tiro and the freeborn members of the household. But, because the criticisms of Terentia's behaviour just before the divorce in Plut. *Cic.* 41.2 may derive from Tiro, a longstanding hostility has been posited. See Fowler 1908: 151: 'as Cicero obviously loved this man much more than his wife, we can understand why the two should dislike each other', and cf. Shackleton Bailey 1971: 133.
69 Treggiari 1969: 259–63 assembles most of the data. Note, however, that Tiro's manumission must be dated to 53; that before it he was ill at Formiae, not Tusculum. Nobody seems to have accepted McDermott's conjecture (1972: 265) that Tiro was a natural child of Cicero's own, by a slave-woman. If true, that would have affected the attitude of Terentia and Tullia, and I see no trace of this.
70 E.g., Quintus governed Asia 61–58. He was on campaign 57–56, 54–52, 51–50, 49–48. Pompey commanded in Spain 77–71 and in the East 66–61.
71 *Dig.* 24.1.32.13.
72 *A* 5.1/94.1, 3, Minturnae, 5 or 6 May 51.
73 It seems to have been usual for married women to recline on couches for dinner. See further Roller 2003, esp. 398.
74 See Bradley 1991: 186–98 on the marriage.
75 *F* 3.3/66.1, to Ap. Claudius, Brundisium, shortly after 22 May 51; cf. SB *A* iii.191–2.
76 *F* 8.1/77.4, Caelius to Cicero, Rome, c. 26 May 51.

8 Finding the right man

1 *QF* 2.4/8.1, Rome, mid-March 56.
2 Nep. *Att.* 5.3.
3 Nep. *Att.* 12.2; App. *BC* 5.53.
4 Treggiari 1991: 136.
5 Treggiari 1991: 134.
6 Dixon 1983: 105–6, 107–8; 1988: 215.
7 The only possible evidence known to me would be the epitaph quoted above (Ch. 4, n. 1). If we could be sure that 'Tullia, freedwoman of a woman' had been freed by Cicero's daughter, then she would have to have been emancipated, since daughters- and sons-in-power could not manumit (cf., e.g., Suet. *Tib.*15.2). But we cannot postulate this and the evidence of the letters supports the orthodox view.
8 *Dig.* 23.2.2, Paul.

Notes to pages 86–90   189

9   SB *A* iii.203. For agents in Cicero's day, see the lucid account of Crook 1967: 236–42.
10 *A* 5.8/101.3, Brundisium, 2 June 51; cf. 6.1/115.19, Laodicea, 20 Feb. 50; 6.5/119.1–2, in camp on the Pyramus, 26 June 50.
11 *A* 11.23/232.1, Brundisium, 9 July 47; 13.6/310.1, Tusculum, 3 June[?] 45; Shatzman 1975: 423; Andreau 1999: 18–19.
12 Pearce 1974.
13 *A* 2.4/24.7, Antium, early Apr. 59. Treggiari 1969: 263–4 (to be corrected on some points in the light of Shackleton Bailey) summarises his functions.
14 *A* 5.9/102.1, Actium, 14 June 51.
15 *A* 5.17/110.1, en route, 15 Aug.[?] 51; cf. *F* 3.8/70.10, to Ap. Pulcher, in camp near Mopsuhestia, 8 Oct. 51; 2.10/86.1, to Caelius, in camp near Pindenissum, 14 Nov. 51; *F* 2.7/107.3, to Curio, in camp at Pindenissum, soon after 17 Dec. 51.
16 In conjecturing how long letters took in either direction, we rely on the information that a fast courier reached Cybistra (on the far side of his province) in forty-six days from Rome (*A* 5.19/112.1, camp outside Cybistra, 21 Sept. 51), while the Rome *Gazette* of 7 March reached Cicero in Laodicea on the western border by late April (*A* 6.2/116.6, Laodicea, latter part of April[?] 50). The calendar was a month ahead of the true season. Winter conditions would slow down couriers. See SB *A* iii.222–3.
17 *A* 5.11/104.4, Athens, 6 July.
18 *A* 5.13/106.3, Ephesus, 26 July 51; 5.14/107.3, Tralles[?], 27 July 51; Dixon 1983: 106–7; Treggiari 1991: 127–34.
19 *F* 8.4/81.1, Rome, 1 Aug. 51.
20 *A* 5.15/108.1, 3 Aug. 51; cf. similar sentiments expressed to Caelius, *F* 2.11/90.1, 4 Apr. 50; 2.13/93.3, early May 50; all Laodicea.
21 *A* 5.17/110.3, en route, 15 Aug.[?] 51; 5.20/113.9, camp at Pindenissum, 19 Dec. 51.
22 *Brut.* 246.
23 *A* iii.195.
24 Suet. *Aug.* 63.2; cf. Treggiari 1991: 93. Julius Caesar was engaged as a boy to a rich equestrian woman (Suet. *Jul.* 1).
25 *Am.* 69. The definition is from *OLD s.v.* 'grex'.
26 *Brut.* 151–5; *Phil.* 9; see also Hutchinson 1998: 65.
27 Syme 1986a: 260.
28 *A* 5.21/114.9, Laodicea, 13 Feb. 50; Suet. *Jul.* 50.1, perhaps Catullus 27.3; Syme 1980: 430 = *RP* iii.1243.
29 *F* 4.2/151.1, 4, 28 or 29 Apr. 49; *A* 10.9/200.3, 3 May 49; 10.10/201.4, 3 May 49; all Cumae; *A* 12.22/261.2, Astura, 18 March 54.
30 *A* 9.18/187.2, Formiae, 28 Mar. 49, etc.; *F* 4.3/202.4, Rome[?], first half of Sept.[?] 46, etc.
31 He was probably, like Messalla, a friend of Horace (Hor. *Sat.* 1.10.85–6).
32 Stemma xxiv in Syme 1986a.
33 Cf. *A* 6.2/116.10, Laodicea, latter part of April[?] 50; 6.3/117.10, en route to Tarsus, May or beginning of June 50; 6.4/118.3, en route, mid-[?] June 50; 6.5/119.4, in camp on the Pyramus, 26 June 50; 6.8/122.5, Ephesus, 1 Oct. 50.
34 Nep. *Att.* 9.4, 12.4; *A* 10.10/201.5, Cumae, 3 May 49.
35 *F* 3.64/138, Laodicea, April[?] 50.
36 SB *F* i.136.
37 Both claimed descent from the famous Appius Claudius the Blind, censor 312 (Suet. *Tib.* 3.1) and other important figures.
38 Barrett 2002: 4, 10–11.

39 Sall. *Cat.* 50.4.
40 *QF* 3.1/21.15, Arpinum and Rome, Sept. 54; 3.2/22.1, Rome, 11 Oct. 54.
41 Barrett 2002: 11.
42 *F* 2.13/93.1–2, Laodicea, early May 50.
43 *F* 3.10/73, Laodicea, first half of Apr. 50.
44 We know nothing more of these. Cf. *Phil.* 11.9; Alexander 1990 nos. 316, 317.
45 *F* 3.10/73.5; cf. 6.11/224, to Trebianus, Tusculum[?], first half of June 45.
46 It is possible that Fabia was a third wife, Tullia's sucessor or that a different Dolabella was meant, but the orthodox view seems more likely.
47 Quint. *Inst.* 6.3.73.
48 Plut. *Ant.* 84.1; Syme 1986a: 316. The son Tullia bore to Dolabella at the beginning of 45 would be too young to be negotiating with Cleopatra. It is unlikely that he lived for more than a few months.
49 *PIR*[2] C1345, C1348.
50 *A* 15.29/408.2, Formiae, 6 July 44; 16.2/412.5, Puteoli, 11 July 44.
51 The only full sketch of his life known to me in English is TP iv.xcv–ci, to be used with caution.
52 One had a consulship in 283, another in 159.
53 Gruen 1966: 386.
54 Frier 1985: 44–7.
55 Badian 1965.
56 Dio 42.33.3.
57 App. *BC* 2.129.
58 Syme 1986a: 316; cf. 1980: 430–5 = *RP* iii.1244–8.
59 Sumner 1971: 364; but see further Syme 1980: 432–3 = *RP* iii.1245–6.
60 Pace Groebe in *RE* 7A 1331.
61 Suet. *Jul.* 1; Syme 1980: 422 = *RP* iii.1236.
62 P. 95. Syme 1980: 433 = *RP* iii.1245.
63 Syme 1980.
64 Syme 1980: 434 = *RP* iii.1247.
65 *F* 4.5/248.5, Athens, mid-March 45. That word is somewhat vague and might include leading *equites* in another context.
66 1980: 434 = *RP* iii.1247; as often, it is hard to penetrate the layers of irony.
67 SB *A* iii.244.
68 Cf. Dixon 1983: 104
69 *Phil.* 2.47, 44–6. Cf. [Sall.] *Inv.* 5.
70 *Cael.* 6–7.
71 *A* 6.9/123.2, 15 Oct. 50; 7.1/124.9, 16 Oct. 50; both Athens.
72 Cicero left Side in August; called at Rhodes for the sake of the boys' education; was delayed at Ephesus by unfavourable winds; left for Athens on 1 October and arrived on the 14th; travelled on via Patrae. Tiro fell ill and was left there. The Cicerones sailed on 2 November and, with various delays caused by the weather, went up the coast, with stops at Alyzia, Leucas, Actium and Corcyra (and Atticus' estate at Buthrotum for the Quinti). On 22 November the Marci left Corcyra after dinner and, enjoying a fair wind, reached the Italian coast on the 23rd and Brundisium on the 24th.
73 *F* 16.1/120.1, to Tiro, between Patrae and Alyzia, 3 Nov. 50.
74 Augustus was not present at two of his daughter's weddings (Dio 53.27.5, 54.6.4–5).
75 *A* 7.5/128.3, mid-Dec. 50, Formiae.
76 This may suggest that he did not aim at a political career.
77 *A* 5.2/95.1, Pompeii, 10 May 51.
78 Pompey also had a villa there (Shatzman 1975: 390).

79 *A* 7.5/128.3, Formiae, mid-Dec. 50. Shatzman (1975: 405) wrongly thinks the villa at Alba belonged to Cicero.
80 *A* 7.8/131.3, Formiae, 25 or 26 Dec. 50.

9 Public and private quarrels

1 For the possibility of such family policies in difficult times, see Wiseman 1974a: 180–1, 186–9.
2 E.g., *A* 7.1/124.3, Athens, 16 Oct. 50; 7.7/130.5–7, Formiae,19[?] Dec. 50.
3 *A* 7.8/131.4, Formiae, 25 or 26 Dec. 50.
4 He could not enter the city as he still held a military command.
5 *F* 16.11/143.2, outside Rome, 12 Jan. 49.
6 *A* 7.10/133, near Rome, 18 Jan. 49. For details of his movements 18 January–19 May, see SB *A* iv.428–37 and Shackleton Bailey 1971: 156–66.
7 See Shackleton Bailey 1971: 145–565; Brunt 1986.
8 By 45, he had a villa at Baiae, but this was probably a reward from Caesar after Pharsalus (*A* 13.52/353.2, Puteoli[?], 19 Dec. 45; 15.13a/417.1, Puteoli or Cumae, c. 28 Oct. 44; *F* 9.12/263.1, to Dolabella, a villa, Dec. 45[?]; D'Arms 2003: 169–70).
9 Soranus *Gyn.* 1.46–56.
10 *A* 15.1/377, Puteoli, 17 May 44.
11 *A* 12.33/269.2, Astura, 26 Mar. 45.
12 Treggiari 1976: 87.
13 Nep. *Att.* 13.4.
14 *A* 7.12/135.6, Formiae, 22 Jan. 49.
15 *Mulieres*, a generic term for sexually experienced women or wives in relation to husbands. Cicero uses it often in writing to Atticus to mean 'Terentia and Tullia', the women of his family. It sometimes included Pomponia, as a member of Atticus' family. It is not disrespectful. I translate *feminae* (women, females) as 'ladies' when it seems tinged with additional respect.
16 *A* 7.12/135.6, Formiae, 22 Jan. 49.
17 *A* 7.12/135.3.
18 *A* 7.11/134.3, Formiae[?], 21 Jan. 49; 7.13/136.1, Minturnae, 23 Jan. 49; *F* 16.12/146.1, to Tiro, Capua, 27 Jan. 49.
19 Cicero clarifies this later: he thought of doing this when it appeared that the Pompeians would go to Spain (*A* 7.17/141.1, 4, Formiae, 2 Feb. 49).
20 *A* 7.13a/137.3, Minturnae, 24 Jan. 49.
21 Note that Pomponia's safety and honour are of joint concern to the Cicerones and her brother.
22 *A* 7.16/140.1, Cales, 28 Jan. 49.
23 *A* 7.16/140.2.
24 *A* 7.16/141.5, Formiae, 2 Feb. 49.
25 *A* 7.21/145.2, Cales, 8 Feb. 49.
26 Cf. *A* 7.17/141.3, Formiae, 2 Feb. 49.
27 *A* 7.21/145.2, 3, Cales, 8 Feb. 49; cf. 7.23/147.3, Formiae, 10 Feb. 49.
28 Letters to other correspondents survive sparsely, apart from some to and from Caesar and Pompey which were copied into the correspondence with Atticus.
29 Later, he thought villas too would be destroyed because Pompey would invade Italy (*A* 9.9/176.4, Formiae, 17 March 49; cf., e.g., 9.7/174.4, Formiae, 13 March 49).
30 *A* 8.3/153.7, Cales, night of 18–19 Feb. 49; on this lodge or overnight stopping-place (not in Shatzman 1975), cf. SB *A* iv.429.
31 *A* 8.11D/161D.2–4, to Pompey, Formiae, 27 Feb. 49.

192 *Notes to pages 105–7*

32 *A* 8.3/153.5, Cales, night of 18–19 Feb. 49; cf. *A* 8.11D/161D.7; 9.1/167.4, Formiae, 6 March 59.
33 *A* 8.6/154, Formiae, 20 Feb. 59.
34 (All the letters cited are from Formiae, unless otherwise noted.) L. Manlius Torquatus (*A* 7.12/135.4, 22 Jan. 49; 7.23/147.1, 10 Feb. 49), praetor 50 or 49; C. Cassius Longinus the tribune (*A* 7.23/147.1); C. Sosius the praetor (*A* 8.6/154.1, 20 Feb. 49); M. Pomponius Dionysius, Atticus' freedman, who refused to return to teaching the boys (*A* 8.5/157.1, 22 Feb. 49; 8.10/159.1, 24 Feb. 49); the younger Cornelius Balbus (*A* 8.9a/160.2, 25 Feb. 49); M. Fabius Gallus, an erudite *eques* and friend of both Pompey and Cicero, carried a letter to Atticus in Rome, so may have called on 28 Feb. (*A* 8.12/162.1, 28 Feb. 49). Sosius was in Rome by 6 March and Lepidus left for Rome on 7 March. Many others left Formiae at that time (*A* 9.1/167.2, 6 March). Curtius Postumus and Q. Fufius Calenus called on their way to join Caesar (*A* 2a/169.3, 8 March 49; cf. 9.3/170.2, 9 March 49; 9.5/171.1, 10 March 49). Q. Furnius, a friend, came with a message from Caesar (*A* 9.6/172.6, 11 March 49; cf. 9.6A/172A, from Caesar, between Arpi and Brundisium, c. 5 March 49); Crassipes on 16 March 49 (*A* 9.11/178.3, 20 March 49); C. Caecius; C. Matius, *eques* and friend of Caesar and Cicero (*A* 9.11/178.1, 2, 20 March 49); Matius and C. Trebatius Testa (a lawyer whom Cicero had recommended to Caesar) on the 21st (SB *A* iv.381); a certain Baebius (*A* 9.14/182.2, 24 or 25 March 49); Trebatius again (*A* 9.17/186.1, 27 March). These will be just the tip of the iceberg, the important callers worth mentioning to Atticus. Cicero liked to get away into the country to think (*A* 9.9/176.1, 17 March 49).
35 *A* 8.9a/160.1; 9.1/167.2; cf. 7.12/135.4; *A* 7.23/147.1; 8.14/164.3.
36 *A* 8.13/163.2, Formiae, 1 March 49; cf. 8.16/166.2, Formiae, 4 March 49.
37 *A* 2.14/34.2, Formiae, c. 26 Apr. 59; 2.15/35.3, Formiae, c. 28 Apr. 59.
38 *A* 8.3/153.6, Cales, night of 18–19 Feb. 49; 8.4/156.3, Formiae, 22 Feb. 49; 8.11B/161B.1, to Pompey, Formiae, 15 or 16 Feb. 49.
39 *A* 7.13a/137.3, Minturnae, 24 Jan. 49; 7.14/138.1, Cales, 25 Jan. 49; 8.12/162.1, Formiae, 28 Feb. 49; 8.13/163.1, Formiae, 1 March 49; 10.14/206.1, Cumae, 8 May 49; 10.17/209.2, Cumae, 16 May 49.
40 *A* 8.1/151.4, Formiae, 15 or 16 Feb. 49; cf. 9.7/174.7, Formiae, 13 March 49; 9.10/177.1, Formiae, 18 March 49; 10.14/206.1, Cumae, 8 May 49.
41 *A* 8.16/166.1–2, Formiae, 4 March 49; 9.1/167.3, Formiae, 6 March 49.
42 *A* 9.3/170.1, Formiae, 9 March 49.
43 *A* 9.5/171.1, 10 March 49; 9.6/172.1, 11 March 49; *A* 9.17/186.1, 27 March 49; all from Formiae.
44 *A* 9.6/172.4
45 *A* 9.7/174.2, 6, Formiae, 13 March 49.
46 *A* 9.15/183.3, Formiae, 25 March 49.
47 *A* 9.11/178.3, Formiae, 20 March 49.
48 *A* 9.13/180.1,2, Formiae, 23 March 49; 9.13a/181, Formiae, 24 March 49.
49 *A* 9.18/187.1, 2, Formiae, 28 March 49.
50 *A* 9.16/185.3, Formiae, 26 March 49, copying Caesar's letter.
51 D'Arms 2003: 190 and SB *A* v.395, respectively.
52 *A* 13.52/353, 19 Dec. 45.
53 *A* 9.18/187.3, Formiae, 28 March 49.
54 *A* 8.9/188.3, between Formiae and Arpinum, 29 or 30 March 49.
55 Cicero had given young Quintus the white toga at Laodicea on that day in 50 (*A* 5.20/113.9, camp at Pindenissum, 19 Dec. 51; 6.1/115.12, Laodicea, 20 Feb. 50).
56 Terentia was in Rome by about 14 April (*A* 10.4/195.12).
57 Shackleton Bailey 1995: 103 notes that 'young man', *iuvenis*, is used of young

Quintus once (*A* 10.10/201.6, Cumae, 3 May 49, with 'our'). The previous sentence in *A* 10.1a/191.1 refers to Atticus' relative (possibly brother-in-law) Celer, so it would be natural to think Cicero then turns to *his* relations. (But, equally, if young Caesarians in general were meant, Celer, who had been in Caesar's company when Cicero saw him [*A* 9.18/187.2, Formiae, 28 March 49], might lead in to that topic.)

58 *A* 9.19/189.1, Arpinum, 1 or 2 Apr. 49.
59 *A* 9.19/189.2, Arpinum, 1 or 2 Apr. 49.
60 *A* 10.1/190.1.
61 For fake inscriptions to the Tullii from there (with one possibly genuine one) see Syme 1955b: 160 = *RP* i.270; 1979: 1–2 = *RP* iii.1122.
62 *A* 10.2/192.1, Laterium or *Arcanum*, 5 or 6 Apr. 49. Cicero may be thinking of the meaning of *arcanum*, 'secret'.
63 *A* 10.4/195, Cumae, 14 Apr. 49. During this time, young Quintus left his father, perhaps on the pretext of escorting his mother to Rome, and had a talk with Caesar's friend A. Hirtius. It was a terrible blow to his father and uncle. They were afraid Quintus had leaked their plans, but from one of Dolabella's letters to Curio, telling him how pleased Caesar was with him for wanting Cicero to come to Rome, it appeared that the secret was still safe (*A* 10.4/195.5–6, 11, Cumae, 14 Apr. 49).
64 *A* 9.17/186.1, Formiae, 27 March 49.
65 *A* 10.5/196.3, Cumae, 16 Apr. 49.
66 *A* 10.7/198.1, Cumae, 22 Apr.[?] 49.
67 *A* 10.4/195.12, though *F* 4.1/150.2, to Sulpicius Rufus, Cumae, c. 21 Apr. 49, is more pessimistic.
68 Young Quintus had come back. Marcus was braver and put Cicero's good name first.
69 *A* 10.10/201.1, Cumae, 3 May 49.
70 Did Cicero remember that Caelius had used this word, *optimus*, of Dolabella (p. 95)?
71 *TP* iv.236 explains these as 'settling days', the Kalends and the Ides of each month.
72 E.g., *Cat.* 82.4.
73 *F* 16.12/146.5, Capua, 27 Jan. 49.
74 *F* 16.10/43.1, to Tiro, Cumae, 17 Apr. 53; cf. Treggiari 1977b: 67–8.
75 Shatzman 1975: 406.
76 *A* 10.16/208.4, Cumae, 14 May 49.
77 E.g., *A* 6.3/117.9, en route to Tarsus, May or beginning of June 50.
78 *A* 10.10/201.5, Cumae, 3 May 49; 10.15/207.3, Cumae, 10[?] May 49; 10.16/208.5, Cumae, 14 May 49; *Phil.* 2.58.
79 *A* 10.16/209.3, Cumae, 16 May 49.
80 Soranus *Gyn.* 1.55.
81 Soranus *Gyn.* 2.2–3; Dixon 1988: 106–7.
82 *A* 10.18/210.2.
83 This was usual for a man going abroad, especially in dangerous times. Cf., e.g., *F* 5.11/257.2, to Vatinius, Rome, early Dec.[?] 45 (Vatinius had commended his wife to Cicero); *F* 12.16/328.4, from Trebonius, Athens, 25 May 44 (Trebonius commends his mother and family). Later, Cicero thanked the Caesarians Oppius and Matius for their attentions to his family (*F* 11.29/335.2, to Oppius, Anagnia[?], July [beginning] 44; 11.27/348.4, to Matius, Tusculum, mid-Oct.[?] 44). Such mentions are 'the tip of the iceberg'.
84 *A* 10.7/198.3, Cumae, 22 Apr. 49.
85 Frederiksen believes Cicero got the money from the Mint, perhaps by selling plate (1966: 132 n.36).

86 She may even have been expected to receive cash when she was in Rome and take it to Cicero (*A* 10.4/195.12, Cumae, 14 Apr. 49, but the text is corrupt).
87 Macrob. 2.3.8.
88 In 49 reduction of interest rates; valuation of property at pre-war levels when it was transferred to creditors; later, probably in 48, cancellation of interest due since the start of the war and of one year's rent, up to 2000 sesterces. See Frederiksen 1966: 132–41; Rawson 1994: 457–8.
89 *Off.* 2.84.
90 Frederiksen 1966: 131.
91 E.g., *A* 7.23/147.1, Formiae, 10 Feb. 49; 9.7/174.6, Formiae, 13 March 49.
92 *A* 6.4/118.3, en route, mid-June 50; 6.5/119.2, in camp on the Pyramus, 26 June 50; 6.7/120.1, Tarsus[?], July 50; 6.9/123.2, Athens, 15 Oct. 50.
93 E.g., *A* 7.3/126.7, near Trebula, 9 Dec. 50.
94 *A* 7.1/124.9, Athens, 16 Oct. 50; *F* 14.5/119.2, Athens, 16 Oct. 50.
95 *Hort. frag.* in Mueller 1904: F v.59, p. 319.
96 *Cic.* 41.2.
97 Cf. Claassen 1996: 218.
98 See, e.g., Dixon 1986: 103; SB *A* v.265.
99 *A* 1.2/211.2, Epirus, second[?] week in Jan. 48.
100 *A* 11.2/212.4, Epirus, middle of March[?] 48; cf. *A* 11.13/224.4, Brundisium, mid-March[?] 47.
101 Cf. Dixon 1986: 103–4.
102 Dixon 1986: 103 thinks it was deducted from the amount set aside for the second and third instalments.
103 Dixon 1986: 118 n.35.
104 Gardner 1986: 68–70; Crook 1990; Treggiari 1991: 332–40; Saller 1994: 210–11.
105 1986: 103–5.
106 I am not following Dixon 1986: 105, who suggests he settled a property on her so that she could use the income. Cf. Mitchell 1991: 265.
107 In later law, this would be a gift from husband to wife (Crook 1990: 156).
108 *A* 11.2/212.3.
109 SB *F* i.499.
110 *F* 9.9/157, from Dolabella, Caesar's camp near Dyrrachium, May 48.
111 *A* 11.4/215, Pompey's camp, 15 July 48.
112 Shackleton Bailey notes that this heading, which is almost certainly authentic, avoids giving names because the letter might be intercepted. He characterises the letter as 'notably curt and uncordial'. Cf. Dixon 1986: 104.
113 Dixon 1986: 104.
114 He said he was not surprised by her brave and loving behaviour in 58 (*F* 14.2/7.2; p. 65). *Contra* Schmidt 1898: 180. For a different view, Claassen 1996: 217.
115 *Off.* 2.45.
116 *A* 11.7/218.2, Brundisium, 17 Dec. 48.
117 On this traumatic quarrel, see Shackleton Bailey 1971: 179–85.
118 SB *F* i.500; *F* 7.3/183.3, Rome, mid-Apr. 46).

10 Three divorces, a wedding, a funeral and a baby

1 The brackets < > mark a conjectural addition to the text by Shackleton Bailey.
2 Atticus did not visit Cicero at Brundisium either (SB *A* i.45).
3 *A* 11.5/216.3.
4 Claassen 1996 argues persuasively against the common view that the marriage was 'crumbling'.

5 Dio 42.29.1; Asc. 5C ('P. Lentulus'). See Shackleton Bailey 1976: 29–32, 112 = 1991: 18–20, 91.
6 *A* 13.23/331.3, with SB *A* v.377–8, who argues rightly that he is not thinking here of what he might leave Marcus by will.
7 It would be odd if Cicero had not met his old friend Eutrapelus' freedwoman and (probably) mistress in the pre-Antonius days. She was in Brundisium with Antonius on his return with the legions after Pharsalus, when Antonius refrained from having Cicero killed (*Phil.* 2.5, 59–61). Cicero and Cytheris were both at a dinner-party in 46, when he was not married (*F* 9.26/197, to Papirius Paetus, Rome, shortly before 17 Nov. [true calendar] 46).
8 *A* 10.10/201.5, Cumae, 3 May 49; 10.16/208.5, Cumae, 14 May 49; *Phil.* 2.58.
9 Money worries continued to be discussed with Atticus (*A* 11.14/225.3; 11.15/226.2, 4; 11.17a/229.3, Brundisium, 14 June 47).
10 *A* 11.12/223.4, Brundisium, 8 Mar. 47.
11 *A* 14.21/375.4, Puteoli, 11 May 44; Livy *Epit.* 113; Plut. *Ant.* 9.1–2; Dio 42.29.1, 32.2.
12 *Phil.* 2.99, Oct.–Nov. 44.
13 Pelling 1988: 137.
14 Pelling 1988: 141.
15 Gardner 1998: 220–1 elegantly puts Terentia's will in context. See too Pölönen 2002. We do not know who her guardian was. (Philotimus could have been.)
16 Gardner 1986: 167–8; Crook 1986: 63–4.
17 E.g., Weinstock 1934: 713.
18 'To satisfy' (*satis facere*) is often used for paying debts. But Shackleton Bailey convincingly rejects a reference to paying off creditors here, for why should Cicero care about them? Claassen 1996: 219 suggests the children are meant. It was a clear duty to put kin first (*Off.* 1.44).
19 Schmidt 1898: 182 supposed Terentia had not put her children down as primary heirs, or at all, but meant to favour her own family. Lacey 1978: 116 thinks Terentia intended to ignore Tullia. Either of these would certainly provoke Cicero, but both seem unlikely. For the expectation that mothers would and should pass on their property to their children, see Dixon 1988: 50–60. Cf. Pölönen 2002: 172.
20 The letter was supposedly sent from Caesar in Alexandria, but Cicero was sure it was not authentic (*A* 11.16/227.1; 17a/229.3).
21 *Cic.* 41.2.
22 Cf. *A* 11.17a/229.1. Sallustius (who had been such a good friend in 58 [*F* 14.4/6.6; *Div.* 1.59]) would have gone too.
23 Known only by his *cognomen*, Sicca is first mentioned in 58 (*A* 3.2/48, Nares Lucanae, 27 March) and appears frequently in 45, helping Cicero with his planned purchase of land for a shrine and as a companion at Astura and host near Rome (12.23/262.3–12.34/273, *passim*) and occasionally in 44.
24 Cf. similar hyperbole about Brutus' dead wife, Cato's daughter, Porcia (*ad Brutum* 1.9/18.2 = SB *Cicero's letters to his friends: Letters to M. Brutus* 19.2).
25 SB *A* v.412–13.
26 *A* 12.52/294.2, Tusculum, 21 May 45; *A* 13.7/314, Tusculum, 10 June 45. Spinther may have been abroad in 47/6.
27 Wiseman 1974a: 112, 188–91.
28 Treggiari 1991: 443–6, 459–61.
29 Carcopino 1947: i.274–5 blames Cicero's selfish unwillingness to risk trouble with Caesar. But the decision does not seem to have been imposed on Tullia. Nor can Dolabella have been in such favour with Caesar as before. In the uncertainty about whether the family's property would be confiscated (which

might be – and was – settled when Caesar returned), it might have been inopportune for Tullia to be unmarried. So there was an argument for not proceeding hastily.
30 TP iv.335 explains the procedure. Both recipient and sender of a draft (*permutatio*) were said 'to exchange', *permutare*. For Cicero's practice, cf. *A* 15.15/393.4, where Cicero sends Tiro to tell the steward Eros to pay cash to Atticus, who will send a draft to Athens for young Marcus' allowance. The accusation is taken seriously in Fantham *et al.* 1994: 271. This money might represent what Cicero had asked Terentia to raise in March (p. 122), but, in view of the interval, is more likely to be the next tranche of money for his expenses.
31 Crook 1990.
32 *A* 11.21/236.2, Brundisium, 25 Aug. 47
33 *Lig.* 7.
34 *Planc.* 97; *Sest.* 131; *F* 14.4/6.2, Brundisium, 29 Apr. 58.
35 Plut. *Cic.* 39.3–4.
36 It was common sense to warn a host in advance, since it took time to stoke up the bath furnace (*F* 9.5/179.3, to Varro, Rome, [late] May 46; 9.16/190.9, to Paetus, Tusculum[?], mid-July 46). Cf. p. 50 above. The basin, *labrum*, is a standard item in the hot room, a large shallow basin on a pedestal: there are examples in the Forum Baths and the Stabian Baths in Pompeii (Yegül 1992: 376–7).
37 Cicero would usually stop overnight at the town of Venusia (above, p. 82). Other letters written on the road are short (e.g., *A* 3.6/51, from the territory of Tarentum, 17 Apr. 58).
38 George Long *ap.* TP iv.347. Cf. TP iv.347: 'almost brusque'; Shackleton Bailey 1971: 177, 'the bleakest of notifications to the wife he had not seen for over two years'; cf. Carcopino 1947: i.240–1; Rawson 1983: 208. I used to wonder if we might suppose that this was merely a quick message about practicalities of the 'your dinner is in the oven' variety, and that other more loving letters had not survived, but it is hard to get away from the absence of the usual four- or five-word wish for her health.
39 Balsdon 1964: 173 is perceptive: 'The strain of the Civil War had taken its toll, combined, perhaps, with the emotional instability which sometimes besets the sexagenarian. He developed quite fantastic obsessions about his wife Terentia: that she should have come from Rome to join him at Brindisi in the winter of 48/7; that she was stealing his money.' (Balsdon was born in 1901.)
40 The uxorious Pompey (born 106), widowed in 54, in 52 married the much younger Cornelia after she had lost her first husband. The Emperor Claudius (born 10), after executing his wife, married Agrippina in AD 49.
41 E.g., the divorces of Cn. Pompeius and Mucia (*A* 1.12/12.3, Rome, 1 Jan. 61), Paulla Valeria and an unidentified husband (*F* 11.8/92.1, from Caelius, Rome, mid-Apr. 50), P. Cornelius Lentulus Spinther and Caecilia Metella (*A* 12.52/294.2, 21 May 45; 13.7/314, 10 June 45; both Tusculum).
42 This is the general view: e.g., Carcopino 1947: i.241; Balsdon 1964: 173; SB *A* v.309; Mitchell 1991: 273. Shackleton Bailey 1971: 201 is cautious: apparently 'within a year of Cicero's return . . . in October 47'.
43 Plut. *Cic.* 41.4; Dio 46.18.3.
44 Plut. *Cic.* 41.2. Plutarch may be following Tiro's biography of Cicero (as in *Cic.* 41.3) as, e.g., Fowler 1908: 151 and Shackleton Bailey 1971: 201 suggest.
45 Claassen 1996: 230 rightly stigmatises Plutarch's list as a 'palpably inadequate deposition by a biographer who wrote well over a century after the divorce took place'. Cf. 210–11.

46 Respectively, Mitchell 1991: 265, cf. 273; Boissier 1892: 102 and TP i: 43; SB A i.46; Dixon 1986: 103, and cf. Ciaceri 1930: 380; Lacey 1978: 116.
47 Balsdon 1964: 173; Crook 1990: 165.
48 Below, pp. 133–4; Shackleton Bailey 1971: 201–2, but Rawson 1983: 225 reserves judgement and Mitchell 1991: 273 is sceptical.
49 Schmidt 1898: 180–1.
50 *Cic.* 29.3; Weinstock 1934: 714.
51 Respectively, Carcopino 1947: i.239–42; Neubauer 1909: 228.
52 *Phil.* 2.75.
53 E.g., *F* 9.1/175.2, late 47 or early 46; 9.2/177.5, c. 22 Apr. 46; both to Varro from Rome.
54 *A* 12.2/238, Rome, early Apr.[?].
55 *F* 9.7/178, to Varro, Rome, late May 46.
56 E.g., *F* 9.16/190.7, to Paetus, Tusculum, mid-July 46.
57 *F* 9.17/191.2, to Paetus, Tusculum, c. 23 July 46.
58 *F* 7.33/192.2, to Volumnius Eutrapelus, Rome, end of July[?] 46.
59 We have to allow for 46 being the long year of the reform of the calendar, when Caesar inserted two intercalary months between November and December.
60 *F* 16.19/184, to Tiro, Tusculum, July[?] 46.
61 *F* 16.22/185.1, to Tiro, Tusculum, July[?] 46.
62 Treggiari 1991: 422.
63 *F* 9.20/193.2–3, to Paetus, Rome, early Aug. 46; 7.28/200.2, to Curius, Rome, Aug.[?] 46.
64 *A* 12.7/244.2, Tusculum, Oct.[?] [by the sun] 46.
65 Shackleton Bailey 1971: 203 puts the divorce in the autumn or early winter.
66 Carcopino 1947: i.276 says it was and puts it no later than October.
67 Treggiari 1991: 448, 472.
68 'We shall never know what emotional or psychological effects the divorces had on his daughter: Cicero's cries of "poor little thing" may be suspected of at least exaggeration, and we are not in the least obliged to suppose that Tullia's death . . . was due to unhappiness' (Crook 1990: 164).
69 *F* 5.13 /201.4, to Lucceius, Rome or Tusculum[?].
70 *A* 12.10/247, 21 Nov. [by the sun].
71 *A* 12.1/248.1, Arpinum, 27 Nov. [by the sun] 46.
72 Shackleton Bailey 1971: 202.
73 *B. Afr.* 95; App. *BC* 2.100. Caesar had once asked Pompey for her hand, although she was already engaged to Faustus (Suet. *Jul.* 27.1).
74 She later (perhaps in 44) married the L. Cornelius Cinna, brother of Caesar's first wife, who had won the praetorship for 44, but who sided with the conspirators after the murder of Caesar. A mob wanted to murder him, but lynched Cinna the poet by mistake. See *MRR* ii.320–1.
75 Boissier 1892: 104 dates this offer to after the divorce from Publilia.
76 Wiseman 1971: 235.
77 Pompeia was to give Cinna a son, the future consul of AD 5.
78 SB *F* ii.373 (keeping the reading of the mss.) suggested that this is L. Cassius Longinus, brother of the future assassin of Caesar, C. Cassius. (This would mean Licinia was a half-sister by their mother.) In 1995: 61 Shackleton Bailey preferred to adopt the conjecture of another editor, correcting 'Cassius' to "Crassus' (twice) and supposes this to be M. Licinius Crassus (cos. 30), since L. Cassius was probably dead by 46. This conjecture has the advantage of making Licinia share the brother's family name and means she is a daughter of the famous Crassus, cos. 70 and 55. I accept the correction.
79 Hoffmann 1959: 1918–19; SB *F* ii.407; in SB *A* v.314 he put it 'shortly before Tullia's death'.

80 Cicero first mentions Publilia as his wife in March 45 (Dixon 1986: 106).
81 This sort of language better fits the Quinti. But the parallel with the new marriage forces us to understand Terentia.
82 Respectively, Syme 1978b: 294 = *RP* iii.1088, as a minimum; Hoffmann 1959: 119.
83 E.g., Stockton 1971: 276; Rawson 1983: 224. It was only later that it became illegal for a guardian (*tutor*) to marry his ward.
84 As suggested by Carcopino 1947: i.243–4 (though the view does not originate with him). Cicero, he thinks, therefore married her in order to avoid transferring the property to her! See above, p. 15, for the law.
85 Syme 1978b: 294 = *RP* iii.1087.
86 *A* 12.18a/256.2, Astura, 13 Mar. 45.
87 Plut. *Cic.* 41.3.
88 Quint. *Inst.* 6.3.75.
89 Plut. *Pomp.* 55.1–3.
90 An age at which a man might be relieved of public duties. See Harlow and Laurence 2002: 118.
91 Shackleton Bailey 1971: 203.
92 Rawson 1983: 209–22, at 209.
93 *F* 6.18/218.5, to Q. Lepta, Rome, Jan. 45.
94 *F* 6.16/218.4, 5.
95 Shackleton Bailey 1971: 204; Dixon 1985b: 368.
96 Treggiari 1991: 467.
97 *A* 12.18/254.1, Astura, 11 Mar. 45; brief account of Cicero's reactions in Treggiari 1998: 14–23.
98 *A* 12.23/262.1, Astura, 19 Mar. 45.
99 SB *A* v.404–13.
100 *A* 12.12.36/275.1, Astura, 3 May 45.
101 *A* 15.15/393.3, Astura, 13[?] June 44.
102 It has been much admired as a literary composition. As efficacious consolation it is less admirable. See especially Hutchinson 1998: 65–77.
103 *F* 4.5/248.1–2, Athens, c. mid-Mar. 45.
104 *Tusc.* 1.84.
105 Hutchinson 1998: 76.
106 1978: 128.
107 *A* 12.18a/256.2, Astura, 13 Mar. 45.
108 *A* 12.19/257.4, Astura, 14 Mar. 45.
109 *A* 12.20/258.1, 2, 15 March 45; 12.12/259.1, 16 March 45; both from Astura.
110 *A* 12.21/260.3, Astura, 17 Mar. 45.
111 *A* 12.22/261.1, 18 Mar. 45; cf. 12.23/262.2, 19 Mar. 45; 12.26/265.2, 22 Mar. 45; 12.28/267.1, 24 Mar. 45; 12.34/273.2, 30 Mar. 45; 12.37/276.3, 4 May 45; all from Astura.
112 *A* 16.6/414.3, Vibo, 25 July 44.
113 16.15/426.5, Arpinum, after 12 Nov. 44.
114 *F* 16.24/350.1, to Tiro, Arpinum, mid-Nov. 44.
115 *A* 12.32/271.2, Astura, 28 Mar. 45; 15.17/394.1, Astura, 14 June 44; 15.20/397.4, Tusculum, 20 June 44; 16.1/409.5, Puteoli, 8 July 44; cf. Dixon 1986: 108–10.
116 E.g., *Mil.* 100; *A* 11.9/220.3, Brundisium, 3 Jan. 47.
117 *A* 12.28/267.3, Astura, 24 Mar. 45.
118 The child would eventually have been sent to his father's house to be raised.
119 Cf. *A* 12.33/269.2, Astura, 26 Mar. 45, for the servants surrounding Attica. I agree with Gardner 1998: 86 that these are not dotal slaves, but doubt whether they are the same as Castricius' slaves mentioned in *A* 12.28/267.3, Astura;

12.30/270.2, Astura, 27 March 45. If they were made part of the baby's 'property' (*peculium*, the possessions a son-in-power had for his own use), they would in law belong to Dolabella.
120 *A* 12.30/270.1, Astura, 27 Mar. 45.
121 Shackleton Bailey (1971: 213) suggests Tullia may have wanted this. Carcopino 1947: i.290–306 paints a black picture.
122 Macrob. 2.3.3.
123 *F* 13.36/307.1, to Acilius, 46 or 45; *F* 6.11/224, Tusculum, first half of June[?] 45.
124 Suet. *Gr.* 14; SB *A* iii.297; *F* ii.373. For Nicias, see Syme's entertaining account 1961: *passim* = *RP* ii.518–29 *passim*.
125 *F* 9.13/311.2, Rome, end of 46 or beginning of 45.
126 *F* 9.10/217, Rome, beginning of 45.
127 In reply to one from him (cf. *A* 12.38/278.2, Astura, 6 May 45).
128 *F* 9.11/250, Atticus' villa near Nomentum, late Apr. 45.
129 *A* 13.9/317, Tusculum, 17[?] June 45.
130 *A* 13.10/318.2, Tusculum, 18[?] June 45; *A* 13.13–14/321.2, Arpinum, 24 June 45; *A* 13.21a/327.3, Arpinum, 30 June or 1 July 45.
131 *A* 13.45/337.2, Tusculum, c. 11 Aug. 45; *A* 13.47/339, Tusculum, 13 Aug. 45.
132 E.g., *A* 13.50/348.1, Tusculum, 23 Aug. 45; 13.21/351.2, Astura, c. 27 Aug. 45.
133 *A* 14.15/369.1, Puteoli, 1 May 44, calling him 'my Dolabella'; 14.16/370.2, Puteoli, 2 May 44; 14.17a/371a, to Dolabella, Pompeii, 3 May 44.
134 *A* 16.15/426.1–2, Arpinum, after 12 Nov. 44.
135 *Phil.* 11.9–10.
136 Gardner 1998: 85–6.
137 Treggiari 1991: 352–3.
138 *A* 12.8/245, Tusculum, end of second intercalary month 46; *F* 6.18/218.5, to Lepta, Rome, Jan. 45; *A* 12.29/300.2, Tusculum, 27 May 45.
139 But cf. Dixon 1986: 107.
140 *A* 14.19/372.5, Pompeii, 8 May 44; 14.18/373.1, Pompeii, 9 May 44; 14.20/374.2, Puteoli, 11 May 44; 14.21/375.4, Puteoli, 11 May 44; 16.3/413.5, Pompeii, 17 July 44; 15.13a/417.1, Puteoli or Cumae, c. 28 Oct. 44; 16.15/426.1–2, 5, Arpinum, after 12 Nov. 44; *F* 16.24/350.2, to Tiro, Arpinum, mid-Nov. 44. See, e.g., Shatzman 1975: 332, 416.
141 Plut. *Cic.* 41.5.
142 The brackets < > mark conjectural additions to the text by editors.
143 *A* 12.34/273.1, Astura, 30 Mar. 45.
144 In July, according to Shatzman 1975: 414.
145 *A* 13.25/333.2, 12 July 45; 13.43/335, 14 July 45; both Tusculum.
146 *A* 14.19/372.4, Pompeii, 8 May 44, with SB *A* vi.236.
147 *A* 15.1/377.4, Puteoli, 17 May 44.
148 *A* 16.2/412.1, Puteoli, 11 July 44; SB *A* vi.286. I am unconvinced that we can deduce that the total dowry was of 1.2 million (Shatzman 1975: 414). There could have been real estate, returned at once.
149 Shatzman 1975: 410–12; D'Arms 2003: 61–2.

11 Death and survival

1 Cicero's bequest was bigger: after buying out his co-heirs, he had an income of 80,000 from his share in the first year alone (Shatzman 1975: 410).
2 Christes 1979: 64–7.
3 Treggiari 1969: 259, 254.

Notes to pages 144–50

4 E.g., Boissier 1892: 96–7; Fowler 1908: 153; *contra*, Neubauer 1909: 231.
5 1983: 25.
6 Modern authorities who call Terentia 'widow of Cicero' are inaccurate (e.g., *OCD s.* Tyrannio the Younger).
7 *A* 15.25/403, Tusculum, 29 June 44; 15.29/408.1, Formiae 6 July 44, etc.
8 *A* 16.7/415.1–7, on board ship near Pompeii, 19 August 44.
9 1.7, 2.1.
10 Plut. *Cic.* 46.2; App. *BC* 4.5; Syme 1939: 191.
11 Nep. *Att.* 10.1–5.
12 Nep. *Att.* 9.4–7, 11.4.
13 Val. Max. 6.7.3; App. *BC* 4.15, 22, 23; Dio 47.8.1.
14 App. *BC* 4.12–18, 22–3. His detailed account is rhetorical and much may be invented.
15 Cf. Sen. *Con.* 1 pr. 11.
16 Sen. *Con.* 7.2.
17 Sen. *Suas.* 6–7.
18 *Suas.* 6.14–5.
19 Sen. *Suas.* 6.16–17.
20 Sen. *Suas.* 6.18–19.
21 Asinius Pollio was specific about the consulship and Cicero's success as an orator (Sen. *Suas.* 24); Cornelius Severus, in hexameter verses, celebrated his suppression of the Catilinarians, his eloquence, his championship of the Senate, etc. (Sen. *Suas.* 6.26). Neither has anything about his family life.
22 2.66.2–5.
23 *Cic.* 47–49.2; cf. *Comparison of Demosthenes and Cicero 5.*
24 46.18.2–3. Cf. Quint. *Inst.* 11.3.143. For Cicero's precepts on deportment and grooming, see *Off.* 1.130–1.
25 *BC* 4.19–20.
26 47.10.6–7; 47.8.4. On both Appian and Dio, see Gowing 1992: 154–7. For all the narratives, Homeyer 1964.
27 Tac. *Dialogus* 17.
28 *Anthologia Latina/Latin Anthology* ii.608, 611, 614; Davis 1958; Treggiari 1973: 246–51.
29 Vell. 2.14.3; Syme 1939: 221.
30 Pliny *NH* 31.6–8; D'Arms 2003: 75–6, 166, 189–90.
31 *Ad Brutum* 1.11/16.1, from Brutus, camp in Macedonia, June 43.
32 App. *BC* 4.32–4; cf. Val. Max. 8.3.3; Quint. *Inst.* 1.1.6.
33 App. *BC* 5.2, 4.51; Syme 1939: 206.
34 Sen. *Suas.* 6.27.
35 Cf. Hemelrijk 1999: 237 n.65. The passage will also be found as Seneca *frag.* 13.61 (Haase) and in Bickel 1915: p. 390.
36 *Mil.* 47 with Asc. 49–50C.
37 At least one modern writer who accepts the match as a fact has dated it to 47 (Pareti 1934: 204), which would demand very swift action on Terentia's part, since she was certainly Cicero's wife at the beginning of October.
38 Syme 1964: 10–12.
39 Rowland (1968: 134) conjectures that Terentia was born in about 94, which would reduce the age gap.
40 E.g., Carcopino 1947: i.232–3.
41 Syme 1964: 284: 'an engaging and ridiculous fabrication'; 1978a: 292–5 = *RP* iii.1085–9; Shackleton Bailey 1971: 278: 'St Jerome's statement ... is more interesting than plausible'.
42 Rowland 1968: 134.
43 *A* 14.19/372.4, Pompeii, 8 May 44.

44 Rowland 1968: 134; Syme 1978a: 294 = *RP* iii.1088.
45 Syme 1986a: 200–26.
46 *Ad Brutum* 23/23.1, Rome, July 43.
47 Syme 1986a: 230–2, 240.
48 Syme 1978b: 295 = *RP* iii.: 1089.
49 Dio 57.15.6–7.
50 *CIL* 14.2556; cf. 2557–8.
51 *AE* 1907.78; cf. 79.
52 1978b: 292–4 = *RP* iii.1086–7; 1981: 367–9 = *RP* iii.1425–7; cf. Syme 1986a: 225. Further bibliography in Raepsaet-Charlier 1987: i.531–2.
53 Syme 1978a: 85–6; 1981: 371–6 = *RP* iii. 1430–5.
54 Cf. Vogel-Weidemann 1982: 280–2.
55 *A* 13.28/299.4, Tusculum, 26 May 45.
56 8.13.6.
57 *NH* 7.158.
58 E.g., Shackleton Bailey 1971: 278; for centenarians in general, see Parkin 1992: 108–11.
59 Münzer 1999: 276.
60 *Dig.* 1.2.2.44; *A* 13.37a/340, Tusculum, Aug.[?] 45; *F* 7.21/332.1, to Trebatius, Tusculum, June [latter half] 44; 16.24/350.1, to Tiro, Arpinum, Nov. [middle] 44.
61 Tac. *Ann.* 3.76.
62 Plut. *Cic.* 49.4, with Pelling 1988: 323.
63 29–27 or 27–25? (Syme 1939: 302–3).
64 Pliny *NH* 14.147; cf. Sen. *Suas.* 7.13.
65 Sen. *Ben.* 4.30.2.
66 Nep. *Att.* 12.1–2, 19.4, with Horsfall 1989.
67 Nep. *Att.* 22.3.
68 Syme 1939: 498. Rowland (1968: 134) throws out the interesting but unprovable suggestion that Marcus' wife could have been the 'wife of Cicero' who went on to marry Vibius Rufus, who encouraged the misconception that this was the great orator's wife. I think this unlikely. Young Marcus must have married at least once, but we know nothing of it.
69 Euseb. *Chron.* on 4 BC; Treggiari 1969: 259–60; SB *F* i.344–5.
70 Nep. *Att.* 16.3.
71 SB *A* i.59–76.
72 SB *F* i.20–6.
73 *A* 16.5/410.5, Puteoli, 9 July 44; *F* 16.17/186.1, to Tiro, Tusculum, July[?] 46.

12 Conclusions

1 Given the lack of new evidence, it would be depressing to attempt a methodical survey of the opposing viewpoints based on interpretations of sometimes ambiguous texts preserved partly by accident. Much interpretation derives from views formulated in standard handbooks a century or more ago. (Drumann's dates are 1786–1861.)
2 1991: 233, 265–6, 273.
3 1971: 201–2.
4 1983: 222.
5 1939: 24 n.4; 1980: 434 = *RP* iii.1247; 1986: 225, thinking of Terentia in old age.
6 1971: 63; 263.
7 E.g., Dixon 1986: 103.
8 Terentia's tolerance is plausible; her responsibility in running the house is

Notes to pages 156–60

  patent. How far she shared his interests is speculative, but I tend to think the relationship was stronger and warmer than Balsdon suggests.
9 It is true that Terentia had an attack of arthritis in her youth, which would presumably recur, but the other illnesses mentioned might well be the normal transient ills which most people suffer. If she lived to 103, she must have had an excellent constitution.
10 The best defences of Terentia are those of Neubauer (1909) and Claassen (1996).
11 Herodotus 1.33.7.
12 *A* 13.21a/327.2, Arpinum, 30 June or 1 July 45.
13 *Leg.* 1.9–10.
14 *A* 13.38/341.1, Tusculum, c. 15 Aug. 45; cf. Balsdon 1964: 175–6.
15 See Hemelrijk 1999: 237–8 n.66, citing Sid. Ap. *Epist.* 2.10.5: 'that in the olden days when their husbands read and meditated Marcia held a candle or candelabrum for Hortensius, Terentia for Tullius, Calpurnia for Pliny, Pudentilla for Apuleius, Rusticiana for Symmachus'.
16 *De or.* 3.45, *Brut.* 211.
17 *F* 14.7/155.1, Caieta, on board ship, 7 June 49.
18 Cf. Hemelrijk 1999: 64–79; 237 n.65.
19 Hemelrijk 1999: 64–7; Plut. *Pomp.* 55.1–2; Sall. *Cat.* 25. Fowler (1908: 153) would not agree that Terentia could be cultured: 'Terentia and Pomponia and their kind seem to have had nothing in the way of "higher education", nor do their husbands seem to have expected from them any desire to share in their own intellectual interests. Not once does Cicero allude to any pleasant social intercourse in which his wife took part; and to say the truth he would probably have avoided marriage with a woman of taste and knowledge.'
20 E.g., *F* 14.4/6.3, Brundisium, 29 Apr. 58; 14.18/144.1–2, Formiae, 22 Jan. 49; 14.14/145.1, Minturnae, 23 Jan. 49; 14.12/159, Brundisium, 4 Nov. 48.
21 E.g., *Laud. Tur.* ii.4–6.
22 *A* 15.11/389.1–2, Antium[?], c. 7 June 44. Servilia took a leading role and attempted to bully Cicero, though Brutus was in the chair.
23 Plut. *Cic.* 20.2.
24 Petersson 1920: 206; *F* 9.26/197.2, to Papirius Paetus, Rome, shortly before 17 Nov. [true calendar] 46.
25 1892: 94, citing *Cael.* 45–7.
26 Plut. *Cato min.* 7.
27 E.g., *F* 9.22/189, to Paetus, probably between 46 and 44.
28 For the usual accusations of passive homosexuality, see [Sall.] *Inv.* 1.2; Plut. *Cic.* 7.5 (Verres).
29 [Sall.] *Inv.* 2; Dio 46.18.6.
30 Cicero had used the idea when accusing Sassia of being a mistress to her daughter's husband (*Clu.* 199, cf. 13). Kaster 2006: 152, 409–11 shows, however, that allegations of incest were not merely conventional, as allegations of homosexual behaviour were. To allege brother–sister incest must have been to risk offending a whole family.
31 Dio 46.18.4; SB *A* v.340; cf. Boissier 1892: 94–5.
32 Dio 46.18.6.
33 *F* 14.3/9.2, Dyrrachium, 29 Nov. 58.
34 *F* 14.2/7.4, Thessalonica, 5 Oct. 58.
35 *F* 14.4/6.5, Brundisium, 29 April 58; 14.3/9.1.5; cf. 14.18 *sal.*, Formiae, 22 Jan. 49; 14.3/9.2; 14.4/6.6; 14.5/119.1, Athens, 16 Oct. 50; 14.2/7.2, Thessalonica, 5 Oct. 58; 14.4/6.1; 14.2/7.3; 14.5/119.2.
36 *F* 14.1/8 *sal.*, 2, despatched from Dyrrachium, 25 Nov. 58; 14.18/145.1, Formiae, 22 Jan. 49; 14.14/145.2, Minturnae, 23 Jan. 49.

37 F 14.2/7.2, 3; cf. 14.5/119.2, not entirely formulaic; 14.3/9.5; cf. 14.4/6.3.
38 Cf. Dixon 1991; Treggiari 1991: 253–5. Hemelrijk (1999: 237 n.63), opposing this view, thinks these are 'occasional outbursts of sentiment' in what was 'a business partnership'. Hutchinson (1998: 28) remarks that 'the lover-like language ... shows strikingly how times of crisis can realize the potential for passion in Roman marriages'.
39 E.g., F 14.1/8.5.
40 F 14.3/9.2, Dyrrachium, 29 Nov. 58; cf. 14.2/7.1.
41 F 14.1/8.1.
42 F 14.2/7.2; 14.1/8.1; 14.7/155.2, Caieta, on board ship, 7 June 49. This self-depreciation and portrayal of the wife taking a masculine part and the husband a feminine one has now been skilfully analysed for the *Laudatio 'Turiae'* by Hemelrijk 2004: esp. 188–97, with explicit comparison of Cicero's letters from exile (190–1).
43 F 14.4/6.6; 14.1/8.1; Treggiari 1991: 237–8.
44 F 14.1/8.1.
45 F 14.1/8.3.
46 F 14.4/6.1; 14.7/155.1.
47 F 14.2/7.2.
48 F 14.2/7.1; cf.14/1.8.1.
49 Stockton 1971: 263; Shackleton Bailey 1971: 175; Rawson 1983: 197; Mitchell 1991: 283; cf. Carcopino 1947: i.254 for her sweetness, modesty and intelligence.
50 Mueller 1904: *F* ix.11, p. 335 = Lactantius *Institutiones divinae* 1.15.20.
51 In the letters to Terentia (sometimes addressed to her too), she is always mentioned affectionately: 'our little Tullia', *Tulliola nostra* (*F* 14.1/8.1; 14.7/155.2, on board ship, Caieta, 7 June 49); *nostra Tulliola* (14.2/7.1); 'our Tullia', *Tullia nostra* (14.11/166, Brundisium, 14 June 47); 'my little Tullia', *Tulliola mea* (*F* 14.4/6.3); 'my dearest little daughter', *mea carissima filiola* (*F* 14.4/6.6); '[my] sweetest daughter', *suavissima filia* (*F* 14.18/144 *sal.*). The diminutive *Tulliola* is not used after Cicero went to Greece in 49 (*F* 14.7/155.1). When writing to Atticus, Cicero calls her 'little Tullia, our darling', *Tulliola, deliciae nostrae* (*A* 1.5/1.8, Rome, Nov. 68); 'little Tullia, our little darling', *Tulliola, deliciolae nostrae* (1.8/4.3, Rome, after 13 Feb. 67); simply 'Tullia' (2.8/28.2, Antium, 16[?] Apr. 59, and often from then on); 'little Tullia', *Tulliola* (frequently from 1.10/6.6, Tusculum, c. May 67 onwards); 'little daughter', *filiola* (1.18/18.1, Rome, 20 Jan. 60); 'my little Tullia', *Tulliola mea* (4.1/73.4, Rome, c. 10 Sept. 57; 6.9/123.5, Athens, 15 Oct. 50); '[my] daughter', *filia* (4.2/74.7, Rome, beginning of Oct. 57, etc.); 'my Tullia', *Tullia mea* (4.16/89.4, Rome, c. 1 July 54, and often from then on) or *mea Tullia* (10.1.3/205.1, Cumae, 7 May 49 and occasionally after); '[my] little girl', *pusilla* (4.15/90.4, Rome, 27 July 54). The diminutive *Tulliola* is not found in letters to Atticus after Cicero returned to find her married for the third time (*A* 6.9/123.5, Athens, 15 Oct. 50). Cicero lets Atticus see how much Tullia means to him: there is no pet name for young Marcus or the younger Quintus. To his brother, Cicero calls Tullia 'my daughter and yours' (*QF* 1.3/3.10, Thessalonica, 13 June 58), 'our Tullia' (2.4/8.2, Rome, mid-March 56; 2.6/10.1, en route to Anagnia, 9 Apr. 56), but uses no diminutives. Quintus reciprocates by calling her 'my little Tullia' (*F* 16.16/44.1, Transalpine Gaul, end of May or beginning of June 53), unless this was a slip.
52 E.g., *A* 11.17/228.1, 12 or 13 June 47; *F* 14.11/166, Brundisium, 14 June 47; *A* 10.8.9, Cumae, 2 May 49.
53 F 14.7/155.2.
54 A 11.17/228.1; F 14.11/166.

55 *QF* 1.3/3.3, Thessalonica, 13 June 58; *A* 11.17/228.1; *F* 14.11/166; cf. *A* 10.8.9.
56 *QF* 1.3/3.3.
57 E.g., Lucretius 3.894–901; Hor. *Epodes* 2.39–48.
58 *The orator, Brutus on famous orators* in 46; *On glory, Consolation, Hortensius, Academics, On the ends of good and evil, Tusculan disputations, On the nature of the gods, On fate, On divination* in 45; *Cato the Elder* or *On old age, Laelius* or *On friendship, Topica, On duties* in 44.
59 See Shackleton Bailey 1971: 179–85 for the effects of the quarrel.
60 Tac. *Ann.* 2.86.2.

Bibliography

Alexander, Michael C. (1990) *Trials in the late Roman Republic, 149 BC to 50 BC*, Toronto: University of Toronto Press.
Andreau, Jean (1999) *Banking and business in the Roman world*, tr. Janet Lloyd, Cambridge: Cambridge University Press.
Augarde, Tony (ed.) (1991) *The Oxford dictionary of modern quotations*, Oxford: Oxford University Press.
Badian, Ernst (1965) 'The Dolabellae of the Republic', *Papers of the British School at Rome* 33: 48–51.
—— (1990) 'The Consuls, 179–49 BC', *Chiron* 20: 371–413.
Balsdon, J. P. V. D(acre) (1962, rev. 1974) *Roman women: their history and habits*, London: The Bodley Head.
—— (1964) 'Cicero the man', in T. A. Dorey (ed.), *Cicero*, London: Routledge and Kegan Paul: 171–214.
—— (1969) *Life and leisure in ancient Rome*, London: The Bodley Head.
—— (1979) *Romans and aliens*, London: Duckworth.
Barrett, Anthony A. (1996) *Agrippina: sex, power and politics in the early Empire*, New Haven, CT: Yale University Press.
—— (2002) *Livia: first lady of imperial Rome*, New Haven, CT: Yale University Press.
Berg, Ria (2002) 'Wearing wealth', in Setälä *et al.* (eds): 15–73.
Berger, Adolf (1953) *Encyclopedic dictionary of Roman law*, Philadelphia: American Philosophical Society, Transactions of the American Philosophical Society ns 43, Part 2.
Berry, D. H. (1996) *Cicero. Pro P. Sulla Oratio*, Cambridge: Cambridge University Press.
Bickel, Ernst (1915) *Diatribe in Senecae philosophi fragmenta* i *Fragmenta de matrimonio*, Leipzig: Teubner.
Blom, Henriette Van der (2003) '*Officium* and *Res Publica*: Cicero's political role after the Ides of March', *Classica et Mediaevalia* 54: 287–319.
Boissier, Gaston (1892) *Cicéron et ses amis. Etude sur la societé romaine du temps de César*, Paris: Hachette.
Bradley, Keith R. (1991) *Discovering the Roman family: studies in Roman social history*, New York: Oxford University Press.
—— (1998) 'The Roman family at dinner', in Inge Nielsen and Hanne Sigismund Nielsen (eds), *Meals in a social context*, Aarhus: Aarhus University Press, Aarhus Studies in Mediterranean Antiquity 1: 36-55.

—— (2005) 'The Roman child in sickness and in health', in George (ed.): 67–92.
Brunt, P(eter) A. (1971) *Social conflicts in the Roman Republic*, London: Chatto and Windus.
—— (1982) '*Nobilitas and novitas*', *Journal of Roman Studies* 72: 1–17.
—— (1986) 'Cicero's *officium* in the Civil War', *Journal of Roman Studies* 76: 12–32.
Carcopino, Jérôme (1947) *Les secrets de la correspondance de Cicéron*, 2 vols, Paris: L'Artisan du Livre.
Carney, Thomas F. (1960) 'Cicero's picture of Marius', *Wiener Studien* 73: 83–122.
—— (1961) 'The flight and exile of Marius', *Greece and Rome* 8: 98–121.
Carp, Teresa (1981) 'Two matrons of the late Republic', *Women's Studies* 8: 189–200.
Cherry, David A. (1989) 'The Minician marriage law: marriage and Roman citizenship', *Phoenix* 43: 244–66.
Christes, Johannes (1979) *Sklaven und Freigelassene als Grammatiker und Philologen im antiken Rom*, Wiesbaden: Steiner, Forschungen zur antiken Sklaverei x.
Ciaceri, Emanuele (1930) *Cicerone e i suoi tempi* ii, Milan: Dante Alighieri.
Claassen, Jo-Marie (1992) 'Cicero's banishment: *tempora* and *mores*', *Acta Classica* (Classical Association of South Africa) 35: 19–47.
—— (1996) 'Documents of a crumbling marriage: the case of Cicero and Terentia', *Phoenix* 50: 208–32.
Clark, Patricia A. (1991) 'Tullia and Crassipes', *Phoenix* 45: 28–38.
Coarelli, Filippo (1993) *Lazio*, Rome: Laterza, Guide archeologiche Laterza.
Crook, J(ohn) A. (1967) *Law and life of Rome*, London: Thames and Hudson.
—— (1986) 'Women in Roman succession', in Rawson (ed.): 58–82.
—— (1990) '"His and hers": what degree of financial responsibility did husband and wife have for the matrimonial home and their life in common in a Roman marriage?', in Jean Andreau and Hinnerk Bruhns (eds), *Parenté et stratégies familiales dans l'antiquité romaine*, Actes de la table ronde des 2–4 octobre 1986, Collection de l'École française de Rome 129, Rome: École française.
Cugusi, Paolo (ed.) (1979) *Epistolographi latini minores* ii.2, Turin: Paravia, *Corpus scriptorum latinorum Paravianum*.
D'Arms, John H. (2003) *Romans on the Bay of Naples and other essays on Roman Campania*, ed. Fausto Zevi, Bari: Edipuglia. (Reprint of *Romans on the Bay of Naples*, Cambridge, MA: Harvard University Press, 1970.)
Davis, H. H. (1958) 'Cicero's burial', *Phoenix* 12: 174–7.
Delia, Diana (1991) 'Fulvia reconsidered', in Pomeroy (ed.): 197–217.
Dixon, Suzanne (1983) 'A family business: women's role in patronage and politics at Rome 80–44 BC', *Classica et Mediaevalia* 34: 91–112.
—— (1985a) 'Breaking the law to do the right thing: the gradual erosion of the Voconian law in ancient Rome', *Adelaide Law Review* 9: 519–34.
—— (1985b) 'The marriage alliance in the Roman elite', *Journal of Family History* 10: 353–78.
—— (1986) 'Family finances: Terentia and Tullia', in Rawson (ed.): 93–120. (An earlier version appeared in *Antichthon* 18 [1984]: 78–101.)
—— (1988) *The Roman mother*, London: Croom Helm.
—— (1991) 'The sentimental ideal of the Roman family', in Rawson (ed.): 99–113.
—— (1997) 'Conflict in the Roman family', in Rawson and Weaver (eds): 149–67.

—— (ed.) (2001a) *Childhood, class and kin in the Roman world*, London: Routledge.
—— (2001b) '*Famila Veturia*: towards a lower-class economic prosopography', in Dixon (2001a): 115–27.
—— (2001c) *Reading Roman women: sources, genres and real life*, London: Duckworth.
—— (2001d) 'Women's work: perceptions of public and private', in Dixon (2001c): 113–32.
Drumann, Wilhelm and E. Paul Groebe (1899–1929) *Geschichte Roms in seinem Übergange von der republikanischen zur monarchischen Verfassung oder Pompeius, Caesar, Cicero und ihre Zeitgenossen nach Geschlechtern und mit genealogischen Tabellen*, 6 vols, Leipzig: Borntraeger.
Dunbabin, Katherine M. D. (1999) *Mosaics of the Greek and Roman world*, Cambridge: Cambridge University Press.
Dyck, Andrew R. (1996) *A commentary on Cicero* De Officiis, Ann Arbor: University of Michigan Press.
Dyer, Christopher (2000) 'Woodlands and wood-pasture in western England', in Joan Thirsk (ed.), *Rural England: an illustrated history of the landscape*, Oxford: Clarendon Press: 97–121.
Engels, David M. (2003) 'Women's role in the home and the state', *Harvard Studies in Classical Philology* 101: 267–88.
Evans Grubbs, Judith (1994): '"Pagan" and "Christian" marriage: the state of the question', *Journal of Early Christian Studies* 2: 361–412.
Fantham, Elaine (2004) *The Roman world of Cicero's* De Oratore, Oxford: Oxford University Press.
Fantham, Elaine, Helene P. Foley, Natalie B. Kampen, Sarah B. Pomeroy and H. A. Shapiro (1994) *Women in the classical world: image and text*, New York: Oxford University Press.
Finley, Moses I. (ed.) (1976) *Studies in Roman property*, Cambridge: Cambridge University Press.
Fowler, W. Warde (1908) *Social life at Rome in the age of Cicero*, London: Macmillan.
Frederiksen, Martin (1966) 'Caesar, Cicero and the problem of debt', *Journal of Roman Studies* 56: 128–41.
Friedländer, Ludwig (1907) *Roman life and manners under the early Empire*, 4 vols, tr. Leonard A. Magnus, London: Routledge and Kegan Paul.
Frier, Bruce W. (1985) *The rise of the Roman jurists: studies in Cicero's* pro Caecina, Princeton: Princeton University Press.
Galinsky, Karl (ed.) (2005) *The Cambridge companion to the age of Augustus*, Cambridge: Cambridge University Press.
Gardner, Jane F. (1986) *Women in Roman law and society*, London: Croom Helm.
—— (1993) *Being a Roman citizen*, London: Routledge.
—— (1995) 'Gender-role assumptions in Roman law', *Classical Views/Echos du monde classique* 39 (ns 14): 377–400.
—— (1998) *Family and* familia *in Roman law and life*, Oxford: Clarendon Press.
George, Michele (1997) 'Repopulating the Roman house', in Rawson and Weaver (eds): 299–319.
—— (ed.) (2005) *The Roman family in the Empire: Rome, Italy and beyond*, Oxford: Oxford University Press.

Gordon, W. M. and Olivia F. Robinson (1988) *The institutes of Gaius*, Ithaca, NY: Cornell University Press.
Gowing, Alain M. (1992) *The triumviral narratives of Appian and Cassius Dio*, Ann Arbor: University of Michigan Press.
Griffin, Jasper (1976) 'Augustan poetry and the life of luxury', *Journal of Roman Studies* 66: 87–105 = 1985: 1–31.
—— (1985) *Latin poets and Roman life*, London: Duckworth.
Griffin, Miriam and E. M(argaret) Atkins (1991) *Cicero On Duties*, Cambridge: Cambridge University Press.
Groebe, E. Paul (1939) 'Tullia', in *RE* vii.A: 1329–36.
Gruen, Erich S. (1966) 'The Dolabellae and Sulla', *American Journal of Philology* 87: 385–99.
Günther, Rosmarie (1987) *Frauenarbeit-Frauenbindung. Untersuchungen zu unfreien und freigelassenen Frauen in den stadtrömischen Inschriften*, Munich: Wilhelm Fink Verlag.
Harlow, Mary and Ray Laurence (2002) *Growing up and growing old in ancient Rome: a life course approach*, London: Routledge.
Harrison, Stephen (ed.) (2005) *A companion to Latin literature*, Oxford: Blackwell.
Haskell, Henry Joseph (1942) *This was Cicero: modern politics in a Roman toga*, London: Secker and Warburg.
Hemelrijk, Emily A. (1999) *Matrona docta: educated women in the Roman élite from Cornelia to Julia Domna*, London: Routledge.
—— (2004) 'Masculinity and femininity in the *Laudatio Turiae*', *Classical Quarterly* 54: 185–97.
Hoffmann, W. (1959) 'Publilia', s. Publilius 17, *RE* xxiii.2: 1918–19.
Homeyer, Helene (1964) *Die antiken Berichte über den Tod Ciceros und ihre Quellen*, Baden-Baden: B. Grimm. Deutsche Beiträge zur Altertumswissenschaft 18.
Horsfall, Nicholas (1989) *Cornelius Nepos: a selection, including the lives of Cato and Atticus*, Oxford: Clarendon Press, Clarendon Ancient History Series.
—— (2003) *The culture of the Roman* plebs, London: Duckworth.
Hutchinson, G(regory) O. (1998) *Cicero's correspondence: a literary study*, Oxford: Clarendon Press.
Joshel, Sandra R. (1992a) 'The body female and the body politic: Livy's Lucretia and Verginia', in Richlin (ed.): 112–30.
—— (1992b) *Work, identity and legal status at Rome: a study of the occupational inscriptions*, Norman: University of Oklahoma Press.
Kampen, Natalie (1981) *Image and status: Roman working women in Ostia*, Berlin: Mann.
Kaster, Robert A. (2006) *Marcus Tullius Cicero: 'Speech on behalf of Publius Sestius'*, Oxford: Clarendon Press, Clarendon Ancient History Series.
Lacey, W(alter) K(irkpatrick) (1978) *Cicero and the end of the Roman Republic*, London: Hodder and Stoughton.
Lintott, Andrew (1999) *Violence in republican Rome*, Oxford: Oxford University Press (2nd edn; first published 1968).
Lott, J. Bert (2004) *The neighborhoods of imperial Rome*, Cambridge: Cambridge University Press.
McDermott, William (1972) 'M. Cicero and M. Tiro', *Historia* 21: 259–86.

McDonnell, Myles (2006) *Roman manliness*: virtus *and the Roman Republic*, Cambridge: Cambridge University Press.
McGushin, Patrick (1992) *Sallust. The Histories* 1 Books i–ii, Oxford: Clarendon Press, Clarendon Ancient History Series.
Marshall, Anthony J. (1990) 'Roman ladies on trial: the case of Maesia of Sentinum', *Phoenix* 44: 46–59.
Mitchell, Thomas N. (1979) *Cicero: the ascending years*, New Haven, CT: Yale University Press.
—— (1991) *Cicero: the senior statesman*, New Haven, CT: Yale University Press.
Moreau, Philippe (1987) 'La *Lex Clodia* sur le banissement de Cicéron', *Athenaeum* 75: 465–92.
Mueller, C(arl) F. W. (1904) *M. Tulli Ciceronis Scripta quae manserunt omnia* IV.iii, Leipzig: Teubner.
Münzer, Friedrich (1999) *Roman aristocratic parties and families*, tr. T. Ridley, Baltimore: Johns Hopkins University Press (first published 1920).
Neubauer, Luise (1909) 'Terentia', *Wiener Studien* 31: 211–32.
Nicolet, Claude (1974) *L'ordre équestre à l'époque républicaine (312–43 av. J.-C.)* ii, Paris: de Boccard, Bibliothèque des Écoles françaises d'Athènes et de Rome 207.
Nisbet, R(obin) G. M. (1961) *M. Tulli Ciceronis in L. Calpurnium Pisonem oratio*, Oxford: Clarendon Press.
Papi, Emanuele (1998) '"*Domus est quae nulli villarum mearum cedat*" (Cic. fam. 6,18,5)', in Maddalena Cima and Eugenio La Rocca (eds), *Horti Romani. Atti del Convegno internazionale, Roma 4–6 maggio 1995*, Rome: L'Erma, Bulletino della Commissione archeologica comunale di Roma Supplementi 6: 45–70.
Pareti, Luigi (1934) *La congiura di Catilina. Alle soglie dell' impero*, Catania: V. Muglia.
Parkin, Tim G. (1992) *Demography and Roman society*, Baltimore: Johns Hopkins University Press.
Pearce, T. E. V. (1974) 'The role of the wife as custos in ancient Rome', *Eranos* 72: 16–33.
Pelling, C(hristopher) B. R. (1988) *Plutarch Life of Antony*, Cambridge: Cambridge University Press, Cambridge Greek and Latin Classics.
Petersson, Torsten (1920) *Cicero: a biography*, Berkeley: University of California Press.
Pölönen, Janne (2002) 'The division of wealth between men and women in Roman succession (ca 50 BC–AD 250)', in Setälä *et al.* (eds): 147–79.
Pomeroy, Sarah B. (ed.) (1991) *Women's history and ancient history*, Chapel Hill: University of North Carolina Press.
Potter, David S. (1999) *Literary texts and the Roman historian*, London: Routledge.
Purcell, Nicholas (1994) 'The city of Rome and the *plebs urbana* in the late Republic', in J(ohn) A. Crook, Andrew Lintott and Elizabeth Rawson (eds), *Cambridge Ancient History* ix, Cambridge: Cambridge University Press: 644–88.
Raepsaet-Charlier, Marie-Thérèse (1987) *Prosopographie des femmes de l'ordre sénatorial (Ier-IIe siècles)*, 2 vols, Louvain: Peeters.
Rawson, Beryl (ed.) (1986) *The family in ancient Rome: new perspectives*, Ithaca, NY: Cornell University Press.
—— (ed.) (1991) *Marriage, divorce and children in ancient Rome*, Oxford: Oxford University Press.

—— (2005) *Children and childhood in Roman Italy*, Oxford: Oxford University Press.
Rawson, Beryl and Paul Weaver (eds) (1997) *The Roman family in Italy: status, sentiment, space*, Oxford: Clarendon Press.
Rawson, Elizabeth (1976) 'The Ciceronian aristocracy and its properties', in Finley (ed.): 85–102 = E. Rawson 1991: 204–22.
—— (1983) *Cicero: a portrait*, Bristol: Bristol Classical Press (repr., with corrections; first published London: Allen Lane, 1975).
—— (1991) *Roman culture and society: collected papers*, Oxford: Clarendon Press.
—— (1994) 'Caesar: civil war and dictatorship', in J. A. Crook, Andrew Lintott and E. Rawson (eds), *Cambridge Ancient History* ix, Cambridge: Cambridge University Press: 424–67.
Richardson, John (2003) '*Imperium Romanum* between Republic and Empire', in Lukas de Blois *et al.* (eds), *The representation and perception of Roman imperial power*, Amsterdam: J. C. Gieben: 137–47. (Proceedings of the Third Workshop of the International Network Impact of Empire [Roman Empire, c. 200 BC–AD 476].)
Richardson, L(awrence), Jr. (1992) *A topographical dictionary of ancient Rome*, Baltimore: Johns Hopkins University Press.
Richlin, Amy (ed.) (1992) *Pornography and representation in Greece and Rome*, New York: Oxford University Press.
Rives, James (1992) 'The *Iuno feminae* in Roman society', *Classical Views/Echos du monde classique* 36 (ns 11): 33–49.
Roller, Matthew (2003) 'Posture and sex in the Roman *convivium*', in *American Journal of Philology* special issue, 'Roman dining', ed. Barbara K. Gold and John F. Donahue, 124: 377–422.
Rowland Robert J. (1968) 'Sallust's wife', *Classical World* 62: 134.
Russell, Donald, tr. with introduction and notes (1993) *Plutarch: selected essays and dialogues*, Oxford: Oxford University Press.
Sallares, Robert (2002) *Malaria and Rome: a history of malaria in ancient Italy*, Oxford University Press.
Saller, Richard P. (1994) *Patriarchy, property and death in the Roman family*, Cambridge Studies in Population, Economy and Society in Past Time 25, Cambridge: Cambridge University Press.
Schmidt, Otto E. (1898) 'Cicero und Terentia', *Neue Jahrbucher für das klassische Altertum* 1: 174–85.
Schultz, Celia E. (2006) *Women's religious activity in the Roman Republic*, Chapel Hill: University of North Carolina Press.
Scullard, H. H. (1981) *Festivals and ceremonies of the Roman Republic*, London: Thames and Hudson.
Seager, Robin (1979) *Pompey: a political biography*, Oxford: Blackwell.
Setälä, Päivi (2002) 'Women and brick production: some new aspects', in Setälä *et al.* (eds): 181–201.
Setälä, Päivi, Ria Berg, Riikka Hälikkä, Minerva Keltanen, Janne Pölönen and Ville Vuolanto (eds) (2002) *Women, wealth and power in the Roman Empire*, Rome: Institutum Romanum Finlandiae.
Shackleton Bailey, David R. (1965–70) *Cicero's Letters to Atticus*, 7 vols, Cambridge: Cambridge University Press.

—— (1971) *Cicero*, London: Duckworth.
—— (1976) *Two studies in Roman nomenclature*, New York: American Philological Association.
—— (1977a) 'Brothers or cousins?', *American Journal of Ancient History* 2: 148–50 = 1997: 306–8.
—— (1977b) *Cicero* Epistulae ad Familiares, 2 vols, Cambridge: Cambridge University Press.
—— (1986) '*Nobiles* and *novi* reconsidered', *American Journal of Philology* 107: 255–60 = Shackleton Bailey 1997: 309–13.
—— (1978a) *Cicero's Letters to Atticus*, 2 vols, Harmondsworth: Penguin.
—— (1978b) *Cicero's Letters to his friends*, Harmondsworth: Penguin.
—— (1988) *Cicero's Letters to his friends*, Atlanta: Scholars Press.
—— (1980) *Cicero* Epistulae ad Quintum Fratrem et M. Brutum, Cambridge: Cambridge University Press.
—— (1985) 'More on Cicero's speeches (*post reditum*)', *Harvard Studies in Classical Philology* 89: 141–51.
—— (1991) *Two studies in Roman nomenclature*, New York: American Philological Association (2nd edn).
—— (1992) *Onomasticon to Cicero's speeches*, Stuttgart: Teubner (2nd edn).
—— (1994) 'A Ciceronian Odyssey', *Ciceroniana* ns 8: 87–92 = Shackleton Bailey 1997: 363–8.
—— (1995) *Onomasticon to Cicero's letters*, Stuttgart: Teubner.
—— (1996) *Onomasticon to Cicero's treatises*, Stuttgart: Teubner.
—— (1997) *Selected classical papers*, Ann Arbor: University of Michigan Press.
—— (1999) *Cicero. Letters to Atticus*, 4 vols, Cambridge, MA: Harvard University Press, Loeb Classical Library Cicero 22, 23, 24, 29.
—— (2001) *Cicero. Letters to friends*, 3 vols, Cambridge, MA: Harvard University Press, Loeb Classical Library Cicero 205, 216, 230.
—— (2002) *Cicero. Letters to Quintus and Brutus etc.* Cambridge, MA: Harvard University Press, Loeb Classical Library Cicero 462.
Shatzman, Israël (1975) *Senatorial wealth and Roman politics*, Brussels: Latomus, Collection Latomus 142.
Shaw, Brent D. (1987) 'The age of Roman girls at marriage: some reconsiderations', *Journal of Roman Studies* 77: 30–46.
Short, Brian (2000) 'Forests and wood-pasture in lowland England', in Joan Thirsk (ed.), *Rural England: an illustrated history of the landscape*, Oxford: Clarendon Press: 122–49.
Shumka, Leslie (2000) 'Making women: cosmetics, adornment and the construction of femininity in the Roman world', Ph.D. dissertation, University of Victoria.
Skutsch, Otto (1985) *The Annals of Q. Ennius*, Oxford: Clarendon Press.
Small, Alastair M., Vito Volterra and R. G. V. Hancock (2003) 'New evidence from tile-stamps for imperial properties near Gravina, and the topography of imperial estates in SE Italy', *Journal of Roman Archaeology* 16: 178–99.
Stockton, David (1971) *Cicero: A political biography*, Oxford: Oxford University Press.
Strachan-Davidson, James Leigh (1900) *Cicero and the fall of the Roman Republic*, London: Putnam (previously published 1894).
—— (1912) *Problems of the Roman criminal law*, Oxford: Clarendon Press (repr. Amsterdam: Rodopi, 1969, 2 vols in 1).

Sumner, Graham V. (1971) 'The Lex annalis under Caesar', *Phoenix* 25: 246–71, 357–71
Syme, Sir Ronald (1939) *The Roman Revolution*, Oxford: Oxford University Press.
—— (1955a) 'Review of T. R. S. Broughton, *The Magistrates of the Roman Republic* (1951–1952)', *Classical Philology* 50 127–38.
—— (1955b) 'Review of A. E. Gordon, *Potitus Valerius Messalla consul suffect 29 BC*', *Journal of Roman Studies* 45: 155–60 = Syme, *RP* i.260–70.
—— (1961) 'Who was Vedius Pollio?', *Journal of Roman Studies* 51: 23–30 = Syme, *RP* ii:518–29.
—— (1964) *Sallust*, Berkeley: University of California Press.
—— (1978a) *History in Ovid*, Oxford: Clarendon Press.
—— (1978b) 'Sallust's wife', *Classical Quarterly* 28: 292–5 = Syme, *RP* iii.1085–9.
—— (1979) 'The *patria* of Juvenal', *Classical Philology* 74: 1–15 = Syme, *RP* iii.1120–34.
—— (1979–91) *Roman Papers*, 7 vols, Oxford: Clarendon Press (*RP*).
—— (1980) 'No son for Caesar?', *Historia* 29: 422–37 = Syme, *RP* iii.1236–50.
—— (1981) 'Vibius Rufus and Vibius Rufinus', *Zeitschrift für Papyrologie und Epigraphik* 43: 365–76 = Syme, *RP* iii:1422–35.
—— (1986a) *The Augustan Aristocracy*, Oxford: Clarendon Press.
—— (1986b) 'More Narbonensian senators', *Zeitschrift für Papyrologie und Epigraphik* 65: 1–24 = Syme, *RP* vi.209–231.
—— (1987) 'Marriage ages for Roman senators', *Historia* 36: 318–32 = Syme, *RP* vi.232–46.
Tatum, W. Jeffrey (1999) *The patrician tribune: Publius Clodius Pulcher*, Chapel Hill: University of North Carolina Press.
Taylor, Lily Ross (1960) *The voting districts of the Roman Republic: the thirty-five urban and rural tribes*, Rome: American Academy, Papers and Monographs of the American Academy 20.
Treggiari, Susan (1969) *Roman freedmen during the late Republic*, Oxford: Clarendon Press (reprinted 2000).
—— (1973) 'Cicero, Horace and mutual friends: Lamiae and Varrones Murenae', *Phoenix* 27: 245–61.
—— (1975) 'Jobs in the household of Livia', *Papers of the British School at Rome* 43: 48–77.
—— (1976) 'Jobs for women', *American Journal of Ancient History* 1: 76–104.
—— (1977a) 'Intellectuals, poets and their patrons', *Classical Views/Echos du monde classique* 21: 24–9.
—— (1977b) 'The manumission of Tiro', *Liverpool Classical Monthly* 2: 67–72.
—— (1979) 'Lower class women in the Roman economy', *Florilegium* 1: 65–86.
—— (1991) *Roman marriage: iusti coniuges from the time of Cicero to the time of Ulpian*, Oxford: Clarendon Press.
—— (1994) 'Putting the bride to bed', *Classical Views/Echos du monde classique* 38 (ns 13) 311–31.
—— (1998) 'Home and Forum: Cicero between "public" and "private"', *Transactions of the American Philological Association* 128: 1–23.
—— (1999) 'The upper-class house as symbol and focus of emotion in Cicero', *Journal of Roman Archaeology* 12: 33–56.
—— (2002) *Roman social history*, London: Routledge.
—— (2003) 'Marriage and family in Roman society', in Ken(neth) M. Campbell

(ed.), *Marriage and family in the biblical world*, Downers Grove, IL: InterVarsity Press: 132–82.
—— (2005a) 'Marriage and family', in Harrison (ed.): 372–84.
—— (2005b) 'Putting the family across: Cicero on natural affection', in George (ed.): 9–35.
—— (2005c) 'Women of the time of Augustus', in Galinsky (ed.): 130–47.
Tyrrell, Robert Y. and Louis C. Purser (1885–1933), *The Correspondence of M. Tullius Cicero*, London: Longmans, vol. 1 3rd edn, vols 2–5 2nd edn (reissued Hildesheim: Georg Olms, 1969).
Vasaly, Ann (1993) *Representations: images of the world in Ciceronian oratory*, Berkeley: University of California Press.
Vogel-Weidemann, Ursula (1982) 'Miscellanea zu den Proconsules von Africa und Asia zwischen 14 und 68 n. Chr.', *Zeitschrift für Papyrologie und Epigraphik* 46: 271–94.
Wallace-Hadrill, Andrew (1994a) *Houses and society in Pompeii and Herculaneum*, Princeton: Princeton University Press.
—— (1994b) 'The social structure of the Roman house', in Wallace-Hadrill 1994a: 3–61.
Watson, Alan (1967) *The law of persons in the later Roman Republic*, Oxford: Clarendon Press.
Weinstock, Stefan (1934) 'Terentia' (*s.* Terentius 95) *RE* V.A1 710–16.
Williams, Craig (1999) *Roman homosexuality: ideologies of masculinity in classical antiquity*, New York: Oxford University Press.
Wiseman, T. P(eter) (1971) *New men in the Roman Senate 139 BC–AD 14*, Oxford: Oxford University Press.
—— (1974a) *Cinna the poet and other Roman essays*, Leicester: Leicester University Press.
—— (1974b) 'Legendary genealogies in late-republican Rome', *Greece and Rome* 21: 153–64.
—— (1979) *Clio's cosmetics: three studies in Greco-Roman literature*, Leicester: Leicester University Press.
—— (1987a) '*Conspicui postes tectaque digna deo*: the public image of aristocratic and imperial houses in the late Republic and early Empire', in *L' Urbs: espace urbain et histoire (Ier siècle av. J.-C.–IIIe siècle ap. J.-C)*, Rome: L'École française de Rome, Collection de l'École française de Rome 98: 395–413 = Wiseman 1994: 98–115.
—— (1987b) *Roman studies, literary and historical*, Liverpool: Francis Cairns.
—— (1994) *Historiography and imagination: eight essays on Roman culture*, Exeter: University of Exeter Press, Exeter Studies in History 33.
Yegül, Fikret K. (1992) *Baths and bathing in classical antiquity*, New York: Architectural History Foundation.

Index of persons and Gods

A page number may indicate multiple references.

Acastus, slave of Cicero 96–7
Acilius Glabrio, M'., tribune 122 BC 26
Aculeo, C., Cicero's uncle by marriage 25
Aelia, daughter of Q. Aelius Tubero, married L. Cassius Longinus (cos. suffect AD 11) 26
Aelius Lamia, L., aedile 45 BC 121
Aelius Tubero, L., friend of Cicero and a connection by marriage 25, 26
Aelius Tubero, Q. 26
Aemilius Lepidus, M'., cos. 66 BC 105
Aemilius Lepidus, M., cos. 46, 42, triumvir 43 BC 18, 144
Aemilius Lepidus Paullus, L., cos. 50 BC 97
Aemilius Scaurus, M., cos. 115 BC 23–4
Aesopus, *see* Clodius Aesopus
Agrippa, *see* Vipsanius Agrippa
Agrippina the Younger, mother of Nero, *see* Julia Agrippina
Alexio, doctor 38, 101
Ampia 28
Ampius Balbus, T., tribune 63, praetor 59 BC 28
Annaeus Seneca, L., the Elder, writer on rhetoric 145–7, 151
Annaeus Seneca, L., the Younger, philosopher 132, 144, 149, 157
Annius Asellus, P., senator 38–9
Annius Milo, T., tribune 57, praetor 55 BC 53, 70, 78, 132
Antistius Vetus, C.? 148
Antonia, wife of M. Antonius 122
Antonia the Younger, daughter of M. Antonius (cos. 44 BC) 20
Antonius, C., cos. 63 BC 45, 49

Antonius, M., cos. 99 BC 11, 23, 24, 25
Antonius, M. (Mark Antony) cos. 44, 34, triumvir 43 BC 28, 48, 49, 85, 96, 109, 111, 117, 121, 122, 129, 144–5, 148, 149, 150, 152, 153
Apollonius, slave of P. Licinius Crassus 38, 80
Appian, historian 148
Aristocritus, courier from Terentia 68
Arrius, C., of Formiae 53, 105
Asconius Pedianus, Q., commentator on Cicero's speeches 13, 24, 31, 135
Asinius Pollio, C., cos. 40 BC 144, 149
Atilius Regulus, M., cos. 267 BC 59
Atticus, *see* Pomponius Atticus
Aufidius Bassus, historian 147
Aufilius, *see* Ofilius
Augustus, *see* Julius Caesar, C. (Octavian)
Aurelia, wife of C. Julius Caesar (praetor c. 92 BC) 20, 46, 66, 152
Aurelia, wife (it is deduced) of M. Valerius Messalla Corvinus 151
Aurelius Cotta Maximus, M., cos. AD 20 150–51

Balbus, *see* Cornelius Balbus
Balsdon, J. P. V. D., 129, 156–8
Boissier, Gaston 159
Brutus, *see* Junius Brutus

Caecilia, mother of Atticus 41, 50
Caecilia Attica, daughter of Atticus, 7, 20, 36–7, 41, 85, 88–9, 153
Caecilia Metella, wife of Cornelius Sulla 28, 132

Index of persons and Gods 215

Caecilia Metella, wife of Cornelius Lentulus Spinther 126
Caeciliae Metellae 14, 20
Caecilius Metellus, L., tribune 49 BC 28, 121
Caecilius Metellus Pius Scipio Nasica, Q., cos. 52 BC 134–5
Caecilius Metellus Celer, Q., cos. 60 BC 50, 126, 152
Caelius Rufus, M., tribune 52, praetor 48 BC 32, 37, 80, 82, 85, 86, 89, 93, 95, 100, 104, 109, 159
Caerellia 141, 157, 159–60
Caesonius, M., probably the man who was aedile 69 and praetor 66 BC 132
Calenus, *see* Fufius Calenus
Calpurnia, wife of C. Julius Caesar (cos. 59 BC) 28, 66
Calpurnia, ?wife of M. Valerius Messalla Corvinus 151
Calpurnia, wife of Pliny 33
Calpurnius Piso, C., cos. 67 BC 42
Calpurnius Piso Caesoninus, L., cos. 58 BC 13, 57, 61, 69, 158
Calpurnius Piso Frugi, L., great-grandfather of Tullia's husband 41–2
Calpurnius Piso Frugi, L., grandfather of Tullia's husband 41–2
Calpurnius Piso Frugi, L., father of Tullia's husband 41–2, 69
Calpurnius Piso Frugi, C., Tullia's first husband, 41–3, 47, 52, 54, 56, 57, 61, 64, 65, 67, 68, 69, 75, 93–4
Camillus, C., friend and agent of Cicero 86, 97, 103, 112, 114, 123, 125
Carcopino, J. 150
Cassius Dio, historian 44–5, 129, 134, 148
Cassius Longinus, C., praetor 44 BC 62, 106, 140, 145, 152
Cassius Longinus, L., tribune 44 BC, 27, 133
Cassius Longinus, L., cos. suffect AD 11
Catiline, *see* Sergius Catilina
Cato, *see* Porcius Cato
Catullus, *see* Valerius Catullus
Ciaceri, E. 155, 157
Cicero, *see* M. Tullius Cicero
Cinna, *see* Cornelius Cinna
Claassen, Jo-Marie 130
Clark, Patricia 76
Claudiae, daughters of Ap. Claudius Pulcher (cos. 54 BC) 91

Claudii Nerones 90
Claudii Pulchri 90
Claudius Marcellus, C., cos. 50 BC 66, 97
Claudius Nero, C., cos. 207 BC 90
Claudius Nero, Ti., praetor before 63 BC 90
Claudius Nero, Ti., praetor 42 BC 83, 90–2, 93, 95
Claudius Nero, Ti., the future emperor Tiberius 90, 152
Claudius Pulcher, Ap., cos. 54 BC 89–91, 94–5
Cleopatra 92, 150
Clodia, wife of Q. Caecilius Metellus Celer 20–1, 49–50, 65, 66, 126, 152, 159
Clodia, mother-in-law of L. Caecilius Metellus, probably the divorced wife of L. Licinius Lucullus 28, 159
Clodia, wife of Ofilius 152
Clodius Aesopus, tragic actor 71
Clodius Pulcher, P., tribune 58 BC 20, 48, 49–50, 54, 56, 65–6, 70, 74, 78, 90, 105, 119, 122, 126, 148, 159
Cluvius, M., of Puteoli, 142, 143, 152
Cornelia, mother of the Gracchi 157
Cornelia, daughter of L. Cornelius Cinna, wife of C. Julius Caesar 93
Cornelia, wife of P. Sestius 28, 48, 49
Cornelia, Fausta 132
Cornelia, daughter of Q. Caecilius Metellus Pius Scipio Nasica, 20, 144, 157; as wife of Pompey 28, 134
Cornelius, Q. 48, 49
Cornelius Balbus, L., cos. 40 BC 66, 143
Cornelius Chrysogonus, L., freedman of Sulla 28
Cornelius Cinna, L., cos. 87–4 BC 26, 93
Cornelius Dolabella, stepson of Tullia 92
Cornelius Dolabella, Cn., cos. 81 BC 92
Cornelius Dolabella, Cn., praetor 81 BC 92
Cornelius Dolabella, L., praetor c. 100 BC, probably grandfather of Tullia's husband 92
Cornelius Dolabella, P., praetor c. 69 BC, probably the father of Tullia's husband 92
Cornelius Dolabella, P., cos. suffect 44, Tullia's third husband 77, 83, 86,

216   *Index of persons and Gods*

89–99, chs 9, 10 *passim*, 144, 145, 162–3
Cornelius Dolabella, P., cos. AD 10, 92
(Cornelius) Lentulus, son of Tullia 135, 138, 139, 141
Cornelius Lentulus (Spinther), P., cos. 57 BC 66, 70, 76, 158
Cornelius Lentulus Spinther, P., quaestor ?44 BC 126
Cornelius Lentulus Sura, P., praetor 63 BC 47
Cornelius Nepos, biographer of Atticus 19, 85, 153
Cornelius Scipio Aemilianus, P., cos. 147, 134 BC 10, 88
Cornelius Scipio Asiagenus, L., cos. 83 BC 28
Cornelius Severus, poet 149
Cornelius Sulla, Faustus, quaestor 54 BC 28, 132
Cornelius Sulla, L., cos. 88, 80, dictator 82–?80 BC 11, 24, 26, 28, 92, 132, 144
Cornelius Sulla, P. 50
Cornelius Tacitus, historian 152, 163
Cornificia, daughter of Q. Cornificius 151
Crassipes, *see* (Furius) Crassipes
Crassus, *see* Licinius Crassus
Cremutius Cordus, A., historian 147
Crook, J. A., 129–30
Curio, *see* Scribonius Curio
Curius, Q., senator, 46
Curtius Nicias 140

Deiotarus, king of Galatia 87
Dexius, husband of Licinia 133
Dio, *see* Cassius Dio
Diocles, *see* (Terentius) Tyrannio (Diocles)
Diodorus, Greek historian 46
Diodotus the Stoic 38, 80
Diviciacus the Gaul 38
Dixon, Suzanne 115
Domitius Ahenobarbus, Cn., cos. 32 BC 149

Epictetus, Stoic 43
Eppuleia, wife of Ampius Balbus 28

Fabia, half-sister of Terentia 30–1, 49–50, 61, 92
Fabia, wife of Dolabella 89, 92, 93, 95
Fabii 30

Fabius Gallus, M., *eques* and friend of Cicero 133
Faustus Sulla, *see* Faustus Cornelius Sulla
Fowler, W. Warde 156
Fufius Calenus, Q., cos. 47 BC 129, 134, 148
Fulvia 46, 145
Fulvia, daughter of M. Fulvius Bambalio, wife of Clodius 20, 48, 49, 122, 145, 148, 149, 152
Furii 75
(Furius) Crassipes, second husband of Tullia 75–7, 78, 93, 106

Gabinius, A., cos. 58 BC 61, 90
Gaius, jurist 59
Good Goddess 19, 44, 49, 56
Gracchus, *see* Sempronius Gracchus
Gratidia, grandmother of Cicero 23, ?25
Gratidia, wife of Catiline 24
Gratidius, M. 23–4

Helvia, aunt of Cicero 25
Helvia, mother of Cicero 25, 32–3
Helvii 25
Hirtia, sister of A. Hirtius 132–3, 149
Hirtius, A., cos. 43 BC 130, 132, 145, 149
Horace (Q. Horatius Flaccus), poet 59, 71, 144, 152
Hordeonius, T., co-heir of Cluvius 143
Hortensia, daughter of Q. Hortensius Hortalus (cos. 69 BC) 149
Hortensius Hortalus, Q., cos. 69 BC 57, 62
Hortensius Hortalus, Q., praetor ?45 BC 111

Jerome, Christian writer 38, 132, 144, 149, 152
Julia, mother of M. Antonius 121, 149
Julia, daughter of C. Julius Caesar
Julia, daughter of C. Julius Caesar (Augustus) 20, 66
Julia Agrippina (Agrippina the Younger) 20
Julius Caesar, C., cos. 59, 48, 46, 45, 44 BC; dictator 49, 48–7, 46–5, 45–4 BC 18, 26, 27, 28, 56, 66, 70, 74, 75, 77, 84, 88, 89, 90, 93, 96, ch. 9 *passim*, 123–4, 130, 132, 140,

143, 144, 150, 151, 152, 155, 158, 159, 161
Julius Caesar, C. (Octavian), great-nephew of the dictator, later Augustus 11, 18, 20, 85, 88, 90, 92, 144, 148, 149, 150, 152, 153
Junia, mother of C. Claudius Marcellus 66
Junia, daughter of Servilia, and wife of P. Servilius Isauricus (cos. 48, 41 BC) 117
Junia Tertia, daughter of Servilia, and wife of C. Cassius Longinus (praetor 44 BC) 62, 106, ?131, 152
Junius Brutus, M., praetor 44 BC 62, 91, 95, 145, 148, 152
Junius Brutus Albinus, D., cos. designate 42 BC 77
Junius Silanus, D., cos. 62 BC 66
Juno 16
Jupiter 45, 58, 93
Juventius Laterensis, M., praetor 51 BC 66

Labienus, T., tribune 63 BC 158
Lacey, W. K. 138
Laelia, daughter of C. Laelius (cos. 140 BC) 26
Laelius, C., cos. 140 BC 26, 159
Laelius, D. 121
Lamia, *see* Aelius Lamia
Licinia, wife of P. Cornelius Scipio Nasica (praetor 93 BC) 26
Licinia, wife of C. Marius (cos. 82) 26
(Licinia), probably wife of L. Caecilius Metellus 28
Licinia, (half-)sister of Cassius or Crassus 133
Liciniae, daughters of L. Licinius Crassus (cos. 95 BC) 26
Licinius Crassus, L., cos. 95 BC 25
Licinius Crassus, M., cos. 70, 55 BC 56, 74, 76, 158
Licinius Crassus, M., cos. 30 BC 133
Licinius Crassus, P., cos. 97 BC 51
Licinius Crassus, P. 38, 80, 135, 144
(Licinius) Tyrannio, scholar 74, 77, 80
Livia, wife of P. Rutilius Rufus (cos. 105 BC) 152
Livia Drusilla, daughter of M. Livius Drusus Claudianus, marries Ti. Claudius Nero 20, 90; marries the younger Caesar 90
Livius Drusus, M., tribune 122 BC 152

Livius Drusus, M., tribune 91 BC 11
Livy (T. Livius), the historian 20, 145–7
Long, George 128
Lucceius, L., praetor 67 BC 131
Lucretia 16–17
Lucretius, T., poet 1, 2, 6
Lutatius Catulus, Q., cos. 102 BC 51

Maecenas, C. 85
Marcius Censorinus, L., cos. 39 BC 148
Marcius Philippus, L., cos. 56 BC 107
Maria 24
Marius, C., cos. 107, 104–100, 86 BC 11, 24, 26
Marius, M., praetor c. 102 BC 24
Marius, M., friend of Cicero 116
Marius Gratidianus, M., praetor ?85, ?84 BC 24
Mescinius Rufus, L., quaestor 51 BC 103
Messalla, *see* Valerius Messalla
Messallinus, *see* Valerius Messallinus
Metellus, *see* Caecilius Metellus
Milo, *see* Annius Milo
Minerva 58
Mitchell, Thomas N. 155
Mucia, wife of Pompey 132
Mucia, wife of Acilius Glabrio 26
Mucia, wife of L. Licinius Crassus 26
Mucius Scaevola, Q., cos. 117 BC 26
Mucius Scaevola, Q., cos. 95 BC 26
Munatius Plancus, L., cos. 42 BC 144

Nepos, *see* Cornelius Nepos
Neubauer, Luise 130
Nicias, *see* Curtius Nicias

Octavia, daughter of C. Octavius and Atia 28, 149
Octavius, C., *see* C. Julius Caesar (Octavian)
Of(f)ilius, A. 152
Oppii, bankers 112–13
Orpheus, ?dotal slave of Terentia 64
Ovid (P. Ovidius Naso), poet 20, 53, 58, 151

Paetus, *see* Papirius Paetus
Pansa, *see* Vibius Pansa
Papirius Paetus, L., friend of Cicero 78
Petersson, T. 159
Philippus, *see* Marcius Philippus
Philodamus 17

218 Index of persons and Gods

Philotimus, see Terentius Philotimus
Pilia, wife of Pomponius Atticus 7, 28, 77–8, 89, 97, 118, 132, 163
Piso, see Calpurnius
Plancius, Cn., aedile 55/4 BC 78, 130, 133
Pliny (Plinius Secundus, C.) the Elder 75, 152
Pliny (Plinius Secundus, C.) the Younger 33
Plutarch (Mestrius Plutarchus, [L.?]), biographer 20, 22–3, 25, 32, 37, 44–5, 47, 49–50, 58, 114, 122, 123, 129–30, 134, 148, 156, 158
Pollex, confidential slave of Cicero 116
Polybius, Greek historian 10
Pompeia, wife of Faustus Sulla 28, 132–3
Pompeius, Sex., cos. designate 35 BC 149
Pompeius Magnus, Cn. (Pompey), cos. 70, 55, 52 BC 32, 51, 54, 57, 66, 70, 74, 75 77, 79, 84, 98, ch. 9 *passim*, 134, 144, 158, 159
Pompeius Magnus, Cn., son of the foregoing, 91, 95
Pompey, see Cn. Pompeius Magnus
Pompeius Strabo, Cn., cos. 89 BC 26
Pomponia, wife of Quintus 31, 41, 50, 55, 74, 75, 76, 79, 80, 81–2, 85, 98, 103, 105, 148, 162–3
Pomponius Atticus, T., after adoption in 58 Q. Caecilius Atticus, 26, 44, 45, 52–4, 56, 67, 102, 145, 153, 156, 159, 163; correspondence with Cicero 40, *and see under* Cicero; as confidant of Cicero 40, chs 8–9 *passim*; daughter, *see* Caecilia Attica; estate at Buthrotum 26, 40, 52, 53, 61, 70, 78, 87, 108, 111, 113; frugality 35; house 67, 153; performs tasks for Cicero 43–4, 61–70, 85–91, 97, 108, 115–16, 119, 123, 125–6, 138–9, 141; relationship with Cicero, *see under* Cicero; staff 86, 102, 114, 132; villa 141; wife, *see* Pilia
Pomponius Dionysius, M., freedman of Atticus 78, 80, 108, 143
Pontidia 83, 85, 87, 90, 91, 98
Pontidius, M. 87
Pontius, L., host of Cicero 98

Porcia, daughter of M. Porcius Cato 62, 152
Porcius Cato, M., 'the Elder', cos. 195, censor 184 BC 27
Porcius Cato, M., 'the Younger', praetor 54 BC 121, 159
Postumia, wife of Ser. Sulpicius Rufus (cos. 51 BC) 85, 87–8, 132
Precius 97
PUBLILIA, second wife of Cicero, 1, 18, 21, 131; marries 134–5; as Cicero's wife 140–41, 160, 161, 163; divorce 141; during proscriptions 145, 148–9; later life and possible marriages 149–51,152; character 161; dowry 134, 141–2, 150; wealth 134
Publilii 134
Publilius, ?brother of Publilia 131, 134, 141, 152, 161
(Publilius, M.) father of Publilia 134
Publilius Strato, M., joint freedman of Publilia and C. Vibius Rufus 151
Pupius Piso Frugi, M., cos. 61 BC 42

Rabirius Postumus, C., banker, praetor c. 48 BC 66
Rawson, Elizabeth 144, 155
Regulus, see Atilius Regulus
Roscius, Sex. 28
Rubrius 17
Rufus, see Caelius, Mescinius, Sulpicius, Vibius
Rutilius, probably P. Rutilius Rufus cos. 105 BC 152

Sallust, see Sallustius Crispus
Sallustius Crispus, C. (Sallust), praetor 46 BC, historian 5, 19, 20, 44, 149–51
Sallustius, Cn. 122, 150
Sallustius, P. 122, 150
Scribonia 85
Scribonius Curio, C., tribune 50 BC 48, 96, 148
Sebosus of Formiae 53, 105
Sempronia, allegedly involved in Catiline's plot 19, 20–21, 157
Sempronius Gracchus, C., tribune 123, 122 BC 11
Sempronius Gracchus, Ti., tribune 133 BC 10, 11
Seneca, see Annaeus Seneca

Index of persons and Gods 219

Sergius Catilina, L., praetor 68 BC 31, 45–6, 48
Servilia, mother of Brutus 20, 62, 66, 83, 85, 87–8, 117, 145, 152, 158
Servilius Isauricus, P., cos. 48, 41 BC 117
Sestius, P., tribune 57 BC 28, 48, 67, 70, 85, 87
Sextilius Ena, poet 149
Shackleton Bailey, D. R. 155
Sicca, friend of Cicero 124
Sidonius Apollinaris, Bishop of Clermont 157
Soranus 42, 101–2
Sositheus, slave of Cicero 80
Statilia, perhaps the daughter of T. Statilius Taurus (cos. 37 BC) 152
Statius, *see* (Q. Tullius) Statius
Stockton, David 155
Suetonius Tranquillus, C., biographer 20
Sulla, *see* Cornelius Sulla, L.
Sulpicia, daughter of Ser. Sulpicius Rufus (cos. 51 BC) 26
Sulpicia, poet, daughter of Ser. Sulpicius Rufus (son of the cos. 51) 20–21, 88
Sulpicius Rufus, Ser., cos. 51 BC 26, 83, 87–8, 93, 136–8
Sulpicius Rufus, Ser., son of the foregoing 83, 85, 87–8, 91
Syme, Sir Ronald 94, 151, 155

Tacitus, *see* Cornelius Tacitus
TERENTIA, first wife of Cicero, 1, 7, 14, 18, 21; background and family 25, 29, 30–31; youth 12, 24; marries Cicero 27–9; birth of Tullia 36–7; interval between her children 36, 44, 159; birth of Marcus 44; during Cicero's consulship 45–7; in crisis of 58 and during Cicero's exile 31, 56–70; in search for Tullia's new husband 83–94; during civil war ch. 9; during Cicero's stay at Brundisium 118–28; divorce 34, 114, 128–30, 131–2, 134, 138–9, 143, 156, 159,163; during proscriptions 145, 148–9; later life 152–4; age at death 13, 152.
character 155–61; in charge of Cicero's property 33, 60, 64–5, 102, 128–9, 159; confidante and adviser of Cicero 40, 44–5, 61–2, 158–9, 161; conversation 38, 157; and couriers 68–9, 86, 96–7, 104, 116, 119, 128; and cult 35–6, 44–5, 49–50, 111; dines out 38, 77, 81, 144; dinners at home 38, 106, 144, 157; dowry 34–5, 120, 138–9, 150; freed slaves 30, 33–4, 35, 102; friends 41, 44, 102, 122, 158.
at games 36, 44, 56, 71, 78; her generosity 65, 66, 68, 161; health 41, 44, 63, 66, 68, 69, 112, 115, 119, 122–3, 156; holidays 52–3, 77–8, 79; hostess, *see* receives; hosts 98; housekeeping 33, 37, 129, 158, 159; inherits legacies 143; intellect 38, 156; intellectual interests 44, 143–4; journeys 28–9, 36, 38, 52–3, 60, 73, 82, 98–9, 101, 104, 107–8, 110, 116, 118–19; her letters 40–1, 63–9, 96–7, 116, 119, 120–21, 157, 158, 160, *and see under* Cicero; in literature: Dio on 44–5; *Invective against Cicero* on 48; Jerome on 38, 144, 149, 152; Plutarch on 32, 37, 44–5, 47, 49–50, 114, 123, 129–30, 156, 158; Seneca on 144, 149; *see also* Balsdon, Ciaceri, Crook, Dixon, Mitchell, Neubauer, E. Rawson, Shackleton Bailey, Stockton, Syme; manages Cicero's affairs 60, 64–5, 74, 86, 112–13, 116, 118, 121–2, 129, 155–6, 159; money 68; as mother of the household 32–6, 131; patronage and mediation 46, 48–9, 143, 158; in politics 37, 44–50, ch. 6, 108, 130, 144–5, 150, 158–9; property 23, 30, 52, 66, 68, 118, 120, 127, 130, 143; receives visitors and guests 36, 45–6, 50, 52, 66, 71, 79, 94, 106, 107, 111, 143, 157; residences: houses 32, 35; villas 44, *see also under* M.Tullius Cicero; relationship with Atticus 41, 52, 61, 98, 163; with Cicero 49–50, 52, ch. 6 *passim*; 74, 82, 100, 118–19, 122, 127–9, 159–61; with Marcus 159, 162; with Pomponia 41, 55, 75, 163; with Quintus 67–8, 163; with young Quintus 163; with Tiro 80, 163; with Tullia 55, 63, 116, 159, 162; reputation 48, 64, 102–3, 104; rural estates 34–5, 52, 68; semi-detachment 18, 36, 80, 118, 164; slaves 35, 36,64, 68, 102, 111;

urban property 34–5, 139, 162; virtues 64, 67, 112, 160; visiting 36, 44, 66, 158; will 122–3, 125, 127, 128
Terentii 25, 30
(Terentius) Philotimus, freedman of Terentia 33, 78, 86, 97, 102, 112–14, 123, 128, 129–30
(?Terentius) Tyrannio (Diocles), ?freedman of Terentia 143–4
Terentius Varro, C., cos. 216 BC 30
Terentius Varro, M., 30
Tertia, wife of M. Licinius Crassus (cos.70, 55 BC) 66
Teucris 49
Thyillus 49
Tiro, see M. Tullius Tiro
Trebonius, C., cos. suffect 45 BC 96, 140
Tubero, see Aelius Tubero
Tullia, cousin of Cicero 24
TULLIA, daughter of Cicero 1, 7, 13, 14, 18, 21, 40, 41, 45, 46, 49, 52, 130, 132; birth 27–9, 36–7; childhood 37, 38–9, 41, 55; education 161; first engagement 41–4; during Cicero's consulship 45–7; marries Piso 27, 43, 46, 47; as wife of Piso 52–3, 56, 63, 56–70; in crisis of 58 and during Cicero's exile 56–70; supplication of consul 65, 69; widowed 69; engaged to Crassipes 75; ?married and divorced 76–7, 84, 137, 163; search for new husband 83–94; engaged to Dolabella 91–7; married 97–8; as wife of Dolabella 98–131 *passim*; unhappy situation 100, 122–7; pregnancy 101–11; premature baby 111; idea of divorce 125–7, 131; second pregnancy 130–31; divorce from Dolabella 77, 120, 131–2, 137; birth of son 135; death 135–6, 138, 147, 162.
appearance 62, 84; character 62, 161–2; childlessness 69, 76, 84, 94, 97; conversation 62, 74, 137, 161; and cult 46, 49; as daughter of the household 85–6, 120, 122, 126; dines out 77; dinners at home 106, 131; dowry 68, 69, 84, 97–8, 113, 114–16, 125, 126, 135, 140; friends 102, 126, 131, 133; at games 44, 53, 56, 71;

receives guests 131; health 78, 112, 119–20, 135–6; holidays 52–3, 77–8; incest, alleged 131, 159; intellect 55, 62, 84, 161–2; intellectual interests 44; letters 40–41; in literature: 161; Livy on 147, *and see* Lacey, Syme; journeys 28, 52–3, 60, 71–3, 82, 104, 107–8, 110, 111, 118, 123–4, 128–9; negotiating 133, 160; parties 85; in politics ch. 6 *passim*, 100, 108–9, 161; receives visitors and guests 66, 106, 131; relationship with Cicero 50, 62, 67, 74, 109, 110, 119, 131, 136–8, 160, 161–2; with Publilia 140; with Terentia 55, 63, 116, 119, 129, 131, 159, 162; with Marcus 163; with Quintus 75, 120, 163; with young Quintus 163; with Atticus 41, chs. 8–10 *passim*, 163; reputation 63, 102–3, 103, 104, 131, 159–60; semi-detachment 118, 164; slaves and freed slaves who served her 71–2, 139; virtues 62, 95, 108–9, 123, 125, 161; visiting 44, 66
Tullius, Servius, king of Rome 23
Tullius Cicero, L., uncle of Cicero 24, 25
Tullius Cicero, L., cousin of Cicero 24, 29
Tullius Cicero, M., grandfather of Cicero 10, 22, 23, 32
Tullius Cicero, M., father of Cicero 22–5, 32, 34, 43
TULLIUS CICERO, M. 151; family 22–5; childhood 25; as son of the household 32; education 25–6, 28–9, 37, 38, 159; early career 26–9; marries Terentia 27–32; in Greek lands 24, 26–8; quaestor 27, 29, 86; aedile 40; praetor 29; consul 5, 29, 45–7, 106, 147; exile 40, 56–73, 106, 147; governor 77, 83–94, 114; during civil war ch. 9; at Brundisium 118–28; divorce from Terentia 34, 114, 128–30, 131, 134; plans for remarriage 131–3; marriage to Publilia 134–41; divorces Publilia 141; death 145–8; clients 37, 49, 50, 140, 143; complaints against Terentia 74, 113, 114, 127–30, 155–7, 160; couriers 68, 71, 72, 104, 119, *see also under*

Index of persons and Gods   221

Terentia; and cult 45, 73, 144; dines out 76, 78, 130; dinners at home 38, 53, 106, 107; as father of the household 36, 83, 85–6; 94, 120, 122, 126, 138, 139, 140, 162; finances: 32, 74, 78, 84, 98, 112–16, 120, 124, 127, 131, 134, 138–9, 141–2, 152; friends 20, 26, 30, 37, 50, 61, 64, 66, 67, 91, 118, 137, 143, 153, 158; at games 51, 56, 78; health 26, 36, 37, 106, 111, 113, 115, 119, 128; holidays 56, 77, 79, 157; honour, *see* reputation; hosts 61, 63–4, 77, 82, 98, 113, 114, 116; houses in Rome 32, 35, 43, 44, 47, 48, 50, 51, 57, 60–61, 64, 66, 73, 74, 77, 79, 84, 86, 99, 101, 102, 104, 105, 112, 115, 124, 129, 132, 133, 135, 137–8, 139, 148, 153, 162, at Antium 44, 50, 51, 52–3, 77, 78; inherits 48; is heir/executor 98, 142; incest, alleged 131, 159; invective against 48, 131, 159–60; journeys 52–3, 61–4, 67, 72–3, 77, 78, 79, 82, 91, 97–9, 112–13, 128–29; legacies to him 38; lodges 105, 108, 110; on love of children 41, 57, 73, 78; parties 37–8, 138; posterity 71; property 63, 66, 105, 115–16, 120, 127, 135, 139, 149; receives guests 38, 53–4, 71, 77–8, 79, 105–6, 107, 143 ; receptions 46, 50, 53, 105; relationship with Atticus 50; with Terentia, *see under* Terentia; with Publilia, *see under* Publilia; with Quintus 40, 50, ch. 6 *passim*; 74, ch. 9 *passim* esp. 116, 118; with young Quintus 163; with Tullia, *see under* Tullia; reputation 29, 37, 48, 63, 89, 102–3, 104–6, 110, 120, 122, 131; secretaries etc. 38, 136, 157; sexuality 31, 134, 15960; slaves 7, 25, 27, 35, 37, 38, 60, 61, 64, 68, 102, 112, 114, 139, 147; freed slaves 30, 35, 102, 114; staff: 71, 132; his villas 51, 60, 61, 71, 77–8, 79, 84, 102, 103, 107, 112, 119, 129, 132, 148; *see also* Arpinum, Astura, *Cumanum, Formianum, Pompeianum, Puteolanum, Tusculanum*; his will 134, 138, 141; work 267, 37, 38, 40, 48, 50, 56, 78, 79, 86, 135, 137, 162; working day 27, 37–8, 78, 157; writings 20, 25, 78, 136.

letters 21, 31, 40–41, 64, 79, 83, 84, 86, 104, 105, 144, 157, 158, 163; to and from Atticus 40–1, 43, 45, 53–4, 56, 74, 76, 79, 91, 101, 104–5, 119, 123, 125, 127, 136, 139, 153–4, 158 ; to and from Terentia 40–41, chs 6, 8 *passim*, 100, 116, 118, 128, 153–4, 157, 158, 160 ; to Quintus 40, 76, 79; to Tiro 80; survival of letters 80, 153–4.

speeches 13, 38, 46, 157; *On behalf of Quinctius* 28; *Defence of Sex. Roscius* 28; *On the agrarian law* 45; *Speeches against Catiline* 46–7; *After his return to the People* 24; *After his return to the Senate; Defence of Sestius* 72; *Defence of Plancius; Philippics*.

treatises: 10, 140, 157, 162; *On invention* 26; *On the orator* 25; *Consolatio* 161; *On Duties* 24; *Laws* 54.

lost or fragmentary works: *Consulatus suus* 44; *Hortensius* 25; *Marius* 24; *Uxorius* 54

Tullius Cicero, M., son of Cicero 24; birth 36, 44; childhood 37, 46, 47, 50, 52, 57, 60–68; adolescence 79, 81, 87, 98, 103, 104, 105; coming of age 106–7; during civil war 109–10, 112, 116, 119, 122, 123–4, 129, 139, 161; in Athens 29, 34, 115, 140, 144, 145, 148, 150, 162; returns 149; later life and death 152–4; idea of marriage 32

Tullius Cicero, Q., brother of Cicero *passim*; death 145, 147–8; divorce 81; estates 78; *see also* Laterium; houses 50, 55, 74, 163; marriage 41, 812; in politics 77; relationship with Cicero, *see under* Cicero; freedmen 70; slaves 70; youth 24, 25, 26, 29, 31, 33

Tullius Cicero, Q., nephew of Cicero 32, 55, 62, 63, 74, 75, 79, 81, 87, 92, 98, 103,104, 105, 106, 107, 109, 112, 143, 145, 147–8

Tullius Laurea, freedman of Cicero, 143

(Tullius) Statius, (Q.), freedman of Q. Cicero 80, 81,163

222 Index of persons and Gods

Tullius Tiro, M., freedman of Cicero 33, 79–80, 101, 105, 110, 130, 131, 143, 148, 153–4
Tullus Attius 23
'Turia', the anonymous wife eulogised by her husband 18, 66, 138
Tutia 92
Tyrannio, *see* (Licinius)

Valeria, wife of Sulpicius Rufus 88
Valeria Paulla (Polla) 77
Valerius, P., friend of Cicero 65
Valerius Catullus, C., poet 20
Valerius Messalla Corvinus, M., cos. 31 BC 88, 149–51
Valerius Messalla Messallinus, M., cos. 3 BC 150–51
Valerius Maximus, writer 152
Valerius Triarius, brother of Valeria Paulla 77
Vatinius, P., cos. 47 BC 52
Velleius Paterculus, historian 147
Venus Verticordia 107
Vergil (P. Vergilius Maro), poet 152

Verginia 17
Verres, C., praetor 74 BC 17, 24, 29, 38–9, 40, 158
Vettius, L., informer 54
Vibius Pansa Caetronianus, C., cos. 43 BC 145
Vibius Philippus, C., dedicator 151
Vibius Rufus, C., cos. suffect AD 16 151
Vibius Rufinus, C., cos. suffect ?AD 21 or 22 151
Vipsania Agrippina, grand-daughter of Atticus 152
Vipsanius Agrippa, M., cos. 37, 28, 27 BC 20, 85, 153
Visellius Varro, C., cousin of Cicero, aedile c. 59 BC 25, 26, 30, 31, 67
Volumnia Cytheris 36, 90, 111, 121
Volumnius Eutrapelus, P., *eques* 36, 89–90, 121, 145

Xanthippe, wife of Socrates 149
Xenophon 33

General index

A page number may indicate multiple references.

Actium 86
actors 71
actresses 36, 111, 121
adoption 92, 119
adultery 16, 100, 122, 159–60
adulthood 19; *see also* puberty
Aec(u)lanum 98
aediles 25, 40
Aesernia 105
'Africa' (province) 10, 11, 28, 130, 132, 150
age at marriage: legal minimum 20, 27, 150; in practice 20, 27, 37, 42, 84, 93, 134–5, 150, 151
Alba 57, 98
Alban Mount 45
Amiternum 150
Anagnia 77
ancestors 23, 27
Antium 44; *see also under* M. Tullius Cicero: houses
Apennines 22, 26
Apulia 71, 105
Aquinum 81
Arcanum 81, 98, 108, 147
architects 9
Argiletum 34–5, 139, 162
Arpinum 2, 4, 11, 26, 30, 44, 107–8; Cicero's villa near 22, 50, 51, 53–4, 77, 79, 81, 82, 106, 107–8, 112; leading families of 22–5, 87–8, 91
Arx 81, 98, 108, 147
'Asia' (province) 10, 26, 28, 29, 62, 83, 114, 128, 151
assemblies of the People 5, 8; Centuriate 71; Tribal 27

Astura 132, 136, 140, 141, 147
Athens 24, 26, 28, 29, 86, 88, 140, 144, 149
attractiveness 41, 43, 84, 93–5, 98, 107, 132, 141; *see also* beauty, deportment
avarice 20
Aventine Hill 34–5, 139, 162
aviaries 79

babies 36–7, 73, 89, 101, 111–12, 135, 139
Baiae 51
ballot 23
Basilica, Porcian 65
baths 34, 50, 78, 79, 128
Bay of Naples 51
beauty 43, 134, 135; *see also* attractiveness
beds 8, 35, 46, 81, 159, 162
Beneventum 82
betrothals, *see* engagements
birthdays 27, 37, 38, 72, 98, 120
boating 6–7
boni 10
books 44, 51, 52, 77, 78; *see also* literature
British 3
brothers (in general) 2, 4, 6, 15, 17, 63, 84, 85
Brundisium 28, 52, 61, 63, 64, 71–2, 76, 82, 86, 97, 98, 105, 106, 116, 118, 122, 123, 124, 128, 153, 157, 162
business 9, 15
businessmen 9, 17
butchers 16

224 *General index*

Buthrotum, *see under* Pomponius Atticus

Caieta 106, 147, 111, 147
calendar 118
Cales 105
Capene Gate 73
Capitoline Hill 8, 45, 73
Capua 104, 105
Carinae 32, 50, 74
carriages 53, 72, 74, 101, 111
Carthage 10, 59
cash, *see* money
Casinum 30
censors 16
chaperonage 16, 19, 29
charm, *see* attractiveness
chastity, *see pudicitia*
childbirth 13, 25, 111, 164
childlessness 16, 18, 69, 84, 94, 97
child-minders 10, 19, 139
children 8, 13, 15, 16, 57, 62, 73, 136–7, 164
Cilicia 10, 25, 53, 76, 80, 83, 84, 86, 89, 94, 106, 113, 116, 124, 158
circus 8, 44, 53
cities 2, 13, 81, 83, 137
citizens, Roman 1, 10, 14, 58–60; *see also* citizenship
citizenship, Roman 3, 4, 11, 58–9, 60, 140, 143; *see also* citizens
clans 14
clients 8, 14, 37, 38
clothes 23, 69; *see also* dress
coemptio 122
Compitalia 50–51
consent to marriage 15–16, 162
consummation 20, 31, 42–3
control of husband over wife, *see manus*
conubium, *see* rights of Roman citizens, private
conventions 16, 62, 163
conversation 19, 26, 38, 62, 137, 157, 161
copyists 137
Corcyra 133
Corinth 10
Corsica 10
courage, *see* manliness,
couriers 8, 115, 119; *see also under* Terentia, M. Tullius Cicero
craftsmen/women 8, 9, 15, 16
cremations 148

cult 35–6, 44–6, 49, 144; domestic 8, 35; *see also* sacrifices
Cumanum, Cicero's villa at Cumae 7, 75, 77, 78, 79, 82, 88, 98, 107, 108, 110–11, 114, 148
custom 15, 16

dancers 9, 19
dancing 19, 101, 157
daughters 2, 6, 7, 15, 16, 17, 37, 38–9; *passim*
daughters of households 14–15, 59, 122; *see also* Tullia
deportment 42, 43, 62, 148
dignitas, *see* status
dinners 6, 17, 19, 36, 38, 53, 77, 107, 131, 162; *see also* food, meals, parties *and under* Terentia, Tullia, M. Tullius Cicero
divorces 15, 16, 18, 31, 33–4, 76–7, 84, 92, 122, 126, 129, 151, 163, 164; *see also under* Publilia, Terentia, Tullia
doctors 9, 13, 101–2, 111, 139
dowries 2, 15, 16, 31–4, 37, 97, 129, 148; *see also under* Publilia, Terentia, Tullia
dress 4, 6, 8, 16, 27, 33, 45, 93, 107
dressers 10, 33
dressing-sets 69
Dyrrachium 67–8, 72, 116

education 1, 6, 19, 37, 42, 80, 81, 84, 135, 144, 157
elections 5, 44, 71
elegance 19, 43, 148
emancipatio/emancipation 15, 85–6, 120
empire 3, 10, 15, 137
endearments 50, 63, 65, 67, 68, 96, 102, 106, 112, 160
engagements 20, 41, 43, 94–5
Ephesus 86
Epirus 34, 113, 114; *see also* Buthrotum
epitaphs 18, 20, 21, 66, 138
equites 5–8, 9, 11–12, 32, 46, 56, 84, 85, 87–8, 91, 152
etiquette 49, 127, 133–4, 162, 163
Eulogy of 'Turia' 18, 66, 138
evidence, *see* sources
exile 15, 24, 28, 58–60; *see also under* M. Tullius Cicero
ex-slaves, *see* freedmen/women

facilitas, good nature 125, 161–2
faith 16, 18, 136, 160, 161
families 5, 6, 16, 100; Cicero's *passim*
farmers 9, 33, 162
farming 10, 22, 79
farms 6, 10, 33, 34, 51, 69, 112
fatherhood 29
fathers *passim*
fathers of households 14–15, 16, 69, 73; *see also under* M. Tullius Cicero
Ferentinum 132
festivals 19, 27, 38, 45, 46, 50–51, 71, 73, 81, 107
Fibrenus R. 22, 79
Ficulea 141
fides, see faith
fishing 52
fishponds 79
food 6, 13, 51, 78, 86, 130; *see also* dinners, meals
Formiae 106, 107, 108, 145
Formianum, Cicero's villa at Formiae, 44, 51, 52–3, 60–61, 64, 73, 74, 79, 98, 101, 104, 105, 107, 112, 114, 145–8
Formians 53, 105, 106
Forum 18, 27, 38, 42, 44, 50, 51, 66, 70, 73, 79, 86, 107, 137–8, 139, 145, 149
Forum Appii 53
freedmen/women 3, 8, 10, 81
freedmen 6, 15, 33, 38, 49, 107
freedom 59
freedwomen 14, 19, 36, 90, 121
Fregellae 22
friends *passim;* of women 19; *see also under* Terentia, Tullia, M. Tullius Cicero
Frusino 22, 115
fulling 23
funerals 5, 18, 152
furniture 6, 61, 75, 125, 151

games 8, 19, 27, 36, 37, 44, 53, 56, 71, 78; gladiatorial 8, 44, 51, 56, 71; Secular 152
gardens 6, 44, 51, 75
Gaul 66, 76; Cisalpine 28, 144; Narbonese 10, 28, 144
gifts 15
glory 1, 5, 44
gods and goddesses 23, 35–6, 44, 49, 72, 95, 111, 151; household 19, 35–6, 60–61, 96

gold 18
good behaviour, *see modestia*
good nature, *see facilitas*
gossip 26, 84, 89, 92, 104, 140, 141, 156
governors 3, 11, 12, 17, 28, 71, 77, 80, 89, 90, 92, 95, 144, 151, 153
graciousness 16, 18
Greece 26, 28, 61, 40, 91, 103, 107, 112, 116
Greek (language) 3, 19, 23, 25, 157
Greeks 10, 17, 19, 38
guardians 14, 15, 39, 122, 134
guardianship (*tutela*) 14, 15, 34, 39, 122, 134
guests 17, 38, 51, 71, 81

Hernici 2
holidays 7, 51–4, 77–8; *see also under* Terentia, Tullia, M. Tullius Cicero
honour 16–18, 64, 103, 104, 108, 115, 136, 138
horses 53, 71–2; *see also* riding
hosts 71, *see also under* Terentia, M. Tullius Cicero
hostesses 19, 36, 131; *see also under* Terentia, Tullia
households 16
housekeeping 19, 33, 81
houses 6, 8, 18, 22, 26, 28, 33, 51, 60, 69, 75, 76, 79, 101, 105, 115, 122, 133, 135, 145, 149; *see also* villas *and under* Pomponius Atticus, Terentia, M. Tullius Cicero, Q. Tullius Cicero
'humanity' (*humanitas*) 93, 98, 123–4, 160, 161
husbands *passim;* abroad 18, 28, 37, 78, 80, 81, 129, 133

illegitimacy 2, 17
imagines, family portraits 8, 152, 154
immigrants 3, 9, 10
imperium, see empire
ingenium, character and inborn abilities 62, 98, 161
inheritance 16, 59; by women 7, 15, 69, 134; by Caesar 143; by Cicero 143; by Terentia 143; *see also* wills
incest, incestuous marriages 4; brother–sister 20, 159; father–daughter 131, 159
Invective against Cicero 44–5
Italians 11–12

Italy 29, 61, 63, 68, 71, 73, 76, 100, 105, 108, 111, 116, 118, 121, 123, 124, 131, 142

jewels 6, 7, 18, 69
jokes, joking 19, 41, 43, 44, 88–9, 92, 111, 134, 139–40, 159; *see also* wit
jurists 88, 115, 152

kings 71, 81, 87
kissing 37, 59

labourers 8, 9, 10, 50–51
Lampsacus 17, 19
land 6, 10, 15
Lanuvium 2
Laodicea 86, 87, 140
Lares 60–61; *see also* cult, gods
Lares Augusti 151
Laterium 77, 108
Latin 19
Latins 2, 15
Latium 2, 44
Laudatio 'Turiae' 18, 66, 138
law, of all peoples 4; Roman 4, 15, 69; writings on 20
legacies, *see* inheritance
legislation 10–11, 20, 45, 52, 58, 59, 60, 67, 71, 72, 75, 134
Lesbos 28
letters 8, 21, 33, 40–41, 67, 69, 135, 141,163; delivery time 84, 86, 96–7; for Cicero's letters, *see under* M. Tullius Cicero, for Terentia's, *see under* Terentia
liberi, offspring 17, 38–9, 73
liberty 59
life, expectation of 13
Lilybaeum 27
Liris R. 22, 82
literature 6, 19, 38, 78, 79, 80, 157, 161
litters 19, 53, 101, 110, 147–8
livestock 34
living, standards of 6, 10, 37, 51, 74–5
lodgings 29, 32
Luca 77
luxury, *see* living, standards of

Macedon, Macedonia 10, 49
manliness 16, 24, 67, 68, 123–4, 160, 161
manners 19, 98; *see also* etiquette
manumission 3, 15, 64, 79; *see also* freedmen/women, freedmen, freedwomen
manus, control of husband over wife 15, 16, 34
markets 16
marriage, 6, 100, 164; as alliance 27; ideology of 18; invalid 59; legislation on 20; 'mixed' 4; Roman 2, 4, 15–16
Marseille 28
Marsi 26
Matronalia 38
meals 8, 36, 81; *see also* dinners, food
medicine 20, 101–2
memoirs 21
menarche 20, 42
merchants 9
midwives 102, 111
Minturnae 82, 108, 110
mistresses of the house 8; 32–6; in sexual sense 46, 90
modestia, good behaviour 16, 62, 161
money 18, 32, 34, 35, 38, 50, 68, 73, 75, 112–15, 122, 123, 127, 128, 129, 139, 141–2
morality 16, 25
mortality 18
mothers 2, 6, 19, 84, 85; *passim*
mothers-in-law 13, 18, 33, 61
mothers of households 14, 32–6, 133
mourning 72, 75
mourning-clothes 56, 60, 65, 66, 69, 71
mules 8
music 19, 157

names 14, 30, 98, 139
Naples 3, 6, 78
New Men 5, 6, 27, 29, 30, 88, 147, 151
nobles 1, 5, 21, 30, 41, 50, 84, 85, 90, 93
nomenclature 14
nurses 10, 19, 33; *see also* wetnurses

officium, duty, attentions 66, 138, 158
Oppian Hill 32
Optimates 10, 100
ordines, orders 4–8

Palatine Hill 50
parties, 36, 37, 75; drinking 17, 19; engagement 75
Patrae 101, 116

patricians 6, 23, 75, 83, 84, 88, 90, 92, 93
patrons 14
People, Roman 5, 9, 11, 17, 27, 45, 46, 47, 57, 66, 73, 105; *see also* assemblies, elections
Pergamum 10
Pharsalus, Battle of 116, 117
Philippi, Battle of 149, 150, 152
pietas 36, 62, 67, 69, 115, 123, 137, 138, 160, 161
picnics 6–7
plays 8, 53, 56, 71, 78; *see also* games
plebeians 14, 30, 41, 50, 84, 92, 93
plebs 5, 73, 119, 148
Pompeianum, Cicero's villa at Pompeii, 44, 48, 50, 51, 52–3, 77, 78, 98, 110, 141
Pomptine Marshes 98
Pontus and Bithynia 69
Populares 10
Porcian Basilica 65
Portico of Catulus 74
power, paternal 15, 59, 162
prayers 36, 69, 95
pregnancy 13, 28, 29, 36, 44, 76, 101–2, 131, 135, 150
presents 31, 38, 41
prisoners of war 59
probitas, uprightness 160
processions 19
property 1, 15, 18, 33–5, 58, 136–7, 148; separation of 18, 35, 127, 160; *see also* land, wealth
prosecutions 1, 18, 62
proscriptions 11–12, 58, 144–8
protests 9, 17, 56, 60, 61, 69
provinces 1, 3, 28, 40
puberty 14, 20, 31, 42–3
pudicitia 16–18, 33, 43, 62
Puteolanum, Cicero's villa at Puteoli 107
Puteoli 153

races 8, 44, 53
rape 16–17
Reate 30
receptions 8, 38, 46, 50, 53, 105; *see also* dinners, parties
recreation 6, 37–8, 101
religion 16, 18; *see also* cult, gods and goddesses, prayer, sacrifices
rents 34, 139, 162

reputation 16, 29, 37, 129; *see also under* Terentia, Tullia, M. Tullius Cicero
restraint 16
Rhodes 29
riding 5, 53, 116
rights of Roman citizens, private 2, 3, 4, 10; public 14
Rome, City of 73, 74, 86, 101, 103, 104, 105, 121, 148; women in 19
Rubicon 101

Sabines 2
sacrifices 19, 35–6, 44–6, 49; *see also* cult
Salus 72
Samnites 11
Sardinia 10
Saturnalia 46, 50, 51
scent 6
seaside 6–7, 51, 52–3, 75, 77
sea voyages 28, 61, 72, 86, 97, 105, 109, 110, 111–13, 147
secretaries/research assistants 10, 40
sedan chairs 19, 101
Senate 4–8, 11, 17, 27, 32, 45, 46, 47, 48–9, 58, 59, 71, 73, 75, 77, 101, 105, 107, 108, 137, 150; *see also* senators
senators 1, 4–8, 11–12, 20, 32, 50–51, 56, 60, 84, 90, 91, 100, 105, 108
servants, *see* slaves, freedmen/women
sexual life 20–21, 31, 42–3, 95–6, 100, 126, 159–60
shopkeepers 8, 9, 15, 16
shopping 19
shops 8, 145
Sicily 3, 10, 27, 29, 37, 86
Side 94, 96
silver 61, 125
Sinuessa 107
slaves, 3, 6, 8 , 10, 13, 15, 16, 17, 19, 33, 37, 43, 50–51, 58, 81, 107, 160; of Cicero, *see under* M. Tullius Cicero; of Terentia, *see under* Terentia; attending Tullia, *see under* Tullia
sons 12, 14, 15, 41–2, 85; *passim*
sons-in-law (in general) 43, 76, 77, 88, 110, 126, 136; *see also* Calpurnius Piso Frugi, C., (Furius) Crassipes, Cornelius Dolabella, P.
sons of households 14–15, 32, 49–50, 59, 69, 122

General index

sources 7, 8, 13–14, 15, 20–21, 22, 40–41, 129, 145, 150, 163
Spain, 10, 28, 109, 110, 112, 115, 132, 133, 140, 144, 161
spinning, *see* wool
statues 43–4, 51, 79
status 4, 66, 67, 78, 79, 124, 136, 137
status-loss 59
stewards 33, 113; *see also* Terentius Philotimus
Subura 32, 139
succession, intestate 15, 59, 153
Suda 143
swimming 7
Syria 76, 96, 140, 153

Tabula Valeria 65
talent, *see ingenium*
Tarentum 82, 128
Tarracina 53, 98
Tarsus 94
tax on women 148–9
teachers 9–10
Teanum Sidicinum 105
tears 57, 60, 63, 64, 65, 68, 109, 120, 122
Temple of Tellus 32
Temple of Vesta 65
temples 73
textiles 6, 125
thanksgivings 45
theatres, *see* plays
Thessalonica 58, 61, 64
Tiber 70
tombs 22, 18, 138
toys 19
towns, Italian 4, 37, 50, 73, 102, 128
trade 6
travel abroad 28, 86–7, 97; in Italy 28, 71–2; speed of 40, 71, 96–7, 110
Trebula, territory of 82, 98
Tres Tabernae 53
trials 5, 8, 78, 89, 91, 93, 95
triumphs 97, 99

Trojans 102–3
Tusculanum, Cicero's villa at Tusculum, 43–4, 48, 50, 51, 53, 60–61, 64, 73, 74, 81, 126, 128–9, 130–31, 135, 140, 141, 145–7
Tusculum 2, 61, 151

Venusia 82, 128, 153
Vestal Virgins 30–31, 44–6, 61, 92
Via Appia 30, 52, 71, 76, 82
Via Latina 22, 53, 132
villas 6–7, 28, 30, 36, 40, 57, 98, 105; for Cicero's villas, *see under* M. Tullius Cicero *and* individual villas
violence 9, 11, 18, 46, 60–61, 65–6, 70, 74, 77, 122, 145–8, 164
virtus, *see* manliness
visits to friends 19, 36, 71, 132; *see also under* Terentia, Tullia
Voconian law 15, 38–9, 134
Volscians 2, 23

walks 37, 50, 52, 56
wars 5, civil 11–12, 97, chs 9–10 *passim*, 149, 164
Way, Appian 30, 52, 71, 76, 82; Latin 22, 53, 132; Sacred 74
wealth 6, 10, 84; *see also* land, property
weddings 31, 43, 47, 77, 78, 97–8
wetnurses 139; *see also* nurses
widows 2, 15, 69, 72
wills 3, 15, 98; *see also under* Terentia, M. Tullius Cicero
wine 6, 33, 46, 153
wit 19, 157; *see also* jokes
wives 45 and *passim*; intervention by 48–9; private property of 34; of senators 102–3, 105, 106
wool 16, 18, 19, 23, 33
women *passim*; and class 6; gatherings of 6, 85; not to be named in political speeches 13, 73; property of 7–8
working class 8–10

Related titles from Routledge

Cornelia
Mother of the Gracchi
Suzanne Dixon

Cornelia - daughter, wife and mother of famous men - won her own enduring place in Roman history. Her sons' political successors, orators, authors and even Roman emperors revered her as 'Mother of the Gracchi'. In a time of moral upheaval and cultural innovation, Cornelia's drive and education equipped her sons for the new age.

Why, asks Dixon, should the mother of revolutionaries continue to be admired - for her prose style, her fertility, her philosophic calm in adversity, her vicarious ambition - by the same arch-conservatives who blamed her sons for the decline of the Republic?

Dixon reminds us that this iconic Roman mother venerated by later ages for igniting her sons' fatal political ambitions and for proclaiming that her children were her 'jewels', was once a woman, not only a myth. She endured the deaths of her own ambitions with the assassinations of her two famous sons ('the Gracchi') in their prime. Her daughter Sempronia, childless widow of a famous general, was the sole survivor of Cornelia's twelve children. Dixon argues that it was Sempronia, dutiful to the end, who kept the family myths alive.

This concise, pocket-sized book plunges the reader into the turbulent Italy of the second century BCE, when Cornelia and her family were at the centre of the culture wars and political upheavals that followed military conquest. Essential reading for anyone interested in women's history, political myth-making or the politics of the Roman Republic.

Hb: 978-0-415-33147-0
Pb: 978-0-415-33148-7
eBook: 978-0-203-39243-0

Available at all good bookshops
For ordering and further information please visit:
www.routledge.com

Related titles from Routledge

Girls and Women in Classical Greek Religion
Matthew Dillon

'Highly recommended ... no collection of classical, religious or gender studies would be complete without it.' - *Choice*

'A work of considerable scholarship, and one on which the author is to be congratulated.' - *Minerva*

'It makes accessible a substantial body of disparate material.' - *JACT Review*

'Wisely, this important contribution to understanding the female dimension of ancient religion does not make the worship of goddesses a central concern.' - *International Review of Biblical Studies*

It has often been thought that participation in fertility rituals was women's most important religious activity in classical Greece. Matthew Dillon's wide-ranging study makes it clear that women engaged in numerous other rites and cults, and that their role in Greek religion was actually more important than that of men. Women invoked the gods' help in becoming pregnant, venerated the god of wine, worshipped new and exotic deities, used magic for both erotic and pain-relieving purposes, and far more besides.

Clear and comprehensive, this volume challenges many stereotypes of Greek women and offers unexpected insights into their experience of religion. With more than fifty illustrations, and translated extracts from contemporary texts, this is an essential resource for the study of women and religion in classical Greece.

ISBN10: 0-415-20272-8 (hbk)
ISBN10: 0-415-31916-1 (pbk)

ISBN13: 978-0-415-20272-5 (hbk)
ISBN13: 978-0-415-31916-4 (pbk)

Available at all good bookshops
For ordering and further information please visit:
www.routledge.com

Related titles from Routledge

Julia Augusti
Elaine Fantham

Julia, the only daughter of Emperor Augustus, became a living example of the Augustan policy. By her marriage and motherhood she encapsulated the Augustan reforms of Rome and helped secure a dynasty.

An unidentified scandal, distorted or concealed in the ancient sources which led to her summary banishment, has discredited Julia, or at least clothed her in mystery. However, studying the abundant historical evidence available, this biography illustrates each stage of Julia's life in remarkable detail:

- her childhood – taken from her divorced mother to become part of a complex and unstable family structure
- her youth – set against the brilliant social and cultural life of the new Augustan Rome
- her marriages – as tools for Augustus' plans for succession
- Julia's defiance or her father's publicized moral regime, and implicit exposure of his hypocrisy by claiming the same sexual liberty he had once enjoyed

Reflecting new attitudes, and casting fresh light on their social reality, this accessible but penetrating portrait from one of the foremost scholars of Augustan literature and history will delight, entertain and inform anyone interested in this engaging Classical figure.

ISBN10: 0-415-33145-5 (hbk)
ISBN10: 0-415-33146-3 (pbk)

ISBN13: 978-0-415-33145-6 (hbk)
ISBN13: 978-0-415-33146-3 (pbk)

Available at all good bookshops
For ordering and further information please visit:
www.routledge.com

Related titles from Routledge

Julia Domna
Syrian Empress
Barbara Levick

Julia Domna's influence on her age, unlike that of most women of ancient Rome, has not been underestimated. Throughout history she has been regarded as one of the most important figures to operate behind the imperial throne. In fact, as the Emperor Septimius Severus' prized and respected wife and the loyal mother of Caracalla, who joined them and their armies in their travels, she was on hand for all the Emperors' decisions and a figure visible throughout the Empire.

Yet her fame has come at a price. As part of a dynasty which used force and violence to preserve its rule, she was distrusted by its subjects; as a Syrian, she was the object of prejudice; as a woman with power, she was resented. Such judgements have been persistent: some modern historians blame Julia and her dynasty for the century of crisis that followed their rule, for the corruption of the Empire, civil war, oriental despotism, and exotic novelties in the imperial cult.

On the other hand, Domna was the centre of a literary circle considered highly significant by nineteenth-century admirers.

This book contains an overdue reassessment of these assumptions:

- Was Julia more powerful than earlier empresses?
- Did she really promote despotism?
- How seriously is her literary circle to be taken?

This book covers Julia's life, and charts her travels from Aswan to York during a period of profound upheaval, seeking the truth about this woman who inspired such extreme and contrasting views, exposing the instability of our sources about her, and characterizing a sympathetic, courageous, intelligent, and important woman.

Hb: 978-0-415-33143-2
Pb: 978-0-415-33144-9
eBook: 978-0-203-39241-6

Available at all good bookshops
For ordering and further information please visit:
www.routledge.com

Related titles from Routledge

Medea
Emma Griffiths

Medea, the sorceress of Greek myth and Euripides' vengeful heroine, is famed for the murder of her children after she is banished from her own family and displaced by a new wife. Her reputation as a wronged 'everywoman' of Greek tragedy has helped engender her lasting appeal to the modern age. However, this firmly rooted status has also caused many of the intricacies of her timeless tale to be overlooked.

Emma Griffiths brings into focus previously unexplored themes of the Medea myth, along with providing an incisive introduction to the story and its history. Viewed within its context, the tale reveals fascinating insights into ancient Greece and its ideology, the importance of children, the role of women, and the position of the outsider and barbarian.

The critically sophisticated analysis, expressed in clear and accessible terms, proceeds to examine the persistence of the Medea myth through ancient Rome to the modern day. Placing the myth within a modern context and into analytical frameworks such as psychoanalysis, Griffiths highlights Medea's position in current classical study, as well as her lasting appeal. A vivid portrait of a woman empowered by her exclusion from society, alive with passion and the suffering of wounded love, this book is an indispensable guide to a fascinating mythical figure.

ISBN10: 0-415-30069-X (hbk)
ISBN10: 0-415-30070-3 (hbk)

ISBN13: 978-0-415-30069-X (hbk)
ISBN13: 978-0-415-30070-3 (pbk)

Available at all good bookshops
For ordering and further information please visit:
www.routledge.com

Related titles from Routledge

**Olympias
Mother of Alexander the Great
Elizabeth Carney**

The definitive guide to the life of the first woman to play a major role in Greek political history, this is the first modern biography of Olympias.

Presenting a critical assessment of a fascinating and wholly misunderstood figure, Elizabeth Carney penetrates myth, fiction and sexual politics and conducts a close examination of Olympias through historical and literary sources, and brings her to life as she places the figure in the context of her own ancient, brutal political world.

Individual examinations look at:

- the role of Greek religion in Olympias' life
- literary and artistic traditions about Olympias found throughout the later ancient periods
- varying representations of Olympias found in the major ancient sources.

An absolutely compelling read for students, scholars, and anyone with an interest in Greek, classical, or women's history.

ISBN10: 0-415-33316-4 (hbk)
ISBN10: 0-415-33317-2 (pbk)

ISBN13: 978-0-415-33316-0 (hbk)
ISBN13: 978-0-415-33317-7 (pbk)

Available at all good bookshops
For ordering and further information please visit:
www.routledge.com